THE NAVAJO WEAVING TRADITION

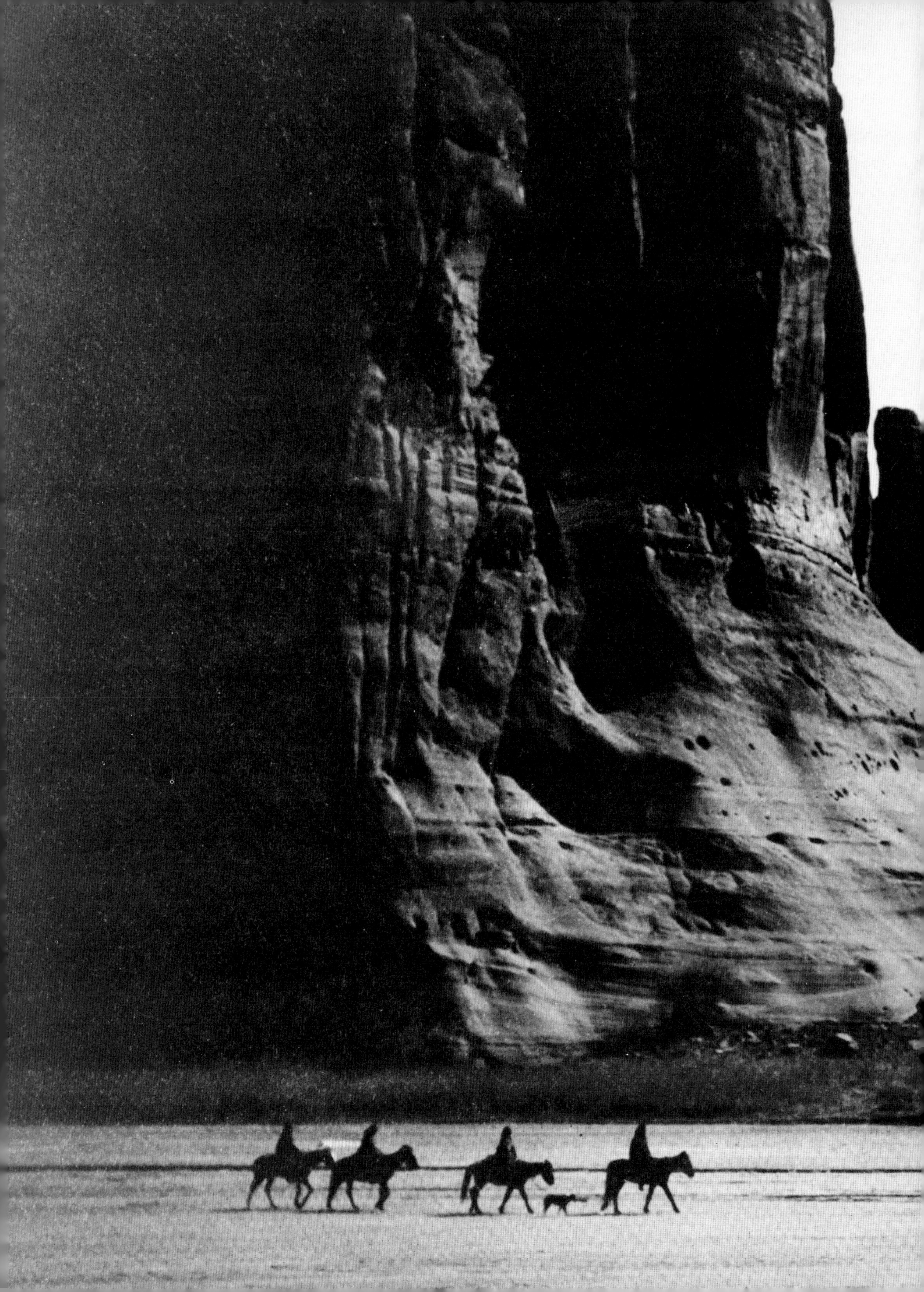

THE NAVAJO WEAVING TRADITION
1650 to the Present

Alice Kaufman and Christopher Selser

E. P. DUTTON, INC. NEW YORK

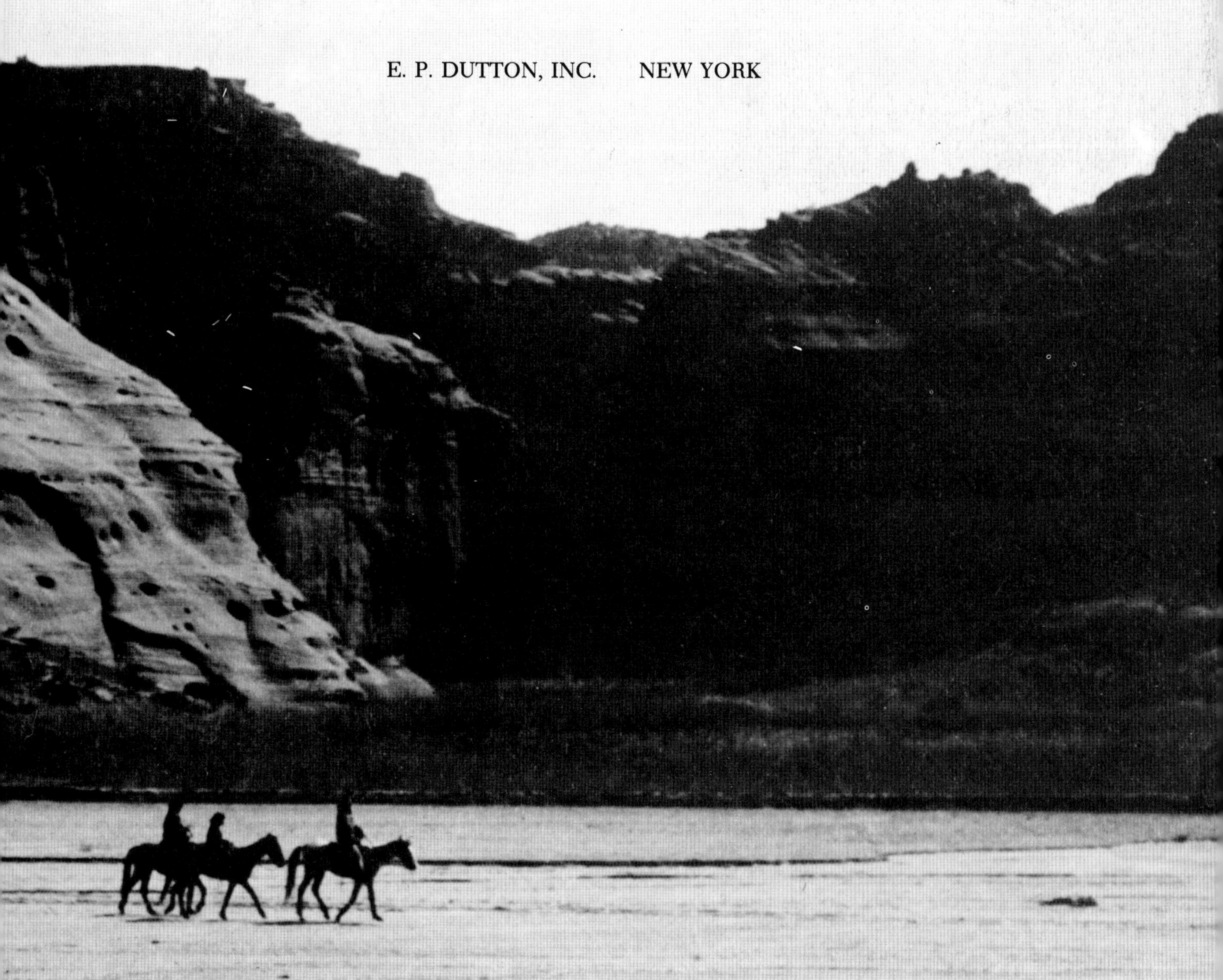

1 (pages ii–iii). Canyon de Chelly, photograph by Edward S. Curtiss, 1904. (Photograph courtesy Smithsonian Institution)

First published, 1985,
in the United States by E. P. Dutton, Inc., New York.

For information contact: E. P. Dutton, Inc.
2 Park Avenue, New York, N.Y. 10016

Library of Congress Catalog Card Number: 84-71645

Printed and bound by
Dai Nippon Printing Co., Ltd., Tokyo, Japan.
ISBN: 0-525-24299-6 (cloth)
0-525-48194-X (DP)
Published simultaneously in Canada by
Fitzhenry & Whiteside Limited,
Toronto

W

Designed by Marilyn Rey

10 9 8 7 6 5 4 3 2 1

First Edition

CONTENTS

ACKNOWLEDGMENTS

An important part of America's recent discovery of its rich folk art heritage is the dramatic increase in the awareness and appreciation of American Indian arts by the public, especially in the field of Navajo weaving.

This project began as the result of a suggestion made by John Macrae III, formerly with E. P. Dutton, Inc., and an ardent fan of Navajo weaving, who believed there was a definite need for a major study of the history and development of Navajo weaving.

The book would not have been possible without the generous cooperation and assistance of many individuals and museum personnel. It is a great pleasure to acknowledge below those who permitted us to photograph textiles in their collections or who provided important research information: Laura Allen, Museum of Northern Arizona, Flagstaff, Arizona; Joshua Baer, Santa Cruz, California; Jan Bell and Ellen Horn, Arizona State Museum, The University of Arizona, Tucson, Arizona; Anthony Berlant, Santa Monica, California; Fred Boschan, Lafayette Hills, Pennsylvania; Nancy and Harry Brorby, Tucson, Arizona; Lee Cohen, Scottsdale, Arizona; Terry DeWald, Tucson, Arizona; John and Margo Ernst, New York, N.Y.; Nancy Fox, Laboratory of Anthropology, Museum of New Mexico, Santa Fe, New Mexico; Gallup Public Library, Gallup, New Mexico; Dan Garland, Sedona, Arizona; Steve Getzwiller, Benson, Arizona; Erwin and Marjorie Goodman, New York, N.Y.; Pamela Hearn, The University Museum, University of Pennsylvania, Philadelphia, Pennsylvania; Andrew Nagen, Corrales, New Mexico; Anne Marshall, Heard Museum, Phoenix, Arizona; Museum of New Mexico, Santa Fe, New Mexico; André Nasser, New York, N.Y.; National Archives, Washington, D.C.; Pendleton Mills, Pendleton, Oregon; Eric Phillips, Corrales, New Mexico; David and Steven Pickelner, Fort Collins, Colorado; Marion Rodee, Maxwell Museum of Anthropology, University of New Mexico, Albuquerque, New Mexico; Edgar Smith, New York, N.Y.; Smithsonian Institution, Washington, D.C.; Barbara Stanislavski, School of American Research, Museum of New Mexico, Santa Fe, New Mexico; David Stock, New York, N.Y.; David Wenger, Denver, Colorado; Mark Winter, Durango, Colorado.

Special recognition is due Dr. Joe Ben Wheat of Boulder, Colorado, whose years of devotion to the field of research in Navajo textiles have resulted in major contributions to this body of knowledge.

Christopher Selser

THE NAVAJO WEAVING TRADITION

1

A BRIEF INTRODUCTION TO NAVAJO WEAVING

> The art of weaving, as it exists among the Navajo Indians of New Mexico and Arizona, possesses points of great interest to the student of ethnolography. It is of aboriginal design; and while European art has undoubtedly modified it, the extent and nature of the foreign influence is easily traced. It is by no means certain, still there are many reasons for supposing, that the Navajos learned their craft from the Pueblo Indians . . . yet the pupils, if such they be, far excel their masters today in the beauty and quality of their work. It may be safely stated that with no native tribe in America, north of the Mexican boundary, has the art of weaving been carried to greater perfection than among the Navajos.
>
> Dr. Washington Matthews
> *Third Annual Report of the Bureau of Ethnology, 1881 1882*[1]

Navajo blankets and rugs have been avidly sought after and collected for more than two hundred years. The first collectors were other Indians. During the nineteenth century Navajo blankets were important status symbols, not only among Navajos but also among many native Americans, especially the Plains Indians, instantly proclaiming the wealth and status of anyone who wore one. Although they hated and feared Navajo warriors, many Spanish colonists in Mexico and New Mexico preferred Navajo blankets and sarapes to those made by their own weavers. Starting in the 1840s American explorers, followed by American soldiers and government agents and then by American tourists traveling in the Southwest bought Navajo blankets and sarapes as souvenirs.

Artists collect Navajo blankets and rugs because of their strong visual statement. To museum curators Navajo blankets and rugs are outstanding examples of both historic and contemporary primitive art. Anthropologists see Navajo textiles as the sum of their diverse cultural parts. Art collectors value the investment potential of Navajo blankets and rugs as well as their beauty, for some rare old Navajo weavings have sold for over six figures, and new rugs and tapestries can sell for five figures or more.

Weaving is an ancient form of artistic expression. The Indians of the Southwest were creating beautiful textiles long before Europeans came to the New World. When Francisco Vásquez de Coronado led his conquistadors into what is now Arizona and New Mexico in the mid-1500s, he found sophisticated native peoples wearing clothing they had woven from cotton. After the invading Spanish brought sheep to the Southwest, wool replaced cotton as the dominant material of Southwest Indian textiles. Spanish sheep and trade goods, Spanish tapestry-weaving techniques, and Spanish-Mexican textile design had a profound influence on Navajo weaving. But the Spanish influence is only part of the story. Navajo weaving may be considered an artistic manifestation of the turbulent history of the Navajos—and of the Southwest itself.

Before the Spanish arrived, the Pueblo Indians were the dominant political and cultural force in the Southwest, and Pueblo weavers were the first models for the Navajos. Eighteenth-century Navajo textiles were probably very similar both technically and stylistically to the Pueblo textiles that inspired them. It was experimental Navajo weavers, however, who excelled in the use of wool, of Spanish indigo dye, and of commercial materials in Southwest weaving. While conservative Pueblo weavers continued primarily to produce traditionally striped blankets, innovative Navajo weavers were creating bold designs featuring terraced diagonals, wavy bands, triangles, and diamonds. Although some of these patterns shared design elements with Mexican textiles, they also bring to mind earlier, more familiar (to the weaver) terraced designs found on historic Navajo baskets. By the nineteenth century the quality, quantity, and variety of Navajo weaving far surpassed Pueblo weaving.

The American presence in the Southwest was felt gradually by Navajo weavers, first through trade. When Mexico won its independence from Spain in 1821, the Santa Fe Trail became a major trade route to the Southwest, bringing in new sources of trade goods from the East. The American influence grew more profound after the United States annexed the New Mexico Territory in 1848. Unable to maintain peaceful relations with the Navajos, the United States government banished virtually the entire tribe and imprisoned them in eastern New Mexico. After a five-year confinement the Navajos were allowed to return to their land of mesas and canyons, but life—and weaving—had changed forever.

By the mid-1870s government-licensed traders were opening trading posts on Navajo land, and by the 1880s the Santa Fe Railroad was carrying eastern tourists through the Southwest regularly. Contact with the Anglo, which had been abrasive and transitory, became a permanent fixture of the Navajo world. This contact completely transformed the function and appearance of Navajo weaving. Instead of weaving wearing blankets, which by the late nineteenth century had limited appeal (by 1900, even Navajos stopped wearing their own blankets, preferring machine-made commercial blankets bought at the trading post), Navajos began to weave floor rugs to sell to Anglos.

Until the twentieth century Navajo designs were an amalgam of Pueblo, Spanish, and Mexican influences as filtered through a weaver with an ancient design tradition of her own. During the 1900s, however, the taste and market expectations of the Anglo trader became the dominant influences on Navajo weaving. Some traders had a taste for Oriental rugs, some for Classic Period nineteenth-century blankets, and some for Pueblo/Rio Grande–style striped blankets, and they all made their preferences known to the weavers. Of course, the weavers usually had ideas and market expectations of their own. Navajo rugs became, in the words of John Adair, "the Indian's idea of the trader's idea of what the white man thought was Indian design."[2] (Adair is speaking here about Zuni jewelry, but the point is well taken.)

Today's regional rug styles can be traced directly back to the personal design preferences of a few influential traders. Juan Lorenzo Hubbell, who ran the trading post at Ganado, Arizona, wanted his weavers to return to the bold patterns of the Classic Period, and he encouraged them to do so by hanging oil paintings of the old blankets on the walls of his trading post. Hubbell's instincts proved correct when hundreds of the rugs he inspired were sold to tourists along the route of the Santa Fe Railroad.

John B. Moore, the trader who ran the post at Crystal, New Mexico, was even more enterprising in his attempt to capture the Anglo market. In 1903 and again in 1911 Moore published mail-order catalogues featuring Navajo rugs. Like Hubbell, Moore provided his weavers with a selection of preferred patterns, some of them Classic Period revivals, some of his own design. Moore's original designs—bordered, ornate geometrics reminiscent of Oriental rugs—are the forerunners of the famous Teec Nos Pos, storm pattern, and Two Gray Hills rug styles.

Today these regional rug styles, so radically different from earlier Navajo blanket styles, have become traditional to both weavers and buyers. Indeed, individual weavers have become well known for their skill at creating examples of these characteristic styles. Because of the diversity of the regional styles and the superb technical aspects of the weaving, the best contemporary rugs are the equal of the finest textiles produced in the history of Navajo textiles. Outstanding contemporary rugs are collected just as avidly as are fine Classic and Late Classic Period (1800–1875) blankets and colorful Transitional Period (1875–1900) textiles, although often not by the same collectors. Well-known contemporary weavers such as Daisy Taugelchee from Two Gray Hills and Margaret Begay from Wide Ruins are booked far into the future with orders from traders, dealers, and private customers. Contemporary Navajo weaving is an inspiring American success story.

From the time of the earliest weavers, who wove to clothe themselves and their families, to the weavers of the 1980s who make rugs and wall hangings for Anglo customers they will probably never see, outstanding Navajo weavers have been able to express their individual artistic sensibilities within clearly defined limits of design. The colors of a Classic Period sarape were largely limited to red, blue, brown/black, and white. But each weaver had her own vision of how to arrange and lay out the pattern of simple terraced design elements, thus creating her own unique visual statement within the art of Navajo weaving. Most collectors would never confuse one sarape with another, and can recognize instantly whether or not they have seen a particular weaving before.

Rather like poets working within the strict confines of the sonnet style, Navajo weavers give free rein to their creative energies to produce something distinctly original within clearly defined limits. When Daisy Taugelchee, the prize-winning Two Gray Hills weaver, sits down at her loom, she will use almost exclusively only natural shades of wool—white, black, brown, and carded tans and grays. She is bound by tradition—merely decades old but firmly rooted nonetheless—to create a multibordered geometric design dominated by a strong central element. Within these limits, Taugelchee will weave a unique yet characteristic work of textile art, as recognizable and collectable as a Classic Period Chief blanket. This ability to transcend form and function is basic to Navajo weaving and has been since the Navajos started to weave some two hundred years ago.

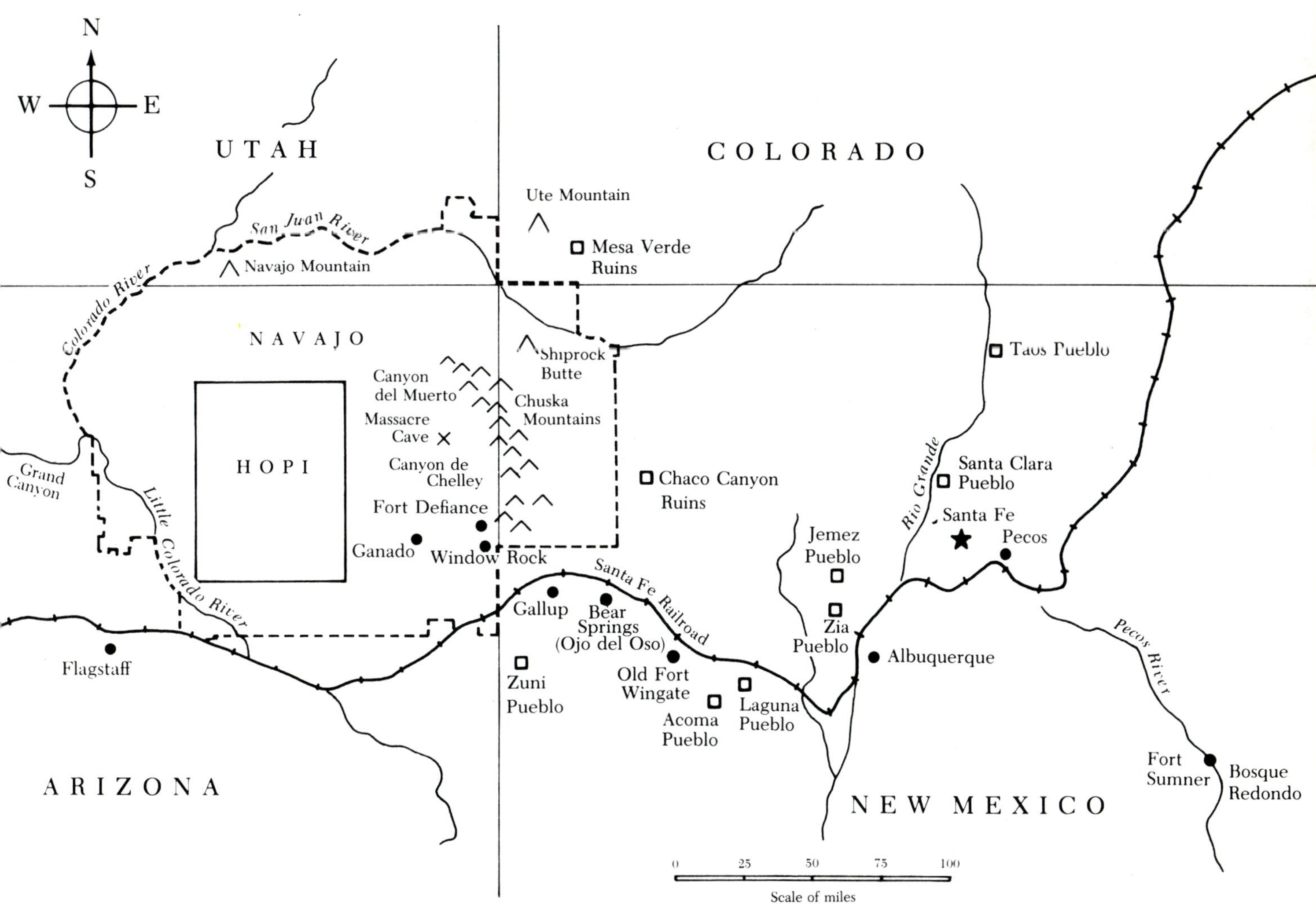

2. The Navajo territory and surrounding area.

2

THE FIRST WEAVERS

The beginning of the world, I am thinking about it
The beginning of the world, I am talking about it

Navajo ceremonial chant[3]

According to Navajo myth, the "Dineh," or the People (which is how Navajos refer to themselves), were led to their home in the Southwest from another world beneath the earth by supernatural spirits called Holy People. Spider Man, one of the Navajo Holy People, taught the Navajos how to make a loom from sunshine, lightning, and rain. Spider Woman taught them how to weave.

Anthropologists say that the ancestors of the Navajos, Athapascan-speaking peoples, like other Indians before them, crossed into Alaska from their ancient homeland in Asia over a land bridge resulting from the formation of glaciers during the Ice Age, some 25,000 years ago. They remained in Alaska and in northern Canada for centuries before starting their long trek south. When groups of Athapascans arrived in the Southwest (scholars date their arrival between the years A.D. 900 and 1400), they found other Indians who had already been living there for centuries.

The Athapascans, who had known only a nomadic life of hunting and gathering, must have been stunned at the sight of the great towns of stone and adobe inhabited by these people, the ancestors of today's Pueblo Indians (*pueblo* is the Spanish word for town). At the height of the Classic Pueblo culture (A.D. 900–1100), 7,000 men, women, and children lived at the Mesa Verde (Colorado) cliff dwellings. Dozens of towns like Mesa Verde existed. The pueblos at Chaco Canyon (New Mexico) housed a population of at least 10,000—1,200 in one huge multiroomed building alone. The Athapascans called the sophisticated, wealthy farmers who lived in cities like these *Anasazi*—ancient ones.

The bands of wanderers from the north ended their long journey to live in the country of the Anasazi. They reinvented their own culture based on what they saw of Pueblo Indian life, myth, and ceremony. What they learned was layered onto the cultural baggage they brought with them to the Southwest. The results were uniquely Navajo.

After observing the irrigated, planted fields of the Pueblo Indians, the People stopped relying solely on gathering wild plants and hunting game for their existence and started planting corn, cotton, and other crops like their neighbors. The name Navajo is said to come from the Tewa (a Pueblo language) word *navaju*, meaning great planted fields. Corn became more than food to the Navajos. As it was for their models the Pueblo Indians, corn became central to Navajo life, legend, and ceremony.

My great corn plants
Among them I walk
I speak to them
They hold out their hands to me.

Navajo ceremonial chant

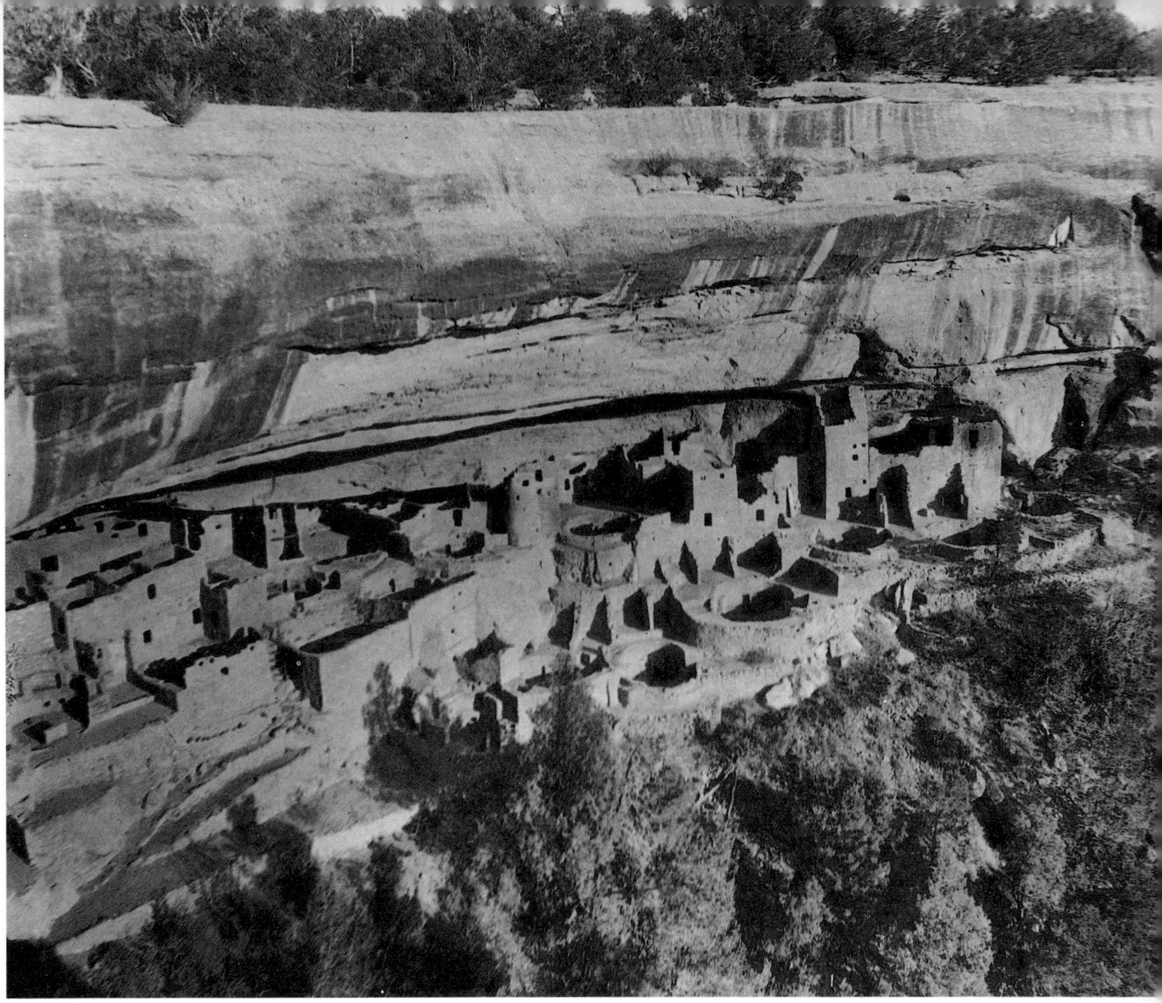

3. Prehistoric pueblo, A.D. 900–1300. Photograph c. 1881. (Courtesy University Museum, University of Pennsylvania)

4. Hopi pueblo of Walpi, northeastern Arizona, late nineteenth century. (Photograph courtesy University Museum, University of Pennsylvania)

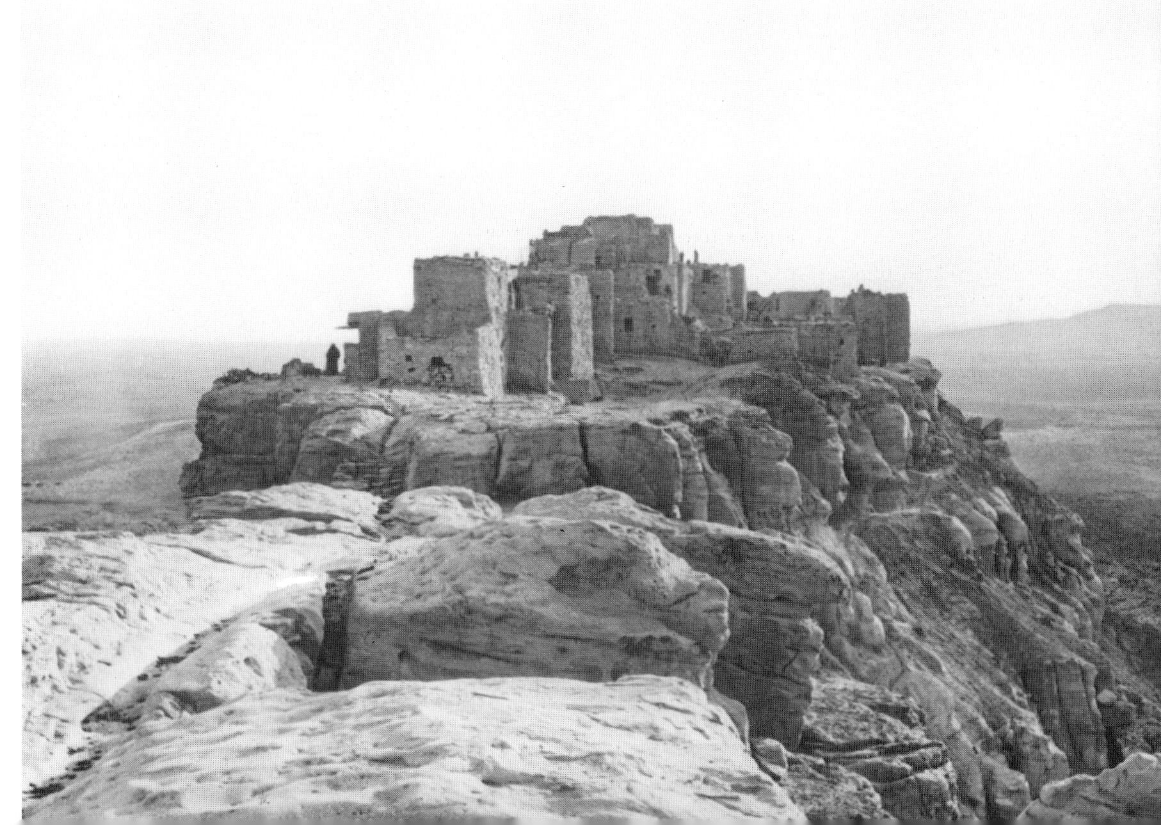

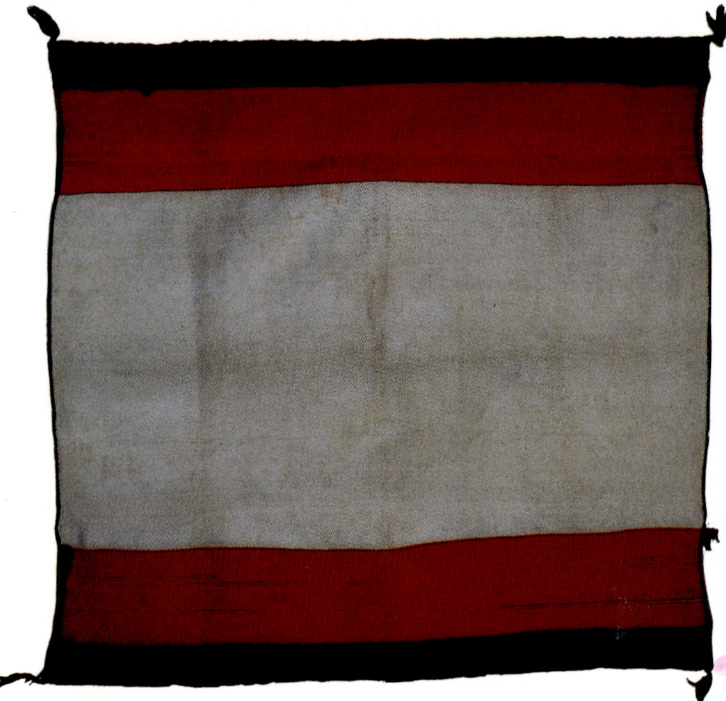

5. Wool-embroidered cotton manta, Hopi pueblo, c. 1880. 35″ x 33″. 16 warp/in.; 16 weft/in. The Pueblo manta or shawl, woven wider than long, became the basis for the development of the Navajo "Chief blanket." Woven of native hand-spun cotton yarn and embroidered with raveled synthetic-dyed red and indigo-dyed blue hand-spun wool yarns. (Private collection)

But the early Navajos never depended on agriculture alone. From the time they entered the Southwest they hunted as they had always done. They also traded with and raided neighboring Indian settlements for food, clothing, pottery, baskets, farming tools, and captives.

In 1540 Coronado, seeking gold, glory, and converts to Christianity, led the Spanish conquistadors into what is now Arizona and New Mexico. By the time the Spanish arrived, the Pueblo Indians, once a rich, proud people, had long abandoned the great cliff dwellings at Mesa Verde, the enormous pueblos at Chaco Canyon, and their other towns. Many anthropologists suspect that a severe drought in the thirteenth century may have caused the Anasazi to desert their towns and disperse to smaller, more scattered settlements. Constant raiding by the Athapascans probably also contributed to the dispersal and decline of the ancient Pueblo culture. Some anthropologists theorize that the nearly inaccessible cliff dwellings and mesa-top towns were built as a defense against raids by hostile bands of Indians.

The earliest Spanish account of the Navajo Indians comes from a report by Antonio de Espejo. In 1583 Espejo led a small Spanish expedition west from Zia, one of the Pueblos near the Rio Grande. According to the account, the "mountain people," as Espejo called the Navajos, "carry on trade with those of the settlements [the Pueblos], taking to them salt, game such as deer, rabbits and hares, tanned deer hides and other things, to trade for cotton mantas [blankets] and other things."[4]

Although many of the People died at the hands of the Spanish or were sold into slavery, most Navajos managed to remain independent of the invaders. Navajos never built towns or villages like those of the Pueblos, preferring to live in semipermanent far-flung clusters of small huts, or hogans. Because they were widely dispersed over a large area of mostly inaccessible land that was not suitable for intensive farming, they were far less vulnerable to Spanish control than the Pueblo Indians, many of whom lived permanently and communally along the Rio Grande, the center of Spanish rule. Navajo land was the wild, nearly barren canyon and mesa land west of the fertile Rio Grande valley. This geographic location, combined with their seminomadic life-style, allowed the Navajos to watch at a distance while the Spanish exploited the more centralized agricultural Pueblos.

The Spanish conspicuously displayed cultural and material wealth that was irresistible to the acquisitive Navajos. During the 1500s and 1600s, as fast as the Spanish colonized Pueblo lands, the Navajos raided the new Spanish settlements. The sheep and horses (both imported to the New World by the Spanish) captured by the Navajos changed their lives as profoundly as the growing of corn had centuries earlier. Mutton became a new diet staple. Navajo raiders on horseback were a constant threat to Spanish settlements and Pueblo villages alike. Navajo shepherds on horseback could control large flocks spread over wide areas. Navajo hunters on horseback could ride for miles tracking game.

When my horse neighs
Different horses follow
When my horse neighs
Different color sheep follow
I am wealthy from my horse

Navajo ceremonial chant

As flocks of Navajo sheep grew, farmland gave way to grazing land. Abandoning much (though not all) of what they had learned about agriculture, many Navajo families left their great planted fields to follow the flocks in constant search of more grazing land. Although the ear-

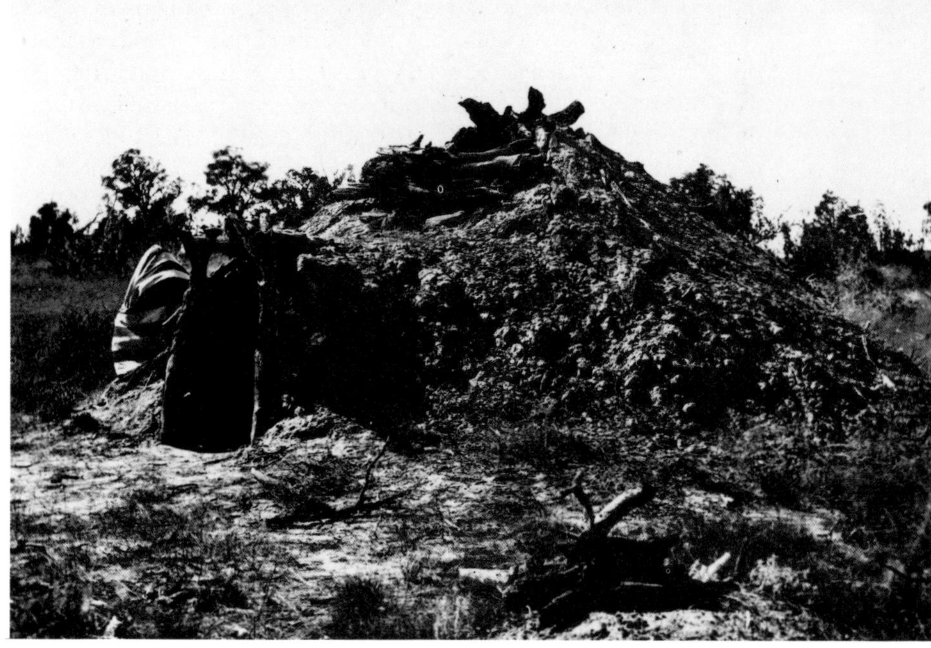

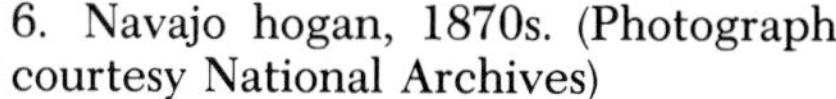

6. Navajo hogan, 1870s. (Photograph courtesy National Archives)

7. Navajo sheep and shepherd at watering hole, c. 1899. (Photograph courtesy University Museum, University of Pennsylvania).

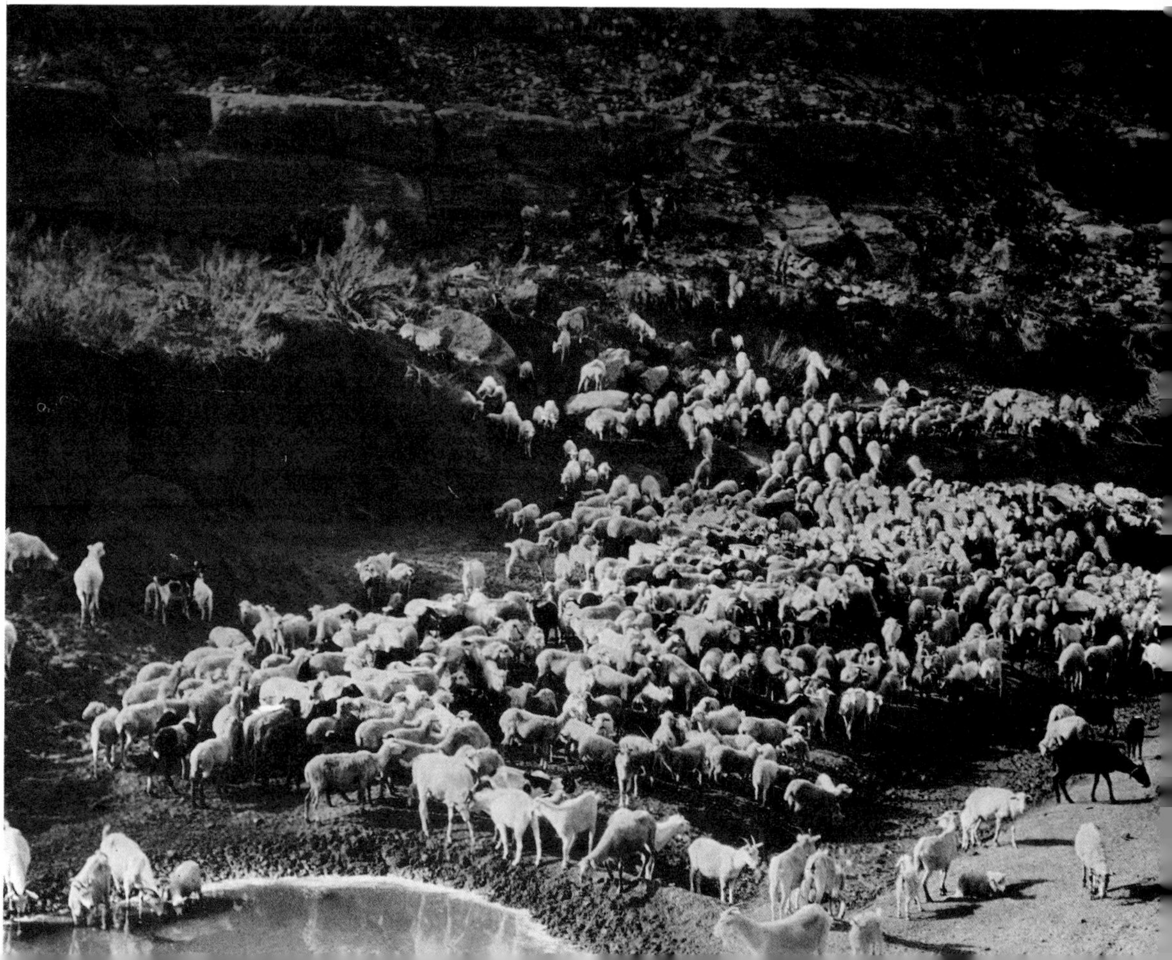

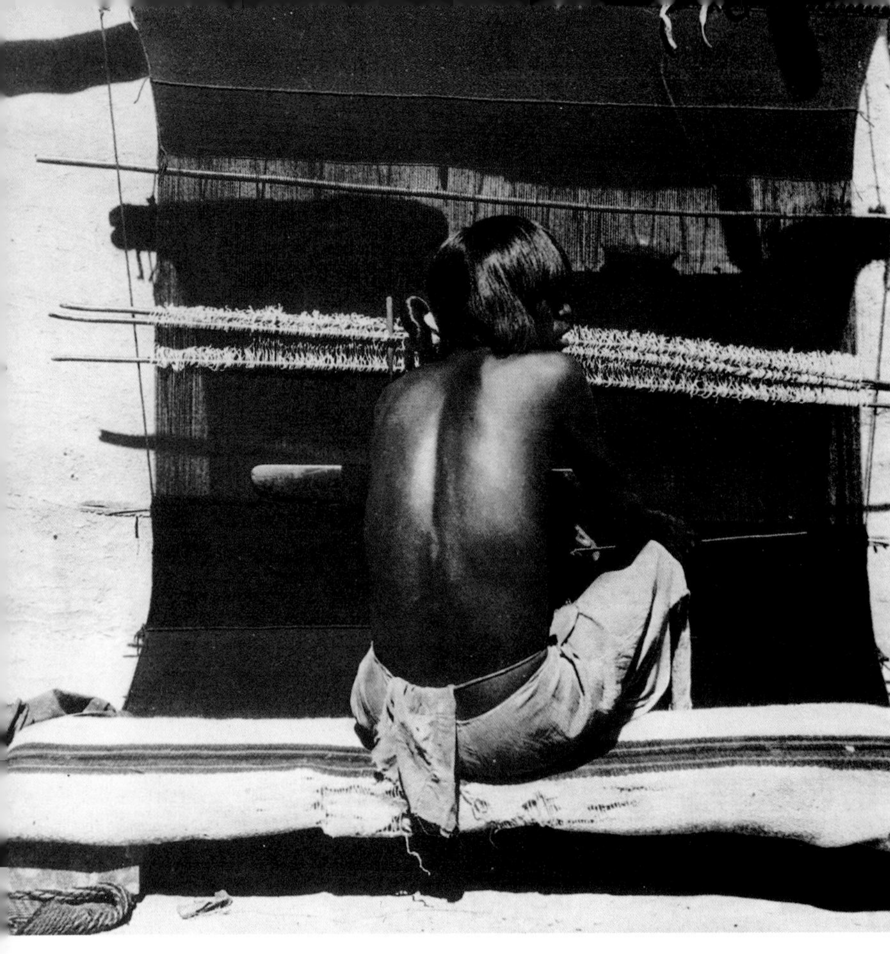

8. Hopi man weaving, late nineteenth century. (Photograph courtesy University Museum, University of Pennsylvania).

9. Navajo woman weaving, late nineteenth century. (Photograph courtesy Smithsonian Institution)

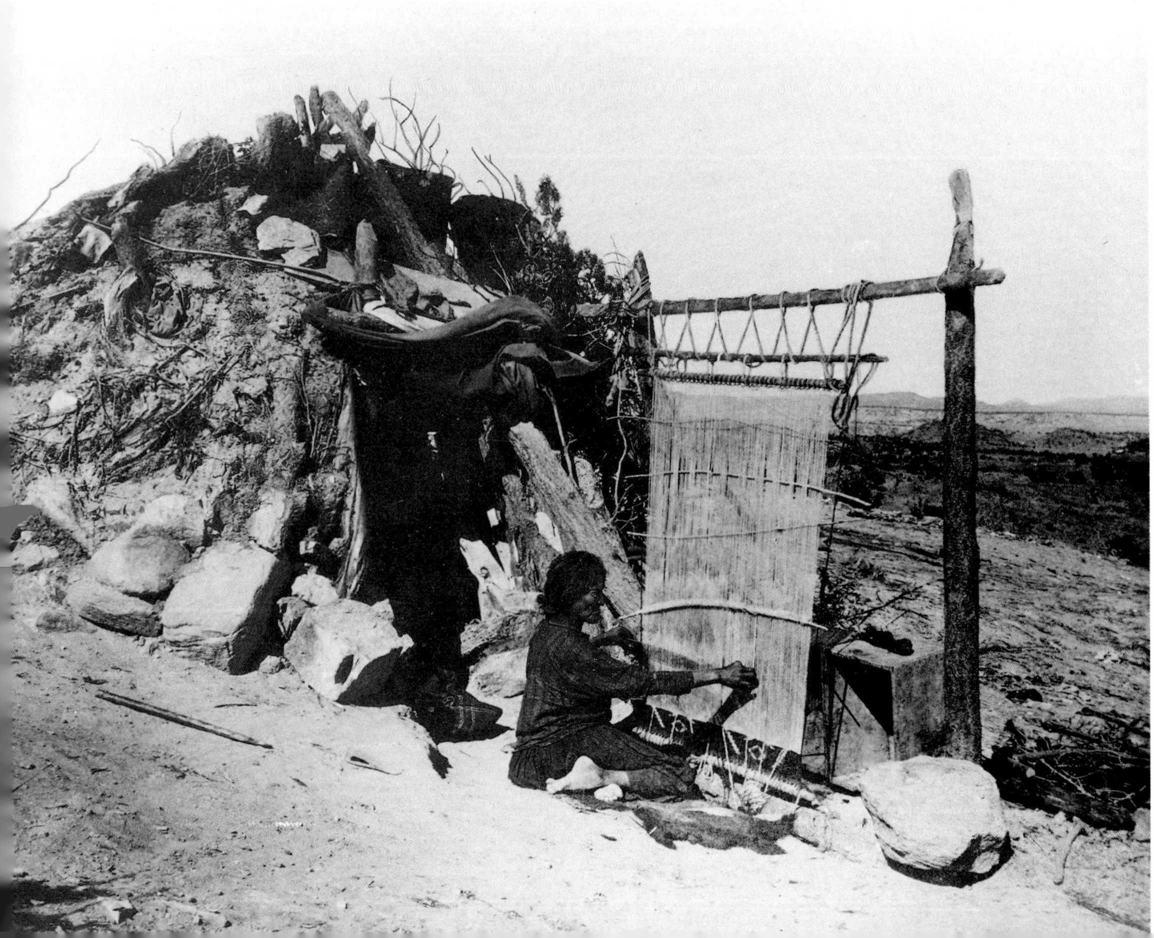

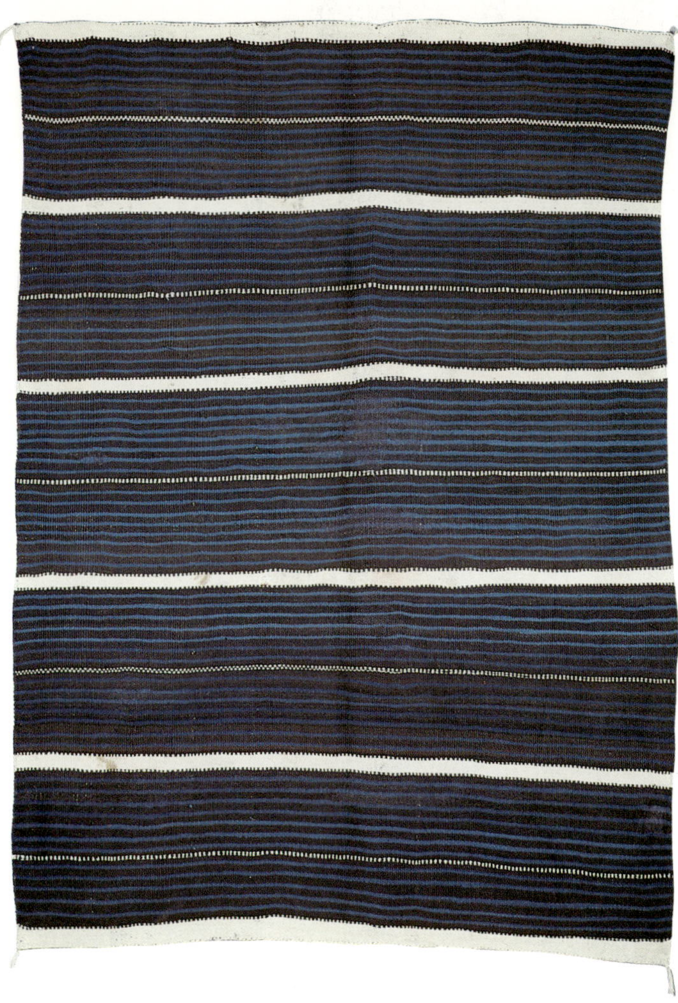

10. Hopi blanket, c. 1870. 69″ x 51″. 7 warp/in.; 32 weft/in. A style of blanket shared by both the Pueblo and Navajo, the Moki stripe pattern remained a favorite until the late nineteenth century. Woven of indigo-dyed blue hand-spun and natural brown and white hand-spun wool yarns. (Collection of School of American Research, Museum of New Mexico).

11. Rio Grande blanket, before 1860. 93″ x 49″. 7 warp/in.; 36 weft/in. Resembling Pueblo and Navajo striped blankets of the eighteenth and early nineteenth centuries, Rio Grande blankets employed a wider range of natural dye colors. Woven of vegetal-dyed green, yellow, and beige, indigo-dyed blue, and natural brown and white two-ply hand-spun wool yarns. (Private collection)

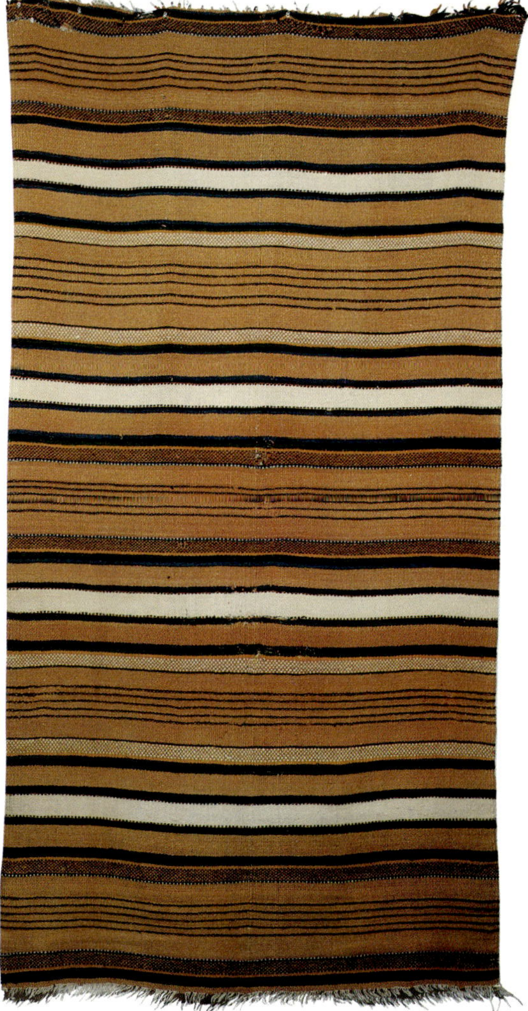

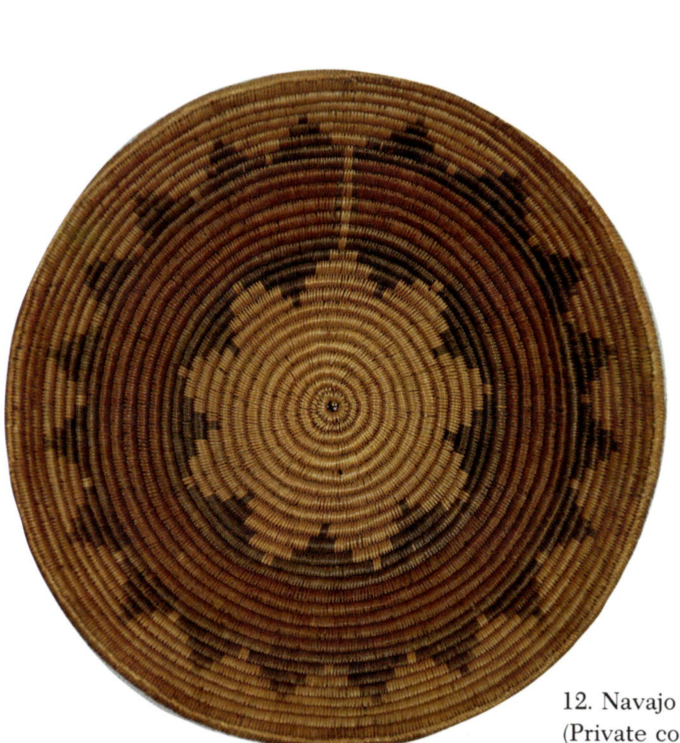

12. Navajo wedding basket, c. 1900. (Private collection)

liest Navajo textiles may have been woven from cotton cultivated by Navajo farmers, Navajo women quickly learned to shear the sheep and to weave cloth with the wool. Their simple, upright looms were modeled after looms used by Pueblo weavers.

Because of increasing hostility between the Pueblos and the Spanish during the middle and late seventeenth century, many Pueblo Indians seeking refuge from the Spanish came to live among the Navajos. As Pueblo men, who were the traditional weavers among the Pueblo Indians, coexisted with and married Navajo women, all the techniques of Pueblo weaving were passed on to the Navajos. Navajo men were occupied with hunting, raiding, and the demands of their spiritual lives, but weaving became a nearly universal occupation among Navajo women.

From the time she is an infant, strapped into her cradleboard and placed next to the loom to watch her mother weave, a Navajo girl is expected to spend time weaving every day. Many become expert weavers by the time they are teen-agers.

Weaving is an ancient tradition in the Southwest. The ancestral Pueblo Indians—the Anasazi—had been weaving with cotton since it was introduced from Mexico sometime between the first and eighth centuries. Before cotton was available, the Basketmaker people, an early manifestation of Anasazi culture, wove mats and sandals of grasses, bark, and other natural materials. When the Spanish arrived, the Pueblo Indians used primarily two types of looms: the simple backstrap belt loom and the upright vertical loom. This upright loom, made of sticks and logs tied together, was easily portable, which made it ideal for the Navajo's nomadic ways, and Navajo weavers adopted it.

Spanish historical accounts confirm that by the eighteenth century the Navajos wove and wore striped blankets, woven shirts for men, breechcloths, leggings, sashes, and one-piece women's dresses nearly identical to those made by their Pueblo teachers. Although many ceremonial Pueblo blankets were still being made from the traditional cotton, by 1700 both the Pueblo and Navajo weavers were using the long, straight, clean, shiny wool of the Spanish churro sheep in most of their textiles. Both Pueblo and Navajo weavers of this era were limited to the same choice of colors: the rich brown, creamy white, and carded gray of the natural churro fleece, and indigo blue, a dye introduced by the Spanish by the 1630s.[5] Occasionally, Pueblo and Navajo weavers alike may have used a yellow dye made from native plants such as rabbit brush, and a green dye that was probably made from rabbit brush in combination with indigo blue. Although vegetal dyes were used by Pueblo weavers in their precontact textiles, there is little surviving evidence that vegetal dyes were used in significant amounts in historic times by either Pueblo or Navajo weavers prior to the twentieth century.[6]

While the Navajos were learning to weave from the Pueblo Indians living among them, the Spanish began producing woven woolen textiles of their own in and around Santa Fe. Although early Rio Grande textiles are similar to Indian textiles in color and weave, Spanish blankets, the product of the Spanish horizontal loom, tended to be longer and narrower than the wider shoulder blankets of the Navajo and Pueblo Indians.

By 1750 Navajo weavers had access to the same wool, dye sources, and Spanish design innovations as did their former teachers, the Pueblo Indians. But in the same way that Navajos rewrote Pueblo myth and restructured Pueblo ceremony to suit their own cultural sensibilities, Navajo weaving soon took on a distinctive Navajo quality and diverged from the weaving of the Pueblo Indians. Surpassing Pueblo weavers in quality, quantity, and variety of design, nineteenth-century Navajo weavers became the outstanding weavers in the Southwest.

Why were the Navajos more creative at their looms than their Pueblo teachers? Perhaps it was because a major part of their creative energies was concentrated on weaving. Instead of making most of their own pottery, Navajo women used pots made by the Pueblos, who had been producing sophisticated, stylized ceramics for centuries.

The Navajos had their own ancient basket-weaving tradition. The designs used on their famous wedding baskets probably originated when the People still lived in the northern forests, and possibly predate that era. It was easier, however, to use baskets woven by neighboring Indians. Many of the baskets used by eighteenth- and nineteenth-century Navajos were probably acquired through raiding and trading.

Although Navajo women did not make the majority of the pots and baskets they used, by 1800 they were very familiar with the intricately patterned designs used to decorate both. What they saw of these designs, what they knew of their own basket designs, and what they learned about Pueblo, Spanish, and Mexican textile design added to their love for their familiar landscape of mountains and mesas and became the inspiration for one of the most creative eras of Navajo weaving, the Classic Period of the nineteenth century.

3

THE CLASSIC PERIOD

> The Navajos . . . work their wool with more delicacy and taste than the Spaniards.
>
> Governor Fernando de Chacon, in a letter written in 1795[7]

> Their woolen fabrics are the most valuable in our province.
>
> Pedro Pino, *Exposición del Nuevo Mexico,* 1812, on Navajo weaving.[8]

Although they retained many of their ancient ways—their language and their dependence on hunting and raiding—nineteenth-century Navajos were quite different from their ancestors, the People who first settled in the Southwest. The original bands of nomadic hunters from the north had numbered no more than a few thousand. Once they developed a stable, seasonal economy planting crops and raising livestock, however, their population swelled. In addition, many defiant Pueblo Indians found refuge from the Spanish among the Navajos prior to, during, and after the Pueblo Revolt (the Spanish were driven out of New Mexico by the Pueblo Indians in 1680 only to return in 1692). According to Navajo legend, all the unmarried women of the Jemez Pueblo (see map, fig. 2) were sent to find Navajo husbands after Spain reconquered the Pueblos. When these women had children, and when their daughters had children, the children were Navajos who belonged to the new Coyote Pass clan. The women from the San Felipe Pueblo became absorbed into the Navajo tribe as the Black Sheep clan.[9]

Although their geographical remoteness from one another and their fierce individuality kept the Navajos from being truly unified, as a tribe they were far stronger, richer, and more united by 1800 than ever before. This was due in large part to the abundance of Navajo horses. Once the People were mobile, the country they called Dinetah (*Dine* is Navajo for the People; *Dinetah* is the home of the Dine) expanded dramatically. The Navajos fanned out, seeking new grazing land for their animals and new land to cultivate for farming. This mobility also led to active trading relationships with other Indians and with Spanish colonists in and around Santa Fe. Both groups wanted to trade for Navajo blankets. Thanks to the horse, by 1800 Navajo blankets were already a commercial success.

Strong and mobile, Navajo raiders became the scourge of the Southwest ("a land that knew its scourging well," to quote Navajo scholar Charles Avery Amsden).[10] The years between 1700 and 1800 were characterized by aggression and retaliation on the part of both the Spanish and the Navajos. A series of peace treaties was signed, but neither side honored them. If one group of Navajo raiders made peace with the Spanish, the agreement had no effect on other Navajo raiders. There was no central tribal authority. The only permanent loyalties were clan loyalties, and by 1700 there were more than sixty clans.[11] At the same time, the Spanish had little respect for the treaties because they thought of Navajo Indians as dangerous heathens, beyond hope for conversion to Catholicism. Spanish slave raids among the Navajos were common occurrences whether or not treaties had been signed.

By the winter of 1804/05 the Spanish Governor, Chacon, decided that the almost constant warfare had become too costly and threatening. He ordered Spanish troops to pursue the Navajos into their traditional physical and spiritual stronghold, the Canyon de Chelly (see map). The sheer red walls of the canyon are among the most spectacularly beautiful natural wonders of the Southwest. The ruins of pueblos precipitously built into the canyon walls are remnants of the Anasazi civilization. Since their arrival in the Southwest, the Navajos planted crops and grazed livestock between the canyon walls.

When the Navajos learned that a powerful force of Spanish troops was approaching the canyon, they decided to avoid a confrontation. Many of them left, and those who remained hid in a remote cave in a branch canyon. The Indians believed their hiding place to be impregnable and they were confident. But as the Spanish soldiers rode by below, it is believed that one of the Indians in the cave may have cried out. The Spanish aimed their rifles at the rocks that formed the roof of the cave and the bullets ricocheted into the cave, killing the men, women, and children trapped inside. When the shooting ended, the soldiers climbed into the cave and clubbed and bayoneted any survivors. The cave became known as Massacre Cave and the branch canyon was named Canyon del Muerto, "canyon of the dead."

Navajos have a dread of the presence of ghosts and will not enter any place where someone has died, so they never returned to Massacre Cave. The skeletons of the Indians killed inside the cave were discovered by Anglos one hundred years after the massacre. Along with the remains of the Indians, some of the clothing they had been wearing was also found. One striped blanket survived intact, and several fragments of other wearing blankets were also found (fig. 13).

13. Blanket fragment, c. 1800. One of the earliest documented examples of Navajo weaving, this fragment was collected from Massacre Cave. Note the clusters of narrow stripes alternating with broader bands, which became the basis for the evolution of more complex designs in the nineteenth century. Woven of natural shades of hand-spun wool yarns. (Collection of Maxwell Museum of Anthropology, University of New Mexico)

To this day, these Massacre Cave fragments are the earliest documented surviving Navajo textiles. Everything that is believed to be true about Navajo weaving prior to 1805, the date of the massacre, is guesswork, no matter how educated.

The simple striped designs and twill patterns of the majority of blanket fragments found in Massacre Cave are believed to be typical of designs found on eighteenth-century Pueblo and Navajo blankets (see fig. 14). But by the early 1800s Navajo weavers, employing almost exclusively the tapestry-weave technique, were experimenting with variations on traditional striped designs. The Classic Period was the most fertile era in the history of Navajo weaving for such experiments.

The earliest Navajo blankets probably displayed many different arrangements of stripes. Weavers probably started by varying the width and number of stripes (figs. 15, 16, and 17). They wove stripes within stripes. They outlined stripes in contrasting colors and contrasted zones of stripes with solid bands of color. This experimentation with striped designs seems to have led the more innovative weavers into interrupting the horizontal lines of the stripes, forming terraced diagonals, wavy bands, triangles, and diamonds. Variations on these are the basic elements of Classic Period Navajo blanket design.

Dr. Joe Ben Wheat, one of the leading contemporary scholars in the field of Navajo textile research, says that the terraced zigzag stripe is "precisely that utilized on decorated Navajo baskets" (see fig. 12). Dr. Wheat goes on to say, "Since Navajo baskets were well known before the Navajo began to weave blankets, it seems probable that the basketry design system was simply transferred."[12]

Although ancient basket designs were an important influence on nineteenth-century Navajo weavers, more contemporary influences were also significant. During the years between 1800 and 1864 political change led to cultural change for the Navajos, and these changes were reflected in Classic Navajo weaving.

In 1807 two Spanish weavers, the Bazan brothers, were sent to Santa Fe from Mexico City to teach local colonial weavers to imitate the Saltillo-style sarape (fig. 18) so popular with affluent Mexicans—and also to create a New Mexican sarape that could compete in the marketplace with the increasingly popular Navajo sarape. The dimensions and designs of these New Mexican sarapes possibly inspired Navajo weavers to make their sarapes even more elaborate.

In 1821 Mexico won its independence from Spain

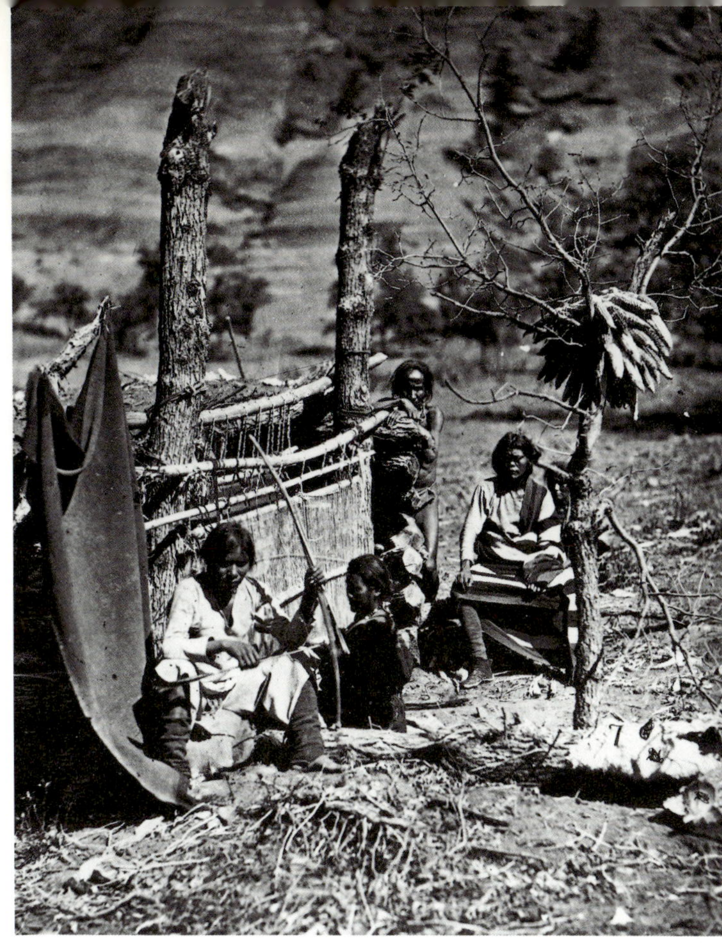

14. Navajo weaver with family, c. 1873. (Photograph courtesy National Archives)

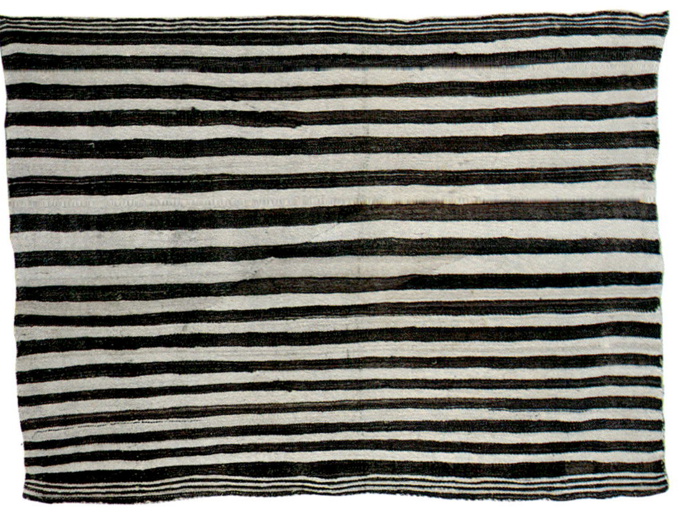

15. Shoulder blanket, 1750–1800. 49″ x 69″. 9 warp/in.; 16 weft/in. Woven wider than long, this plain-weave striped blanket shows early Navajo zoning characteristics at the top and bottom, which later become more clearly identifiable in the Chief pattern blankets. Woven of natural brown and white hand-spun and a tiny amount of indigo-dyed blue hand-spun wool yarn. (Collection of School of American Research, Museum of New Mexico)

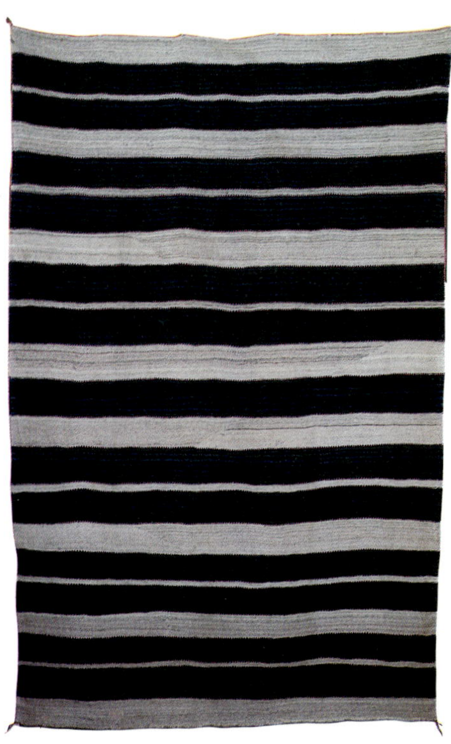

16. Striped Moki blanket, 1860–1880. 78″ x 51″. 10 warp/in.; 28 weft/in. The presence of "lazy lines" in this Moki-style blanket indicates Navajo origin. Woven of indigo-dyed blue and natural brown and white hand-spun wool yarns. (Private collection)

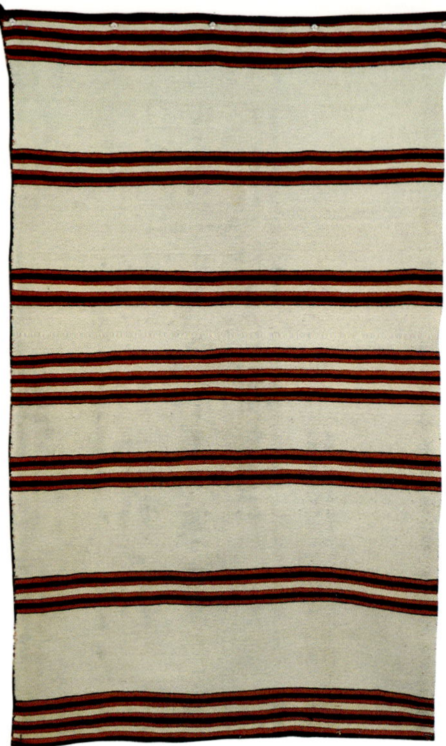

17. Child's sarape, before 1860. 50″ x 30″. 14 warp/in.; 54 weft/in. The grouping of stripes into middle and end zones is an early step in the development of the sarape pattern. Woven of raveled lac-dyed red, indigo-dyed blue hand-spun, and natural white hand-spun wool yarns. (Collection of Heard Museum)

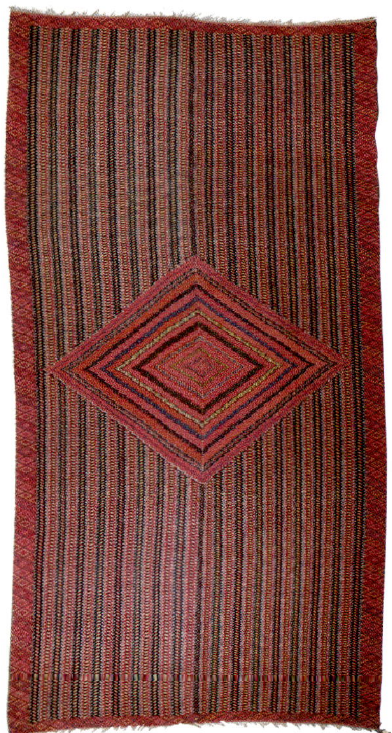

18. Saltillo sarape, 1750–1825. 96″ x 51″. 20 warp/in.; 112 weft/in. Hand-woven in Mexico for Spanish Colonial gentlemen or *caballeros,* some of these very finely woven blankets were shipped north to New Mexico where they influenced both the style and quality of weaving in the Southwest. Woven of natural (presynthetic)-dyed red, pink, green, yellow, and blue and natural (undyed) brown and white hand-spun wool yarns. (Private collection)

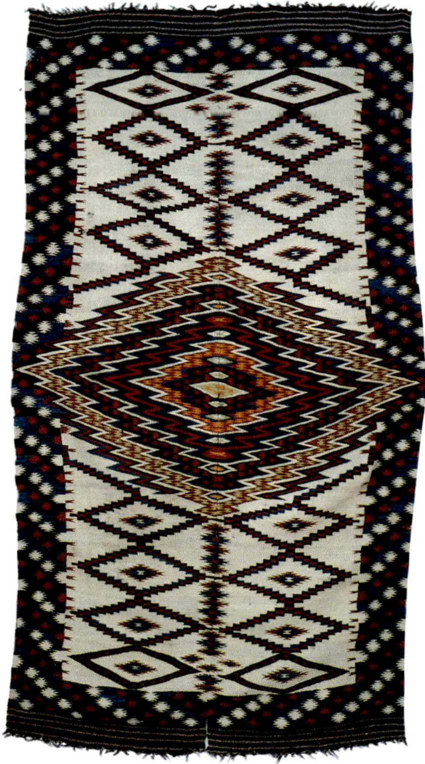

19. Rio Grande blanket, c. 1860. 87″ x 47″. 8 warp/in.; 40 weft/in. Mexican Saltillo sarape design influence is clearly visible in this Rio Grande blanket. Navajos were exposed to and influenced by these textiles in the nineteenth century. Woven of cochineal-dyed red hand-spun, three-ply commercial vegetal-dyed orange and pale green and indigo-dyed blue and natural brown and white hand-spun wool yarns. (Collection of School of American Research, Museum of New Mexico.)

and took control of New Mexico. New trade routes opened under the new regime, giving the Navajos access to new sources of weaving materials. The new dyes, yarns, and *bayeta* trade cloth that arrived in the Southwest in abundance by way of the Santa Fe Trail from St. Louis allowed nineteenth-century Navajo weavers more freedom of creative expression than they had previously known, primarily in the form of access to the color red.

No good red dye was known to be available from the plants indigenous to the canyons and mesas of the Navajos. Two natural sources for the color red were madder, an imported vegetal dye, and lac and cochineal dyes, dyes made from the powdered carcasses of, respectively, Old World and New World cactus beetles. Spanish Colonial weavers and Pueblo weavers were using cochineal dye and madder dye sparingly by 1776, but Navajo weavers apparently never had access to these dyes and therefore had to resort to raveling bayeta, wool trade cloth dyed red with either lac or cochineal dyes.[13]

After raveling the bayeta, Navajo weavers rewove the yarn, either in single strands or loosely twisted together, to form multiple plies as weft elements, in their blankets along with their own handspun wool (see fig. 211). Bayeta became a highly desirable trade item, and Navajo raiders and traders put bayeta high on their "shopping lists." In turn, the fine crimson sarapes woven with bayeta yarn as well as the simpler striped Chief-style blanket were avidly sought after by other Indians as well as by the Spanish colonists (see fig. 20).

Bayeta cloth was but one of many commercial cloths available in the Southwest during the eighteenth and nineteenth centuries. As early as 1788 Navajo weavers were using yarn raveled from commercially woven woolen cloth.[14] Much of the cloth raveled for their blankets may have been produced in the New World as well as in Europe. The Classic Period was characterized by textiles woven from a combination of handspun and raveled yarns.

Along with the availability of lac- and cochineal-dyed bayeta in the Southwest, small amounts of imported European commercially spun three-ply Saxony yarn were also available to Navajo weavers by the 1840s (see fig. 212).

This new wealth of materials resulted in a great number of blankets in a growing variety of styles. The one-piece wraparound blanket dress, or *manta,* woven by eighteenth-century Navajo women was no longer being made as a dress by 1800[15] (although the style lived on as a shawl—see figs. 21 and 39). The new style was a two-piece dress (figs. 22, 23, 37, and 38) of two identical blankets joined at the shoulder and belted at the waist, usually by a woven sash. Two-piece blanket dresses were woven with a large, undecorated center panel of

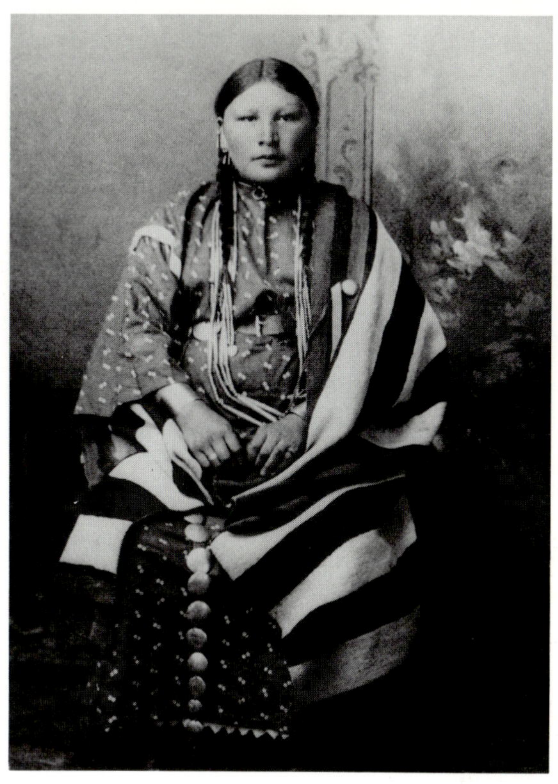

20. Sioux woman wearing a Navajo Ute-style First Phase Chief blanket, 1870s. By the early 1800s Navajo weavers were producing blankets not only for themselves but for trade and sale to both colonists and Indians. (Photograph courtesy University Museum, University of Pennsylvania)

dark-brown wool bordered at the top and bottom by contrasting decorated panels. Designs commonly used in the end panels included plain stripes of varying widths, terraced wavy bands, rows of terraced diamonds, and, late in the Classic Period, rows of crosses, almost always executed in indigo blue on a red bayeta or Saxony field. Occasionally small amounts of vegetal yellow and green were used. Unlike other styles of Classic wearing blankets, the two-piece dress was worn only by Navajo women and was never traded to or worn by other Indians.[16]

With the exception of the blanket dresses and the mantas, whose designs remained basically conservative and unchanging, the design of Classic wearing blankets and sarapes became more elaborate—even florid—as the 1800s progressed. Many of these Classic blankets were both visual and finely woven technological masterpieces of textile art, and many of those that survived are recognized as such by twentieth-century textile scholars and collectors.

Perhaps the most widely recognized and avidly collected style of Classic Navajo blanket is the *Chief blanket.* The name itself is something of a mystery as there were no chiefs among the Navajos. Most contemporary scholars believe the name referred instead to the chiefs of the Plains Indian tribes. Many of these mounted war-

21. Woman's manta, c. 1870. 37″ x 50″. 10 warp/in.; 40 weft/in. Woven entirely in one or more of the twill-weave techniques, the manta or shawl reappears as a popular garment about 1865 as a revival of a much earlier twill-weaving style. Woven of raveled cochineal-dyed red and indigo-dyed blue and natural brown hand-spun wool yarns. (Private collection)

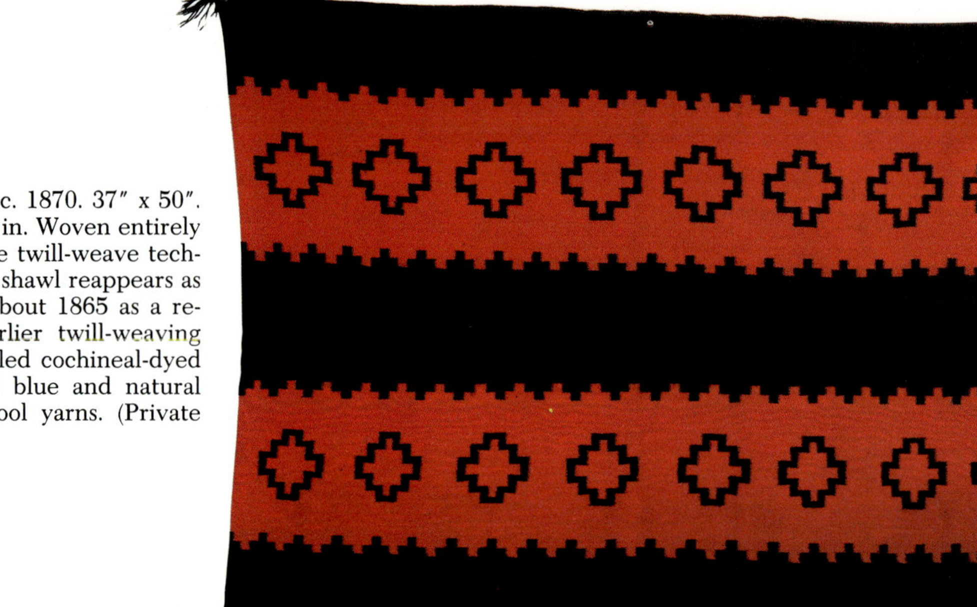

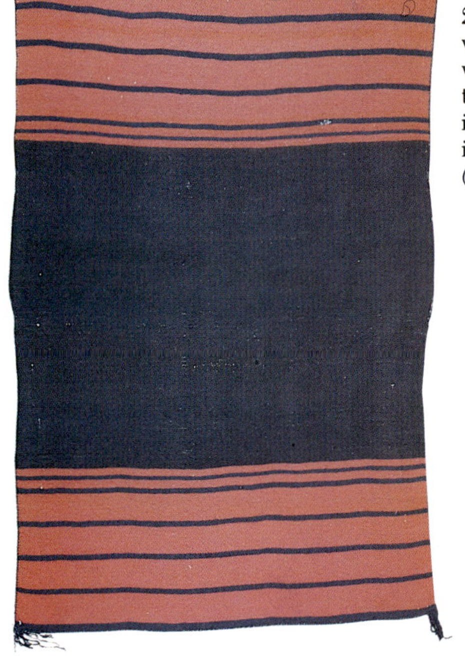

22. Woman's dress half, c. 1865. 52″ x 33″. 12 warp/in.; 48 weft/in. Often woven as finely as the best sarapes, the woman's two-piece dress changed little in design in the nineteenth century until it was replaced by the Anglo-style dress in the 1870s. Woven of raveled cochineal (?)-dyed red and indigo-dyed blue and natural brown hand-spun wool yarns. (Collection of Arizona State Museum, University of Arizona)

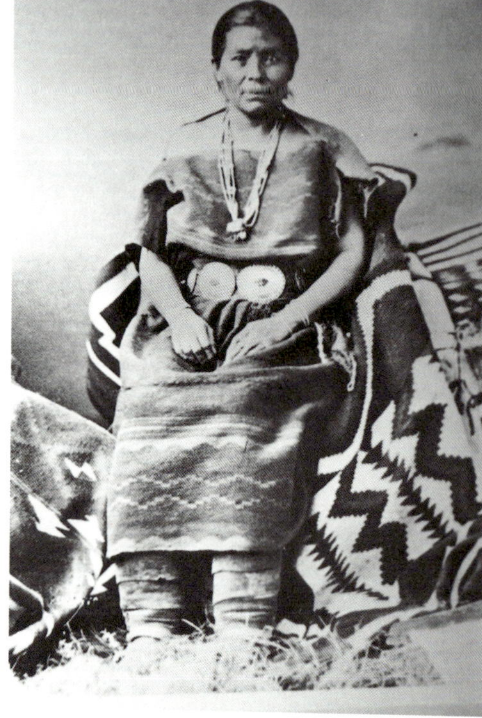

23. Juanita, wife of Navajo leader Manuelito, 1870s. (Photograph courtesy University Museum, University of Pennsylvania)

riors from the north and the east, who typically wore eagle-feather bonnets and beaded and quilled hide war shirts, were proud owners of finely woven Navajo blankets. The striped pattern they favored became known as the Chief blanket. Because these blankets were so highly prized, they became status symbols among Plains Indians. Only chiefs, it was said, could afford them. Actually, anyone who could pay the price (in horses, silver, bayeta cloth, or whatever) could buy or trade for one, and during the 1800s these blankets were the Navajo weaver's "best seller" to the Indian market. A wealthy Plains Indian could outfit his entire family in Navajo Chief blankets (see fig. 24).

During the years between 1800 and 1865 the Chief blanket went through various stages of change in design. These changes characterize the history of stylistic evolution of Classic Navajo blankets.

The earliest version of the popular style, the Ute-style First Phase Chief blanket (figs. 25 and 40), is similar in appearance to the striped shoulder blankets the Navajos had been weaving for one hundred years (fig. 15). During the eighteenth century, many weavers stopped making as many blankets in the old Pueblo proportions in favor of longer, narrower, Mexican-style sarapes that were woven vertically but worn horizontally (fig. 31). During the nineteenth century only Chief blankets and mantas were woven wider than long, and this remained constant through all the phases of design change.

But the First Phase Chief blanket was different from the striped shoulder blankets that preceded it and from the striped *diyugis*, which were somewhat similar in appearance. Chief blankets were more finely woven than other, more ordinary Navajo textiles like the diyugi. The use of bayeta yarn in the bayeta First Phase Chief blanket (see fig. 41) helped trigger this trend. Because the yarn raveled from bayeta cloth was commercially spun, it was often finer than the hand-spun wool. When Classic Period weavers combined raveled bayeta red with their own hand-spun yarn, they tried to spin their own yarn as fine as possible so it would not contrast awkwardly with the commercial product. But even when weavers were limited to the use of brown, blue, and white hand-spun yarn (as in the Ute style), the weaving was technically superior to weaving found in more mundane garments.

As the availability and use of bayeta became more widespread during the 1800s, fewer blankets without bayeta were woven. Using the red yarn sparingly at first, many early Classic Period weavers seemed content to outline the broad indigo stripes of the Chief blanket in red. Blanket fragments dating prior to 1805 woven with wefts of bayeta were found in Massacre Cave. As the weavers grew more daring in design and more proficient in technique, however, their appetite for the red cloth increased. The supply of bayeta seems

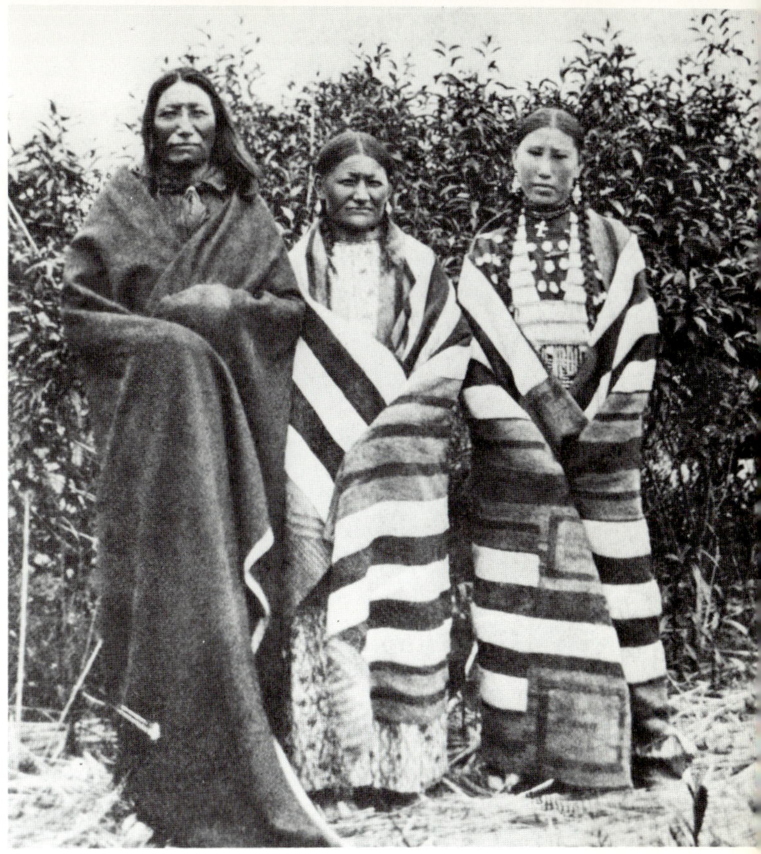

24. Spotted Tail, wife, and daughter, Sioux, 1870s. (Photograph courtesy National Archives)

to have kept pace with the demand, and the use of red bayeta in Classic blankets increased as the nineteenth century progressed.

The use of red stripes in the broad end and center stripes seems to have led to the development of the second stage of Chief blanket design. In the mid-1800s Classic Period weavers began to introduce rectangular blocks of red inside the broad indigo-blue stripes, thus breaking up the continuous flow of the banded design.

The typical Classic Second Phase Chief blanket has twelve divided rectangles, six in the two top and bottom double indigo stripes and six in the two double indigo stripes that decorated the center (see fig. 26). Second Phase Chief blankets are not quite so rare as blankets woven in the earlier First Phase style, but are held in equal aesthetic regard by collectors. The contrast of strong and soft colors and the careful balance and proportion of the minimal design differs markedly from the elaborate sarapes of the same period (figs. 29 and 30).

The controlled design so important to the second design phase of the Chief blanket was to take on added drama and dimension by the 1860s as the crimson rectangles developed into a dominant central diamond surrounded by terraced half diamonds and quarter diamonds (see figs. 27 and 43). The blanket that resulted—the Third Phase Chief blanket—is probably the most widely recognized and most popular Navajo blanket

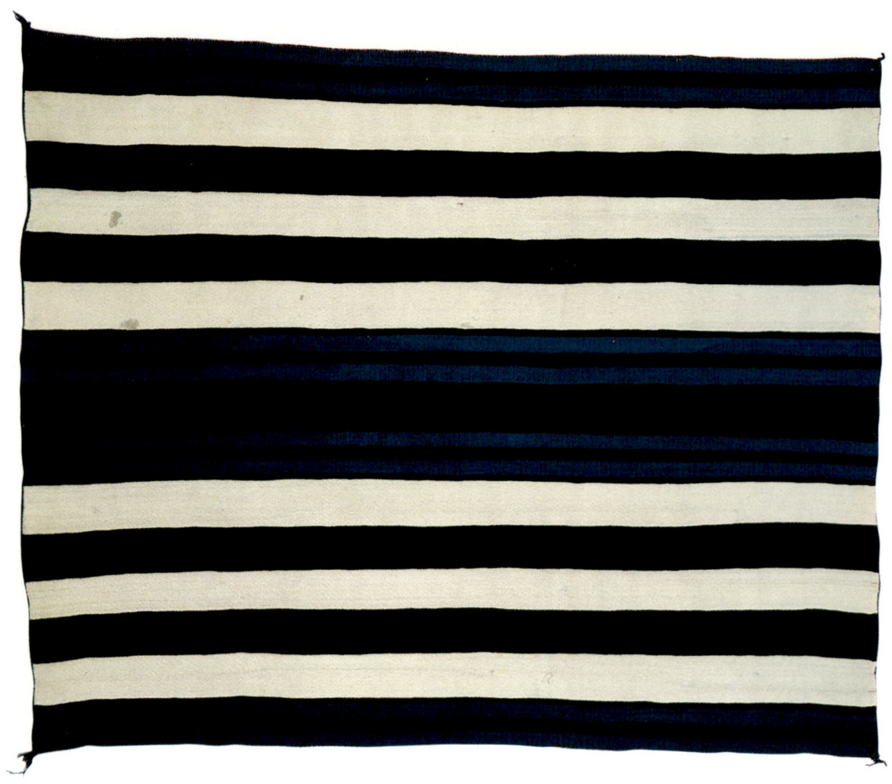

25. Ute-style First Phase Chief blanket, 1800–1850. 56″ x 72″. 10 warp/in.; 68 weft/in. The first recognized style of Chief blanket, the Ute-style blanket is distinguished by its sparing use of color and its minimal but elegant pattern. Woven of indigo-dyed blue and natural brown and white hand-spun wool yarns. (Collection of School of American Research, Museum of New Mexico)

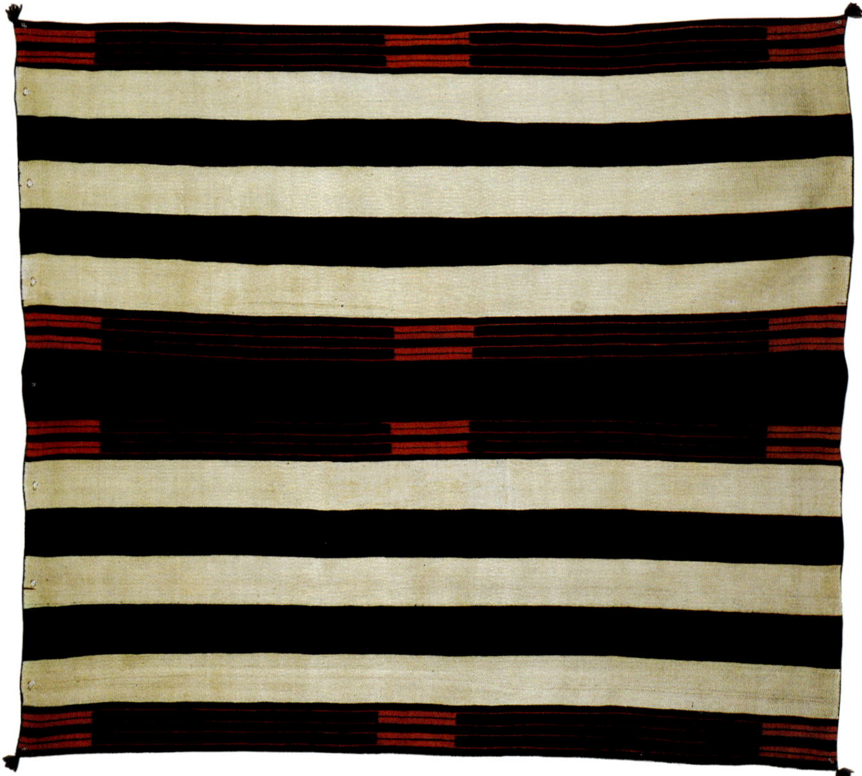

26. Second Phase Chief blanket, c. 1860. 60″ x 70″. 11 warp/in.; 68 weft/in. The interruption of the red-edged broad blue stripes with blocks of red color marks the Second Phase style of Chief blanket. Woven of raveled cochineal with lac-dyed red and indigo-dyed blue and natural brown and white hand-spun wool yarns. (Private collection)

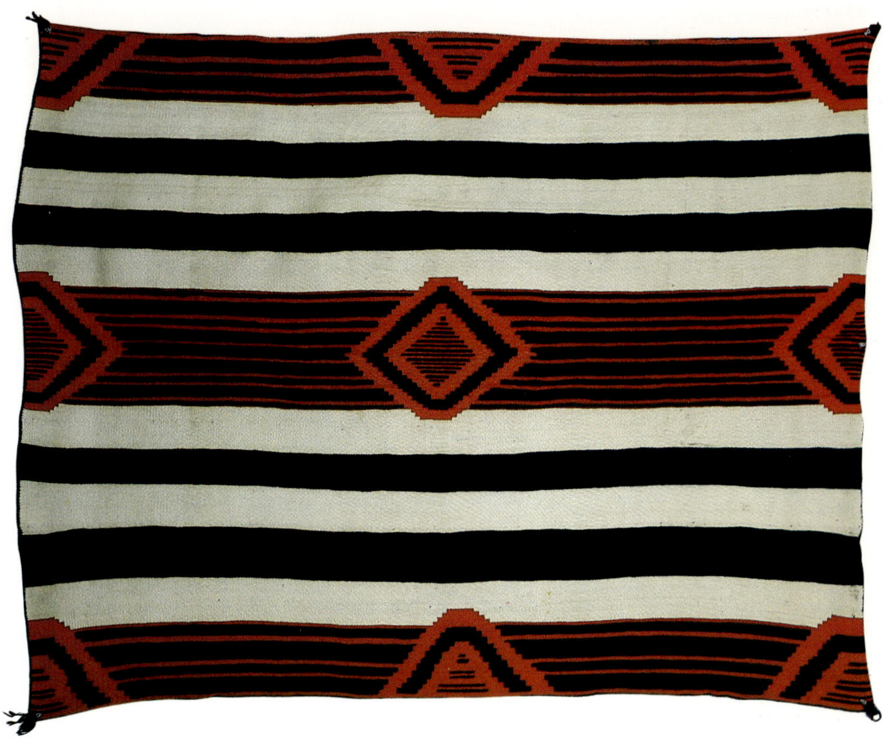

27. Third Phase Chief blanket, c. 1870. 52″ x 70″. 11 warp/in.; 48 weft/in. The central diamond, half diamond, and quarter diamond design elements appear to be superimposed on top of the striped pattern, creating a foreground and background visual effect. Woven of raveled synthetic-dyed red and indigo-dyed blue and natural brown and white hand-spun wool yarns. (Private collection)

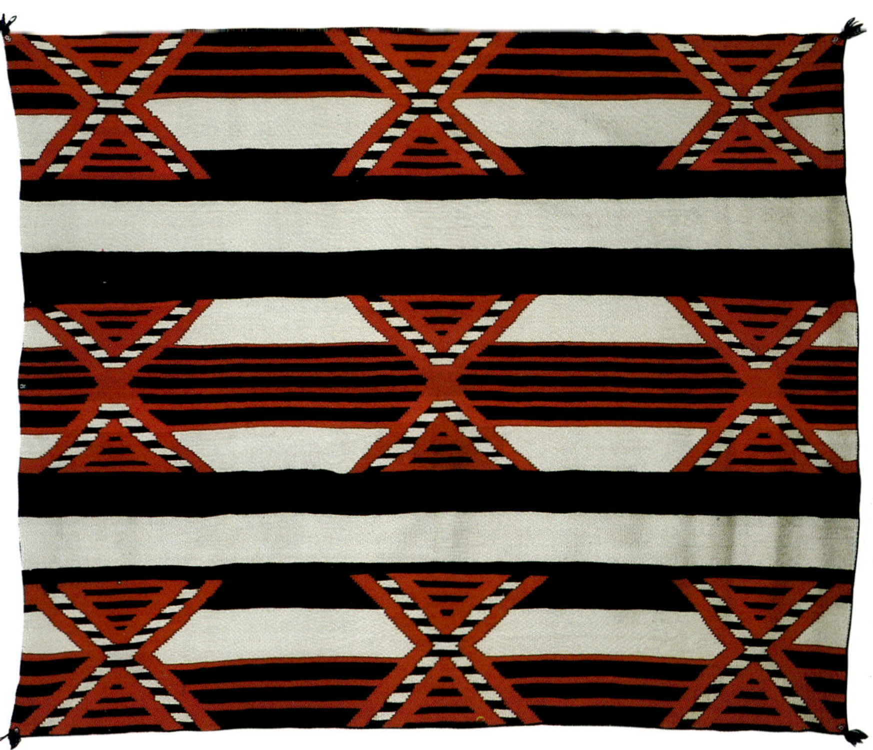

28. Chief blanket variation, c. 1870. 55″ x 68″. 11 warp/in.; 50 weft/in. The blue and white interrupted stripes add extra impact to the X or hourglass design elements which are in fact nothing more than a novel arrangement of typical Third Phase half diamonds. Woven of raveled cochineal-dyed red, three-ply commercial cochineal-dyed red, and indigo-dyed blue, and natural brown and white hand-spun wool yarns. (Private collection)

29. Sarape, 1850–1860. 64″ x 44″. 10 warp/in.; 54 weft/in. Large terraces formed by interrupting the stripes are the stepped building blocks forming the wavy bands, triangles, half diamonds, and diamonds of this Classic Period sarape. Note the weighting of the design in the middle and end zones typical of this period. Woven of three-ply commercial cochineal-dyed red, three-ply commercial vegetal-dyed pale green, and indigo-dyed blue and natural white hand-spun wool yarns. (Collection of Arizona State Museum, University of Arizona)

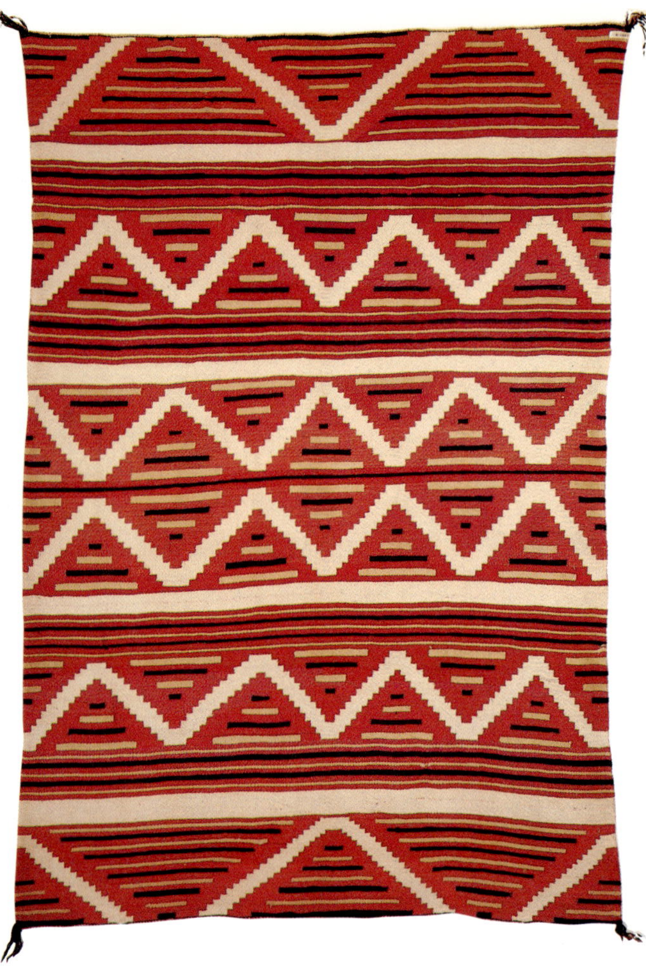

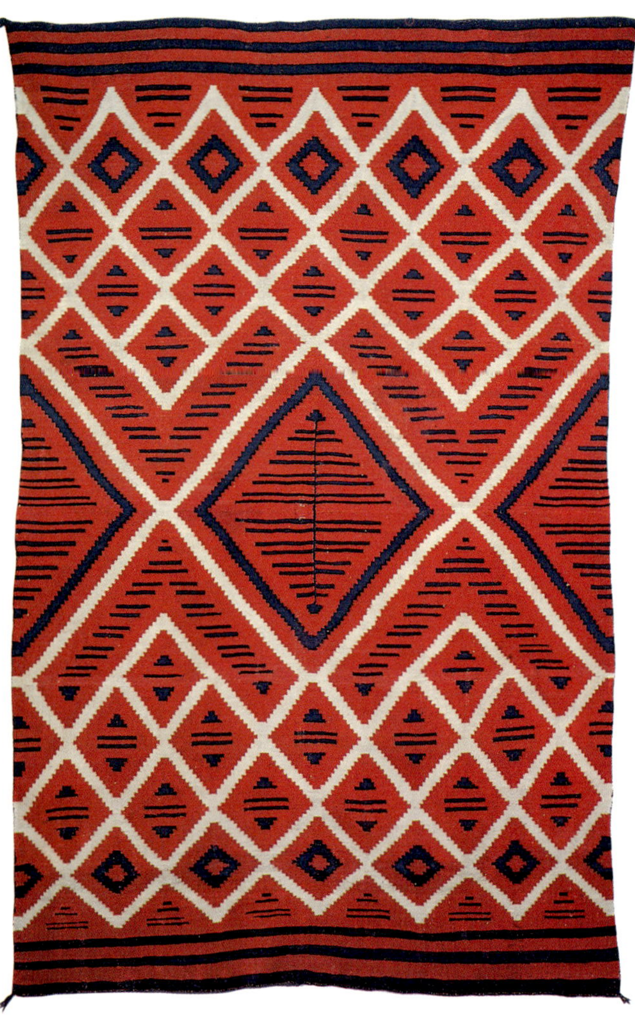

30. Poncho sarape, 1830–1850. 83″ x 55″. 14 warp/in.; 64 weft/in. The essence of Classic Period sarape aesthetics is embodied in this large sarape. Worn as a poncho, these blankets presented a different appearance to the viewer than the standard wraparound sarape shoulder blanket. Woven of raveled lac-dyed red and indigo-dyed blue and natural white hand-spun wool yarns. (Collection of School of American Research, Museum of New Mexico)

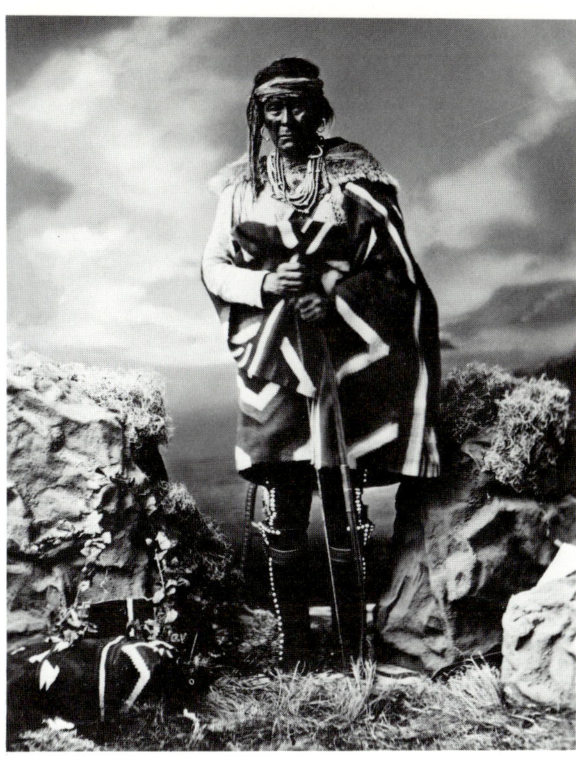

31. Cayatanito, brother of the famous Navajo leader Manuelito, c. 1874. (Photograph courtesy Smithsonian Institution)

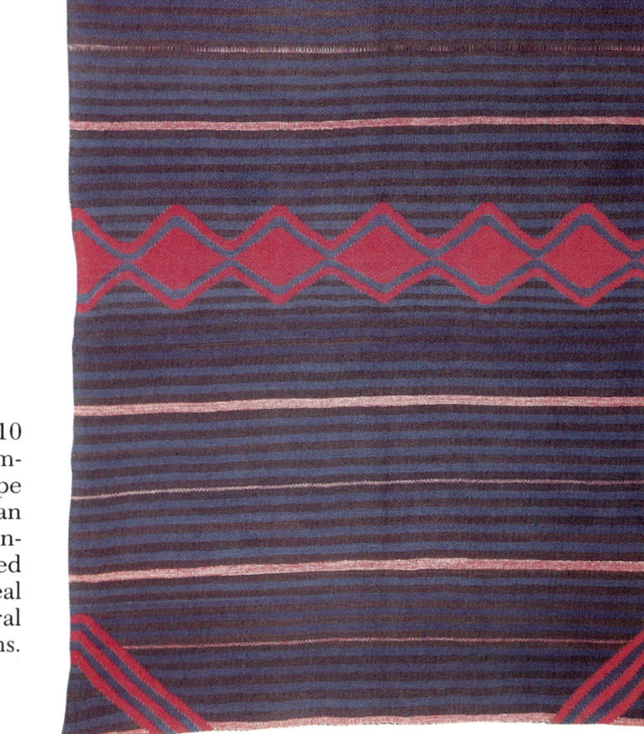

32. Moki sarape, c. 1865. 70″ x 48″. 10 warp/in.; 40 weft/in. This blanket embodies more of the true Navajo sarape design and weave characteristics than the commoner, simply striped Moki blankets. Woven of raveled cochineal-dyed red, raveled and recarded cochineal pink, and indigo-dyed blue and natural brown and white hand-spun wool yarns. (Private collection)

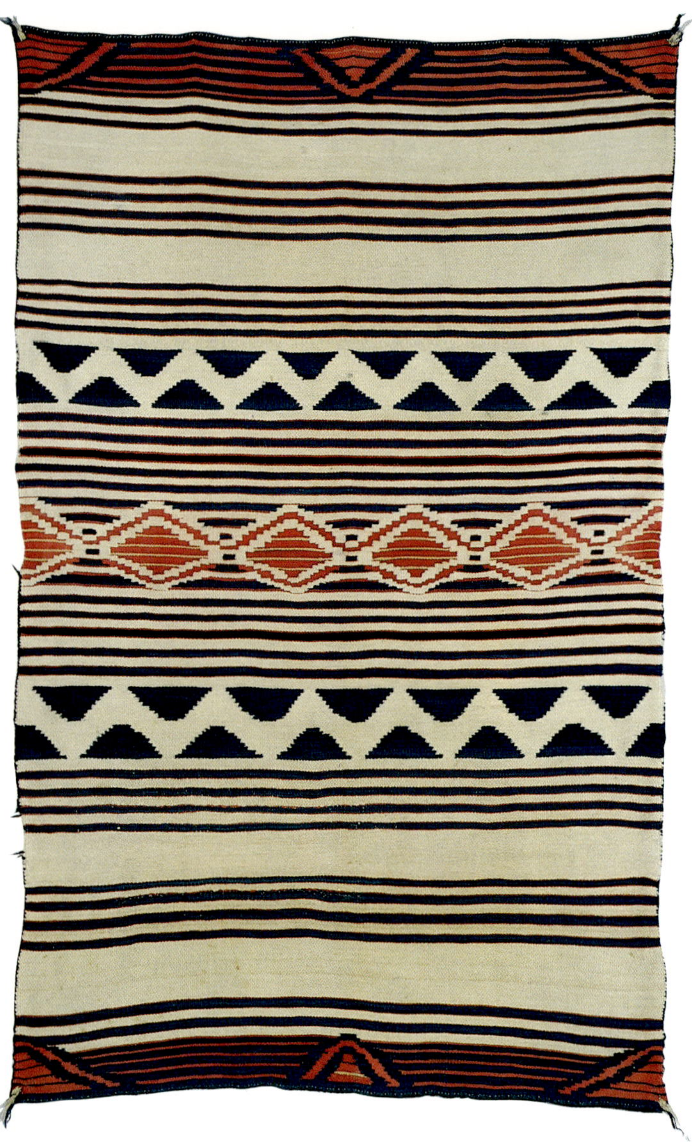

33. Child's sarape, 1850–1860. 51″ x 32″. 13 warp/in.; 56 weft/in. The white background color and use of vegetal yellow in this mostly striped scaled-down sarape indicate it was probably made after 1850. Woven of raveled cochineal-dyed red, vegetal-dyed pale yellow hand-spun, and indigo-dyed blue and natural white hand-spun wool yarns. (Collection of School of American Research, Museum of New Mexico)

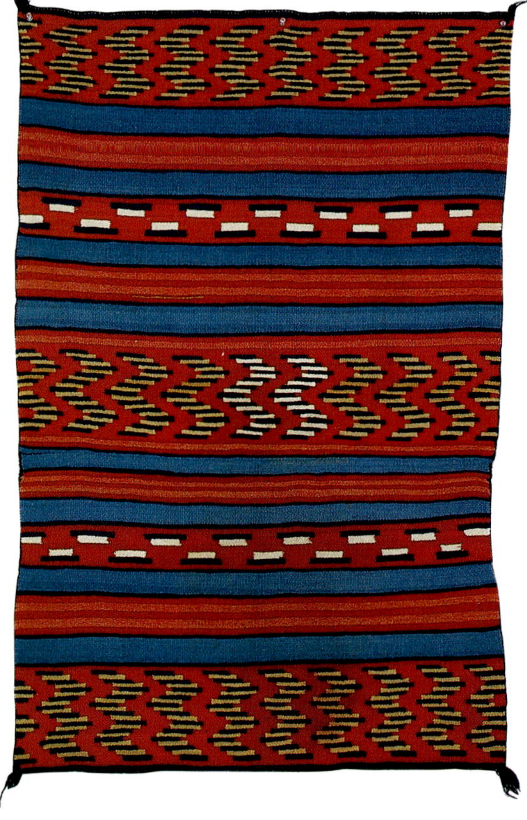

34. Child's sarape/saddle blanket, c. 1870. 48″ x 32″. 9 warp/in.; 30 weft/in. Many of the smaller Navajo blankets may have been woven as multipurpose blankets. Woven of raveled cochineal (?)-dyed red, raveled and recarded cochineal pink, vegetal-dyed yellow hand-spun, and indigo-dyed blue and natural white hand-spun wool yarns. (Private collection)

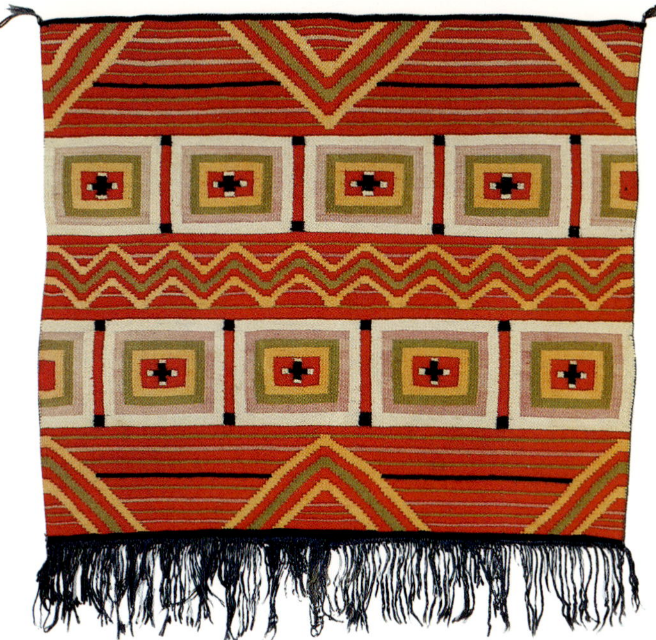

35. Single saddle blanket, c. 1870. 25″ x 30″. 13 warp/in.; 60 weft/in. Reportedly made as fancy saddle blankets for special occasions, most of these small blankets were probably intended as souvenirs for soldiers and government agents stationed in the Southwest in the 1860s and 1870s. Woven of raveled synthetic-dyed red, green, yellow, and lavender and indigo-dyed blue and natural white hand-spun wool yarns. (Collection of School of American Research, Museum of New Mexico)

style ever woven. In fact, the artistic reputation of the Chief blanket, and of the Third Phase Chief blanket in particular, has helped spread the popularity of Navajo weaving in general.

The imagination of the Navajo weaver was not limited to the production of the easily recognized styles of Chief blankets. Beginning with the Second Phase pattern (1850–1865), Navajo weavers began experimenting with numerous pattern variations based on novel combinations of terraced design elements. This process of imaginative experimentation lasted through the 1870s (figs. 44–48).

Many collectors regard the finely woven, colorful, boldly patterned sarapes (fig. 29) and poncho sarapes (fig. 30) woven with a slit for the head as the most exciting examples of Navajo weaving of the Classic Period. Most Classic sarapes are patterned in hand-spun indigo-blue and natural white designs on a red field of raveled bayeta or three-ply Saxony yarn. Small amounts of vegetal yellow- and green-dyed yarns were also occasionally used.

The central terraced diamond found in many Classic sarapes and poncho sarapes is probably an echo of the central diamond found on Mexican Saltillo sarapes (see fig. 18). But the large central diamond was only one popular design for Navajo sarapes. A row of central diamonds was also characteristic of the period.

Large terrace patterns in blue and white on a red field typify the early Classic Period sarape and poncho sarapes, with many having well-integrated, overall patterns that expand from the center of the blanket. Careful study shows that the designs of these sarapes are based on the concept of the interrupted stripe, using color changes to create a pattern composed of a balance of positive and negative space. By 1820 the sarape style had become fully developed.

The sarape woven vertically was worn wrapped horizontally around the body. Poncho sarapes, also woven vertically, were worn draped over the wearer's front and back and viewed vertically as they were woven, but only half at a time (fig. 31). Few poncho sarapes were woven after 1860 (see figs. 30, 52, 54, 56, and 82).

Beginning about 1850, the wavy-band sarape style began to replace the integrated, overall pattern style as the dominant style of Navajo sarape. Three distinct zones of design, usually separated by broad areas of background color containing thin stripes and/or narrow terraced wavy bands, typify the sarapes of the 1850–1865 period. The use of Saxony yarns and of hand-spun white as a background color became more common during those years. Vegetal yellow and green hand-spun yarns were used more frequently than before, but still in small amounts.

One of the distinctive varieties of the Navajo sarape is known as the Moki sarape. (see figs. 16, 32, and 88). The term *Moki* refers to the Pueblo Hopi Indians of northern Arizona. There is no evidence that Hopi weavers in particular made any significant contribution to the design of these subtly striped wearing blankets; in fact, the Moki design style was more likely to have been influenced by the striped Rio Grande blankets of the period. Most Moki sarapes are distinguished by a conservative striping of the field in bands of indigo blue and natural brown, gray, or white. Occasionally these stripes were grouped into repeated zones forming broad repetitious design bands. By the 1860s stripes of bayeta or Saxony red yarn are incorporated. In the late 1860s and 1870s, the Moki style reached its artistic peak when bold terraced and serrated designs were superimposed over the field of stripes (fig. 32).

Classic Period Navajo weavers produced not only full-size sarapes for adults but also smaller sarapes for children (see figs. 17, 33, 55, 61–64, and 67). Similar designs, materials, and high quality of weave appear in the child's sarape, but the design is scaled down to suit the smaller size. Few examples of child's sarapes made before 1860 are known to exist, as it is probable that fewer of the costly sarape-grade blankets were made for

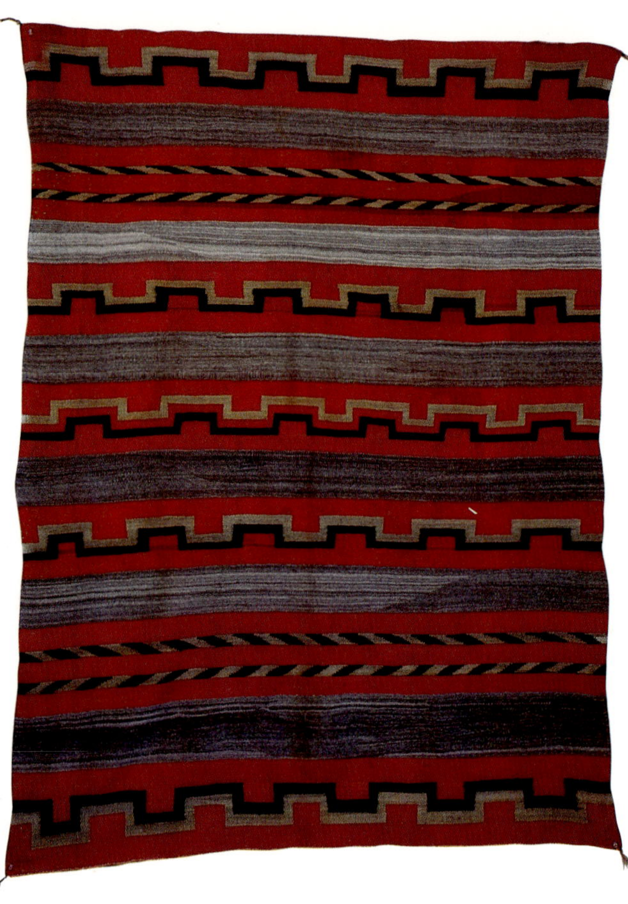

36. Diyugi, 1875–1880. 70″ x 52″. 9 warp/in.; 44 weft/in. Softly woven banded shoulder blankets continued to be made for native use until the late nineteenth century. Woven of four-ply commercial synthetic-dyed red and indigo-dyed blue, indigo with vegetal-dyed green, and natural gray hand-spun wool yarns. (Private collection)

children, and many of those that were made did not survive the wear and tear of actual use by a child. Many of the surviving child's sarapes are of Bosque Redondo vintage or later, and were probably made as souvenirs for sale to soldiers and government agents.

with the child's sarape. Most saddle blankets were woven in a heavier twill weave in a simple striped design. Occasionally, however, fine saddle blankets were woven in a tapestry weave with complex designs, sometimes making it difficult to tell the saddle blanket from the child's sarape (see fig. 34). Double saddle blankets were folded in half before being used under a saddle. Single saddle blankets, which were half the size, were also produced, but in smaller quantities than the double size (fig. 35), and like many child's sarapes of the post-1865 period were probably made as souvenirs.

Although the Classic Period weaver became famous for creating exquisite textiles, fine blankets and sarapes were not the major output of most nineteenth-century Navajo looms—at least, not most of the time. *Diyugis*—soft, loosely woven, simply striped, utilitarian blankets—were made by the thousands for everyday use, both for wearing by day and for sleeping on and under at night. Many diyugis were patterned with broad stripes of natural white or carded gray wool with narrower stripes of indigo blue, red, and natural brown (fig. 36). Occasionally small amounts of vegetal yellow or green were added to the stripes. In addition to the diyugis, women's dresses, mantas, Chief blankets, sarapes, poncho sarapes, child's sarapes, and saddle blankets, Classic Period Navajo weavers also produced woven shirts, sashes, breechcloths, and leggings as everyday wearing apparel.

Owing to their special beauty, costly sarapes and other finely woven wearing blankets were probably worn only on special occasions, and were worn with great care at those times. Taking pride in their ownership, nineteenth-century Indians treated these blankets as valuable garments, if not valuable works of art. Fortunately, because of this special handling, many of the finer blankets have survived. Twentieth-century scholars and collectors can only be grateful that so many extraordinary Classic weavings were treated so respectfully.

During the years before 1864, Navajo weavers produced variation after exciting variation of Classic Period blankets, the patterns of each being the unique product of the weaver's own artistic creativity as expressed within the artistic tradition of her culture. No one knows what direction Navajo weaving might have taken had the art been able to continue to develop without interruption. However, in 1864, politics, Kit Carson, and the U.S. Army would disrupt the natural progress of art and, indeed, of life itself.

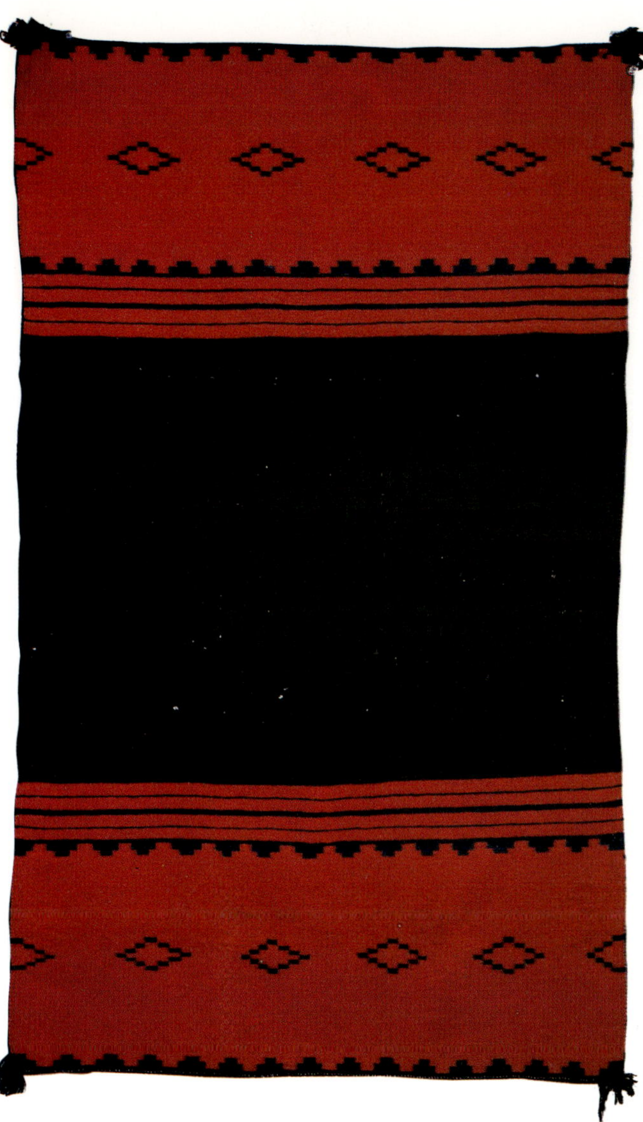

37. Woman's dress half, c. 1860. 53″ x 32″. 10 warp/in.; 50 weft/in. One half of two identically patterned panels, sewn together at the sides and top, leaving openings for the head and arms to pass through. A sash or belt would be worn around the waist. The terraced open diamond was one of the most popular designs on women's dresses. Woven of raveled lac-dyed red and indigo-dyed blue and natural brown hand-spun wool yarns. (Private collection)

38. Woman's dress half, 1865–1870. 50″ x 32″. 14 warp/in.; 50 weft/in. The Spider Woman cross became a popular design element on dresses and other blankets during and after Bosque Redondo. Woven of raveled cochineal-dyed red and indigo-dyed blue and natural brown hand-spun wool yarns. (Private collection)

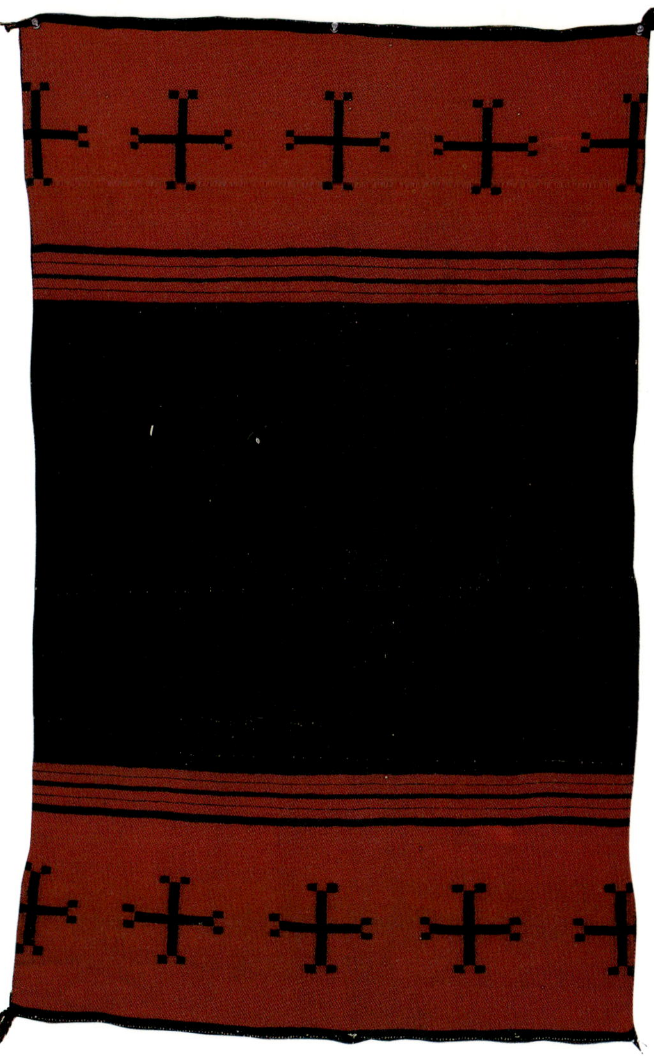

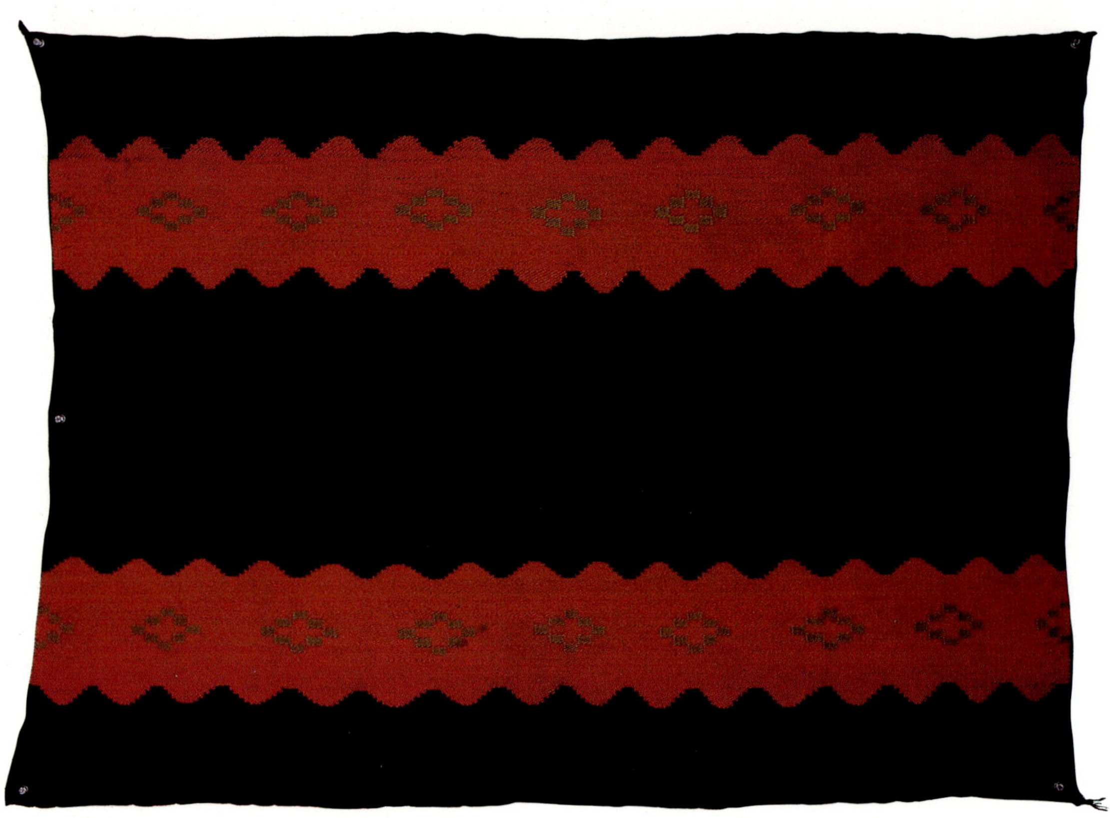

39. Woman's manta, c. 1870. 38″ x 52″. 12 warp/in.; 48 weft/in. The only other Navajo blanket besides the Chief style woven wider than long, the woman's manta or shawl was also worn as a one-piece wraparound dress before the development of the woman's two-piece dress. Woven of raveled cochineal-dyed red, vegetal-dyed green hand-spun, and indigo-dyed blue and natural brown hand-spun wool yarns. (Private collection)

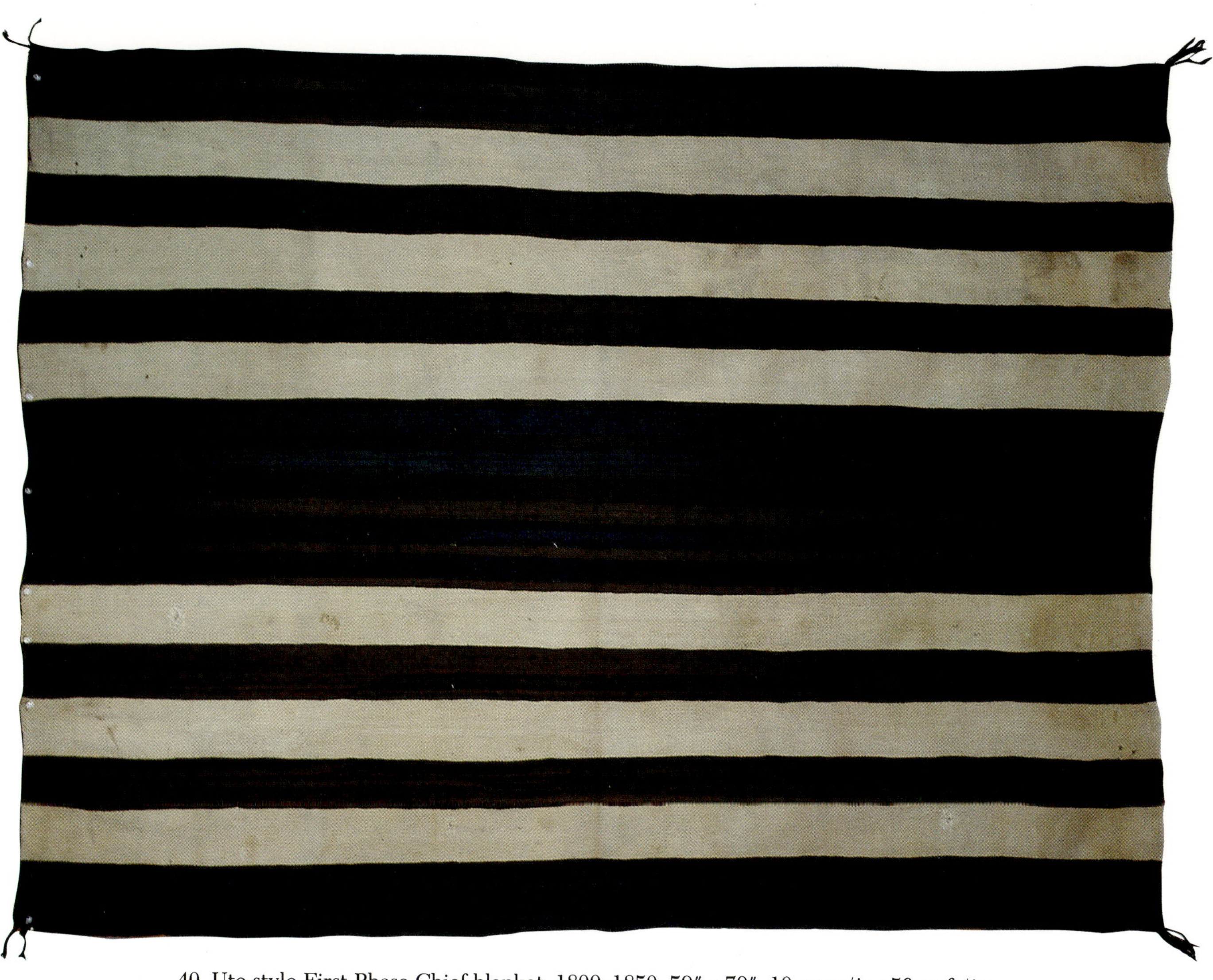

40. Ute-style First Phase Chief blanket, 1800–1850. 59″ x 79″. 10 warp/in.; 56 weft/in. The wide alternating brown and white stripes in this Chief blanket indicate it is a man's wearing blanket. Woven of indigo-dyed blue and natural brown and white hand-spun wool yarns. (Collection of University Museum, University of Pennsylvania)

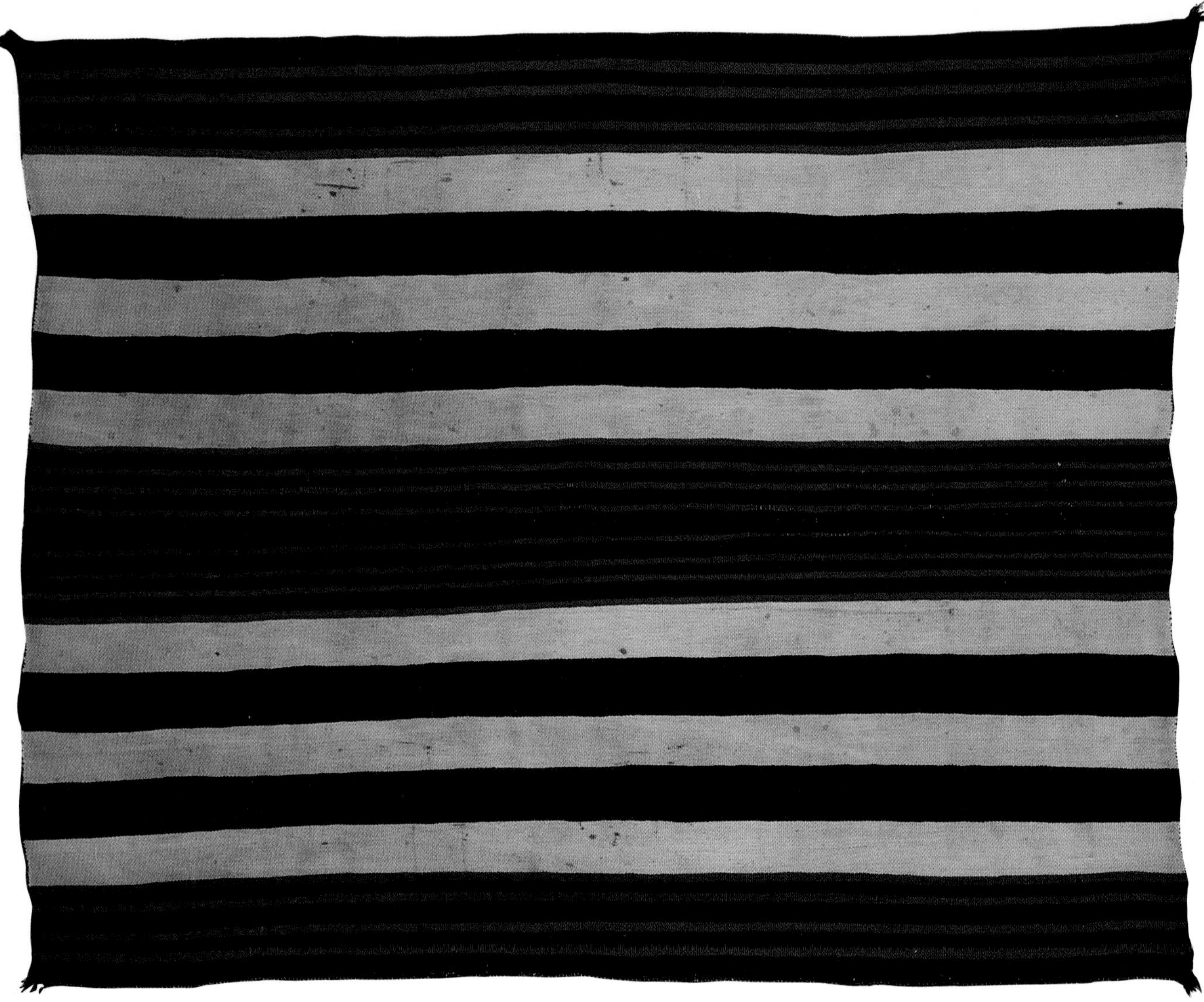

41. First Phase Chief blanket, 1850–1860. 50″ x 63″. 11 warp/in.; 52 weft/in. The addition of thin red stripes outlining the broader blue stripes initiates the trend toward increased complexity in the Chief blanket pattern. Woven of three-ply commercial cochineal-dyed red and indigo-dyed blue and natural brown and white hand-spun wool yarns. (Collection of Maxwell Museum of Anthropology, University of New Mexico)

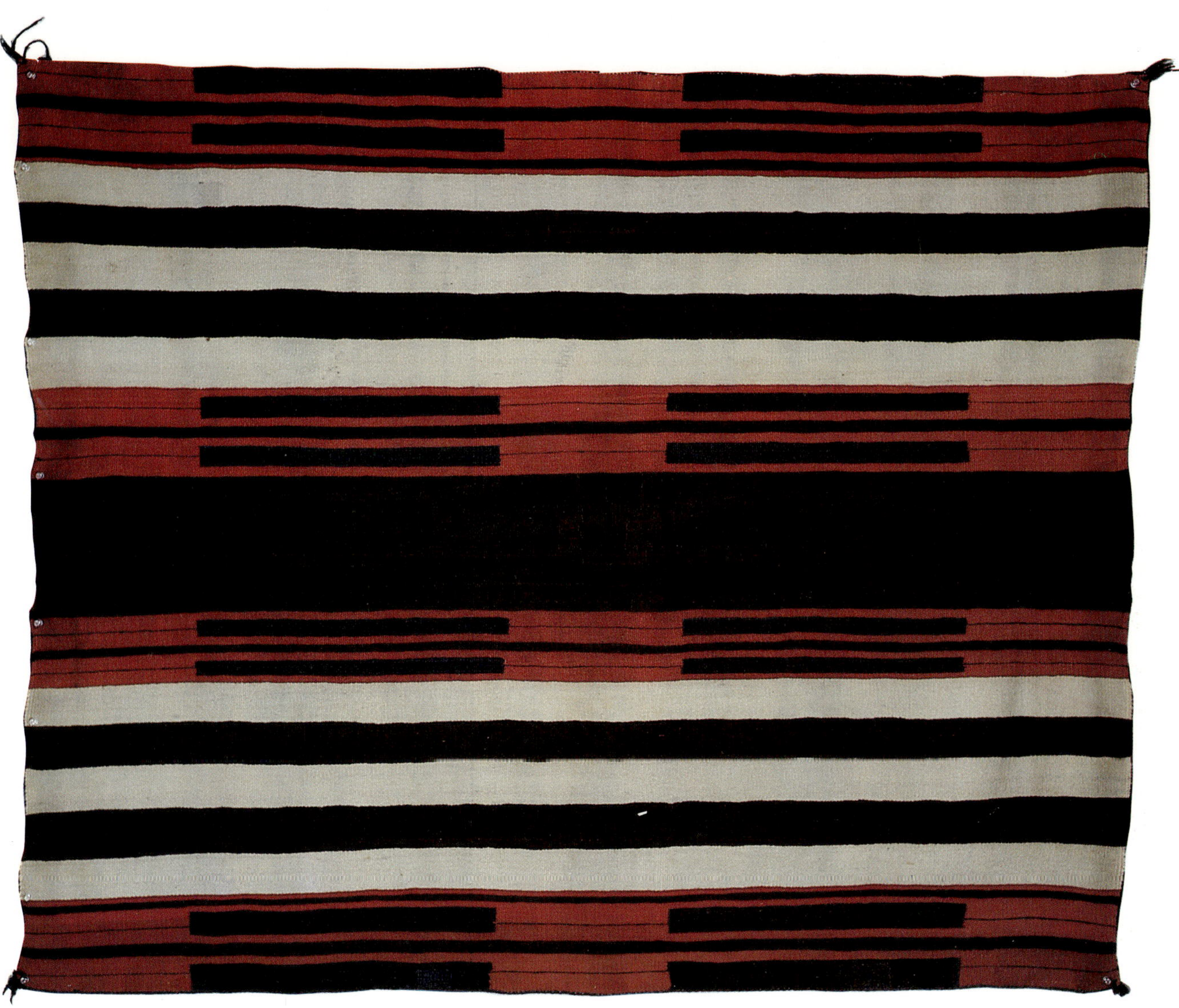

42. Second Phase Chief blanket, c. 1865. 55" x 68". 8 warp/in.; 62 weft/in. The insertion of blocks of red dominates the pattern in this fully developed Second Phase Chief blanket. Woven of raveled lac-dyed red and indigo-dyed blue and natural brown and white hand-spun wool yarns. (Private collection)

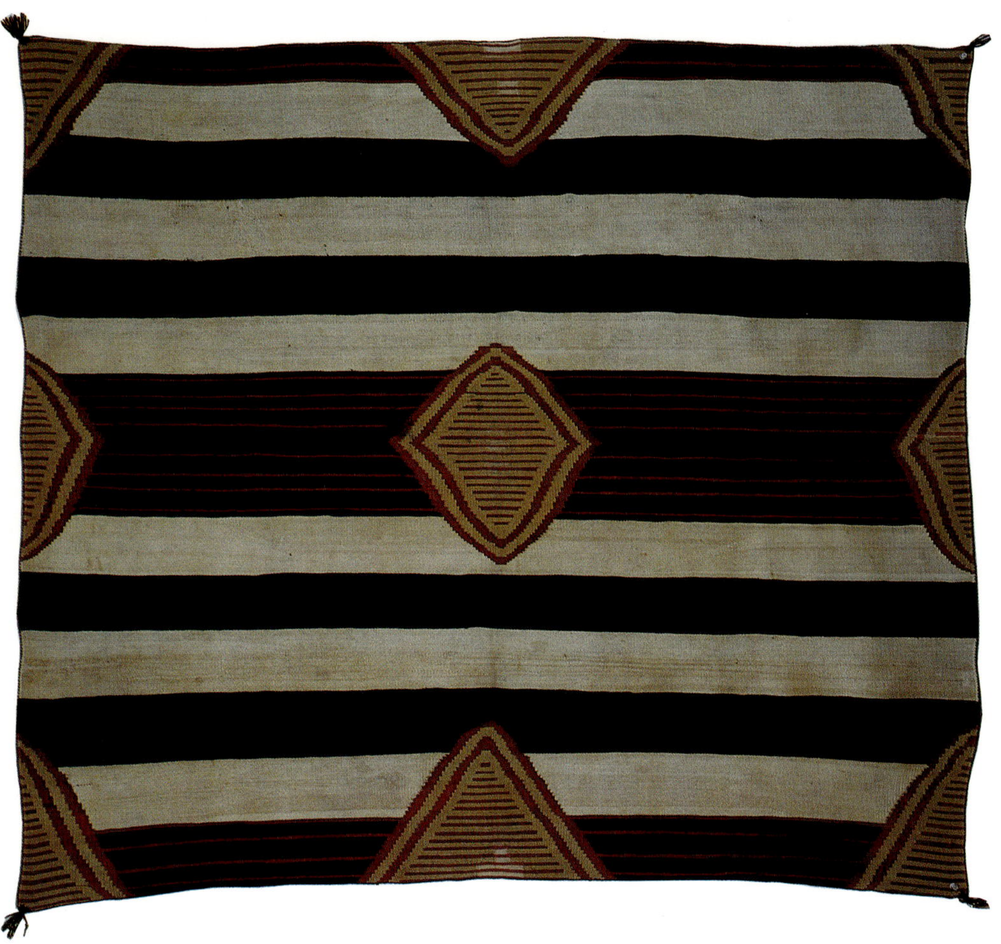

43. Third Phase Chief blanket, c. 1865. 58″ x 68″. 11 warp/in.; 70 weft/in. A rare example of the use of raveled green bayeta, the green terraced designs give added contrast and appear to float above the striped background. Woven of raveled cochineal (?)-dyed red, raveled vegetal-dyed green, and indigo-dyed blue and natural brown and white hand-spun wool yarns. (Private collection)

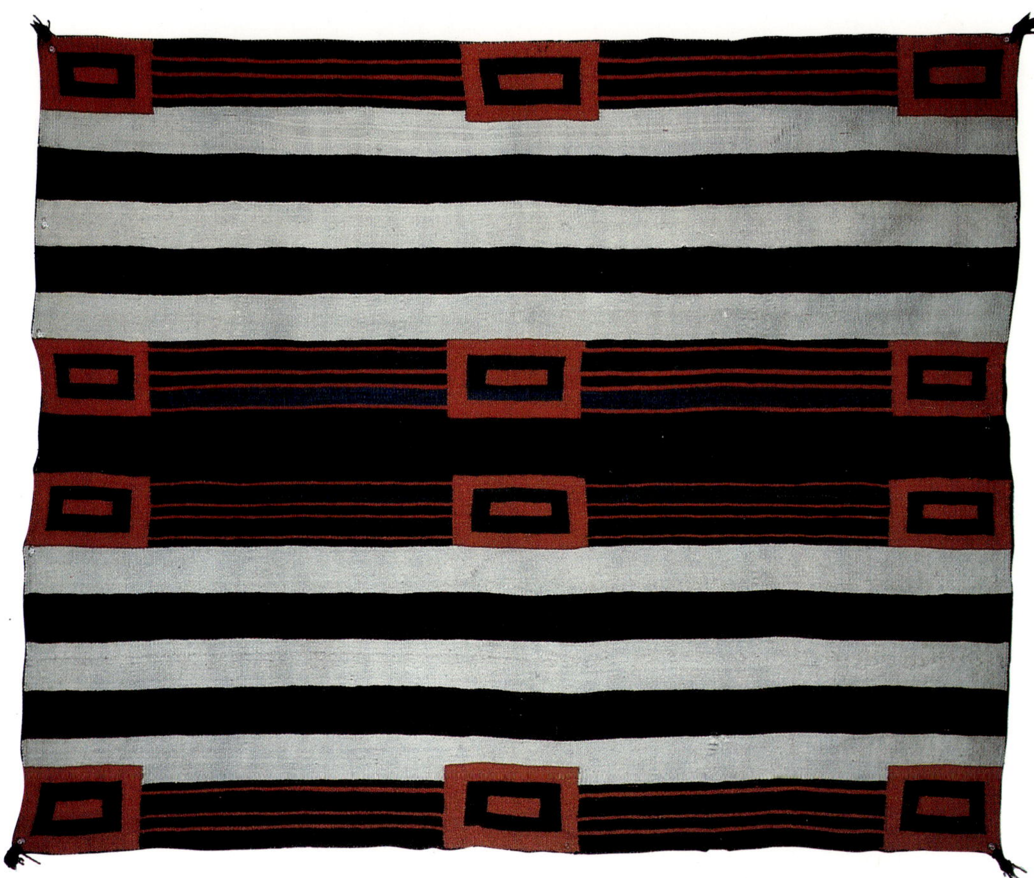

44. Chief blanket variation, c. 1865. 58″ x 73″. 8 warp/in.; 32 weft/in. Often referred to as a variation of the Second Phase pattern, this pattern first occurs by 1860. In this example the boxes of red and blue begin to emerge into the striped field. Woven of raveled lac-dyed red, three-ply commercial cochineal-dyed red, and indigo-dyed blue and natural brown and white hand-spun wool yarns. (Private collection)

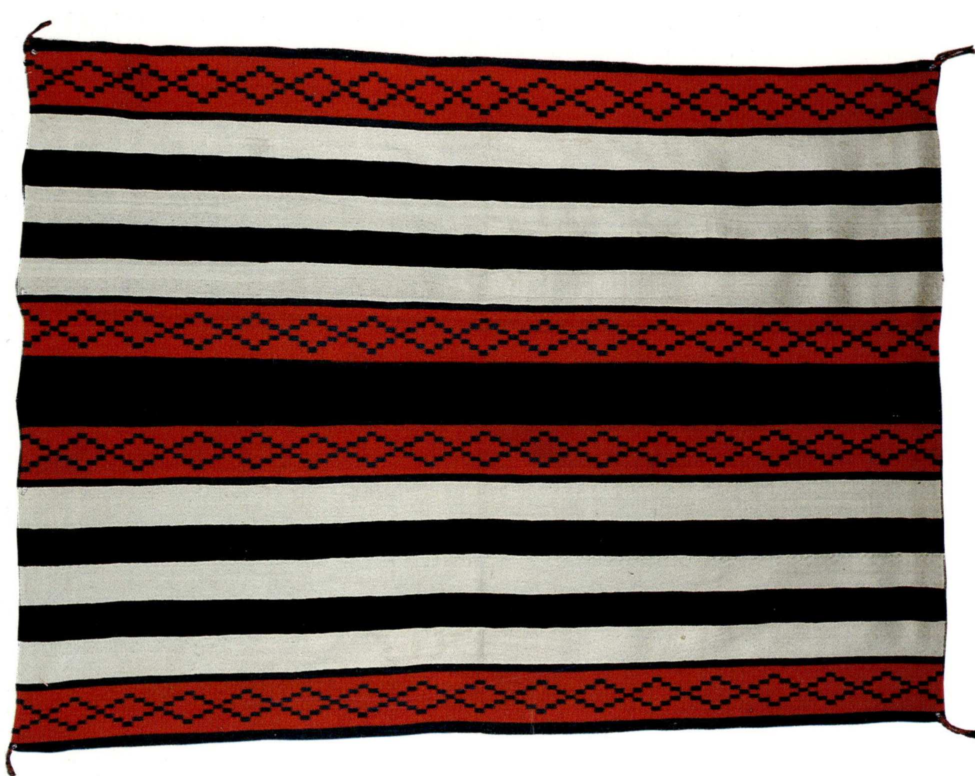

45. Chief blanket variation, 1865–1870. 53″ x 75″. 15 warp/in.; 76 weft/in. This unusual Chief blanket variation employs a common woman's dress pattern in the design bands. (Note the presence of this blanket as a backdrop in the vintage photograph in fig. 102.) Woven of three-ply commercial cochineal-dyed red and indigo-dyed blue and natural brown and white hand-spun wool yarns. (Private collection)

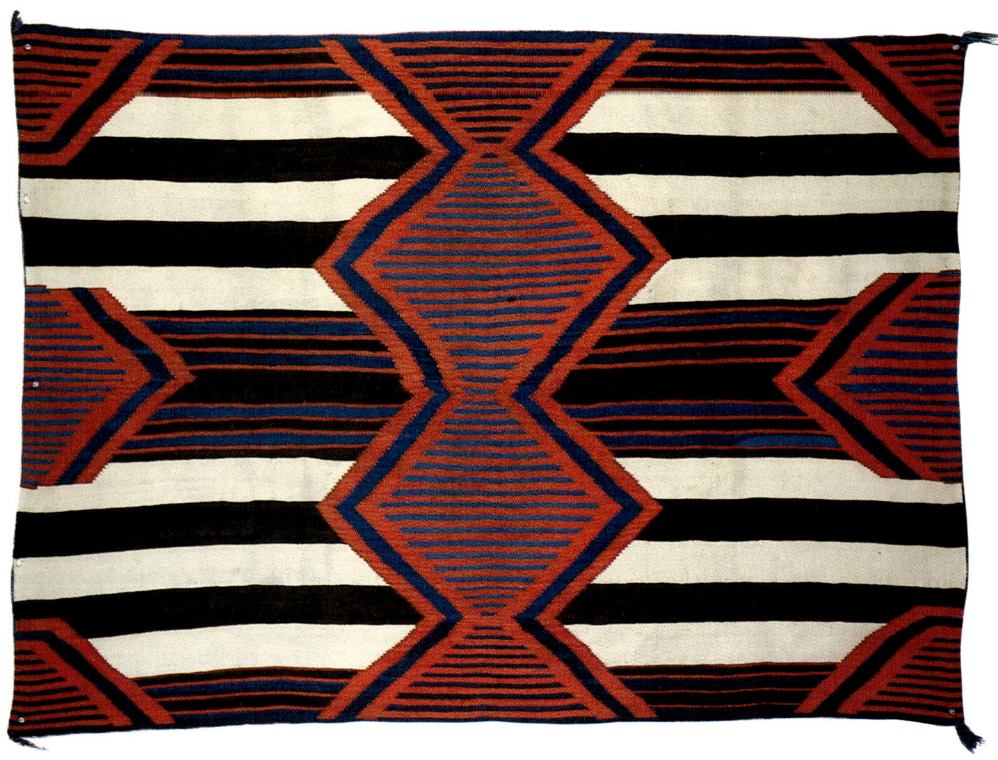

46. Chief blanket variation, c. 1865. 50″ x 71″. 12 warp/in.; 76 weft/in. This blanket clearly shows the sarape design influence on the Third Phase-style Chief blanket pattern. Woven of raveled lac-dyed red and indigo-dyed blue and natural brown and white hand-spun wool yarns. (Private collection)

47. Chief blanket variation, 1865–1870. 55″ x 64″. 9 warp/in.; 50 weft/in. Identified in later years with J. L. Hubbell and the Ganado revival-style rug, the cross design first made its appearance in the 1860s. Woven of raveled cochineal-dyed red and indigo-dyed blue and natural brown and white hand-spun wool yarns. (Private collection)

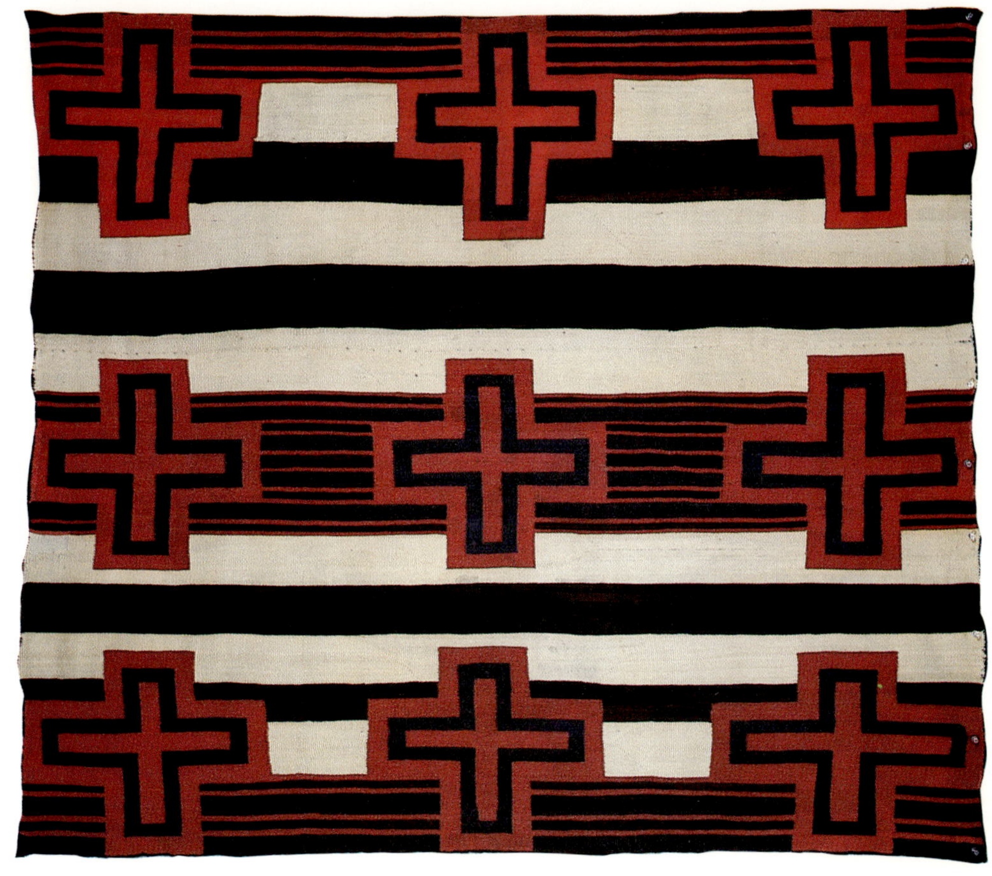

48. Woman's wearing blanket, 1865–1870. 46″ x 61″. 9 warp/in.; 50 weft/in. Distinguished from a man's wearing blanket by the narrower gray and brown stripes and smaller proportions, this woman's wearing blanket, often called a woman's-style Chief blanket, was collected by a Mormon family in Utah about 1870. Woven of raveled lac with cochineal-dyed red and indigo with vegetal-dyed green, indigo-dyed blue, and natural brown and white hand-spun wool yarns. (Private collection)

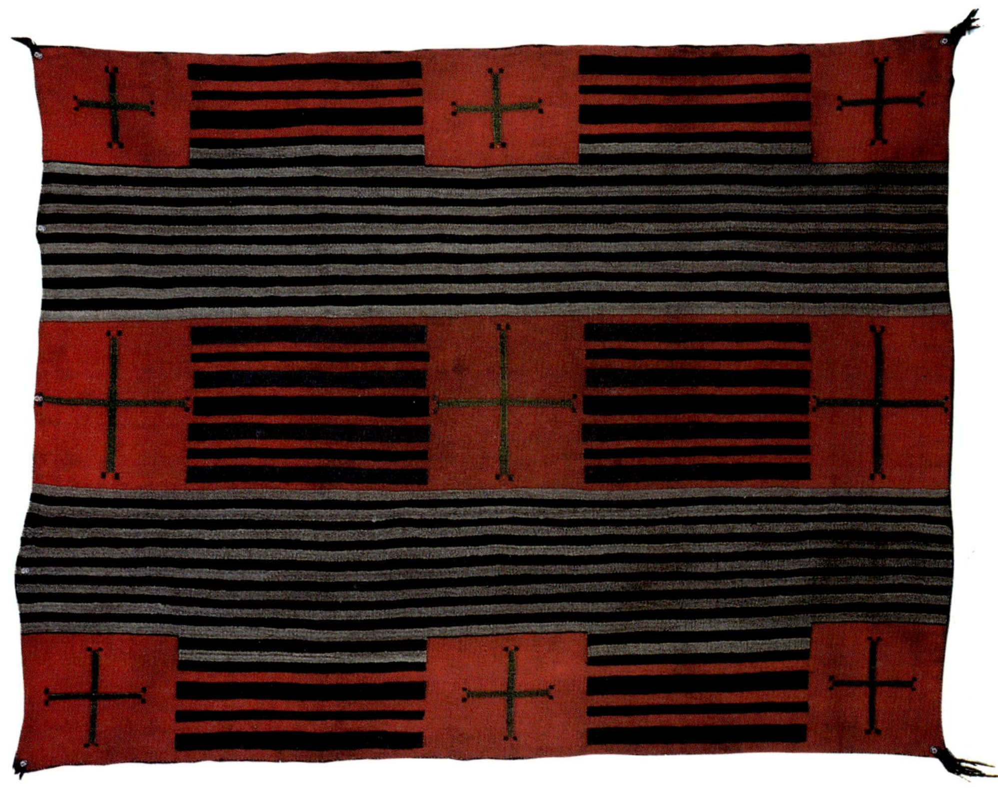

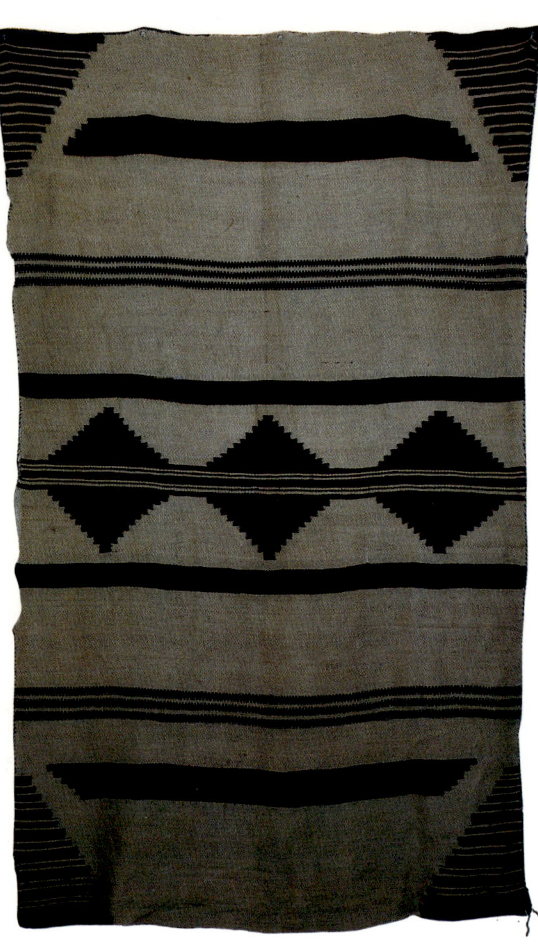

49. Sarape, 1800–1850. 76″ x 44″. 11 warp/in.; 24 weft/in. Contemporary with the Ute-style First Phase Chief blanket, this unusual early sarape combines the simple striped and terraced step design elements without the use of any red bayeta. Woven of indigo-dyed blue, indigo with vegetal-dyed green, and natural white hand-spun wool yarns. (Private collection)

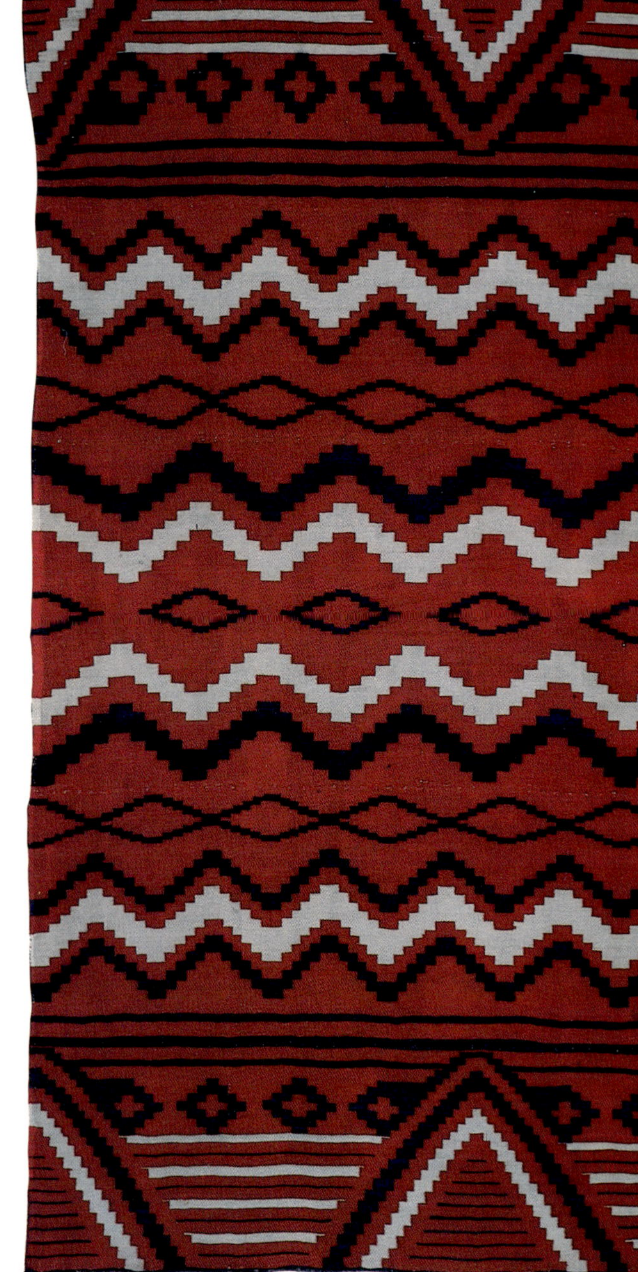

50. Sarape, 1840–1860. 80″ x 54″. 14 warp/in.; 68 weft/in. Excellence in the execution of design and weave characterizes the best sarapes of the Classic Period. Woven of raveled lac(?)-dyed red and indigo-dyed blue and natural white hand-spun wool yarns. (Collection of School of American Research, Museum of New Mexico)

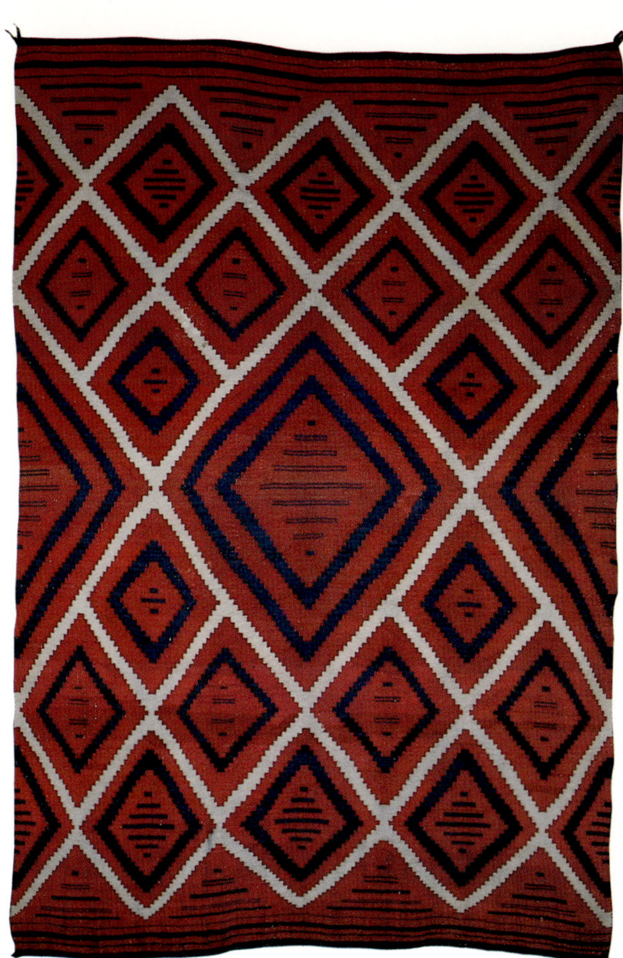

51. Sarape, 1840–1850. 68″ x 47″. 13 warp/in.; 56 weft/in. Strongly resembling the poncho sarape in figure 30, the similarity of the pattern and materials indicates not only similar vintage but also the possibility of both blankets having been woven by the same weaver. Woven of raveled lac-dyed red and indigo-dyed blue and natural white hand-spun wool yarns. (Private collection)

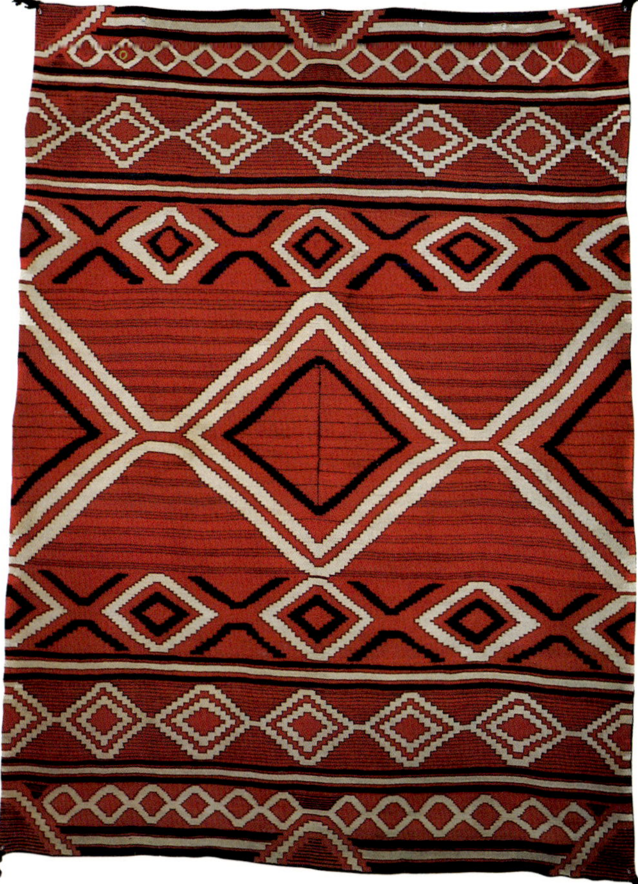

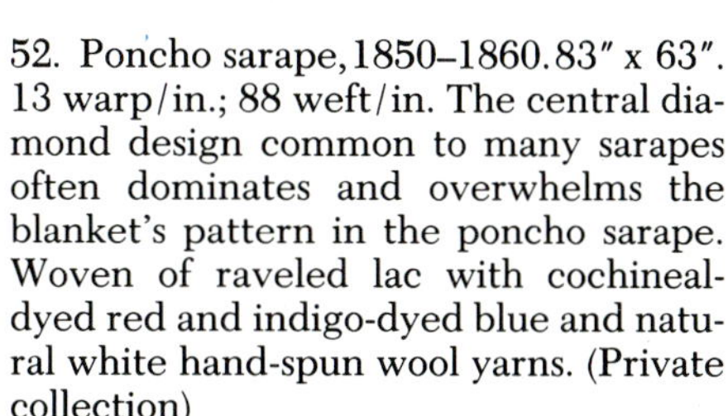

52. Poncho sarape, 1850–1860. 83″ x 63″. 13 warp/in.; 88 weft/in. The central diamond design common to many sarapes often dominates and overwhelms the blanket's pattern in the poncho sarape. Woven of raveled lac with cochineal-dyed red and indigo-dyed blue and natural white hand-spun wool yarns. (Private collection)

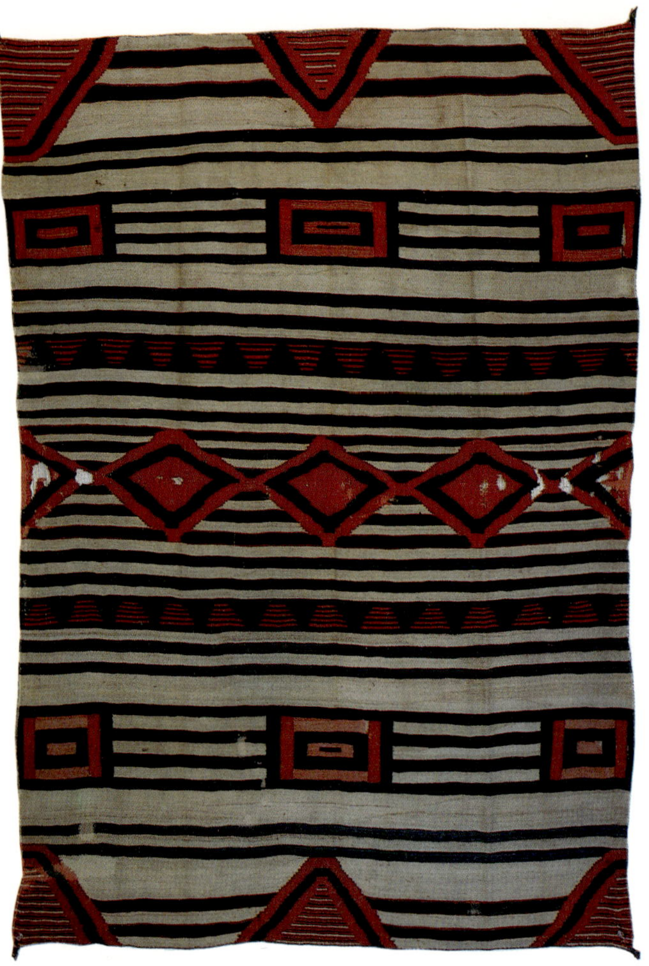

53. Sarape, 1850–1860. 71″ x 51″. 13 warp/in.; 72 weft/in. Similar to the child's sarape in figure 33, this full-size sarape shows signs of having been worn for many years. Many Classic Period blankets show signs of having been repaired many times, for few were casually discarded even when heavily worn. Woven of raveled lac-dyed red, raveled and recarded pink, and indigo-dyed blue and natural white hand-spun wool yarns. (Private collection)

54. Poncho sarape, 1850–1860. 69″ x 58″. 13 warp/in.; 76 weft/in. The three zones of design almost disappear in the expansive patterning of this visually powerful and complex blanket. Woven of raveled lac with cochineal-dyed red and indigo-dyed blue and natural white hand-spun wool yarns. (Collection of University Museum, University of Pennsylvania)

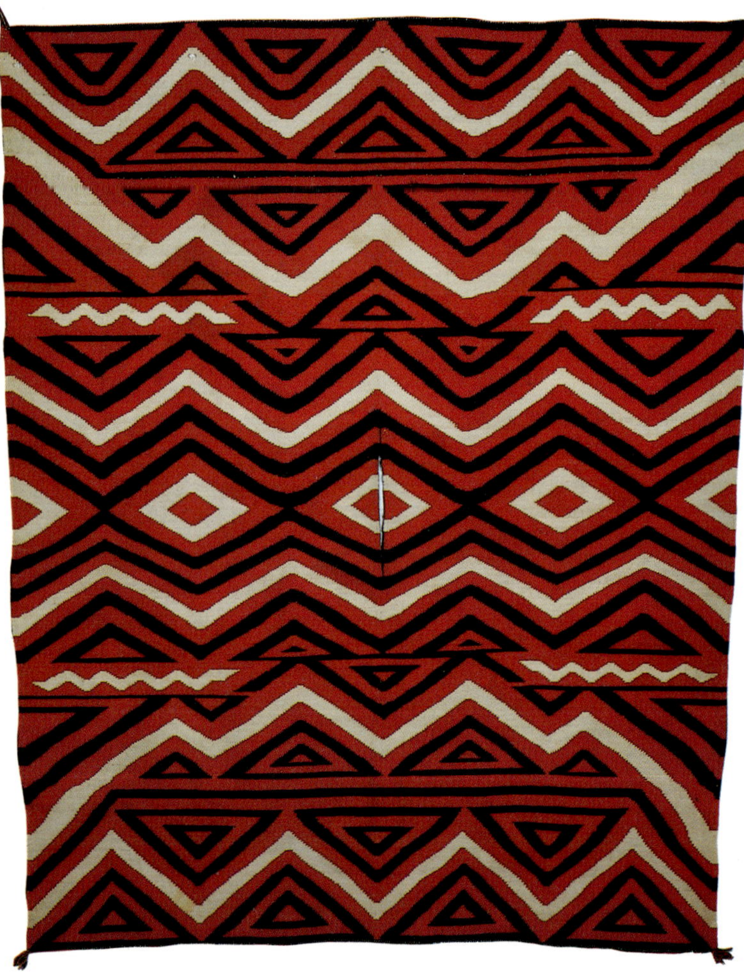

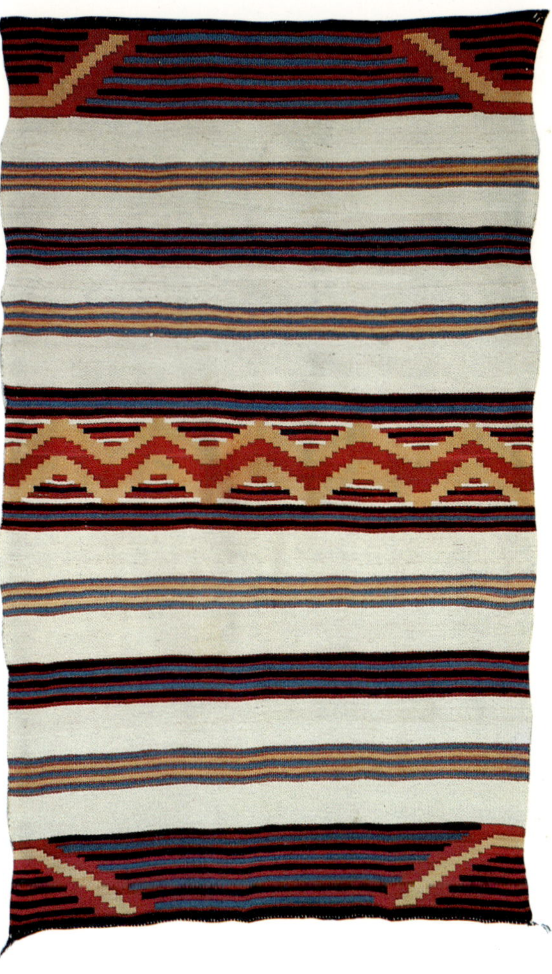

55. Child's sarape, c. 1860. 48″ x 29″. 11 warp/in.; 50 weft/in. The restraint and minimal use of design in multiple colors on a white field make a simple but elegant visual statement. Woven of raveled cochineal (?)-dyed red and pink and indigo-dyed blue (two shades) and natural white hand-spun wool yarns. (Collection of School of American Research, Museum of New Mexico)

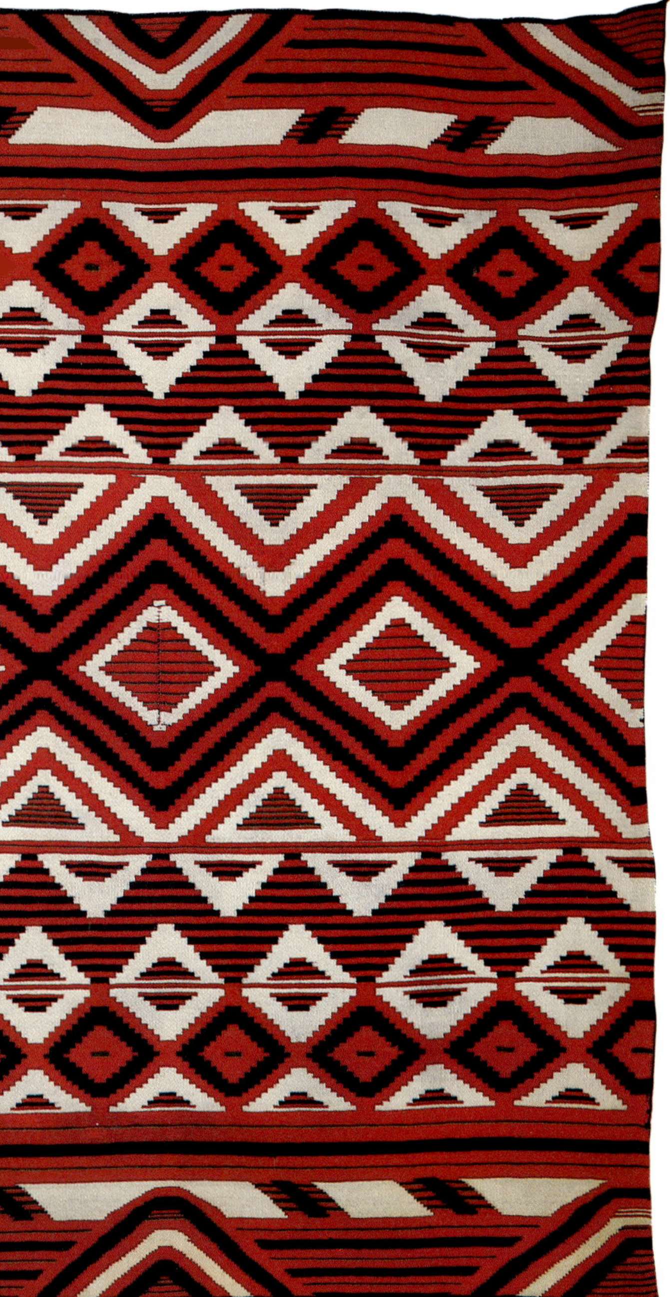

56. Poncho sarape, 1850–1860. 65″x 50″. 14 warp/in.; 84 weft/in. An extraordinary display of the weaver's skill, this small poncho sarape, with narrow opening still sewn together, may have been intended to be worn in the sarape manner. Woven of raveled lac(?)-dyed red, indigo with vegetal-dyed green hand-spun, and indigo-dyed blue and natural white hand-spun wool yarns. (Collection of Arizona State Museum, University of Arizona)

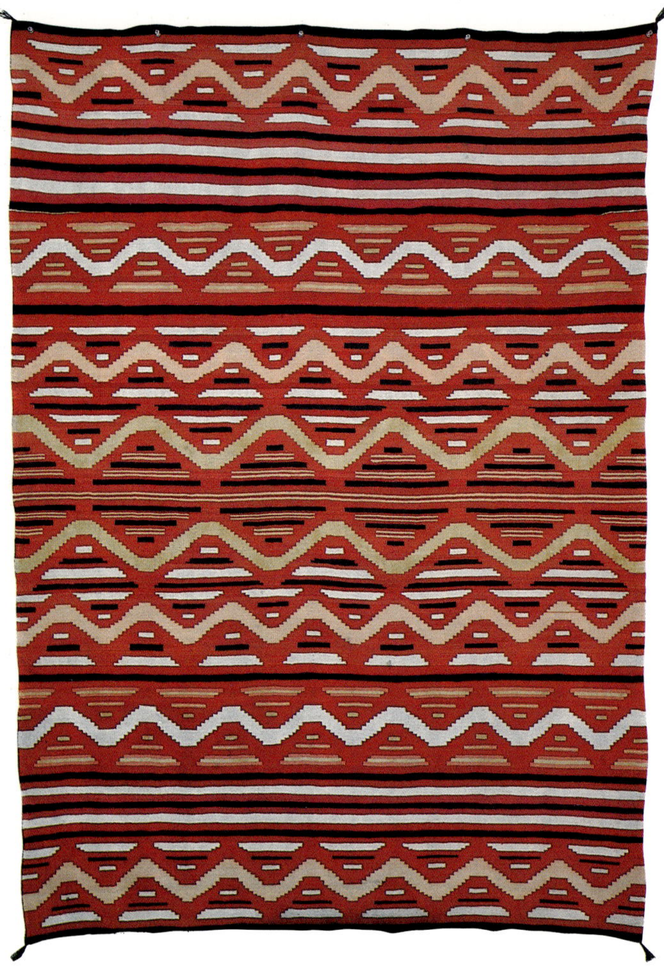

57. Sarape, c. 1850–1860. 69″x 50″. 15 warp/in.; 68 weft/in. The delicacy of pattern resulting from the combination of thin stripes with terraced wavy bands and the use of three-ply Saxony-type commercial yarns are characteristics of Classic Period sarapes produced after 1850. Woven of raveled cochineal-dyed red, three-ply commercial cochineal-dyed red and pink, three-ply commercial vegetal-dyed green and peach, and indigo-dyed blue and natural white hand-spun wool yarns. (Private collection)

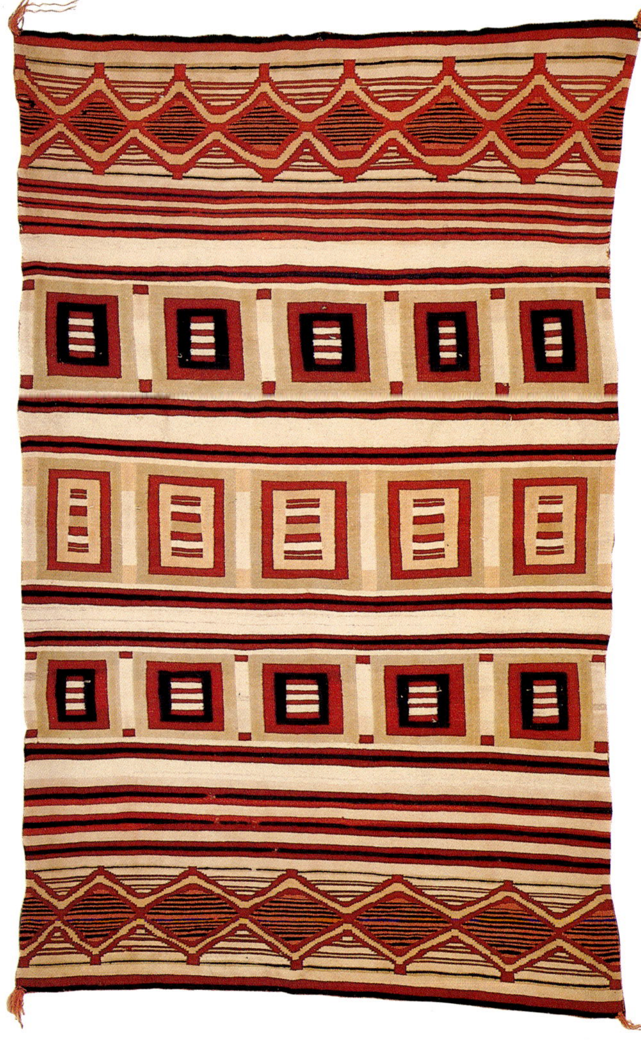

58. Sarape, 1850–1865. 77″x 49″. 13 warp/in.; 40 weft/in. Commonly referred to as Saxony sarapes, sarapes woven largely of three-ply commercial, presynthetic dyed yarns were often atypical in coloration. Woven of raveled and three-ply commercial cochineal-dyed reds, raveled vegetal-dyed green, three-ply commercial vegetal-dyed yellow and beige, and indigo-dyed blue and natural white hand-spun wool yarns. (Collection of Arizona State Museum, University of Arizona)

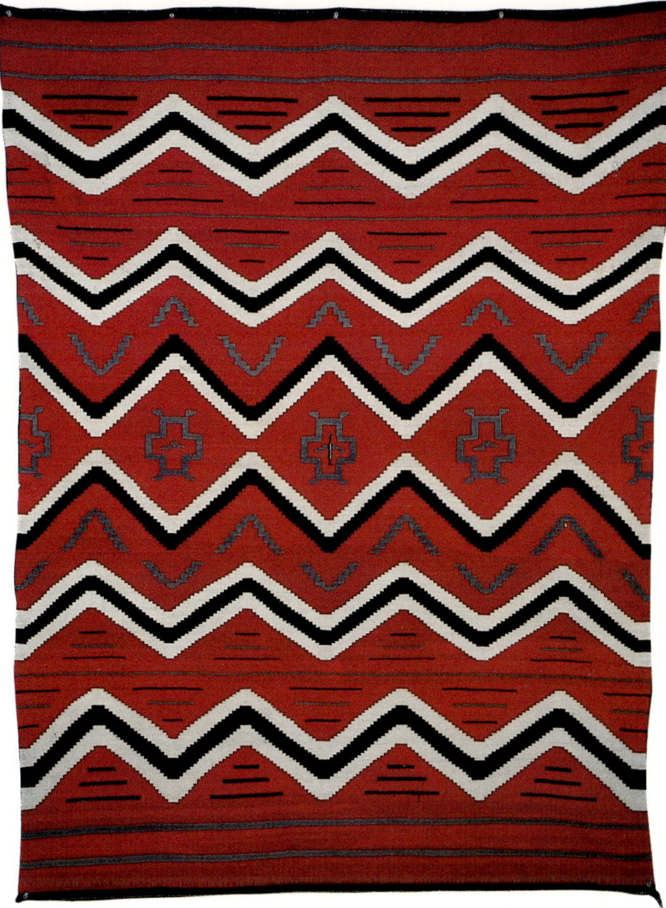

59. Sarape, c. 1865. 70″ x 53″. 14 warp/in.; 88 weft/in. Owned by the Navajo leader Mariano, this finely woven sarape has a small ceremonial opening in the center Spider Woman cross design. Woven of raveled lac with cochineal-dyed red, indigo with vegetal-dyed green hand-spun, raveled indigo-dyed pale blue, and indigo-dyed blue and natural white hand-spun wool yarns. (Private collection)

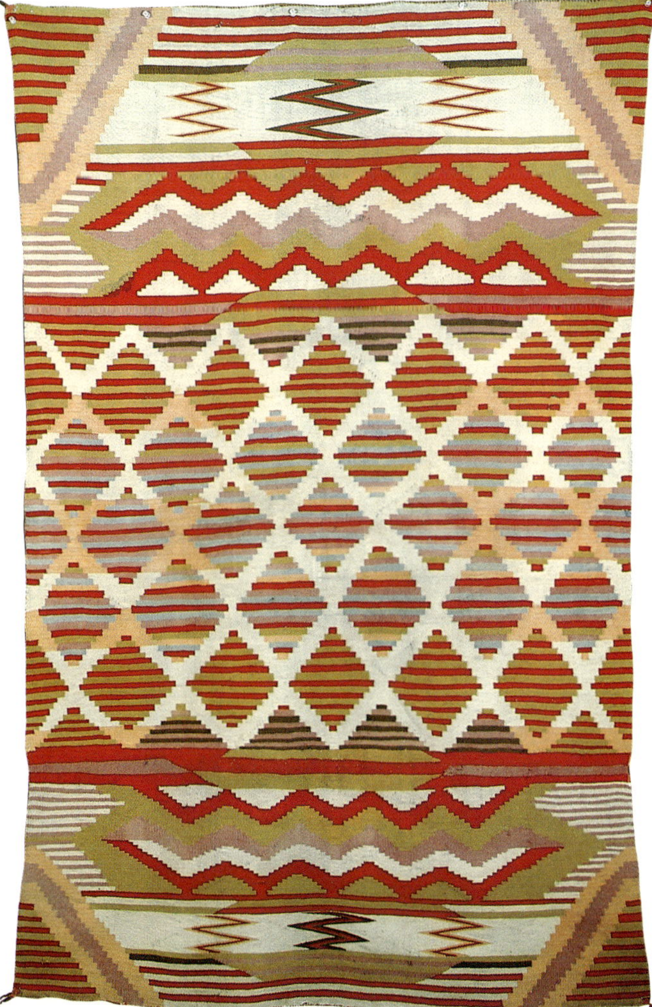

60. Sarape, c. 1865. 68″ x 43″. 14 warp/in.; 52 weft/in. Woven entirely of three-ply commercial Saxony yarns, this sarape, typical in pattern of sarapes of the Classic Period but with Saxony yarn colors, makes a distinctly different visual statement. Woven of three-ply commercial yarns throughout: cochineal (?)-dyed red and pink, synthetic-dyed purple, vegetal-dyed green (two shades), indigo-dyed blue, and natural white wool. (Collection of Heard Museum)

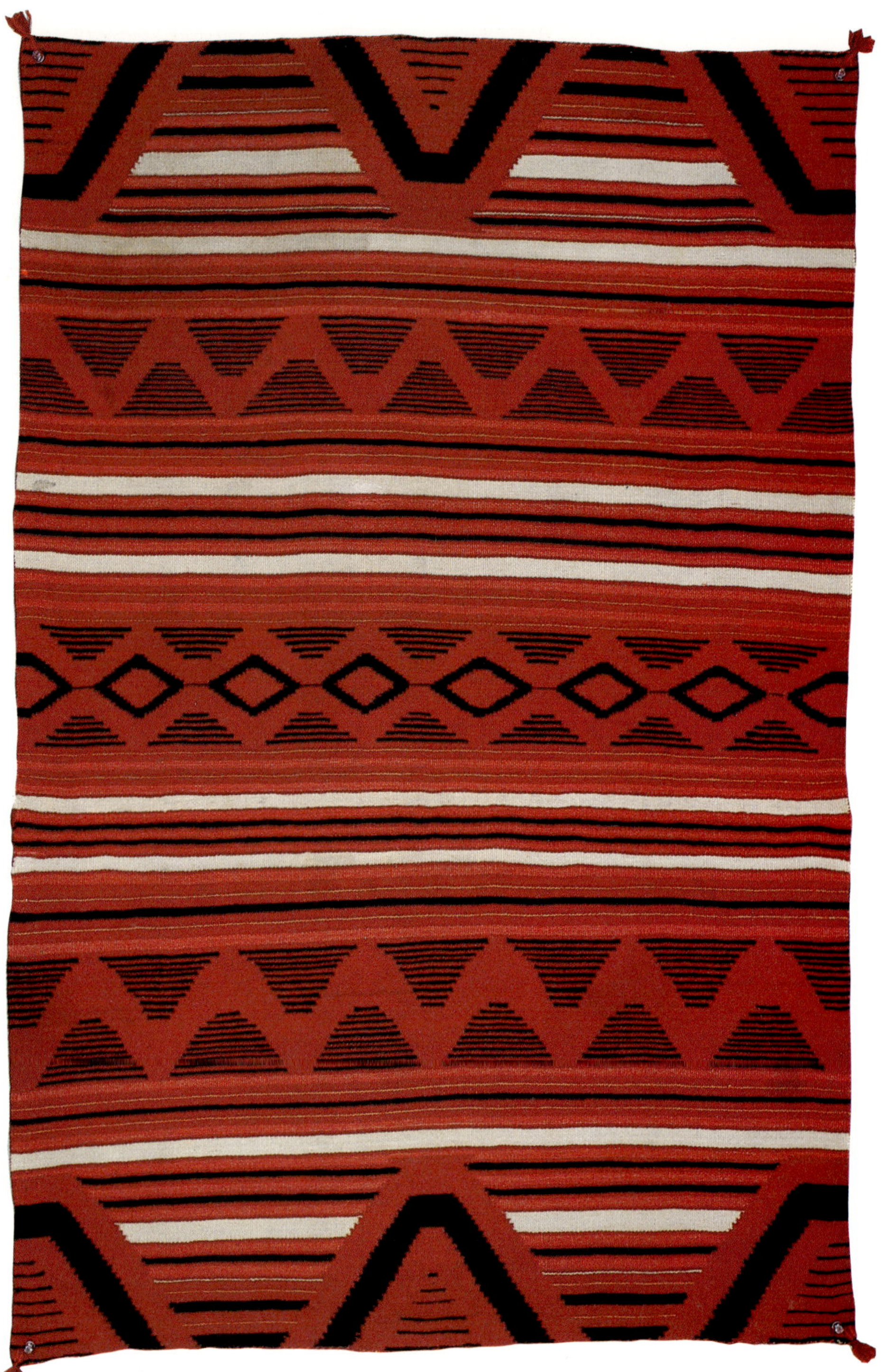

61. Child's sarape, 1865–1870. 53″ x 36″. 12 warp/in.; 60 weft/in. The bands of design in this small sarape create a continuous horizontal movement while the heavier end zones act as a frame. Woven of raveled cochineal-dyed red, raveled and recarded pink, raveled vegetal-dyed yellow, and indigo-dyed blue and natural white hand-spun wool yarns. (Private collection)

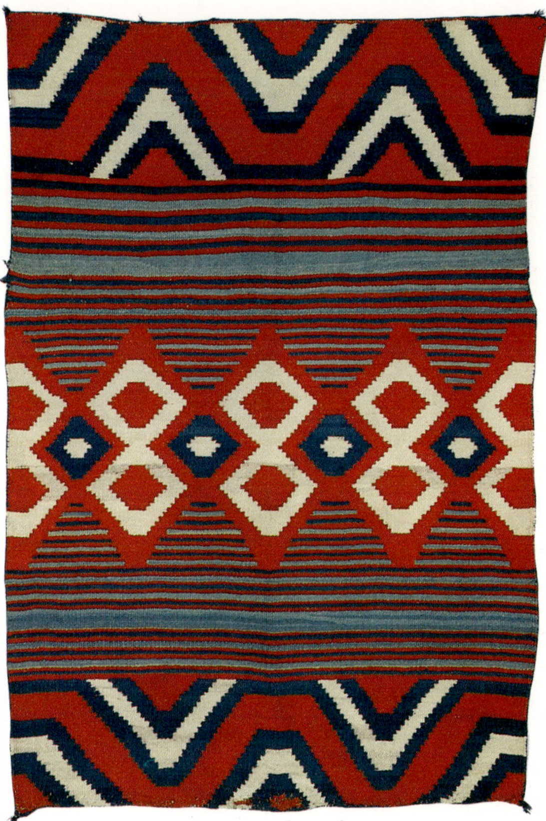

62. Child's sarape, c. 1865. 44″ x 31″. 9 warp/in.; 44 weft/in. Oversize designs and the use of two shades of blue create a large-scale visual impact in this small-scale sarape. Woven of raveled cochineal(?)-dyed red and indigo-dyed blue (two shades) and natural white hand-spun wool yarns. (Collection of School of American Research, Museum of New Mexico)

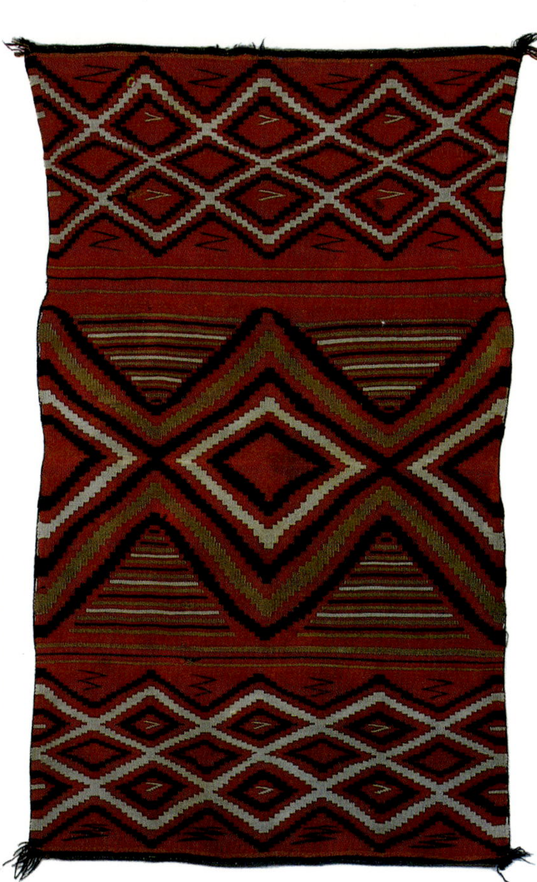

63. Child's sarape, 1865–1870. 54″ x 32″. 11 warp/in.; 64 weft/in. The powerful central diamond design gives this child's sarape the appearance of a scaled-down poncho sarape. Woven of raveled and three-ply commercial cochineal(?)-dyed red, three-ply commercial vegetal-dyed green, and indigo-dyed blue and natural white hand-spun wool yarns. (Private collection)

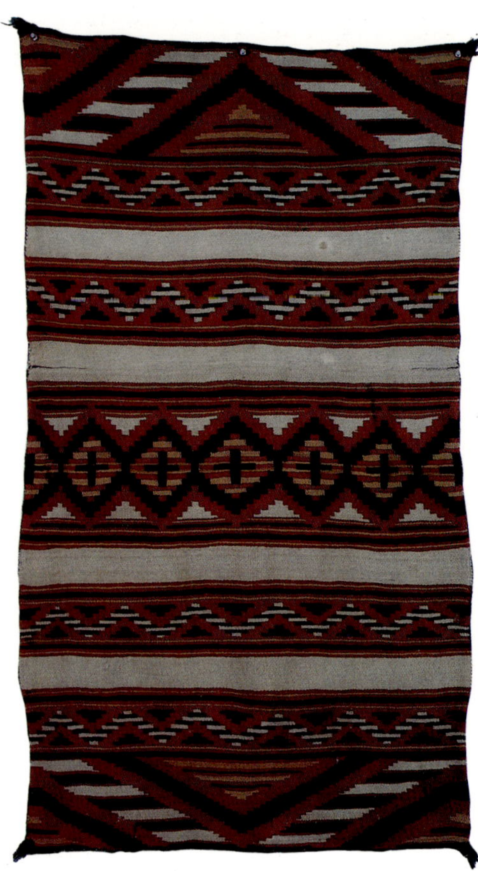

64. Child's sarape, 1865–1870. 49″ x 28″. 11 warp/in.; 56 weft/in. A balance of strength and delicacy is achieved in the best designed Navajo blankets. Woven of raveled cochineal-dyed red, vegetal-dyed yellow, vegetal with indigo-dyed green, and indigo-dyed blue and natural white hand-spun wool yarns. (Private collection)

65. Sarape, c. 1870. 80″ x 58″. 14 warp/in.; 60 weft/in. The popularity of the cross design in Navajo weaving after 1865 was possibly due in part, to the influence of cross designs in Plains Indian beadwork. Woven of three-ply commercial cochineal-dyed red, raveled vegetal-dyed green and peach, three-ply commercial vegetal-dyed brown, and natural white wool yarns. (Private collection)

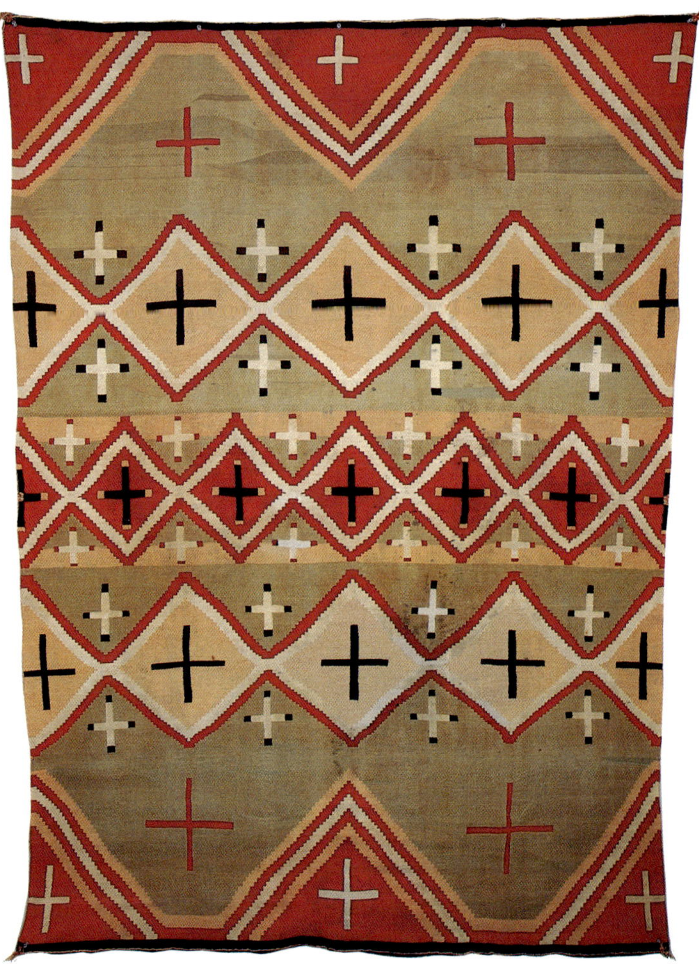

66. Sarape, 1865–1870. 60″ x 38″. 13 warp/in.; 60 weft/in. Bands of serrate designs combined with terraced designs, woven in Classic Period materials, indicate that this is an early example of Navajo weaving employing the diagonal line in design formation. Woven of three-ply commercial Saxony cochineal-dyed red and indigo-dyed blue and natural white hand-spun. (Private collection)

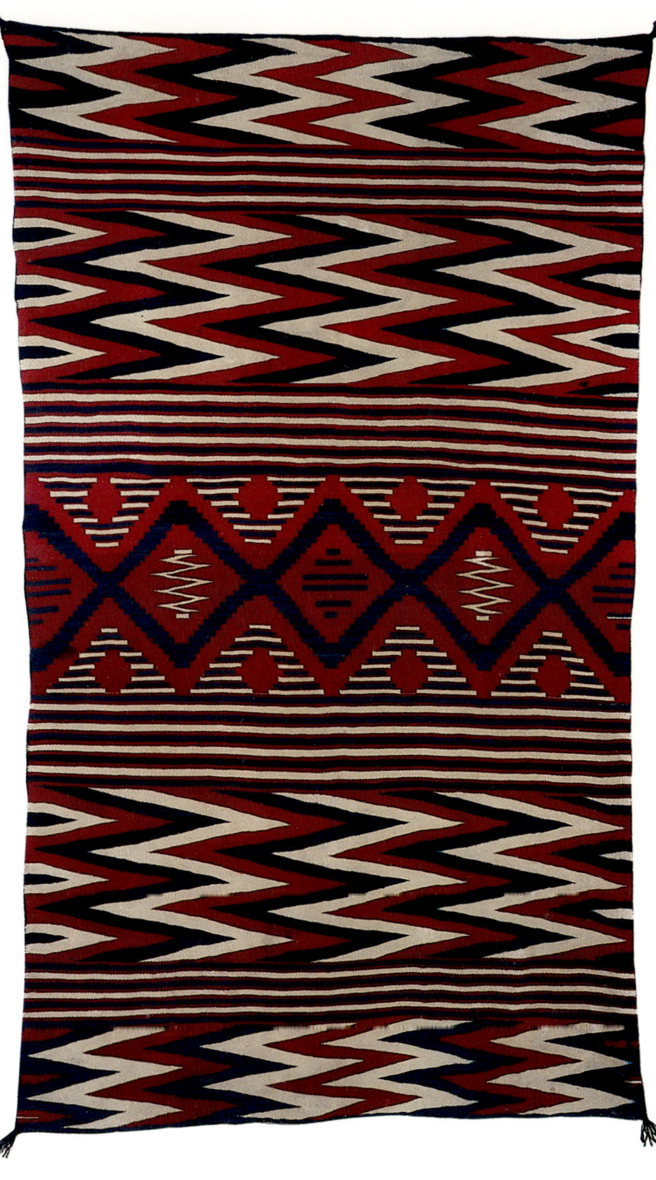

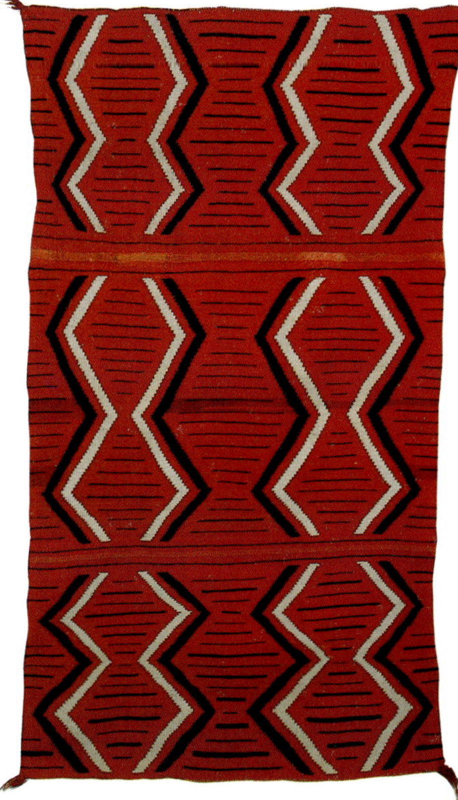

67. Child's sarape, c. 1870. 57″ x 32″. 18 warp/in.; 64 weft/in. The rearrangement of the terraced wavy bands of an earlier period into vertical meanders began to occur at the end of the Classic Period. Woven of raveled cochineal(?)-dyed red, raveled and recarded pink, and indigo-dyed blue and natural white hand-spun wool yarns. (Collection of Maxwell Museum of Anthropology, University of New Mexico)

4

BOSQUE REDONDO AND THE AFTERMATH

I shall endeavor to . . . perform such service among the Navajos as will bring them to feel that they have been doing wrong.

General James H. Carleton,
1862, in a letter to Colonel
John W. Washington[17]

We have shown the Indians that in no place, however formidable or inaccessible in their opinion, are they safe from the pursuit of the troops of this command; and have convinced a large portion of them that the struggle on their part is a hopeless one.

Kit Carson, 1864, in a letter
to his commander written after
invading Canyon de Chelly[18]

After we get back to our country, it will brighten up again, and the Navajos will be as happy and peaceful as the land.

Barboncito, 1868, at the treaty
negotiations at Bosque Redondo[19]

By the middle of the nineteenth century Navajo weavers displayed an artistic confidence rooted in generations of tradition. Many of the textiles they created were extraordinary in terms of weave and design, even when compared to superb textiles woven a mere fifty years earlier. It was not the destiny of these mid-century weavers to make major breakthroughs in terms of technique or design. Rather it was their privilege to enjoy the fruits of their grandmothers' hard-learned lessons. How tragic that the flowering of their creativity would be interrupted so abruptly in 1863 when almost the entire Navajo tribe was rounded up and imprisoned at Bosque Redondo.

The dramatic events of 1863–1864 were the culmination of years of political turmoil in the Southwest. In 1821 Mexico won its independence from Spain and gained jurisdiction over New Mexico. Under Mexican rule, the climate of sporadic violence escalated into nearly constant warfare. Remarkably, each side continued to play both oppressor and oppressed no matter what treaties were in effect. While Mexicans conducted slave raids into Navajo country both with and without official sanction, Navajos on horseback continued their bold raids on Mexican towns and settlements. During the years of Mexican rule Navajos raided not only for livestock and other plunder but also to recover Navajos living among the Mexicans as slaves.

Navajo women taken as slaves were frequently required to weave blankets for their Mexican masters. These "slave blankets" were usually woven to Mexican taste on Navajo looms, often using the yarns and dyes favored by New Mexican weavers. These textiles combined characteristics of both Navajo and Mexican weaving styles and techniques. No one knows how many of these blankets were woven, although the number must have been considerable given the large number of

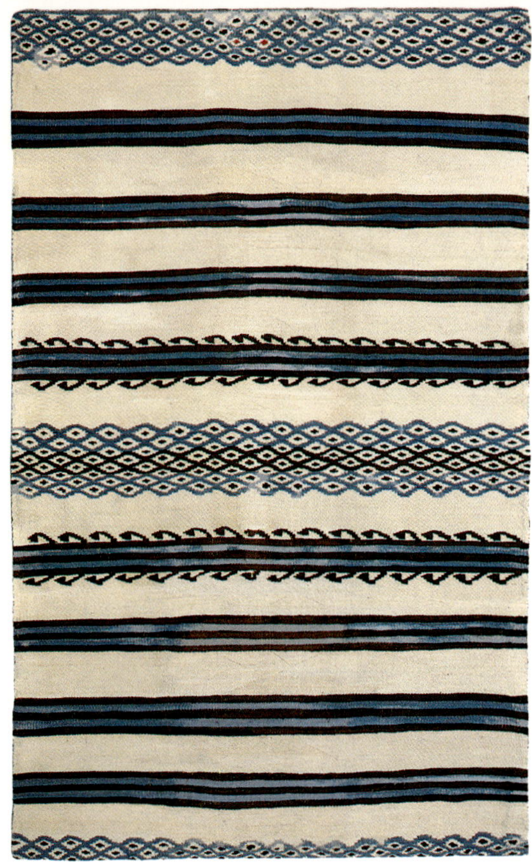

68. Slave blanket, c. 1860. 81″ x 49″. 7 warp/in.; 34 weft/in. A rare documented example of a blanket woven in a Spanish household by a Navajo weaver on the Navajo vertical loom. Woven of indigo-dyed blue and natural brown and white hand-spun and small amounts of cochineal-dyed red hand-spun wool yarns. (Collection of School of American Research, Museum of New Mexico)

Navajo women who were enslaved by the Mexicans. Very few documented slave blankets are known to have survived (figs. 68, 81, and 82).[20]

Perhaps the constant violent warfare with the Navajos helped convince the Mexicans to give up the territory of New Mexico without a fight when challenged by an advancing American army in 1846. When he arrived in Santa Fe, the American commander, Brigadier General Stephen Kearny, told the Mexicans who stayed to live under American rule that they would be considered American citizens and, as such, were entitled to the protection of the U.S. Army. Kearny promised these new Americans that the Army would protect both the settlers and the Catholic Church from Indians, especially the Navajos and Apaches. He did not promise to protect Navajo families from Mexican slave raids.

Less than three months after they occupied New Mexico, American soldiers were sent into Navajo country. This military campaign culminated in the first attempt at reconciliation between the leaders and elders of the Navajo tribe and officers of the U.S. Army. In exchange for permanent cessation of Navajo raiding, the Americans promised to stop Mexican slave raids and offered to open up American trade to the Navajos.

Among the Navajo leaders who met with the Americans to negotiate this treaty at Bear Springs (*Ojo del Oso:* see map, fig. 2) were Narbona, Zarcillas Largo, and Manuelito. Powerful and respected men, they still had no authority over other Navajos. Younger men did not feel bound by the treaty of Bear Springs. They remembered that the *'ricos'*—the wealthy Navajo leaders—who now were asking for peace had originally acquired their sheep, horses, and wealth through raiding. Raiding was also the only way to recover captured slaves.

At the same time, the Mexicans (or the New Mexicans, as they became under American rule) had no intention of giving up their customary slave raids on the Navajos. According to a doctor who practiced medicine in Santa Fe during the 1860s, most New Mexican families owned at least one Navajo slave and many owned four or five. Among New Mexicans, trade in Navajo slaves was as brisk as trade in livestock. The doctor called the Navajos "the most abused people on the continent," and added that "in all hostilities the [New] Mexicans have always taken the initiative with but one exception."[21]

Although the Americans and the individual Navajos who signed the Bear Springs treaty and other treaties that followed were sincere, the treaties were doomed. New Mexicans kept taking Navajo slaves and Navajos kept raiding New Mexican settlements in retaliation. The U.S. Army began to launch regular offensive raids into Navajo country in an effort to keep the peace. In 1848 the American governor advised the New Mexican people to organize their own civilian war parties to ride against the Navajos.

Broken treaties became the rule, not the exception, after New Mexico and Arizona were officially annexed by the United States in 1848. Almost constant hostilities with American soldiers, New Mexican vigilantes, and marauding Utes and Apaches led to severe hardships for the tribe. Navajo flocks were depleted and crops went unplanted, untended, and/or unharvested. Navajos were forced to keep raiding for subsistence. The situation deteriorated even further when the American Army was recalled from New Mexico to fight in the Civil War. Only two companies of American soldiers remained in Navajo country, leaving the hungry, weakened Navajos at the mercy of the Utes, Apaches, and New Mexicans.

By 1862 the Civil War was over in New Mexico and the victorious Union government was forced to consider what had become of its "Indian problem." In the fall of 1862 the U.S. War Department, fed up with the violence in the Southwest, decided that forceful action

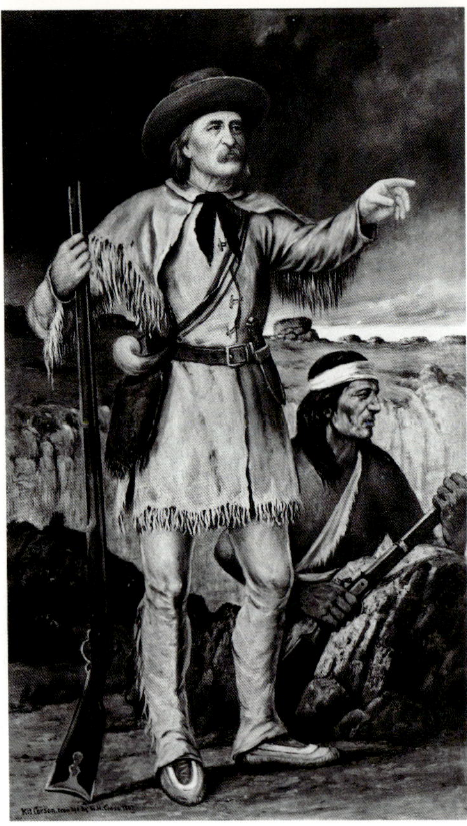

69. *Colonel Christopher "Kit" Carson,* c. 1867, by H. H. Cross. (Photograph courtesy Thomas Gilcrease Institute of American History and Art, Tulsa, Oklahoma)

against the Navajos and Apaches was the solution to the problem. General James H. Carleton, a Civil War hero and veteran of several Indian campaigns, was asked to decide what that forceful action might be. Carleton suggested that both tribes be rounded up and removed to Bosque Redondo ("Circle of trees"), an arid, isolated area in eastern New Mexico (see map, fig. 2).

When the Army sent a team of inspectors to see whether Bosque Redondo was appropriate for the containment of thousands of Indians, the inspectors reported that the site was "remote," lacked pure drinking water, and was subject to flooding. They recommended an alternate site as being more suitable to support a large number of prisoners.

Carleton overruled their objections and convinced the government that the Navajos and Apaches should be sent to Bosque Redondo.[22] There, Carleton surmised, "the old Indians will die off and carry with them all latent longings for murdering and robbing . . . little by little, they will become a happy and a contented people, and the Navajoe Wars will be remembered only as something that belongs entirely in the Past."[23]

Kit Carson, the man Carleton selected to implement his plan, had worked for years as an Indian scout. A few months before he began his campaign against the Navajos, Carson and his army had rounded up and relocated more than four hundred Apaches to Bosque Redondo. When his army moved against the Navajos, they were joined by Carson's allies from his days as a scout, the Ute Indians. Traditional enemies of the Navajos, the Utes needed no encouragement to join the roundup. Warriors from Hopi and Zuni Pueblos also rode with Carson, but they rode against their will and under threat of the destruction of their villages unless they cooperated. The Hopis and Zunis had to be warned not to help the Navajos as they had in the past.

Carson's strategy against the Navajos was harsh, but it was extremely effective. Believing they would choose imprisonment over death, Carson decided to starve the Navajos into submission. To do so, his troops destroyed crops, poisoned water holes, burned peach trees and hogans, killed sheep, and stole horses.

Even as the hopeless, helpless Navajos surrendered to the Americans, they were attacked by vigilante bands of New Mexicans taking their last chance to capture slaves. Carson forbade the Utes to sell their captives to the New Mexicans, but only after receiving orders from Carleton.

Harsh as Carson's measures were, only a few hundred Navajos volunteered to begin the "Long Walk" (four hundred miles) eastward to Bosque Redondo. When Carson took his troops to the heart—and soul—of Navajo country, Canyon de Chelly, in the winter of 1863, however, the Navajos, realizing there was no place left to hide, began to surrender in large groups. In the end, more than eight thousand surrendered to the Americans. Some Navajos eluded capture but most, faced with the choice of certain death or a questionable future at Bosque Redondo, chose Bosque Redondo. With the exception of a few hundred people, by March 1865 the entire Navajo nation was in custody at Bosque Redondo. (See map, fig. 2.)

Those who did surrender found that their problems were far from over. The army posts where the Navajos were held en route to Bosque Redondo quickly ran out of food and clothing. Some of the food that was available —flour, for instance—was so alien to the Navajos that it was inedible without instructions on its preparation (which were not supplied). Already weak and sick, many Navajos died.

Living conditions did not improve when the Indians reached Bosque Redondo itself. An army fort had been built there, named Fort Sumner after a former commander of the military in Santa Fe, but little else had been done to prepare the area to support more than eight thousand prisoners. When Carleton saw the thousands of Indians streaming into his would-be paradise, he sent to Washington for additional supplies. But the U.S. government was preoccupied with supplying the Union Army, which was still fighting the Civil War in the East. The supplies that made their way to New

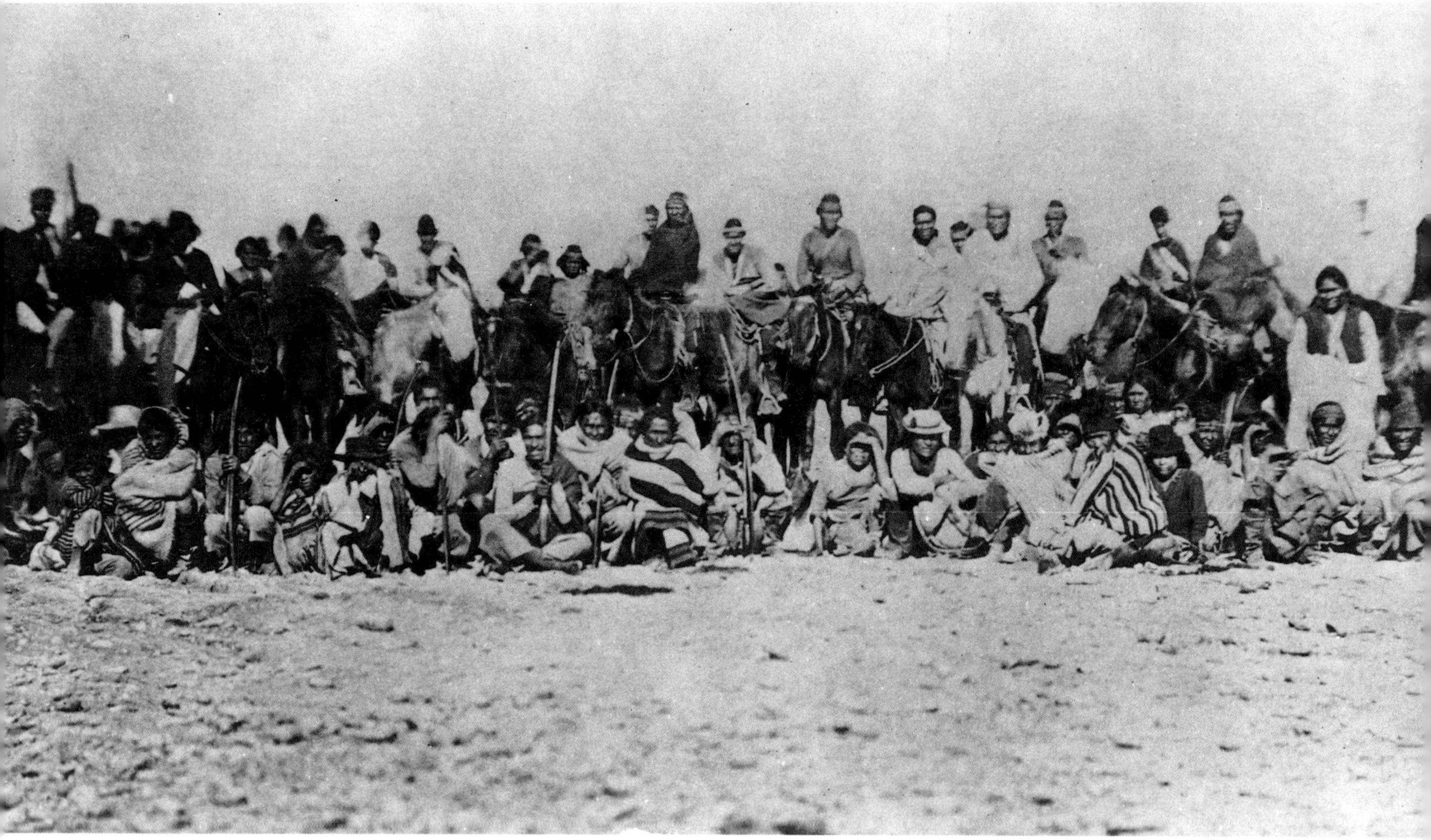

70. Navajo warriors at Fort Sumner (Bosque Redondo), New Mexico, 1864–1868. (Photograph courtesy National Archives)

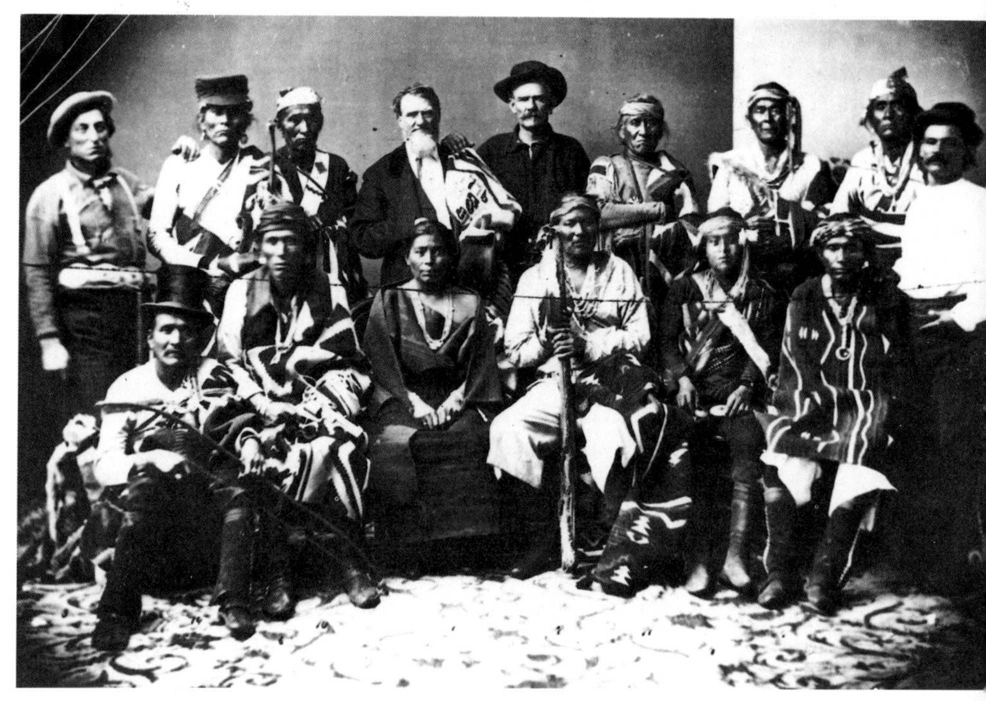

71. Treaty of 1868. Navajo leaders traveling to Washington, D.C., to sign the treaty allowing them to return to their homeland. (Photograph courtesy National Archives)

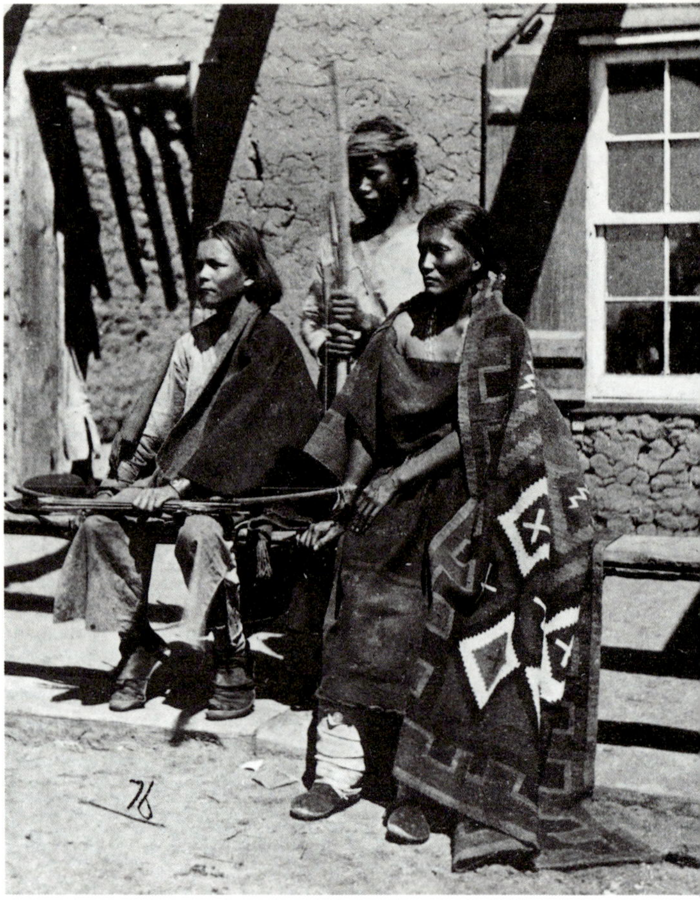

72. Fort Defiance, 1873. After Bosque Redondo, many Navajos became dependent on the United States government for their subsistence. Note the early bordered pattern blanket worn by this young Navajo girl. (Photograph courtesy National Archives)

Mexico were, like the flour, inappropriate or inadequate. Instead of food, seeds, or agricultural tools, goods such as nails and blacksmith tools arrived at Fort Sumner. Carleton's fantasy of a peaceful tribe nourished by their own crops was destroyed when drought, worms, insects, hail, tornadoes, and other natural disasters combined to kill the few Navajo crops that were planted.

Many of the Indians held prisoner at Bosque Redondo were forced to live in holes in the ground. Disease was an enormous problem. Syphilis and malnutrition were rampant, and the drinking water carried dysentery. Many Navajos shunned the hospital at Fort Sumner because of their fear of the ghosts of Navajos who had died there. The Navajos also remembered that friends and relatives who became ill on the Long Walk were either killed by American soldiers or left to die, and were understandably pessimistic about the quality and sincerity of American medical care. To add to these health problems, the soil would not grow crops, the nearest firewood was twenty miles away, and the few sheep, horses, and cattle the Navajos managed to bring with them to Bosque Redondo were virtually unprotected and often fell prey to raiding Comanches and Kiowas from the north and New Mexicans from the west.

Life outside Bosque Redondo was equally difficult for those few Navajos who eluded capture, escaped from captivity, or were the children of Navajo slaves. Slavery, though illegal, was still socially acceptable in New Mexico. Although most Navajos not in captivity at Bosque Redondo were slaves, those who remained free were constantly threatened by New Mexican slavers and Ute Indians.

Even though the Indians at Bosque Redondo were kept in a state of near-starvation, it was still enormously expensive to keep thousands of people confined. Horrified at the expense, local New Mexicans who originally supported Carleton's plan later spoke out against it. An editorial in the Santa Fe *New Mexican* asked why the U.S. government should spend money to starve a people who could do a better job of feeding themselves. Move the Navajos to Arizona, the *New Mexican* advocated, where they could take care of themselves, and give the land at Bosque Redondo to New Mexican ranchers.[24]

Because of the scandalous conditions and the enormous expenses, public opinion in New Mexico became official pressure in Washington against Bosque Redondo and its architect, James Carleton. In September 1866 Carleton was reassigned and, under orders from General Ulysses S. Grant, jurisdiction over the Navajos was transferred from the army to the Bureau of Indian Affairs. The lives of the men, women, and children imprisoned at Bosque Redondo became the responsibility of Theodore H. Dodd. An editor of the *New Mexican* wrote with unconcealed delight, "Our territory will be relieved from the presence of this man [Carleton], who has so long lorded it amongst us."[25]

After assessing the situation at Bosque Redondo, Dodd made a list of essential supplies the Indians needed merely to stay alive. He went to Washington himself to get the necessary funds and then traveled overland to St. Louis where he personally did the buying, supervised the packing, and rode the wagon train west along the Santa Fe Trail himself. Every previous load of supplies had mysteriously shrunk in transit or disappeared entirely. Dodd's supplies arrived intact.

But Dodd's direct, energetic methods were more the exception than the rule, and it took the bureaucracy in Washington almost two more years—years of horror, misery, and death for the Navajos, who called their years at Bosque Redondo *Nabondzod,* "the Fearing Time"[26]—to initiate a final treaty. By 1868, when the treaty was signed, more than two thousand Navajos had

73. Last ration, 1879. Navajos gathering at Fort Defiance for the last government rationing of goods. (Photograph courtesy Smithsonian Institution)

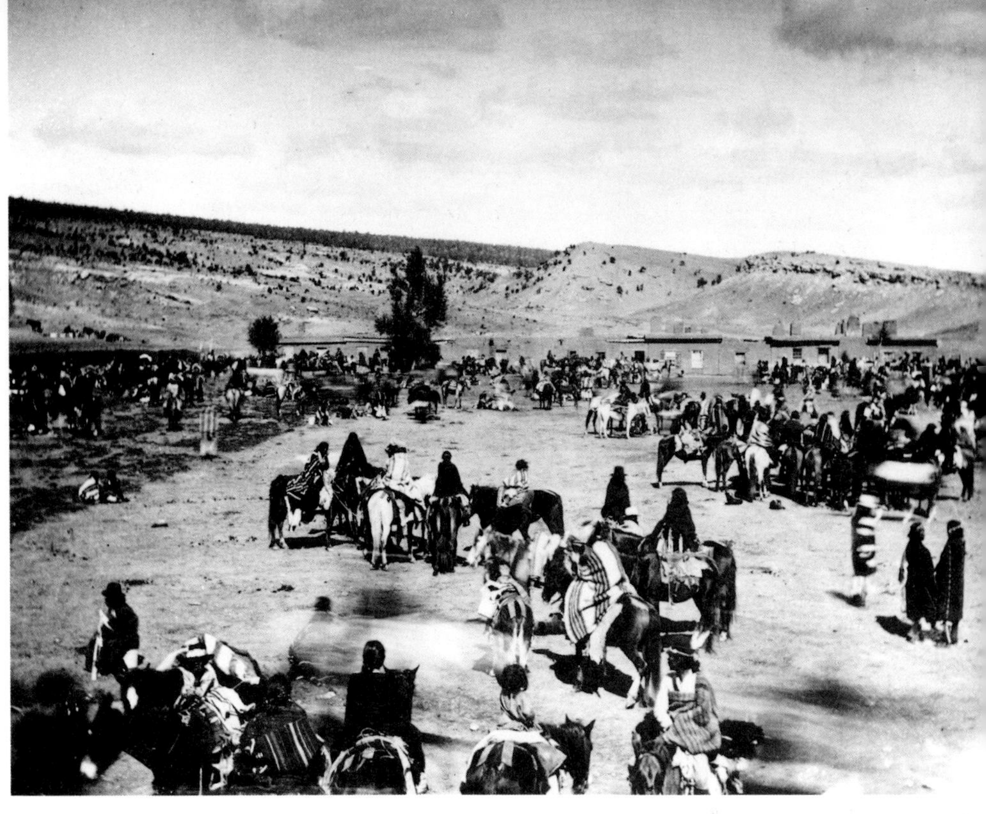

74. Tom Torleno, Navajo boy, as he came to the Carlisle Indian School, Pennsylvania, in the early 1880s.

75. Tom Torleno three years later, at the Carlisle Indian School. (Photographs courtesy Smithsonian Institution)

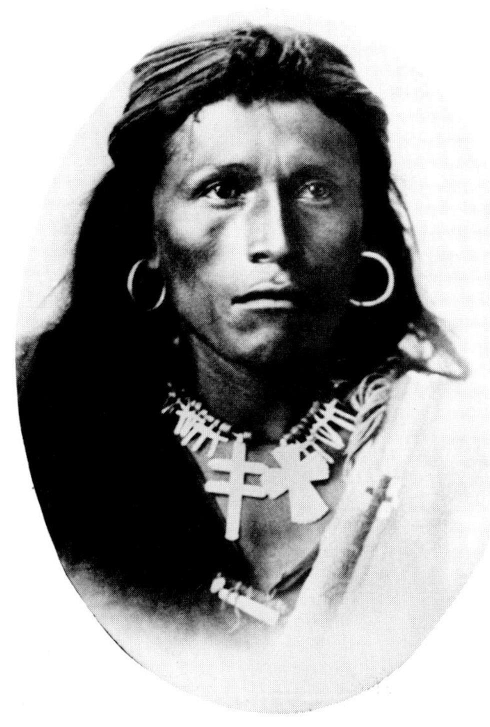

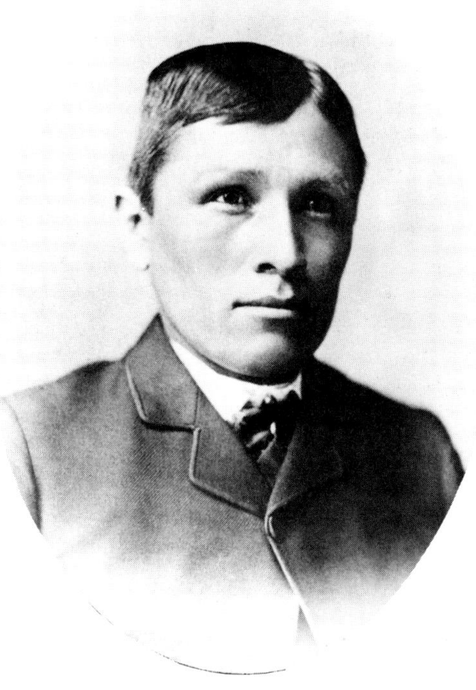

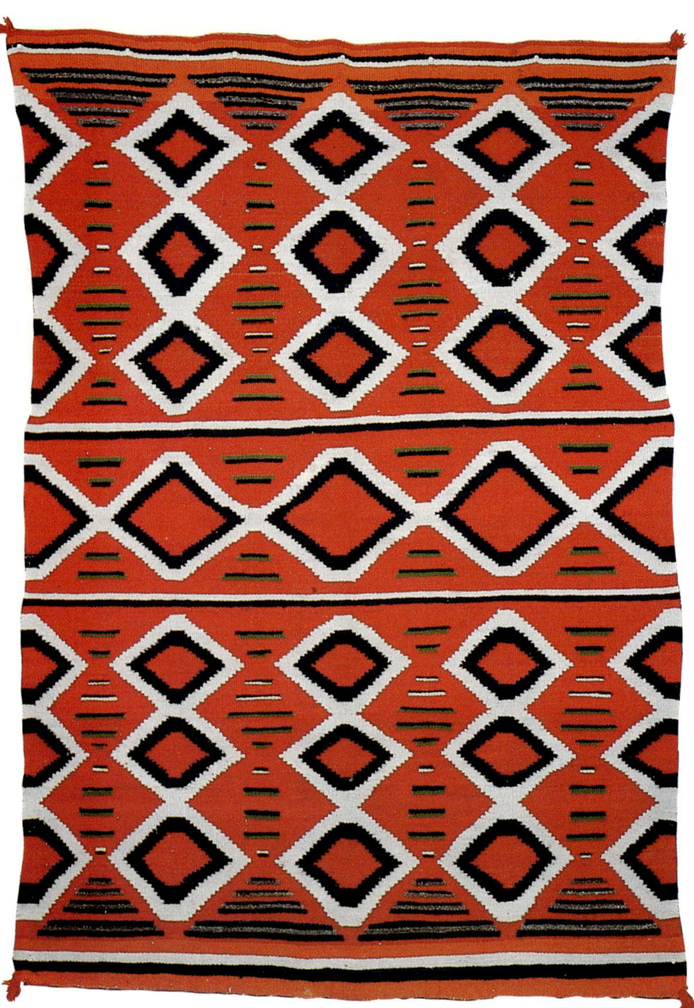

76. Sarape, c. 1875. 75″ x 53″. 7 warp/in.; 44 weft/in. Raveled synthetic-dyed red/orange American bayeta, often called American flannel because of its fuzzy texture, is used in this thick, heavy Late Classic Period-style blanket. Woven of raveled synthetic-dyed red, four-ply commercial synthetic-dyed green, and indigo-dyed blue and natural gray and white hand-spun wool yarns. (Private collection)

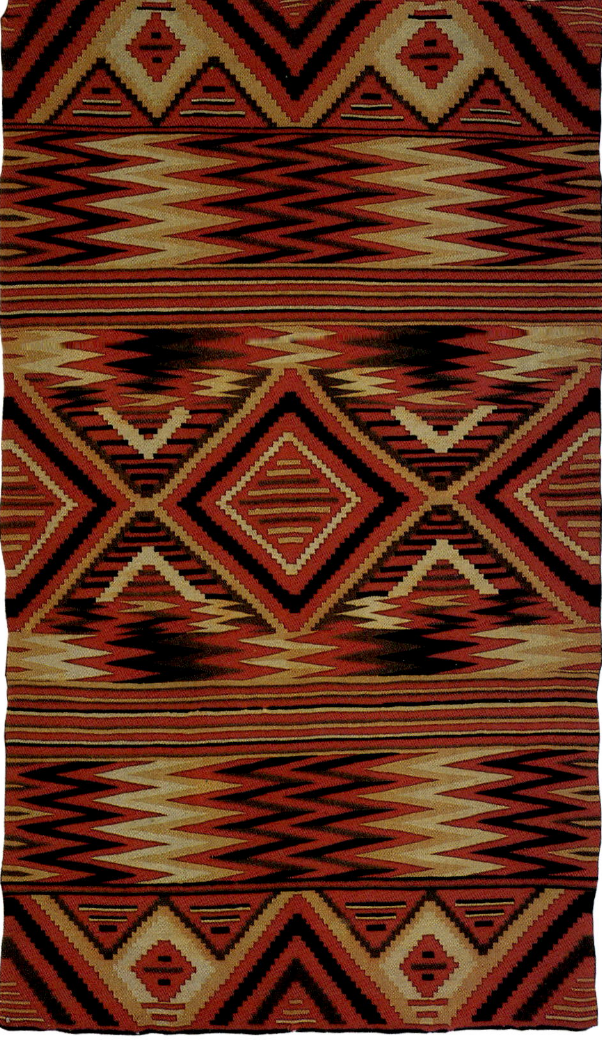

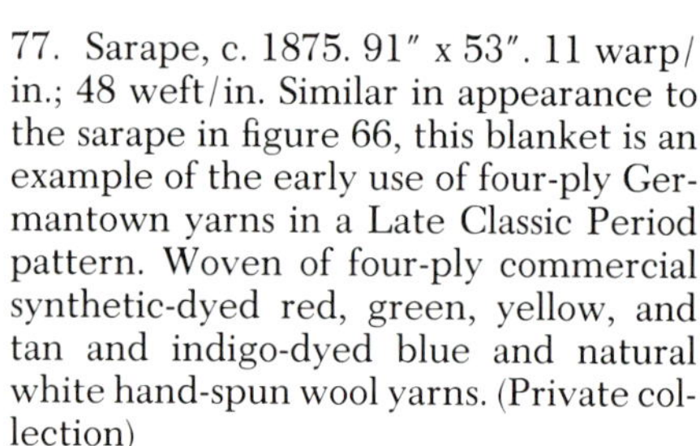

77. Sarape, c. 1875. 91″ x 53″. 11 warp/in.; 48 weft/in. Similar in appearance to the sarape in figure 66, this blanket is an example of the early use of four-ply Germantown yarns in a Late Classic Period pattern. Woven of four-ply commercial synthetic-dyed red, green, yellow, and tan and indigo-dyed blue and natural white hand-spun wool yarns. (Private collection)

died at the prison camp and nearly one thousand had escaped. Before Kit Carson's campaign, the Navajos owned more than two hundred thousand sheep. They left with fewer than a thousand.

During the treaty negotiations, some Americans suggested the Navajos should be sent to live in Oklahoma like the Cherokees, Creeks, and other tribes removed from their land to make way for American settlement. Barboncito, one of the Navajos who signed the final treaty, argued eloquently against such a move, saying, "I hope to God you will not ask us to go to any other country except our own."[27]

In the end, the Navajos were allowed to return to Dinetah. The newly formed Navajo reservation included 3.5 million acres, roughly one-fifth of the area the Navajos originally inhabited. The treaty, signed by twenty-nine Navajo clan leaders (and later by President Andrew Johnson), provided that any Navajo head of family could claim 160 acres anywhere on the reservation (fig. 71). Any Navajo over the age of eighteen could claim eighty acres. Each future farmer would receive $100 worth of farming tools and seeds.

Actually, neither side seemed to be overly concerned about the terms of the treaty. Both the Navajos, who wanted only to go home, and the Americans, who wanted to end the embarrassing suffering and needless expense, wanted a satisfactory resolution. But the terms of the treaty would cause trouble for years to come.

Within days of signing the treaty, the Navajos were on their way back to their country west of the Chuska Mountains. Many of them found they were unable to return to their old homes, however, because they had no livestock, food, or clothing. They were forced to settle, at least for a time, near Fort Wingate in New Mexico (which was built at Bear Springs, the site of the first Navajo-American treaty) or Fort Defiance, Arizona (see map, fig. 2), where they could get the necessities of life from the U.S. government.

After Bosque Redondo, the Navajos never regained economic independence. The reliance on government rations and supplies that started at Bosque Redondo and continued at Fort Wingate and Fort Defiance remains an unpleasant fact of contemporary life. Navajos estimate that unemployment on the reservation reached 80 percent in 1982. Many of these unemployed Navajos are partially or totally supported by the government.[28]

Other changes, equally sweeping and equally permanent, affected the lives of the Navajo people when they returned to Dinetah. Their style of dress, for instance, changed forever. They arrived at Bosque Redondo wearing blankets, sarapes, and two-piece blanket dresses made from wool. Since there was little or no native wool available for weaving clothing at Bosque Redondo, Navajo women began to make clothes for both men and women out of cotton trade cloth supplied by the government. By 1868 the new Navajo women's styles—flounced gingham, velvet, and calico skirts and blouses—resembled the clothes worn by the wives of the soldiers stationed at Fort Sumner. What was "in style" for Anglo women in the 1860s is still in style for Navajo women in the 1980s. Ironically, this style came back into mainstream fashion as "the Prairie Look" in the early 1980s (see fig. 103).

Many of the conditions that made weaving difficult during the years at Bosque Redondo continued to prevail when the People returned home. By necessity, most of the women were concerned with survival, not weaving. Because there were so few sheep, there was very little wool available. It took the government a year and a half after the Bosque Redondo treaty was signed to deliver the 15,000 sheep promised to the Navajos.

78. Child's sarape, 1865–1870. 51″ x 32″. 12 warp/in.; 56 weft/in. A number of raveled and commercial yarns as well as a busy collection of typically Late Classic Period design elements (crosses, vertical zigzags, and diagonal interrupted stripes) are used in this blanket. Woven of three-ply commercial cochineal-dyed red (two shades), raveled cochineal-dyed red, raveled and recarded pink, and vegetal-dyed yellow, indigo with vegetal dyed green, indigo-dyed blue, and natural white hand-spun wool yarns. (Private collection)

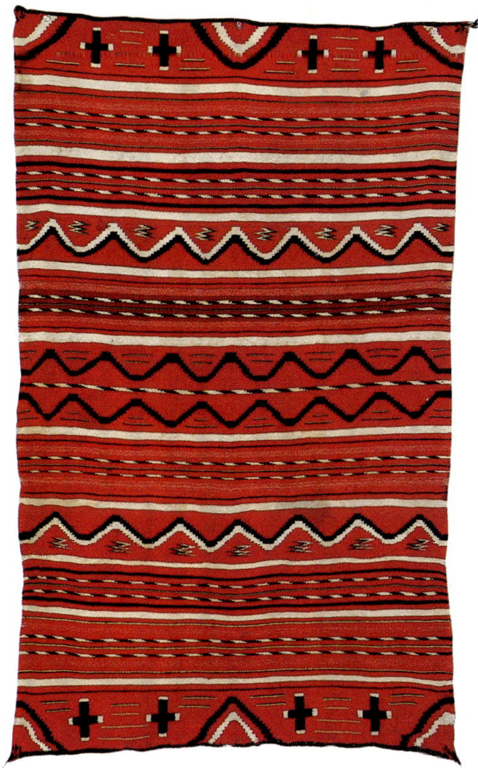

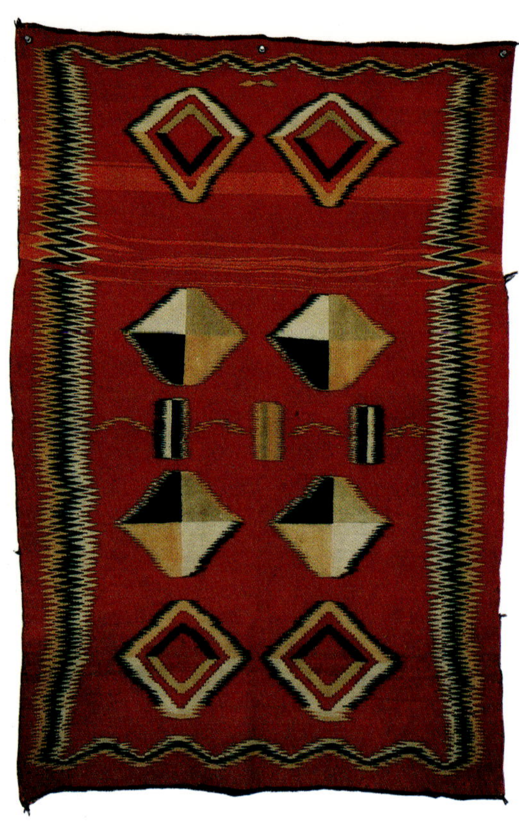

79. Child's sarape, 1870–1875. 50″ x 34″. 13 warp/in.; 76 weft/in. An early example of a bordered pattern, this Late Classic/early Transitional Period blanket incorporates three colors of raveled bayeta. Woven of raveled lac-dyed red, raveled vegetal-dyed green and yellow, and indigo-dyed blue and natural white hand-spun wool yarns. (Private collection)

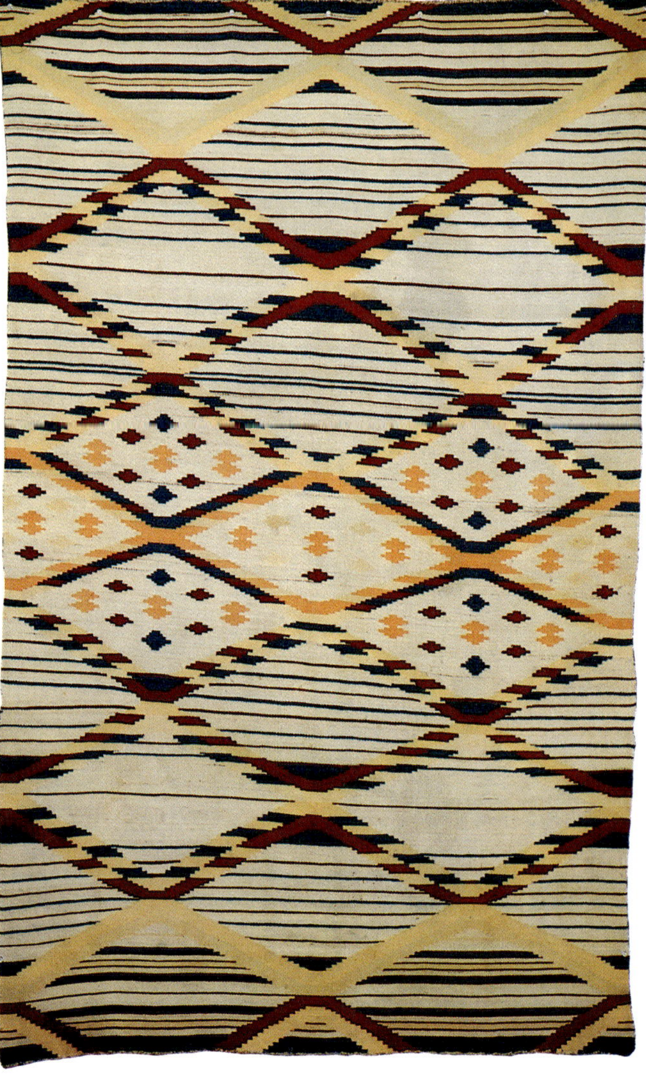

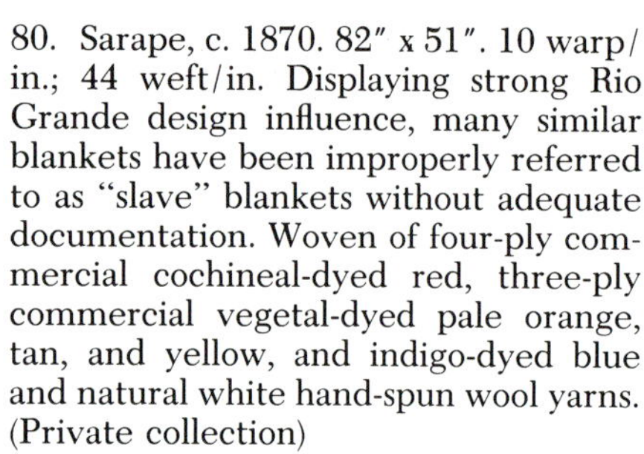

80. Sarape, c. 1870. 82″ x 51″. 10 warp/in.; 44 weft/in. Displaying strong Rio Grande design influence, many similar blankets have been improperly referred to as "slave" blankets without adequate documentation. Woven of four-ply commercial cochineal-dyed red, three-ply commercial vegetal-dyed pale orange, tan, and yellow, and indigo-dyed blue and natural white hand-spun wool yarns. (Private collection)

When the sheep finally did arrive, they were not churros, the hardy sheep introduced by the Spanish and bred by the Navajos, but merinos. Instead of the long, silky churro wool Navajo weavers used in the past, the fleece from merino sheep was short, kinky, and greasy. The lack of hand-spun wool yarn, the result of the poor quality of the merino wool that was available, increased the weavers' dependence on commercial yarns and on commercially woven fabrics which could be raveled.

In the 1870s, yarns raveled from low-grade bayeta, often coarse American flannel cloth, and commercially spun Germantown yarns were almost the only weaving materials available (see figs. 76 and 213). After using these commercial materials for years, many Navajo weavers grew accustomed to them, even preferring to use commercial rather than hand-spun yarn when the latter became widely available again. Younger weavers who had learned to weave with the commercial products had little desire to learn to shear, wash, card, spin, and dye the wool. Older weavers, experienced with churro wool, chose to weave with commercial yarns after they grew frustrated with the problematical merino wool. In 1855 the best weavers used bayeta, Saxony, and hand-spun yarns. By 1880 many of the best weavers were using, almost exclusively, commercial American synthetic-dyed three- and four-ply Germantown yarn (fig. 77).

Navajo dependence on commercial materials continues to this day in many but not all styles of Navajo weaving. Weavers of contemporary Ganado rugs, for example, use packaged synthetic dyes as a matter of course as it has become "traditional" for weavers of Teec Nos Pos and Yei rugs to use commercially spun yarn.

Just as the almost universal use of synthetic dyes and commercial yarns by Navajo weavers of the 1870s and 1880s can be traced directly to the hardships at Bosque Redondo, so can the characteristic textile styles of the same era. Many post–Bosque Redondo weavers were still creating textiles in the Late Classic style, which developed at Bosque Redondo and incorporated such design elements as crosses, interrupted diagonal stripes, vertical zigzags, vertical terraced stripes, and meanders into an otherwise Classic-style blanket (fig. 78). But by 1880 the more innovative weavers were experimenting with textiles dominated by serrated diamonds, serrated wavy bands, and borders on their blankets, often with no discernible horizontal zones of design (figs. 72 and 79). Many of the textiles resembled the old Rio Grande Saltillo-influenced blankets the Navajos had been given at Bosque Redondo.

During the time of their confinement the Navajos were given at least a thousand and possibly as many as four to five thousand Rio Grande blankets. These blankets were the products of a chain of cross-cultural influences. Generations earlier, New Mexican students of the Bazan brothers, the Spanish master weavers, attempted to teach Mexican weavers to re-create the elegance of the fine Mexican Saltillo sarape. Indeed, the Saltillo was so impressive that it indirectly inspired the Navajo weaver to include elements of its design in her blankets. By 1880 that cultural impulse had come full circle. New Mexican weavers were using some design elements borrowed from Navajo sarapes, which had been inspired in part by the earlier New Mexican and Saltillo textiles.

The Rio Grande blankets given to the Navajos at Bosque Redondo were a pale imitation of the original Mexican Saltillos. Coarser and far simpler in design than the earlier, finer textiles, they were still characteristically patterned with large center serrate diamonds and borders. After living with these Rio Grande blankets for years at Bosque Redondo, Navajo weavers incorporated the Spanish designs into their own Navajo design tradition to a far greater degree than they had previously (fig. 80).

But tradition was a thing of the past for the Navajos who started a new life on their reservation after 1868. And just as the past had been wiped away with terrible swiftness, the present and future grew increasingly unpredictable. The establishment of trading posts run by Anglo traders and the new route of the Santa Fe Railroad would bring even more changes to the lives of the Navajos.

To the weavers of the tribe, tradition had been replaced by challenge: the challenge of new yarns and new dyes to master, of new designs to embrace and transform, of new uses and functions for weaving, and, finally, of a new world of customers. Weaving, after all, remained an economic resource to the Navajo.

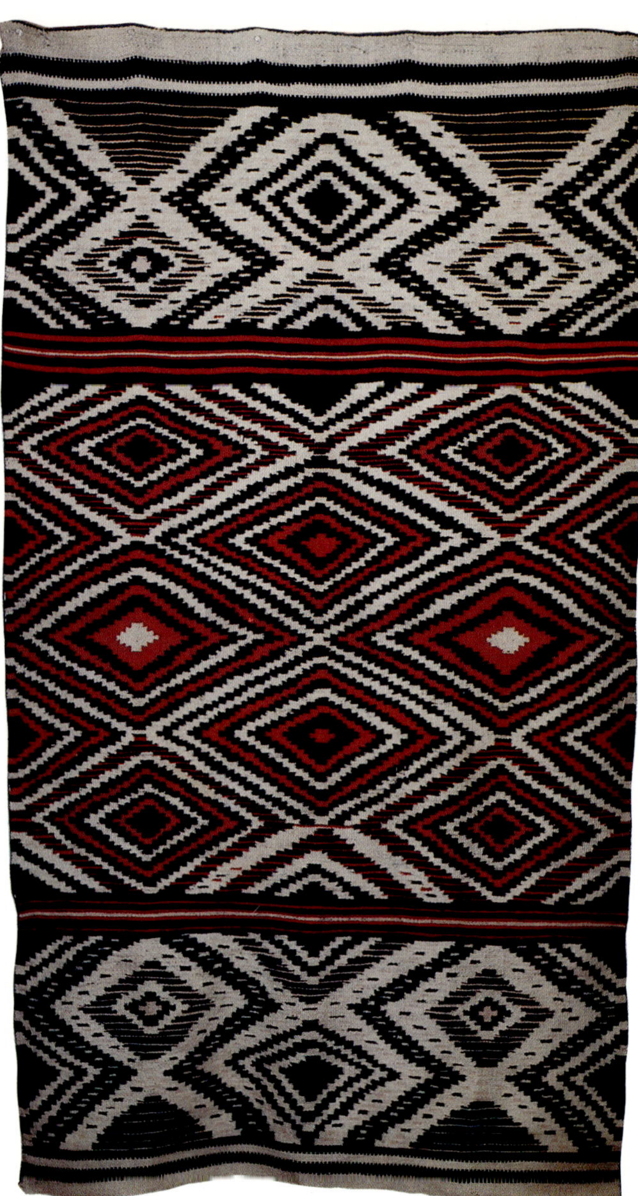

81. Sarape, c. 1860. 85″ x 49″. 8 warp/in.; 32 weft/in. Strong Saltillo design influence and the unusually long proportions of this Navajo sarape suggest that it may have been woven by a Navajo servant for a Spanish patron. Woven of raveled lac with cochineal-dyed red and pink and indigo-dyed blue and natural white hand-spun wool yarns. (Private collection)

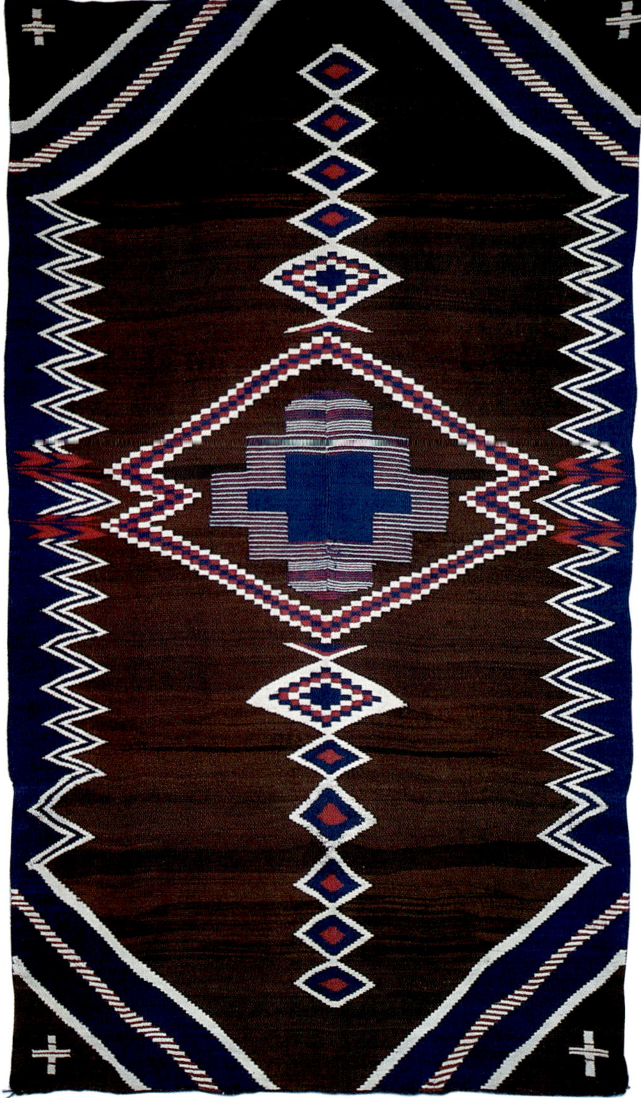

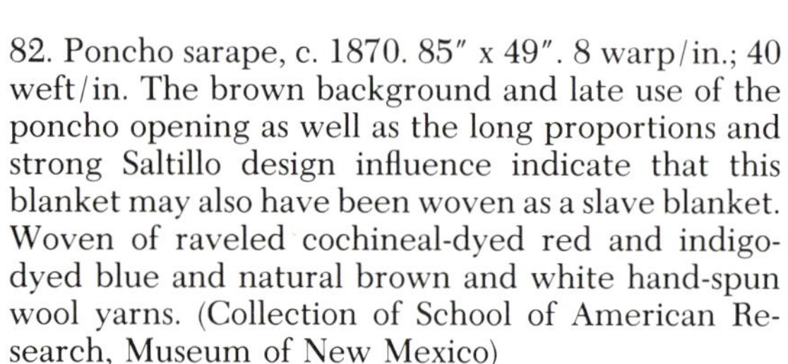

82. Poncho sarape, c. 1870. 85″ x 49″. 8 warp/in.; 40 weft/in. The brown background and late use of the poncho opening as well as the long proportions and strong Saltillo design influence indicate that this blanket may also have been woven as a slave blanket. Woven of raveled cochineal-dyed red and indigo-dyed blue and natural brown and white hand-spun wool yarns. (Collection of School of American Research, Museum of New Mexico)

83. Child's sarape, c. 1875. 54″ x 34″. 11 warp/in.; 54 weft/in. A harbinger of twentieth-century vegetal-dye rugs, the use of vegetal-green hand-spun as a background color is extremely rare in nineteenth-century Navajo blankets. Woven of three-ply commercial synthetic-dyed red and indigo with vegetal-dyed green and indigo-dyed blue hand-spun wool yarns. (Private collection)

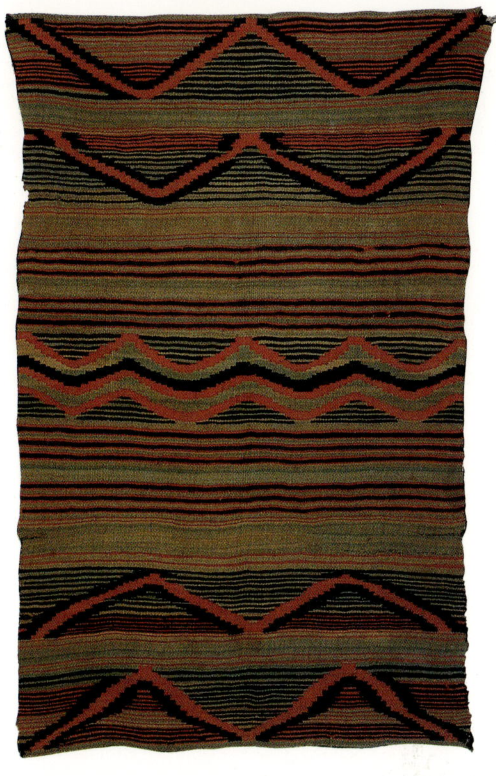

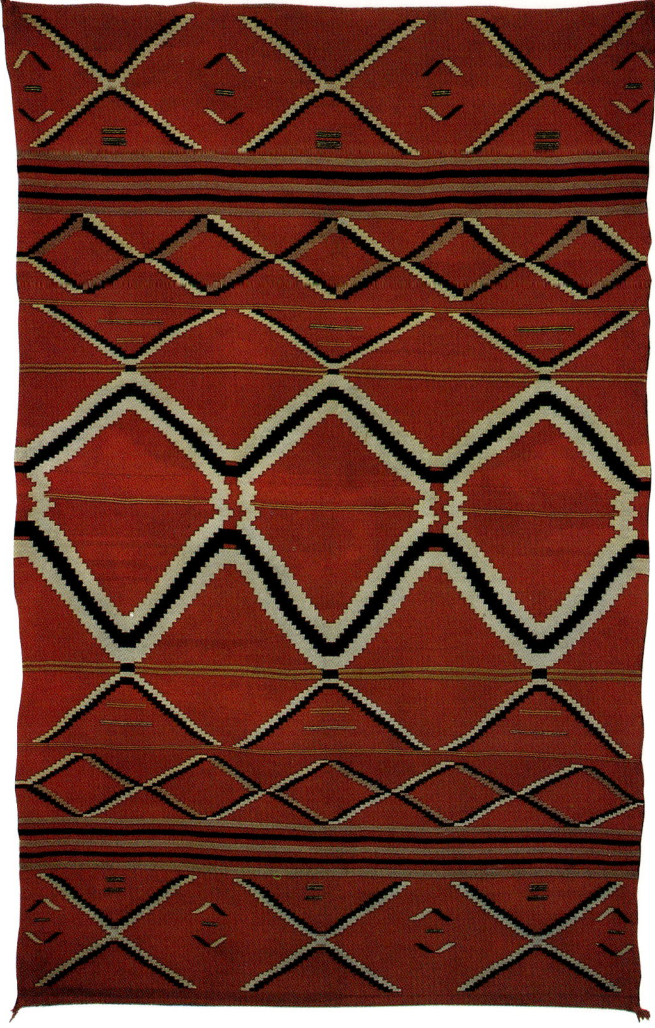

84. Sarape, c. 1870. 78″ x 51″. 13 warp/in.; 68 weft/in. In the Late Classic Period many Navajo weavers began experimenting with new optical design effects, often using the red background color like a canvas on which to create new designs and patterns. Woven of raveled cochineal (?)-dyed red, raveled vegetal-dyed green, synthetic-dyed purple, and indigo-dyed blue and natural white hand-spun yarns. (Private collection)

85. Sarape, c. 1870. 72″ x 54″. 12 warp/in.; 68 weft/in. Beginning about 1870 many Late Classic Period sarapes took on a vertical design orientation. Although the vertical diamonds appear to be serrated, they are composed of many tiny terraces. Woven of three-ply commercial cochineal-dyed red, three-ply commercial vegetal-dyed green, and indigo-dyed blue and natural white hand-spun wool yarns. (Private collection)

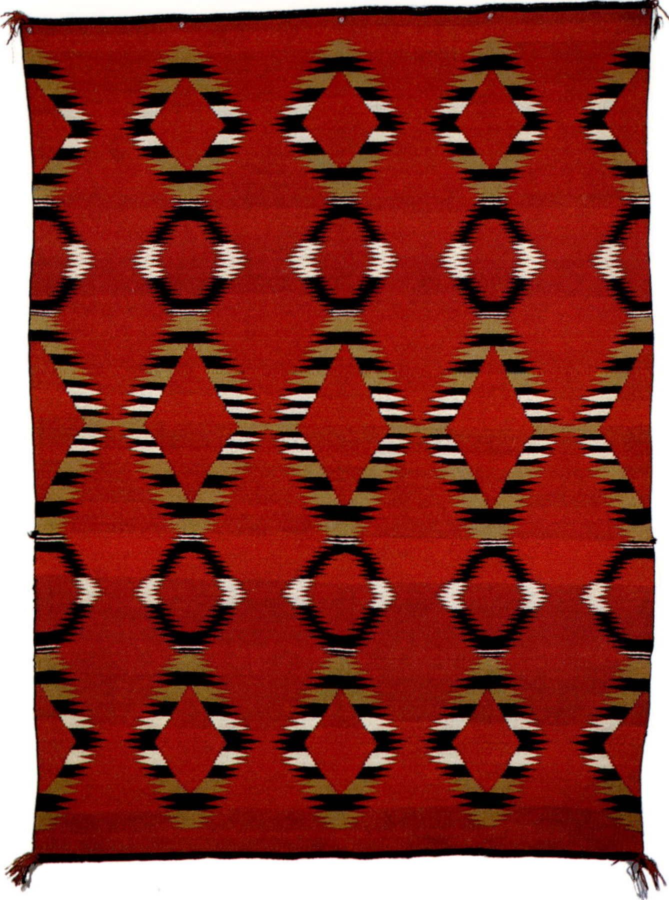

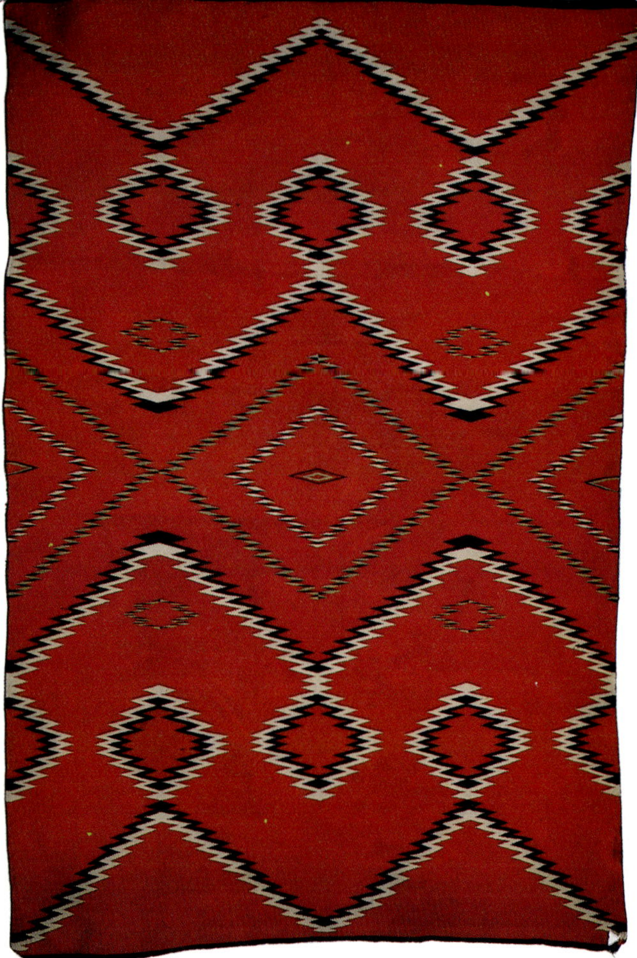

86. Sarape, c. 1870. 79″ x 53″. 11 warp/in.; 88 weft/in. Large open patterns consisting of finely terraced diagonals on a red ground are characteristics of Late Classic Period and early Transitional Period sarapes. Woven of raveled cochineal-dyed red and indigo with vegetal-dyed green, indigo-dyed blue, and natural white hand-spun wool yarns. (Private collection)

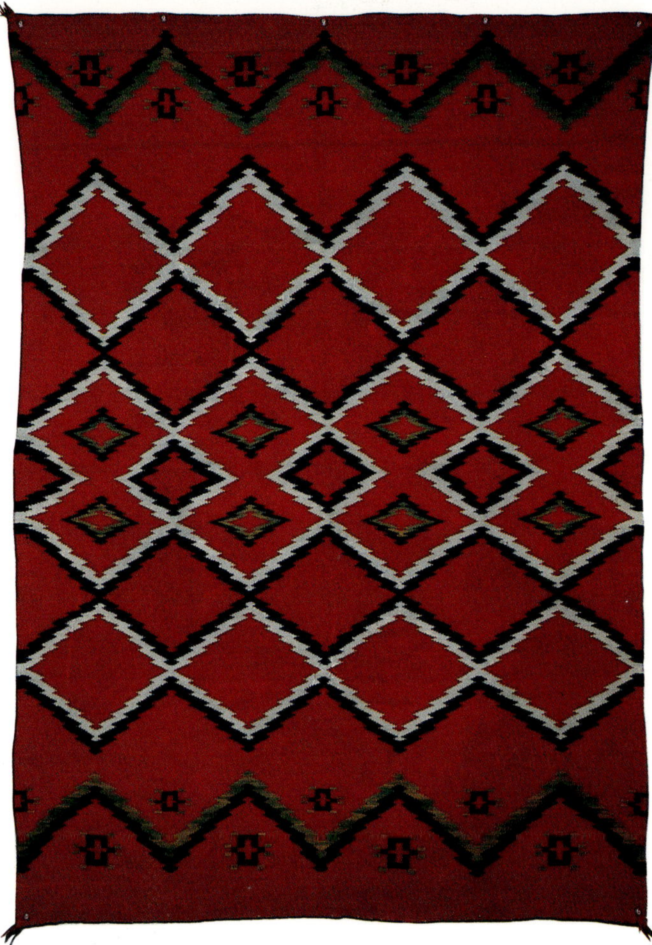

87. Sarape, c. 1875. 77″ x 54″. 12 warp/in.; 48 weft/in. Many Late Classic–early Transitional Period sarapes began to take on an overall patterned appearance reminiscent of early Classic Period design layout but with a different character. Woven of raveled synthetic-dyed red and indigo with vegetal-dyed green, indigo-dyed blue, and natural white hand-spun wool yarns. (Private collection)

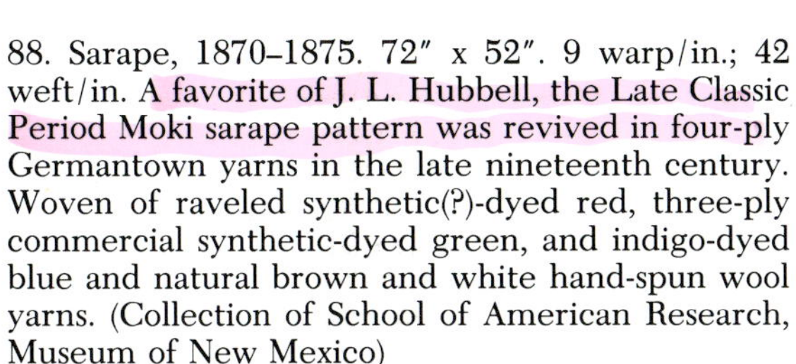

88. Sarape, 1870–1875. 72″ x 52″. 9 warp/in.; 42 weft/in. A favorite of J. L. Hubbell, the Late Classic Period Moki sarape pattern was revived in four-ply Germantown yarns in the late nineteenth century. Woven of raveled synthetic(?)-dyed red, three-ply commercial synthetic-dyed green, and indigo-dyed blue and natural brown and white hand-spun wool yarns. (Collection of School of American Research, Museum of New Mexico)

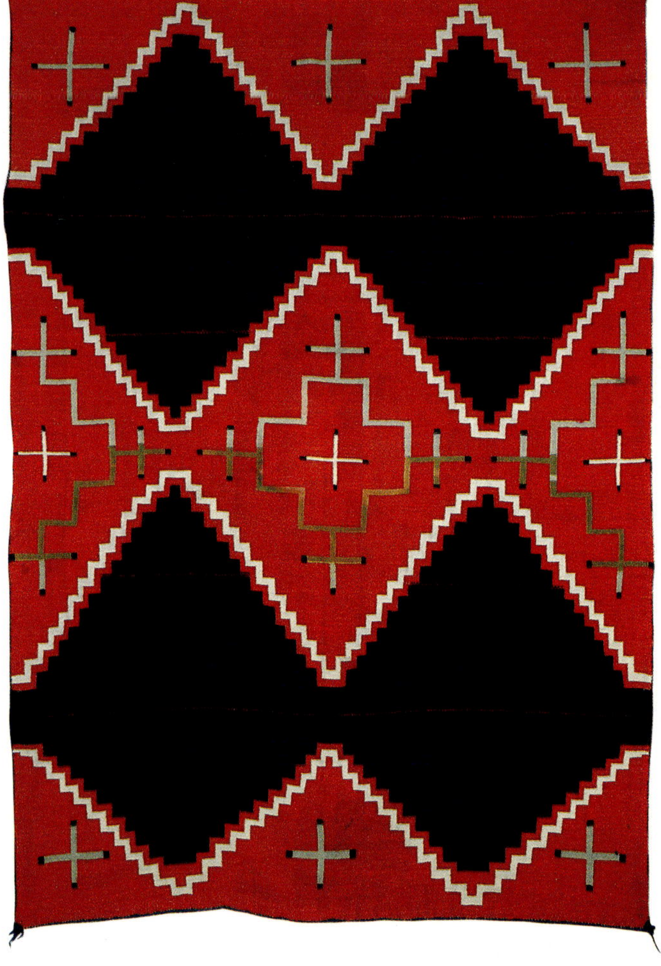

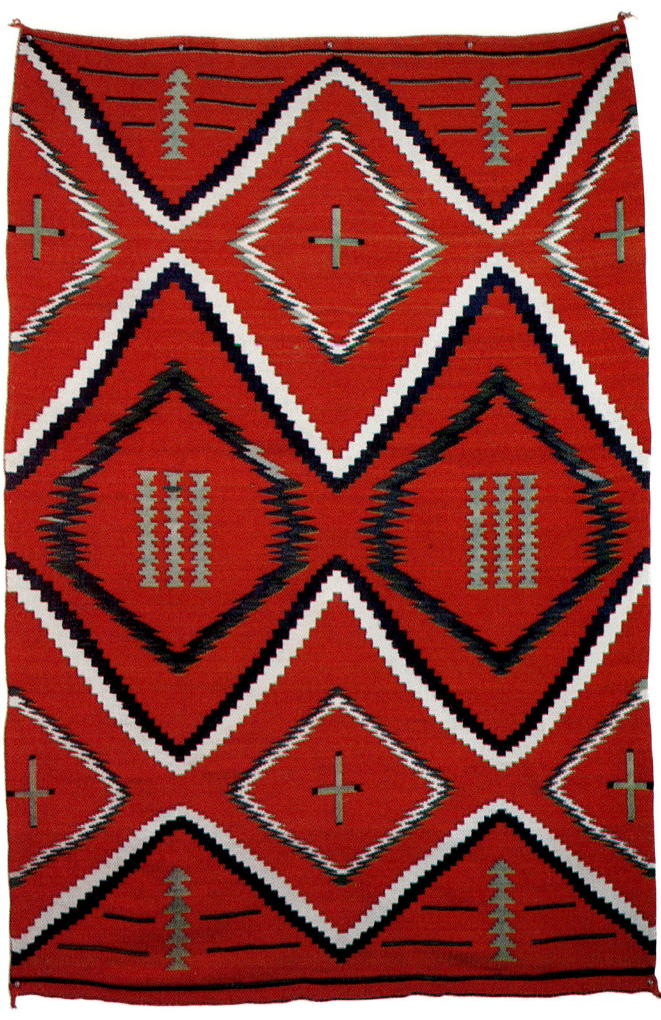

89. Sarape, 1875–1880. 76″ x 53″. 8 warp/in.; 44 weft/in. The combination of terraced and serrated design elements in an all-hand-spun blanket are typical of early Transitional Period blankets. Woven of synthetic-dyed red, indigo with vegetal-dyed green, indigo-dyed blue, and natural white hand-spun wool yarns. (Private collection)

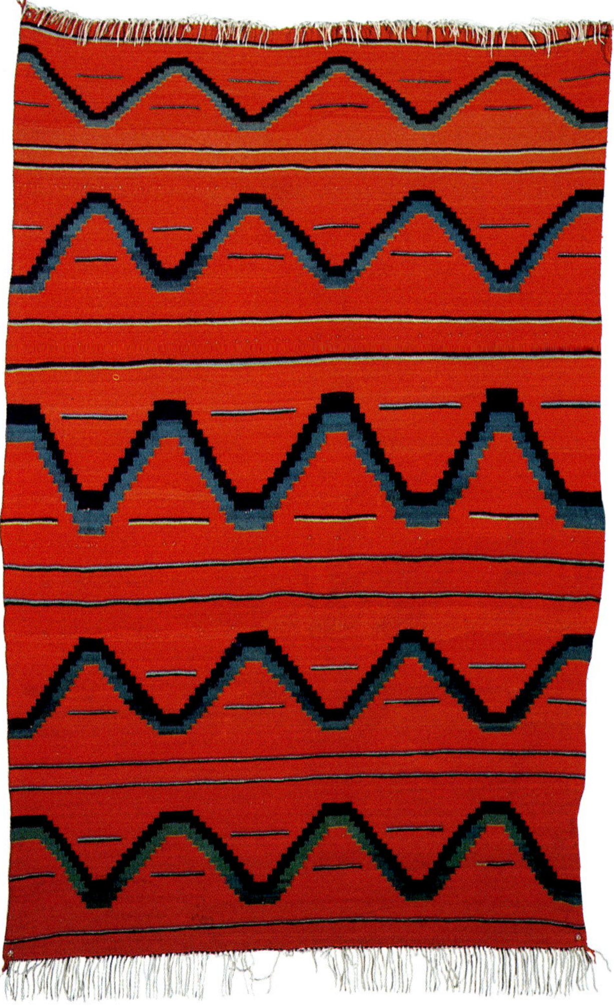

90. Sarape, 1875–1880. 73″ x 48″. 11 warp/in.; 42 weft/in. The use of synthetic-dyed hand-spun yarns in combination with the earlier indigo and vegetal dyes occurs for only a short period of time, as synthetic colors rapidly replaced natural dyes. Note the presence of warp fringe, unusual in Navajo blankets but common in Spanish textiles. Woven of synthetic-dyed red, indigo with vegetal-dyed green, and indigo-dyed blue (three shades) hand-spun wool yarns. (Private collection)

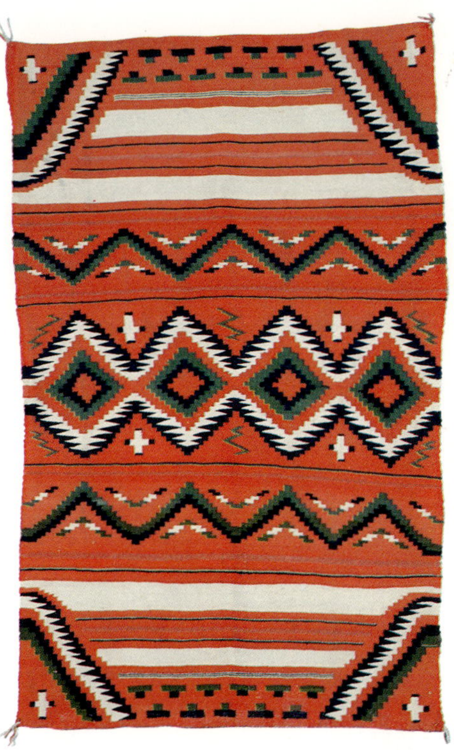

91. Child's sarape, 1875–1880. 49″ x 31″. 11 warp/in.; 45 weft/in. A Late Classic/early Transitional Period pattern executed in all hand-spun yarns is typical of this period. Woven of synthetic-dyed red, indigo with vegetal-dyed green, indigo-dyed blue, and natural white hand-spun wool yarns. (Collection of School of American Research, Museum of New Mexico)

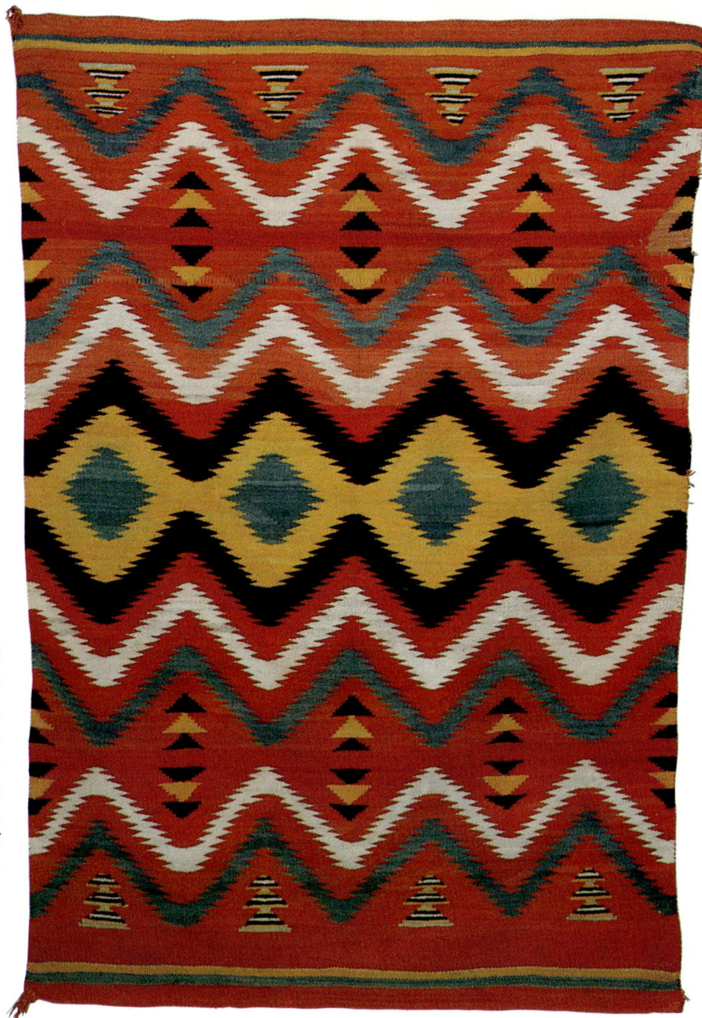

92. Sarape, 1880–1885. 70″ x 49″. 9 warp/in.; 26 weft/in. A soft, thickly woven Transitional Period sarape, woven almost entirely of early synthetic-dyed hand-spun yarns. Woven of synthetic-dyed red, yellow, pale blue, pale purple, and black and natural white hand-spun wool yarns. (Collection of Maxwell Museum of Anthropology, University of New Mexico)

93. Sarape, c. 1880. 69″ x 54″. 7 warp/in.; 40 weft/in. The entire pattern of this Transitional Period blanket is composed of fine serrated designs, some outlined with a thin white line. Woven of synthetic-dyed red, orange, yellow, and green, indigo-dyed blue, and natural white hand-spun wool yarns. (Private collection)

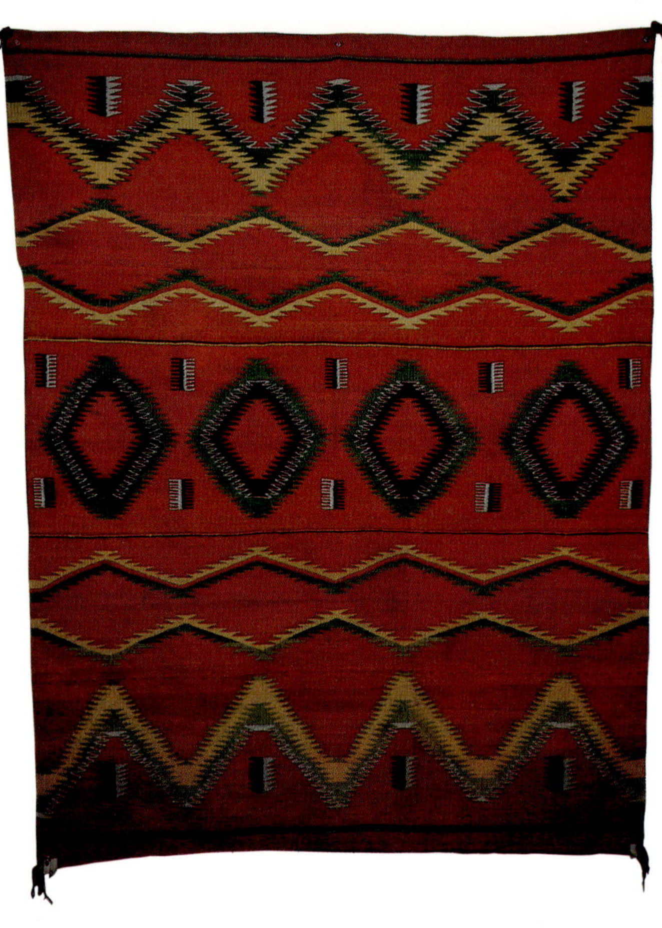

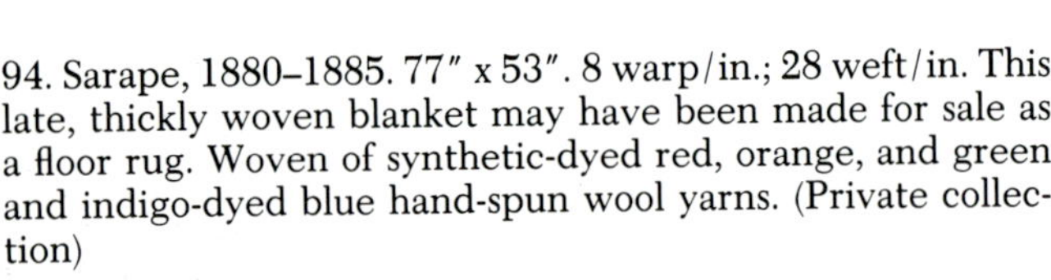

94. Sarape, 1880–1885. 77″ x 53″. 8 warp/in.; 28 weft/in. This late, thickly woven blanket may have been made for sale as a floor rug. Woven of synthetic-dyed red, orange, and green and indigo-dyed blue hand-spun wool yarns. (Private collection)

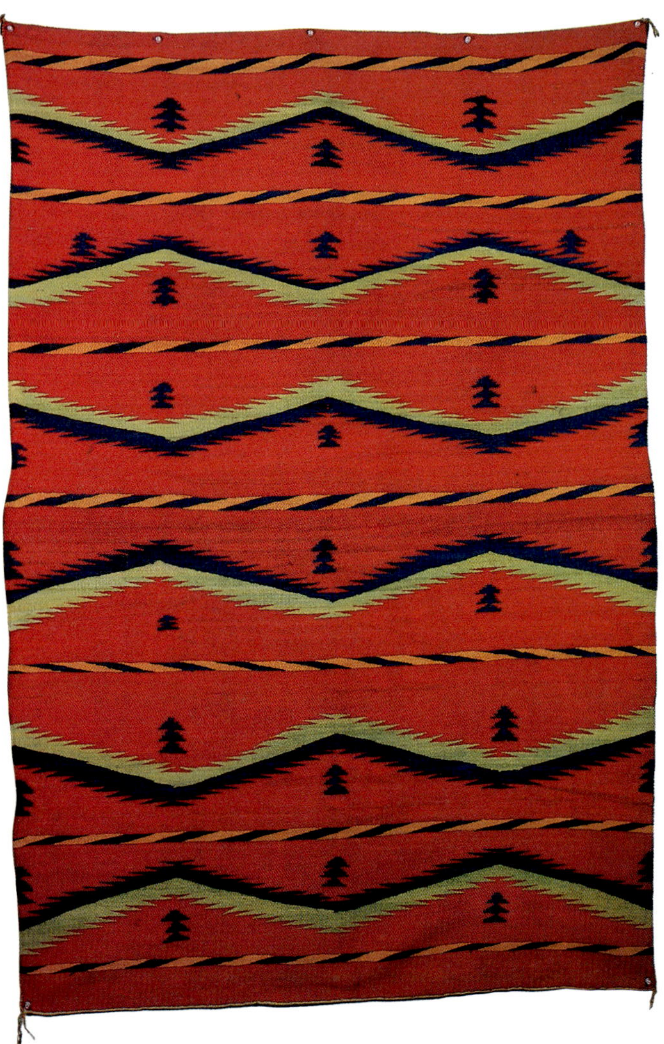

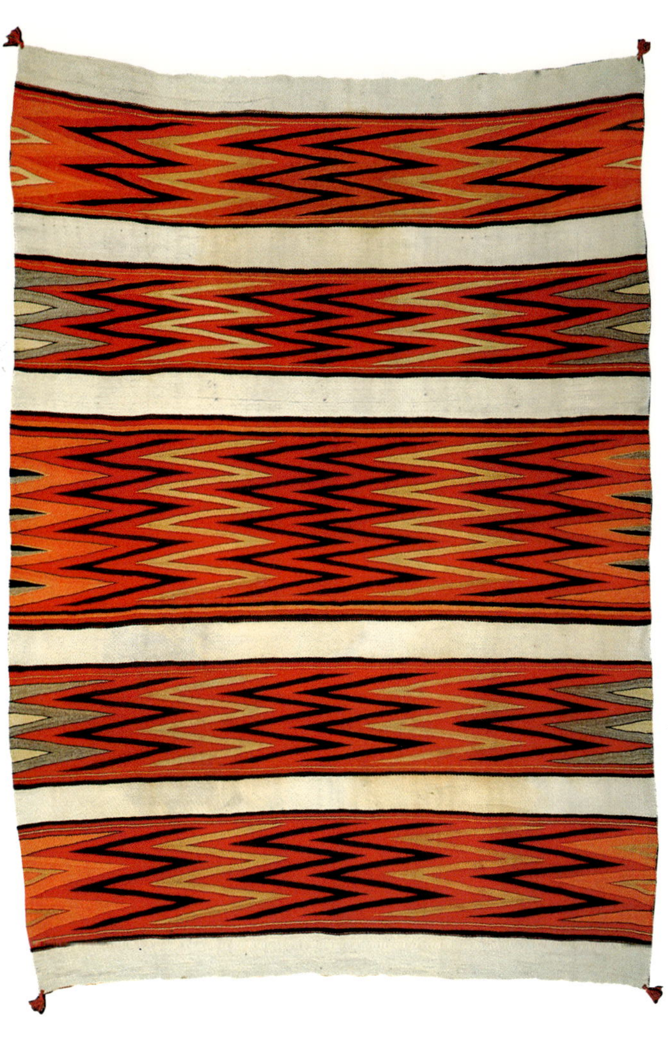

95. Pulled-warp blanket, c. 1880. 82″ x 48″. 10 warp/in.; 44 weft/in. Bands of the pulled-warp technique alternate with plain tapestry weave in the banded "pulled-warp" blanket. Also known as "wedge-weave" blankets, these blankets were produced only from about 1875 to 1890. Woven of synthetic-dyed red (two shades), orange, and black, vegetal-dyed yellow, indigo with vegetal-dyed green, indigo-dyed blue, and natural white hand-spun wool yarns. (Private collection)

96. Pulled-warp blanket, c. 1880. 78″ x 44″. 9 warp/in.; 40 weft/in. In this powerful statement of color and design the weaver has created vertical movement within subtle horizontal bands of color. Woven of synthetic-dyed red, yellow, black, and purple, indigo-dyed blue, and natural gray and white hand-spun wool yarns. (Private collection)

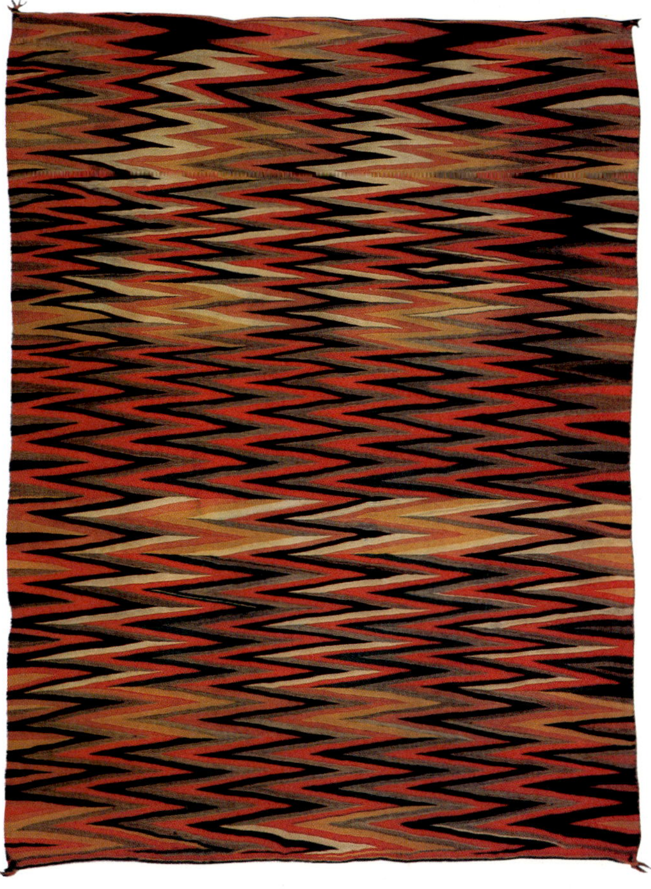

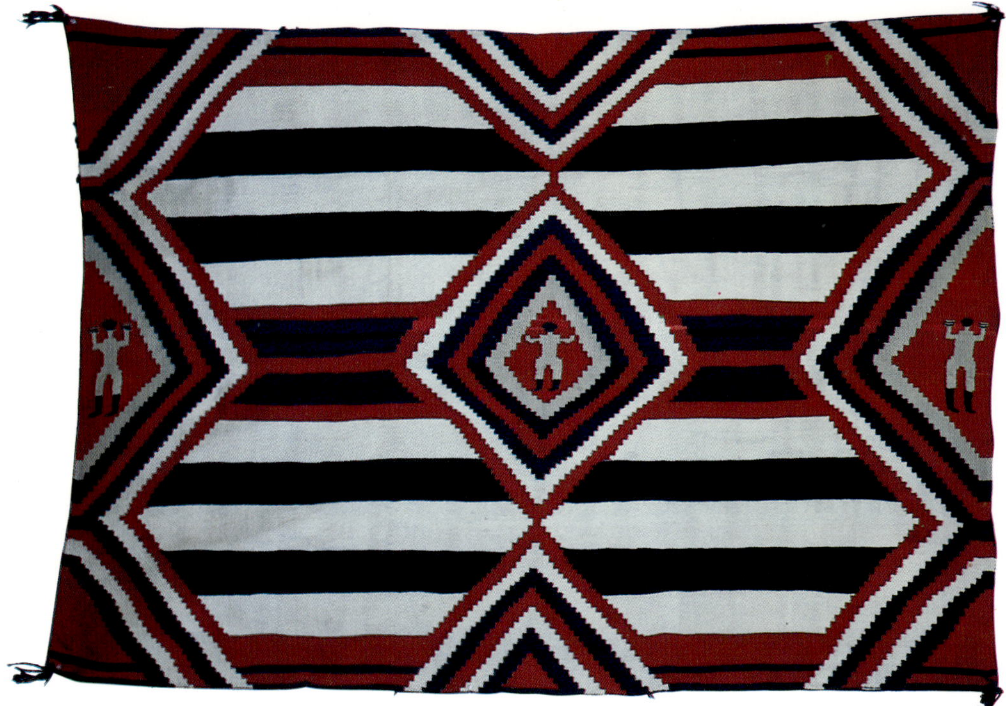

97. Chief blanket variation, c. 1875. 52″ x 72″. 11 warp/in.; 56 weft/in. A late combination of raveled bayeta and four-ply Germantown yarn, this unusual blanket also has early pictorial design elements. Woven of raveled cochineal(?)-dyed red, four-ply commercial synthetic-dyed green, and indigo-dyed blue and natural brown and white handspun wool yarns. (Private collection)

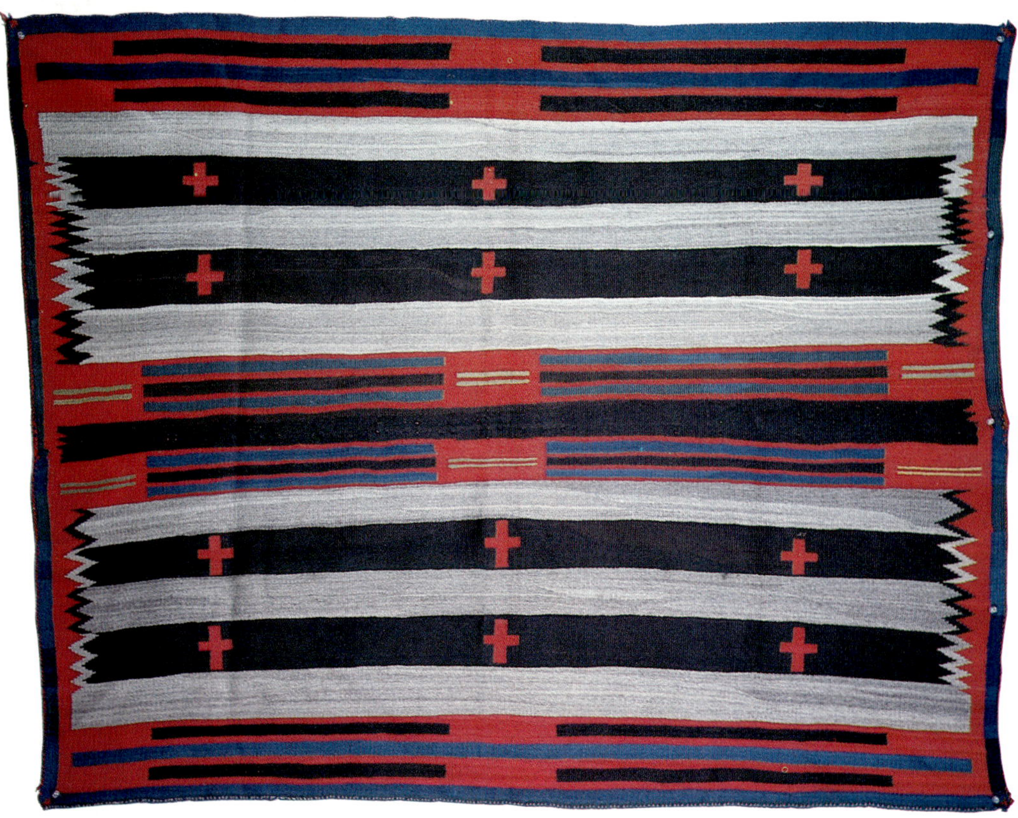

98. Chief blanket variation, c. 1880. 52″ x 67″. 7 warp/in.; 42 weft/in. The Transitional Period is marked by experimental variations on earlier themes. Woven of synthetic-dyed red, pale blue, and black, vegetal-dyed yellow, indigo with vegetal-dyed green, indigo-dyed blue, and natural gray handspun wool yarns. (Private collection)

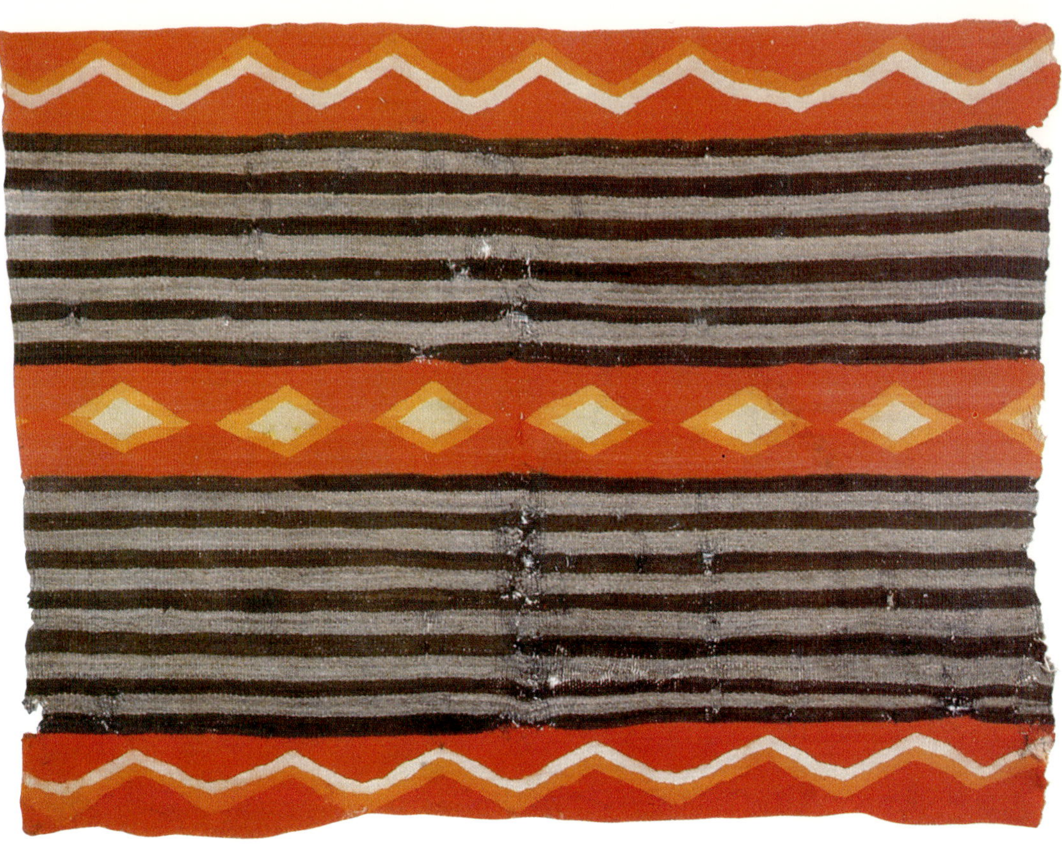

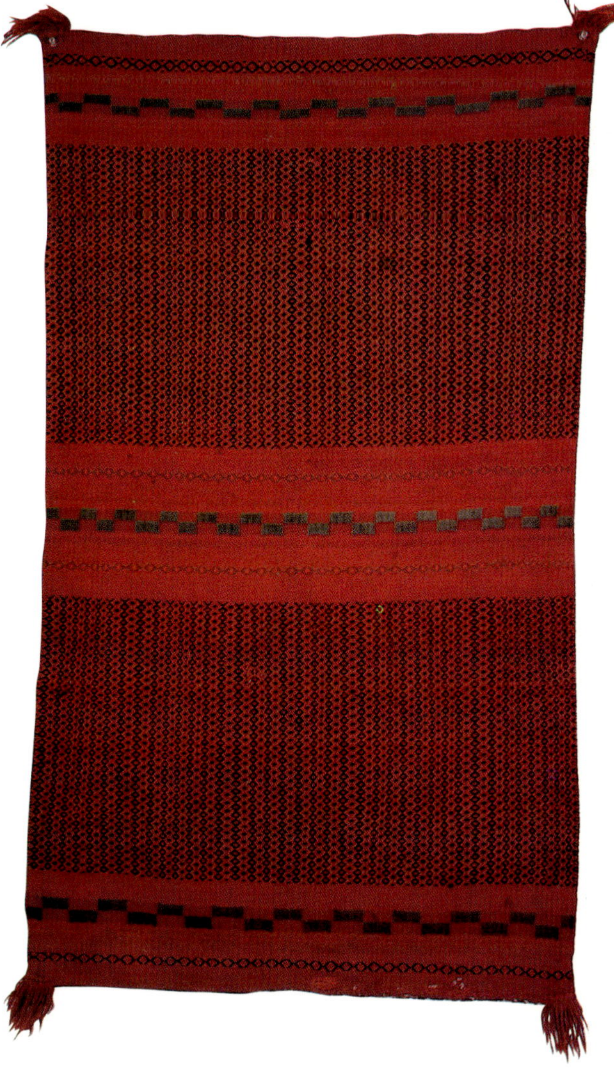

99. Woman's wearing blanket, c. 1885. 38″ x 56″. 6 warp/in.; 32 weft/in. A heavier and smaller version of the woman's wearing blanket was made in the late 1870s and 1880s. Many were probably made as rugs rather than as garments. Woven of synthetic-dyed red, orange, and yellow and natural brown and gray hand-spun wool yarns. (Collection of Arizona State Museum, University of Arizona)

100. Twill blanket, c. 1880. 49″ x 28″. 10 warp/in.; 48 weft/in. Twill-weave techniques were most often employed in the production of saddle blankets. This finely woven example may have been intended as a child's wearing blanket. Note the use of both diamond and herringbone twill techniques. Woven of synthetic-dyed red, orange, and black hand-spun and four-ply commercial synthetic-dyed blue wool yarns. (Private collection)

5

THE RESERVATION TRADERS

> Why couldn't the market for Navajo blankets be enlarged beyond its local orbit, made to include the people back East who had as yet no idea that the savage western Indians were quite civilized craftsmen in their way? The trader would profit doubly, getting a percentage on the goods exchanged to the Navaho for the blanket, as well as on the sale of the blanket to the white man. Later it was discovered that the idea held promise of a third source of gain: the trader could sell the Navaho certain materials needed in weaving, such as dye, spun yarn, cotton twine for warp, then trade for the blanket and sell it on the market—three transactions, three separate profits. If one man thought of all that, his portrait, crowned with laurel, should be over every trader's doorway.
>
> Charles Avery Amsden, 1934[29]

From 1680 to 1880 Navajo weavers drew inspiration primarily from two textile-weaving traditions, Pueblo Indian and Spanish, choosing the elements of each they wished to incorporate into their own weaving. The American influence would be more pervasive. How pervasive becomes clear when we compare a nineteenth-century wearing blanket with a twentieth-century Navajo rug. Functionally, blankets and rugs differed greatly in both use and design. Classic blankets and mantas, worn as clothing, came in three basic sizes: to fit men, women, and children. Rugs, which were used as floor coverings—also came in larger sizes to fit American rooms: ranging from three by five feet to nine by twelve feet and larger. Although the Oriental ruglike patterns of many late nineteenth- and early twentieth-century Navajo weavings were dictated by Anglo marketing strategy rather than Navajo artistic impulse, Navajo weavers attacked these intricate, bordered alien designs with the same appetite for improvisation, innovation, and variety as they once brought to their experiments with the Pueblo stripe and the Hispanic serrated diamond.

After Bosque Redondo, American-made yarns and dyes began to replace the European and Mexican imports. The hand-spun yarns that were available were shorn from merino sheep supplied by the U.S. government to replace the Navajo churro sheep slaughtered by Kit Carson's troops. Merino fleece was short, curly, coarse, greasy, and hard to wash and spin. It was no wonder that during the decades after Bosque Redondo the best weavers abandoned hand-spun wool in favor of commercial yarn. The best commercial yarns available during the years from 1875 through 1915 were manufactured in numerous spinning mills in the Eastern United States, many of them located in or near Germantown, Pennsylvania; *Germantown yarn* is the generic term for these yarns.

Like the weavers of the Classic Period who had been spurred on to greater technical proficiency with the introduction of commercially spun yarns in the form of bayeta and Saxony, the new weavers found that the even machine spin of the Germantown yarn both allowed and invited tight, even weaving. Most Germantown yarns were dyed at the factory with early synthetic dyes. Although these early synthetic dyes used on Germantown yarns were usually of the same quality as the synthetic dyes later sold to Navajos in individual packets with which they dyed their own hand-spun wool, the use of the individual packets did not come into popular use until the late 1870s because of the difficulties in using the earliest synthetic dyes in the wilderness of Monument Valley or Canyon de Chelly.

The use of synthetic dyes and four-ply Germantown yarn is a hallmark of the transition from Late Classic to Transitional Navajo weaving. Late Classic blankets were often woven with indigo blue (and sometimes indigo/rabbitbrush vegetal green) hand-spun yarns and late raveled and early three-ply Germantown yarns, all combined together. Many early Transitional blankets displayed Late Classic design elements (crosses, vertical zigzags and terraced stripes, interrupted diagonal stripes) combined with Transitional serrate design elements laid out in a zoned, borderless blanket pattern executed in a combination of Late Classic and Transitional Period colors and materials and often on a red field (borders appeared as early as 1873; see figs. 89 and 91). Later Transitional blanket/rugs were often woven entirely of hand-spun yarns dyed entirely with brightly colored synthetic dyes (fig. 92). Whether weavers of the Transitional Period used synthetic dyes on their hand-spun yarn or the factory-dyed Germantown yarn, however, the introduction of bright, synthetic, colors brought a revolution to Navajo weaving. Previously limited to sheep colors, indigo blue, native yellows, small amounts of the limited range of Saxony yarn colors, and whatever trade cloth they could acquire and unravel, Navajo weavers suddenly had the full spectrum of color from which to select. Experimenting with a combination of vibrant color and Saltillo-like serrate diamond designs to create pulsating optical effects, late nineteenth century Navajo weavers created the *"eyedazzler"* (figs. 101 and 123–126).

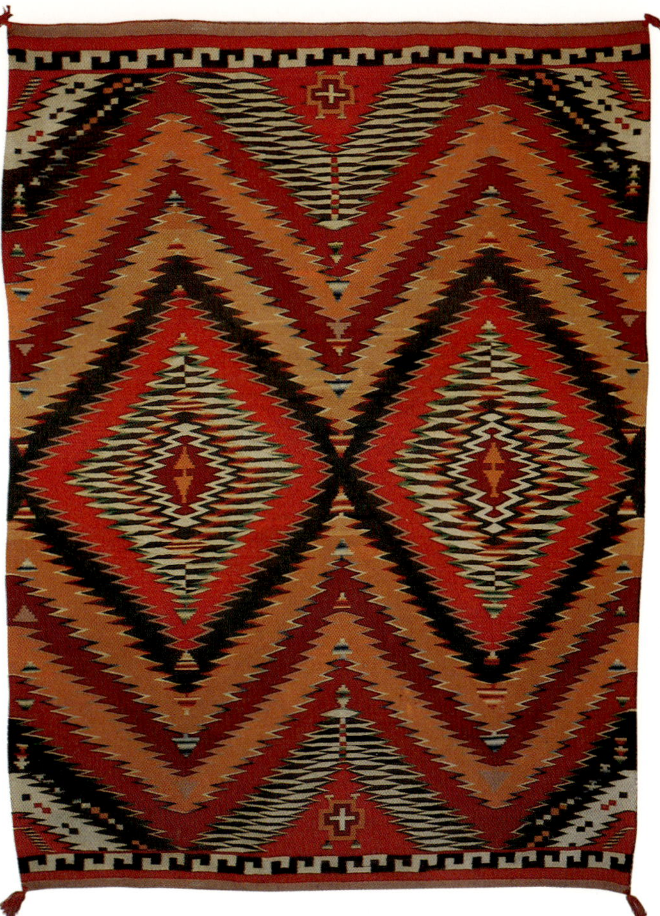

101. Germantown blanket, 1880–1890. 76″ x 57″. 12 warp/in.; 40 weft/in. The term *eyedazzler* could have been coined when the first Anglo viewed this vibrant creation of the Navajo weaver's imagination. Note the use of variegated yarns in the outlining of the Saltillo-like serrate pattern. Woven of four-ply commercial synthetic-dyed red (two shades), green (two shades), yellow, tan, purple, blue, and white wool yarns. (Private collection)

Not every weaver was artist enough to meet the challenge of the new colors and designs, and sometimes "eyedazzlers" were more jarring than dazzling. But many eyedazzlers were outstanding examples of artistic expression, completely different in visual appeal from the blankets that preceded them and the rugs that followed. Today, eyedazzlers have become the pets of twentieth-century color-field painters, art critics, and collectors of Navajo weaving. They have been favorably compared to Op art, a style that reached its peak of popularity with "The Responsive Eye," the 1965 exhibit at The Museum of Modern Art in New York City.

The major source for all this artistic and technical innovation was the Indian trader. Because of the Navajo's growing dependence on American goods and American dollars, trading posts became fixed stars in the ever-shifting Navajo universe. (The dollar was in fact rarely used in trading post business, which was most commonly conducted in the form of barter. Paper money and gold had little appeal to Navajos; silver coins were the only widely accepted U.S. currency. As many Navajo silversmiths melted Mexican silver pesos (pesos contained more silver than did U.S. dollars) to make silver jewelry, pesos were preferable to American coins. Until the 1930s, however, the most common medium of exchange was the *seco,* or token, coins made specifically for each trading post and redeemable only at that post.)

The Navajos, who had traded with other Indians and with the Spanish, started trading with Americans when the first American soldiers and explorers appeared in the Southwest by 1840. Navajos first started selling their

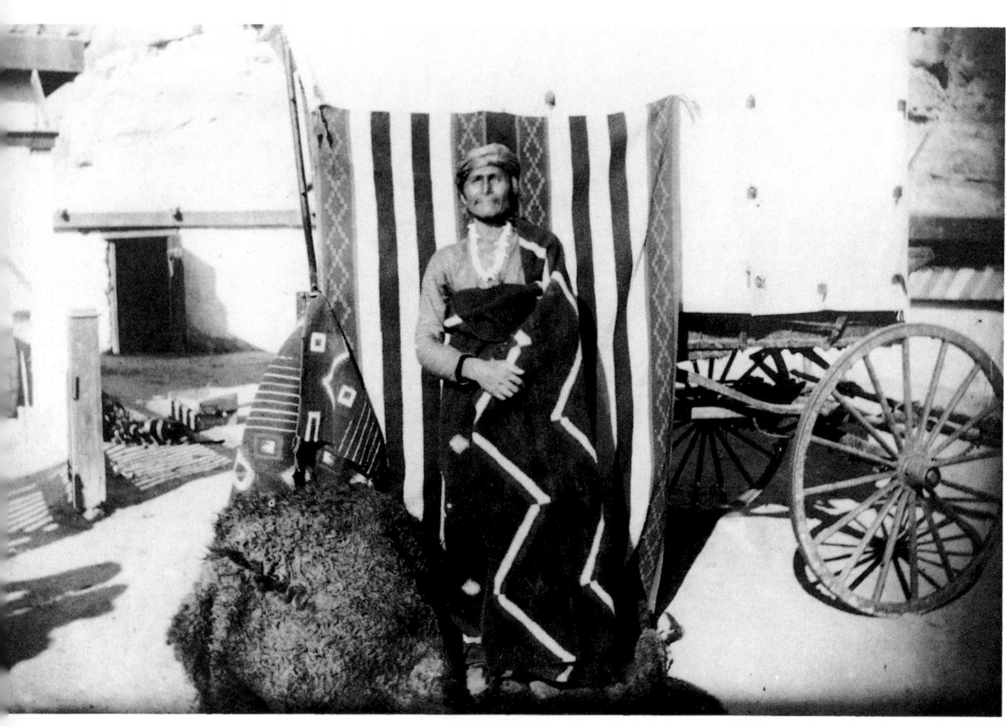

102. Navajo man, c. 1890. Posed in front of one of the many reservation trading posts, this Navajo man still wears the traditional blanket attire. Note that the Chief blanket used as a backdrop is the same as in figure 45. (Photograph courtesy Smithsonian Institution)

103. Ganado Trading Post, c. 1885, photograph by Ben Wittick. Juan Lorenzo Hubbell posed with a young Navajo weaver and her husband in front of the Hubbell Trading Post at Ganado, Arizona. Note the new Anglo style of Navajo attire and the popular Hubbell-inspired Classic revival style of weaving. (Photograph courtesy Museum of New Mexico)

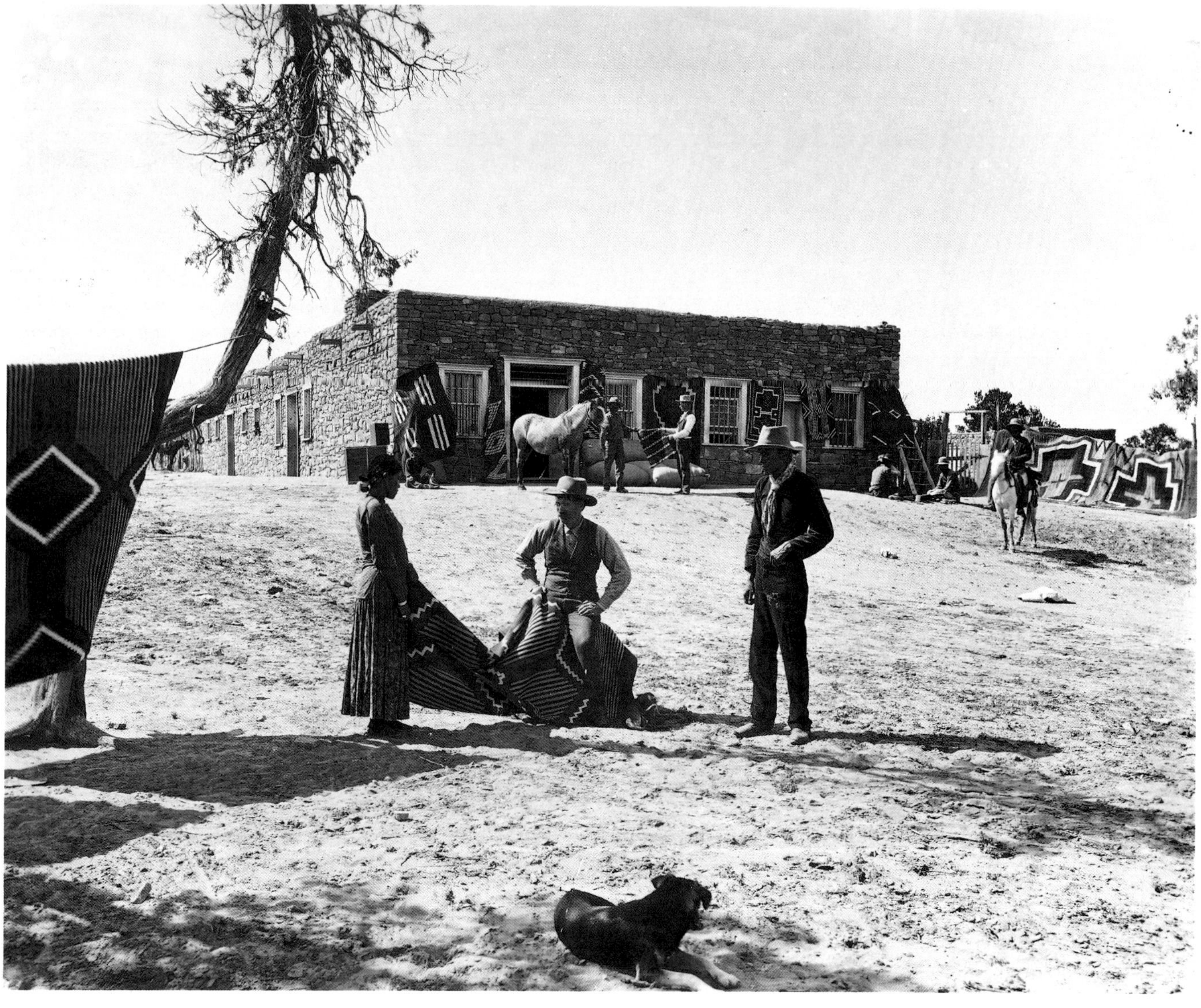

104. J. L. Hubbell's residence, Ganado Trading Post, Arizona, c. 1885. Life on the reservation in the early days was a lonely existence. The Ganado Trading Post, although remote, probably received more visitors than any other trading post, being located along major east-west and north-south trade routes. (Photograph courtesy School of American Research, Museum of New Mexico)

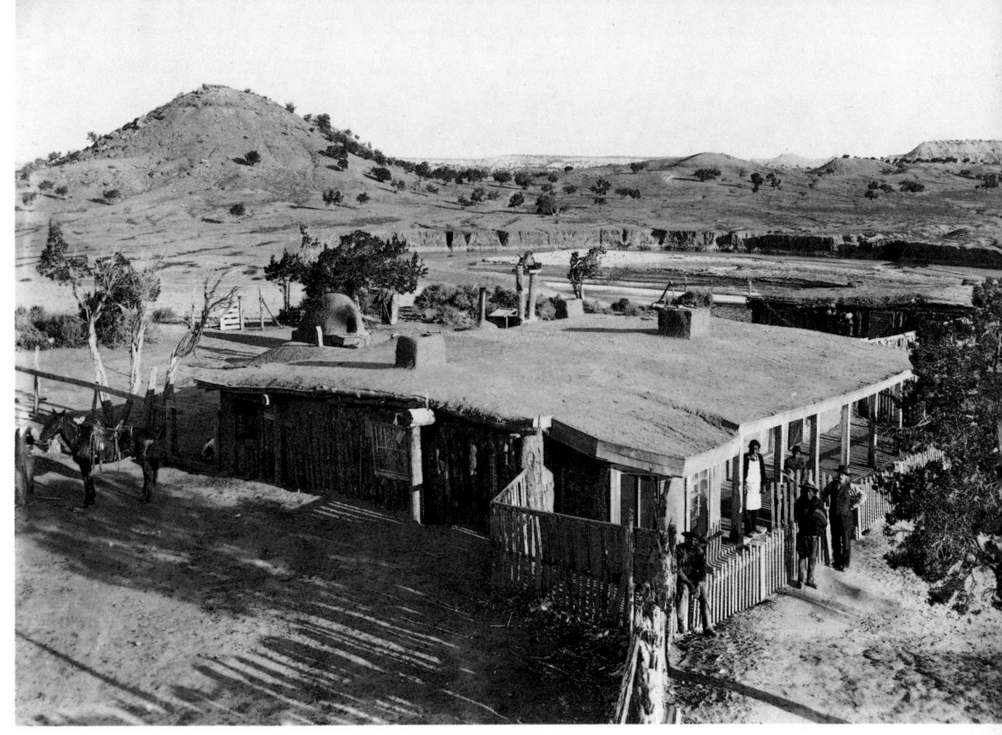

blankets to soldiers at Army post stores in exchange for American goods and silver money. There was a trading post at Bosque Redondo, and many of the traders who went on to open their own posts started their careers working at Army trading posts. In 1868, less than three months after the Navajos left Bosque Redondo, the first license to trade on the Reservation was issued by Major Theodore Dodd to Willi Spiegelberg, member of a famous family of Southwestern entrepreneurs. (Spiegelberg was allowed to trade anywhere on the Reservation, but subsequent traders were limited to one location.)

During the 1870s a handful of trading posts were opened on the Navajo Reservation, while even more posts were doing business just beyond its legal boundaries. The off-Reservation traders were free to make their own rules, while those who traded on Navajo land had to be licensed by the government and had to obey —to some extent—government rules and regulations.

Juan Lorenzo Hubbell became the best-known trader in the Southwest as well as the one who had the greatest early influence on the development of the twentieth-century regional-style Navajo rug. He first traded with the Navajos as a clerk at the Fort Wingate store. By 1876 Hubbell was in business for himself, trading on land outside the Reservation. By 1879 he became a licensed Reservation trader when he took over the post at Ganado, Arizona (fig. 103). During the course of his long, legendary career, Hubbell and his family worked at and/or owned at least fourteen different trading posts, but the post at Ganado was the heart of the Hubbell trading empire. (Hubbell named the post for his friend Ganado Mucho, a prominent Navajo *rico,* or rich man, whose name means many cattle.)

Although to most Americans it would seem like one of the more remote parts of the United States, compared to far-flung posts at Kayenta and Teec Nos Pos, Ganado is practically the crossroads of the Navajo nation (fig. 104). The post is located fifty-five miles north of Gallup, a trip that could take ten days in the winter at the turn of the century. At one point Hubbell owned a stagecoach line that traveled between Albuquerque, Gallup, Ganado, and his other posts.

Hubbell encouraged the weavers who lived in the Ganado area to produce high-quality weaving in a very effective way: he refused to buy any weavings that did not meet his standards. Beginning in the 1870s it was not unusual for weavers, as a time-saving device, to use cotton warps—warps made from ordinary string or wrapping twine instead of stronger, finer warps spun from Navajo native wool—as the foundation for their weavings. Unfortunately for their longevity (cotton deteriorates much faster than wool), many Germantown blankets and rugs woven during this period were woven on cotton warps. A concentrated effort on the part of many of the early traders helped to end this practice.

One of Hubbell's taboos was the use of harsh, gaudy, synthetic dyes. Hubbell wisely limited the weavers in his area to the use of two synthetic dyes: black or blue and red, the colors most often associated with earlier Classic blankets. In fact, he insisted that "his" weavers

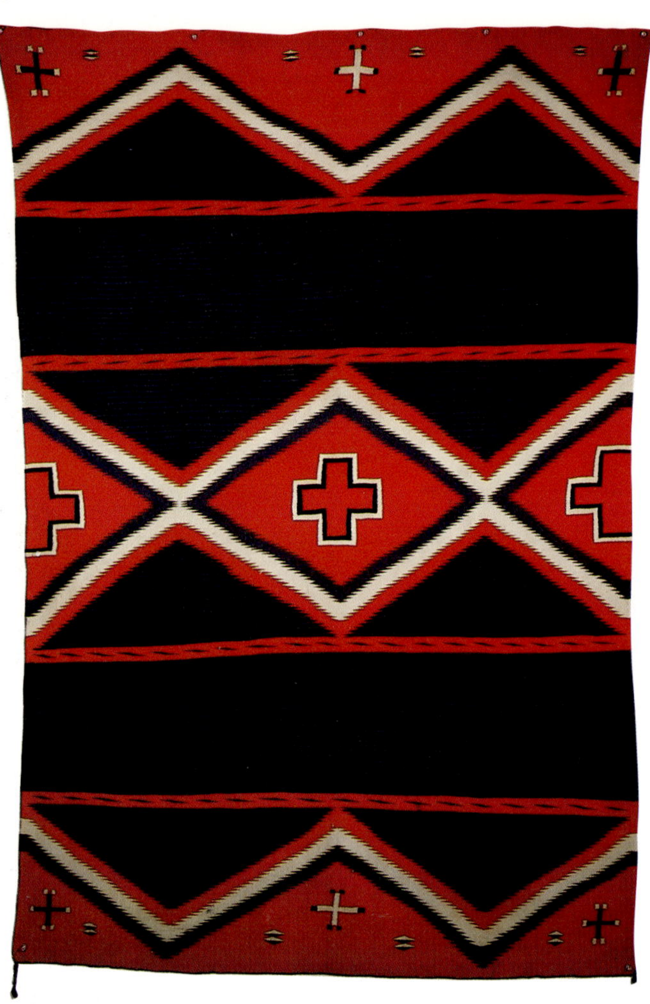

105. Germantown blanket, 1880–1890. 80″ x 54″. 12 warp/in.; 40 weft/in. Copied from the Late Classic Period Moki-style sarape, the Germantown Moki blanket was one of one of the Late Classic styles revived by J. L. Hubbell in the late nineteenth century. Woven of four-ply commercial synthetic-dyed red, purple, black, and white wool yarns. (Private collection)

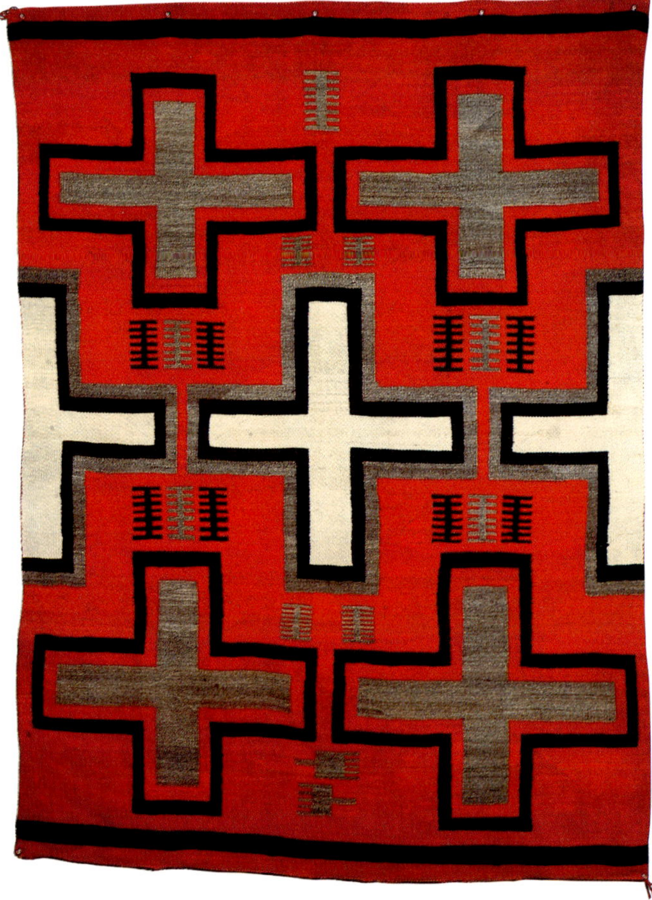

106. Ganado rug, 1890–1900. 83″ x 61″. 8 warp/in.; 24 weft/in. This early rug has the large-outline "Hubbell" crosses associated with Ganado rugs of the period. Woven of synthetic-dyed red and natural gray, white, and brown hand-spun wool yarns. (Private collection)

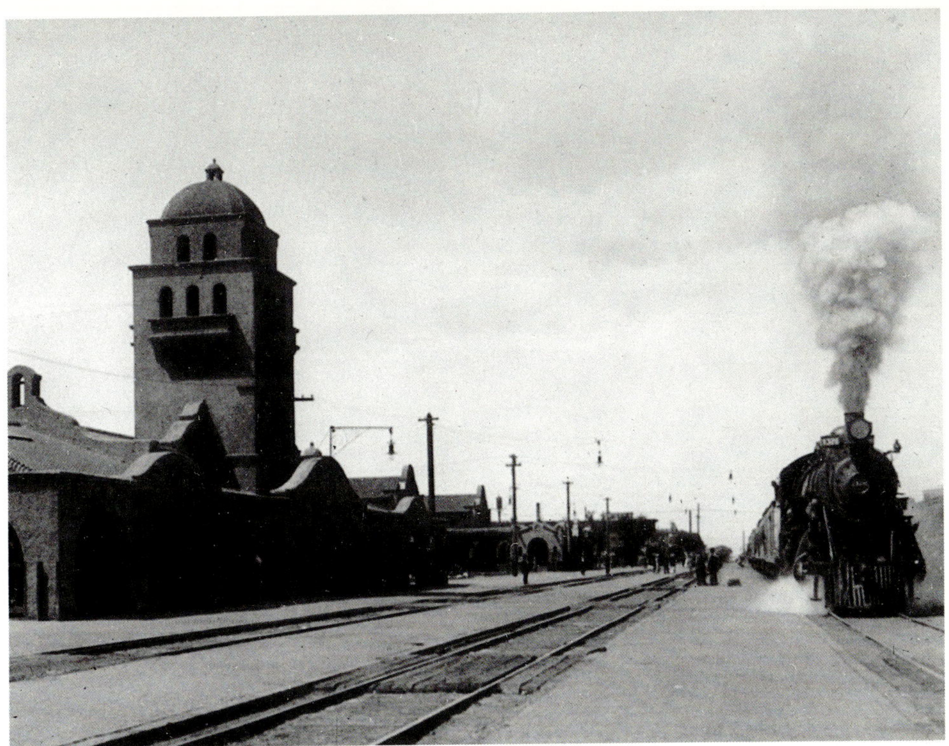

107. Santa Fe Railroad, 1880s: the Albuquerque depot. Throngs of Eastern travelers visited the Southwest once the railroad arrived and provided a safe, inexpensive, and relatively comfortable means of cross-country travel. (Photograph courtesy University Museum, University of Pennsylvania)

use a double portion of red aniline dye so that the handspun yarn would take on a uniquely rich color—the color that would become famous as Ganado red.

Hubbell was as concerned with design as he was with color. He commissioned an artist named E. A. Burbank to paint oil paintings of more than fifty of Hubbell's favorite Classic Navajo blankets and hung the paintings on the walls of the Hubbell Trading Post. The weavers used these paintings as their guides, but instead of the bayeta yarn and indigo dye of the early 1800s, "Hubbell revivals" were usually woven with Germantown yarns (figs. 105, 127, and 128). Many of these "revival" weavings were products of the late Transitional Period: between blanket and rug, with characteristics of each. Blanket styles were woven in rug sizes, for instance, or enclosed within borders, or woven in yarn too heavy to be suitable to wear.

But the weavings that would make the post at Ganado famous were not Transitional pieces. They were clearly meant to be sold and used as rugs. In fact, oversize rugs, rugs made to order in sizes larger than five by seven feet (too large and heavy to use anywhere but on the floor) were a specialty of Hubbell's. The designs of these rugs were not revivals of Classic Period designs but rather the incorporation of Classic Period design elements (crosses, terraced diamonds, and stripes) into a bordered rug pattern that was somewhat Oriental in appearance and complexity. The popularity of these red, black, gray, brown, and white rugs with the Anglo buying public led to the birth of the first regional rug style, as weavers from all over the Ganado area brought Hubbell variation after variation of the Ganado pattern and color scheme (see figs. 106, 135, and 136).

Luckily, Hubbell's ability to inspire attractive, well-woven rugs was matched by his ability to market them. He sold the rugs at his trading posts, of course, but the posts were well off the beaten track and difficult to reach at best. The breakthrough came when Fred Harvey contracted with Hubbell to buy all his blankets and rugs of "good" or "better" quality.

Harvey was a concessionaire who had set up shops, restaurants, and hotels along the route of the Santa Fe Railroad (see fig. 107). At the turn of the century, Harvey opened the Alvarado Hotel in Albuquerque and Hopi House Shop at the Grand Canyon. Both establishments offered local Indian handicrafts—rugs, blankets, baskets, pottery, and jewelry—to Anglo tourists (fig. 108). Harvey hired weavers to work both in Albuquerque and at the Grand Canyon, but they could not meet the demand for their goods, so Harvey turned to Hubbell. Thanks to Fred Harvey, the Ganado rug was exposed to a steady stream of potential customers and collectors (fig. 109). Harvey's standards were as high as Hubbell's. He even disapproved of Germantown yarns, demanding that Germantown weavings bear labels reading, "This yarn is not Indian spun."

Because of his connection with Fred Harvey, Hubbell became the leading rug dealer in America. In 1902, the Harvey organization bought more than $20,000 worth of weavings from Hubbell. Ten years later, Hubbell sold $60,000 worth of rugs to Harvey.

108. Curio Room, Fred Harvey Hotel, Albuquerque, New Mexico, c. 1890. Large quantities of Navajo rugs and Indian relics were sold through the numerous Fred Harvey stores located along the Santa Fe Railroad and at the Grand Canyon, Arizona. (Photograph courtesy University Museum, University of Pennsylvania)

109. Navajo weavers, c. 1909. A group of Navajo weavers and silversmiths displaying the techniques of their craft at the Fred Harvey Indian Building, Albuquerque, New Mexico. (Photograph courtesy Smithsonian Institution)

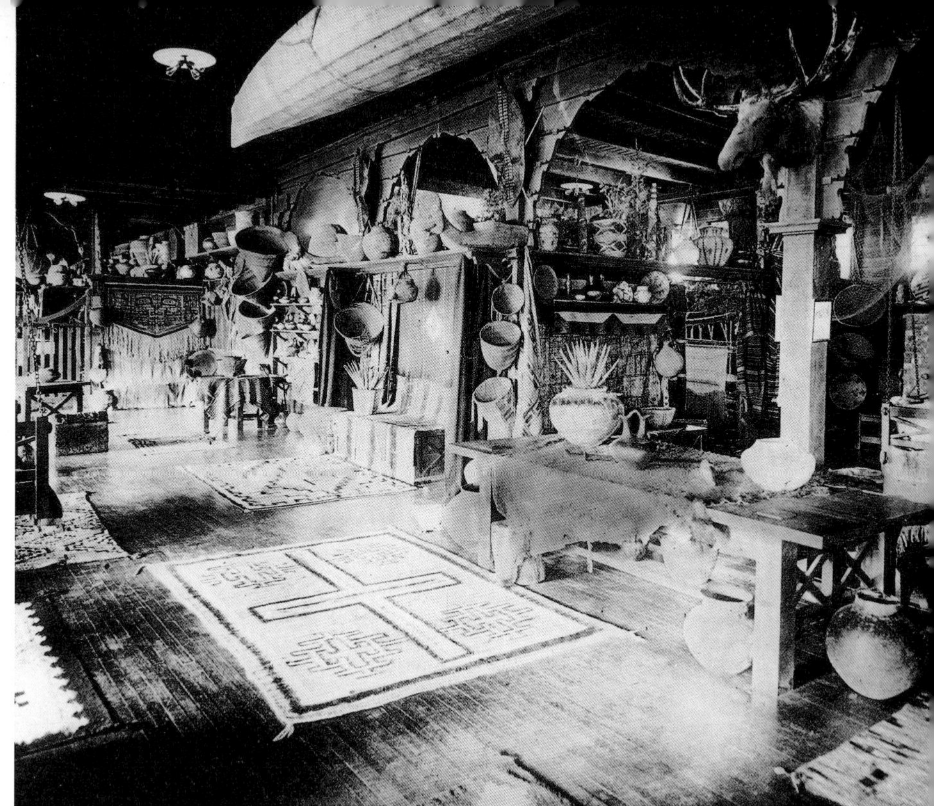

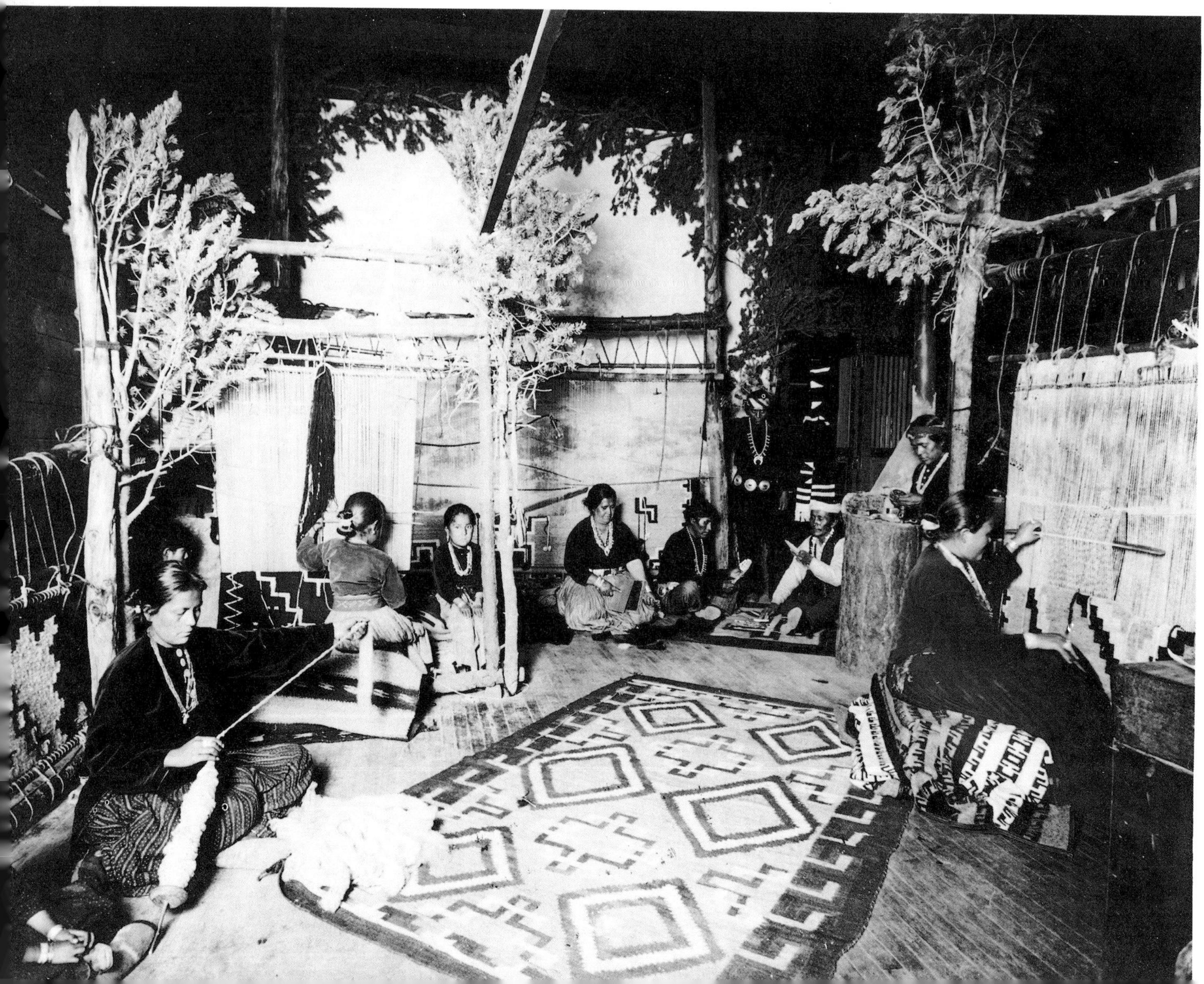

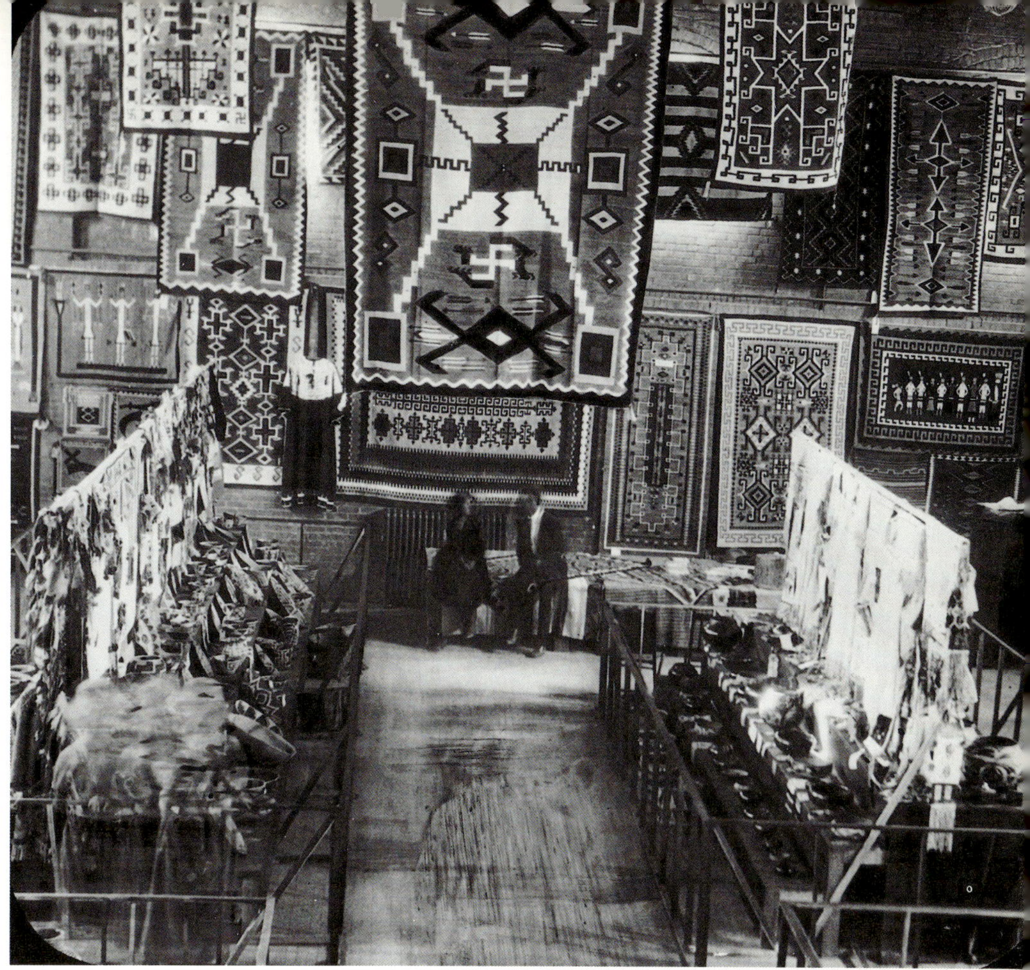

110. Indian fair, Santa Fe, 1915–1920. Beginning about the turn of the century, trade fairs were sponsored by both tribal and Anglo concerns to promote the market for and improve the quality of Navajo weaving and other Indian crafts. (Photograph courtesy University Museum, University of Pennsylvania)

During the first three decades of the twentieth century, Santa Fe and Taos became meccas for artists and writers, who grew very interested in the local Indian cultures. One of the tangible results of that interest was the Southwest Indian Fair. Organized by artists, writers, and archaeologists from Santa Fe's School of American Research, the fair was an outgrowth of the 200-year-old Santa Fe Fiesta. Today we know the Indian Fair as the Santa Fe Indian Market. Competition for prizes and public recognition at the Indian Fair (as well as at the Shiprock Fair and the Gallup Intertribal Ceremonial) spurred weavers, potters, and jewelers to work constantly to improve their skills. At the same time, these fairs enlarged the market, giving the Indian artists important new retail outlets (fig. 110).

Another early major marketer of Navajo weaving was the Hyde Exploring Expedition. Financed by two wealthy brothers from New York, the Expedition is best known for excavating Pueblo Bonito at Chaco Canyon, the richest dig in the history of Southwestern archaeology. Richard Wetherill, who was the driving force behind the project, estimated that the findings included 50,000 pieces of turquoise and 10,000 pieces of pottery that dated to the years from A.D. 900 to 1200. All of it went to The American Museum of Natural History in New York.

The Hyde Exploring Expedition was such a mammoth undertaking, and Pueblo Bonito so remote, that merely in order to keep the scientists, Navajos, and cowboys who worked at Chaco Canyon alive, frequent and regular supplies had to be sent in from Albuquerque, Gallup, Guam, and Thoreau, New Mexico, which were the nearest stops on the Santa Fe Railroad. Because the prices charged at the supply store at Pueblo Bonito were fair, Navajos from all over the reservation started coming to Chaco Canyon to shop. Much to their surprise, the Hyde Brothers and Richard Wetherill found themselves in the trading post business, and soon in the Navajo weaving business. Navajos brought so many weavings to Pueblo Bonito to trade for coffee, flour, and other supplies that the Hydes were soon marketing these weavings at retail outlets in Phoenix, Boston, Philadelphia, New York City, and Paul Smiths, in the Adirondack Mountains of upper New York State, where Navajo weavings were an integral part of the decor of the "Great Camps."

The successful marketing of Navajo rugs to other parts of the country ensured the success of the trading

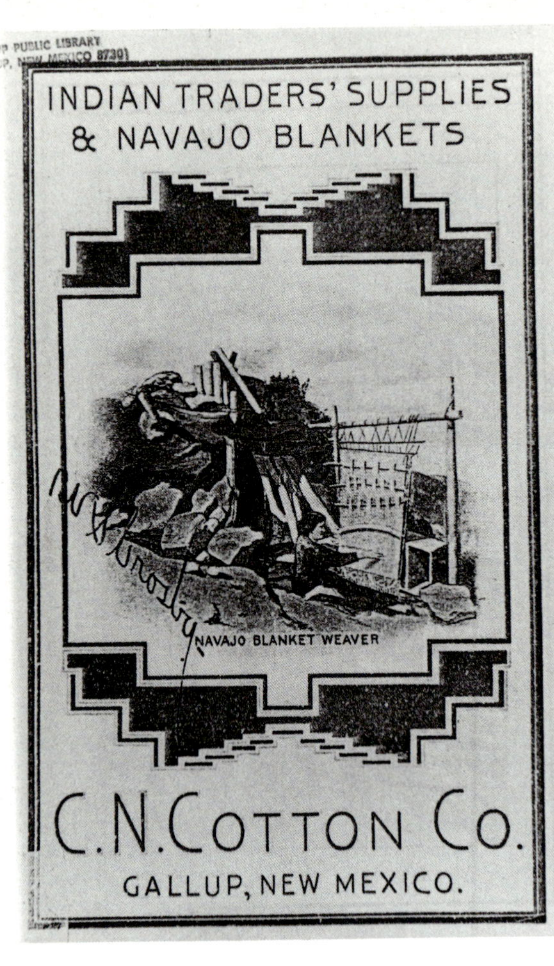

111. C.N. Cotton Co. Catalogue, c. 1897. C. N. Cotton was the first trader to promote Navajo weaving to the Eastern Anglo market by publishing a mail-order catalogue. Note that the illustration of the weaver is based on the photograph shown in figure 9. (Photograph courtesy Gallup Public Library)

112. Oriental Kazak carpet, c. 1880. The Near Eastern Caucasian style of Oriental carpet, popular with late nineteenth-century Victorians, possessed designs that Navajo weavers could easily imitate. (Private collection)

113. Germantown saddle blanket, 1880–1900. 48″ x 34″. 12 warp/in.; 36 weft/in. A Navajo interpretation of an Oriental rug pattern. Drawings and paintings of popular Oriental rug designs were shown to Navajo weavers by the traders. Woven of four-ply commercial synthetic-dyed red, purple, green, orange, yellow, and white wool yarns. (Private collection)

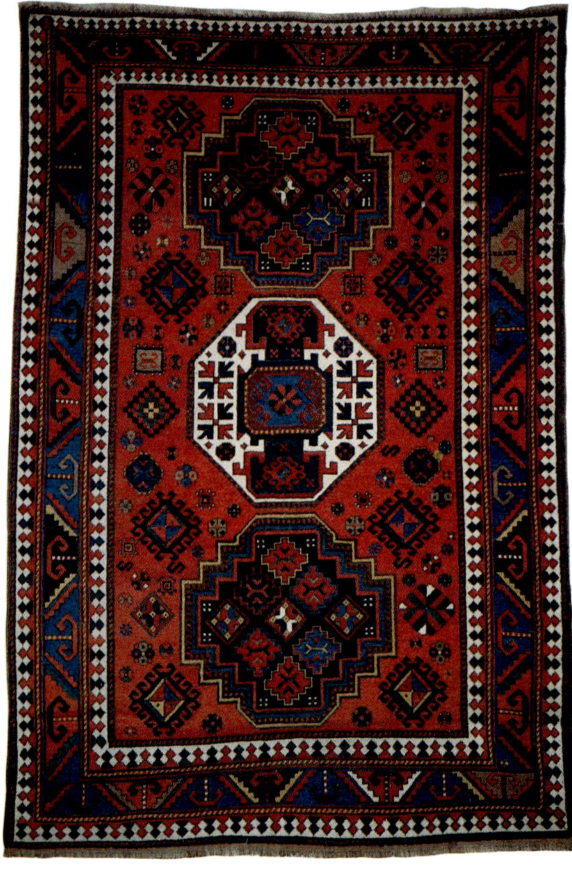

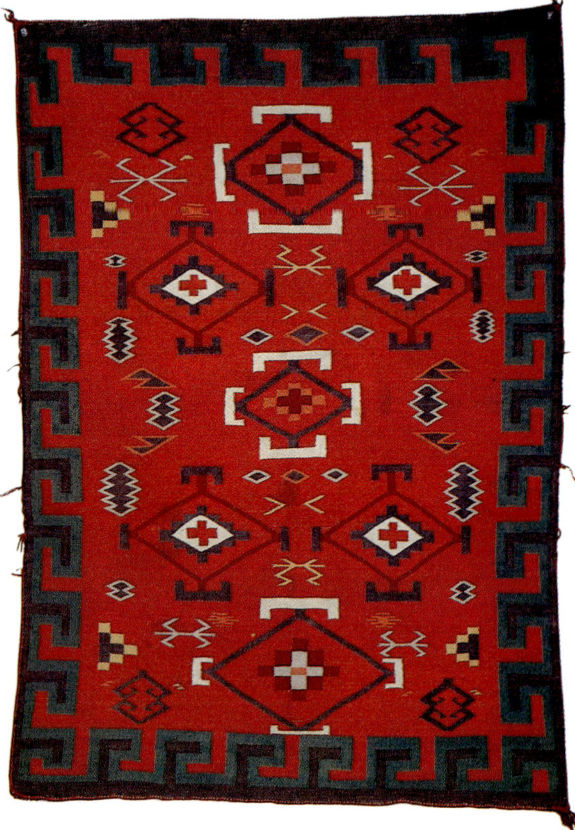

post system. "Money" was both earned and spent at the trading post. The traders supplied Germantown yarns, packets of Diamond brand synthetic dyes, and other post–Bosque Redondo necessities of weaving, as well as flour, Arbuckle's coffee, and other new necessities of life. These traders were also the weavers' outlet to retail sale. Except for annual fairs and competitions, Navajo weavers did not sell directly to Anglos, but to the trader who then sold the weavings at the post, or, more likely, to Fred Harvey or another dealer who had access to the Anglo market. Because of money earned through the sale of these weavings, Navajo Indians became part of the consumer economy and the trading posts became indispensable.

Of course, Hubbell and Wetherill were not the only traders who looked beyond the reservation in order to sell Navajo weavings. C. N. Cotton, who was a one-time partner of Hubbell's at Ganado and at Chinle, was probably the first man to attempt to sell Navajo weavings directly to the Eastern market. He was possibly also the first man to introduce Oriental rug patterns to Navajo weavers (see fig. 113). In 1897, Cotton published the first mail-order catalogue of Navajo blankets and rugs, which he mailed to potential customers in the East (fig. 111).

After a ten-year partnership in the trading post business, it became obvious to Hubbell and Cotton that although they shared the same goal—the commercial success of Navajo weaving—they believed in taking different paths to that goal. The two men differed sharply on the use of synthetic dyes. Realizing that these dyes could be the key to sales success, Cotton encouraged their use. Hubbell saw that the dyes had their practical uses, but believed them to be a threat to the integrity of Navajo weaving. The two men ended their partnership but remained friends and business associates as Cotton went from the retail end of the trading business to the wholesale. He built a large warehouse in Gallup, from which he sold goods to the trading posts on the reservation. After his experiences at Ganado and Chinle, Cotton knew what sold to the Navajos, and he stocked his warehouse accordingly with Arbuckle's coffee, Diamond brand synthetic dye packets, and a new item that captured the fancy and loyalty of many Navajo shoppers: the Pendleton blanket.

"Indian" blankets manufactured by Oregon's Pendleton Mills have been enormously popular with Indians since they were first manufactured before the turn of the century. They are still best sellers among contemporary Indians, particularly among Navajos and Hopis, who are Pendleton's best customers.

The success of the Pendleton Indian blanket is not surprising. The Pendleton company took their Indian customers very seriously and attempted to cater to their taste. In the early 1900s Pendleton sent their textile designer to live with the Indians in order to learn their color and design preferences. Not surprisingly, the designer learned that brightly colored, borderless, banded designs—reminiscent of earlier Navajo blankets—were preferred. Ironically, most early traders did not share the Pendleton company's concern with Indian sensibility and encouraged Navajo weavers to produce bordered rugs that appealed to Victorian tastes.

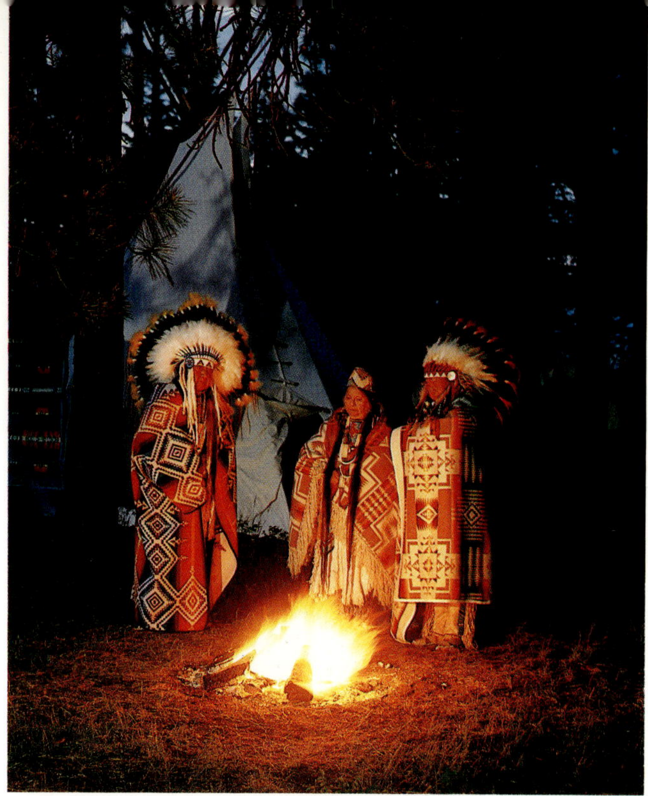

114. Plains Indians wearing Pendleton blankets. Beginning in the late nineteenth century, commercially produced blankets, patterned and colored to suit Indian tastes, replaced the traditional robes and blankets of many Indian cultures. (Photograph courtesy Pendleton Mills, Pendleton, Oregon)

The Pendleton designs are Navajo in feeling but, in the words of the Pendleton company, "the Pendleton Mills never copied an Indian design in producing their blankets; instead, they strove to learn Indian tastes and fancies and then created the blankets to fit these conceptions"[30] (fig. 114).

Colorful, light, warm, and reasonably affordable (according to Pendleton's 1918 price list, women's shawls and men's blankets cost between $8 and $15 each), Pendleton blankets were a natural substitute for the Navajo wearing blankets, which were no longer being made as the weavers preferred to spend their time weaving rugs to sell to Anglos. C. N. Cotton was the only source of Pendleton blankets in the Southwest, and he made $1 profit on each blanket he sold to the traders.

John B. Moore, who became the trader at the Crystal

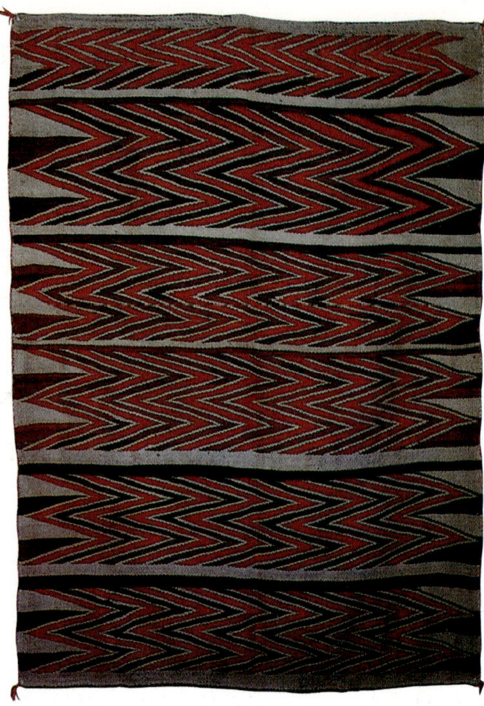

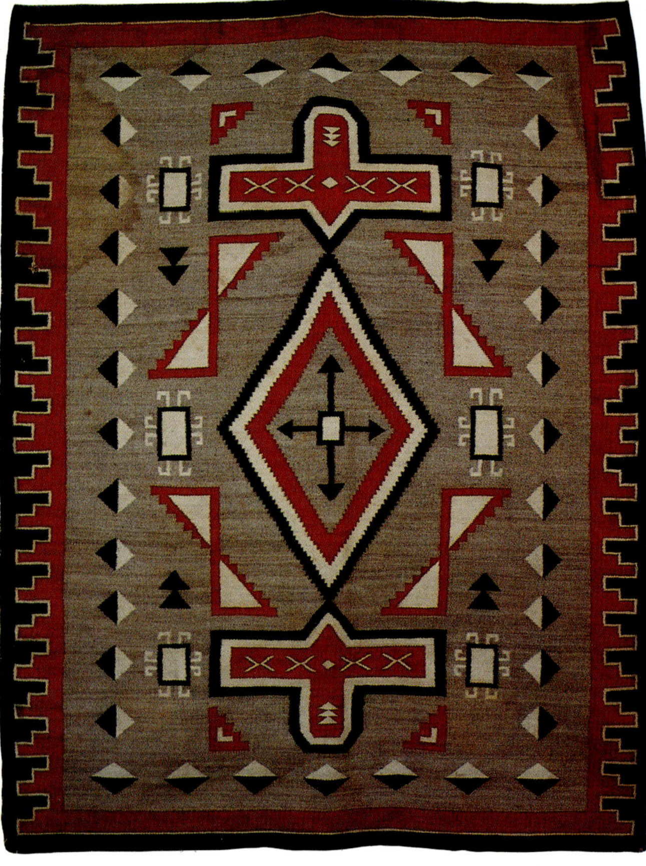

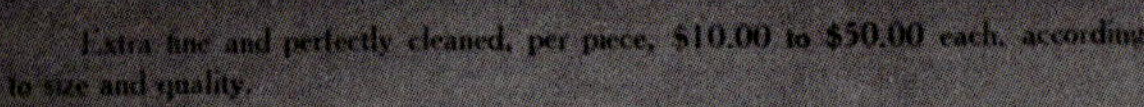

Extra fine and perfectly cleaned, per piece, $10.00 to $50.00 each, according to size and quality.

I have no saddle blankets nor common ones to quote.

Any of the grade will be shipped on approval with the understanding that the customer assumes all transportation costs both ways in case of return; and that no deductions on this account be allowed from invoice price in case of acceptance. We will ship, prepay, allow deductions from invoice price, on the extra fine ones of this grade, priced per piece, just the same as on the "ER-20" class, but only on these, of this "T-XX" class.

A FEW HINTS FOR THE CUSTOMER IN ORDERING

You always get the best value for your money in the higher priced rugs. You will be, and must be, pleased in these, and are assured against the possibility of buying and paying for a thing not satisfactory, by the return privilege allowed on all fine rugs.

You get just the size, the colors, and the pattern wanted, if you order from the "ER-20" class. If it is not in stock when your order comes, and you are willing to allow us a reasonable time in which to have it done, we will have it made for you especially. In this way you get something exclusive without the least danger of any other ever having something just like it.

Do not order the best quality and stipulate the lowest price. We wish in all cases to give the best possible value for the money and know that we do it, but I nor no other can sell our best goods for our lowest prices.

(*Continued on page 25*)

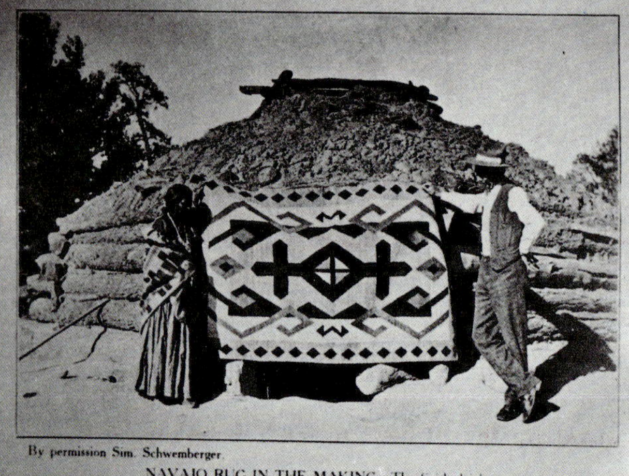

By permission Sim. Schwemberger.

NAVAJO RUG IN THE MAKING. The finished job
(Do you recognize the XXIV pattern?)

115. Blanket/rug, c. 1900. 77″ x 57″. 7 warp/in.; 16 weft/in. Thick and heavy, this early rug may have been sold to the trader by the pound. Similar rugs are commonly referred to as pound rugs. Woven of synthetic-dyed red and natural brown and white hand-spun wool yarns. (Private collection)

116. Crystal rug, c. 1910. 70″ x 55″. 8 warp/in.; 32 weft/in. This J.B. Moore catalogue-type Crystal rug was an example of Moore's ER-20 or best-grade Navajo rug, popular with the Eastern Anglo market. Woven of synthetic-dyed red and natural gray, brown, and white hand-spun wool yarns. (Private collection)

117. Page 8, J.B. Moore catalogue, 1911, *The Navajo.* J. B. Moore with a Navajo weaver showing one of his highest-grade rugs. (Photograph courtesy Gallup Public Library)

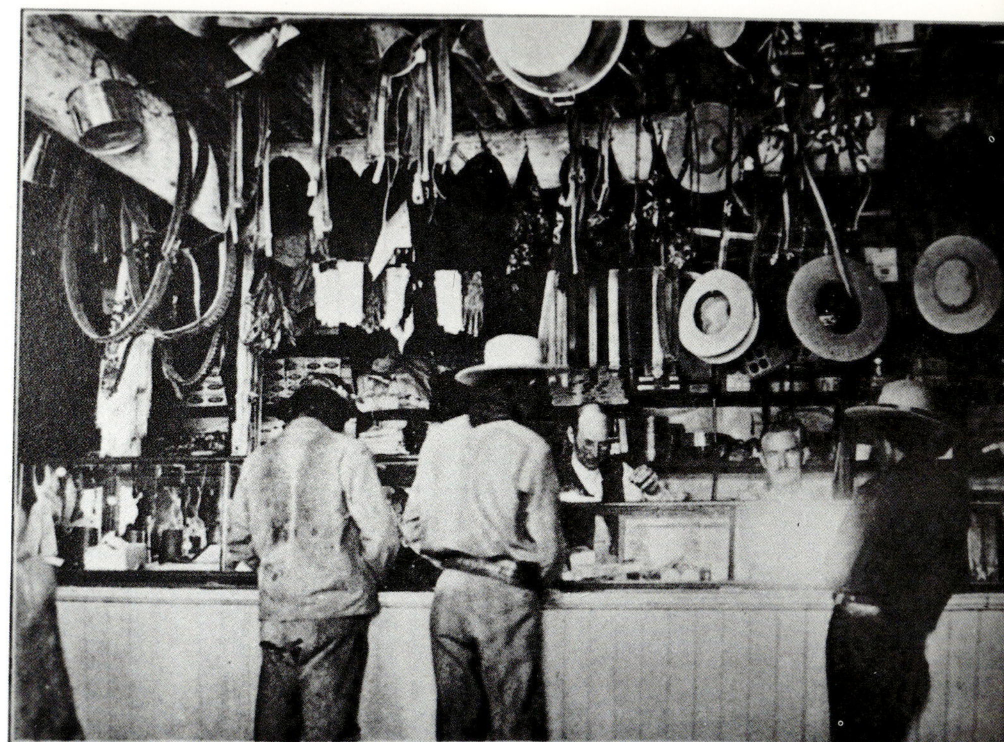

118. Crystal Trading Post interior, c. 1911. An interior view of a typical reservation trading post with J. B. Moore pictured at center behind the counter. (Photograph courtesy Gallup Public Library)

Trading Post in 1896, was as enthusiastic about Navajo weaving and as influential to the course of its history as were Hubbell and Cotton. Although the post first opened in 1873, Moore was the first trader to succeed at Crystal, which is located at the western entrance to the only pass through the Chuska Mountains. In the summer the area is beautiful and very popular with Navajos, but according to Thomas Keam, an early trader, in a letter written in 1884, existence at the post was "impractical," as Crystal is one of the coldest places on the reservation in winter and usually covered by at least two feet of snow.

Although the winter season presented formidable hardships, Moore devoted the lonely months to upgrading the work of the local weavers. He believed that the main obstacle to the commercial success of Navajo weaving was the practice of pricing Navajo textiles by the pound. This led to such evils as using dirty, unwashed wool because it weighed more than clean, fluffy wool, or even adding sand and dirt to the wool to weigh it down (fig. 115). To correct this situation, he would send wool brought to him by local weavers out to be professionally cleaned and then give the clean wool to his best weavers to make into rugs.

Many of the designs of the Moore Crystals came from Moore's own imagination. He believed passionately in the potential commercial success of the busy, bordered, Oriental-like rugs he inspired, and to promote the rugs he published his own mail-order catalogues, first in 1903 and again in 1911 (fig. 117). In the foreword to *The Navajo,* published in 1911, Moore wrote:

> Beginning some fifteen years back as an Indian trader in a rather small way, I have labored unceasingly with and among these Navajo weavers, inducing them to weave better, finer, cleaner and handsomer rugs on the one hand; and just as persistently on the other, to convince the buying public of the real worth and better value of this better product.

Moore's designs are believed to be the forerunners of the Teec Nos Pos, storm pattern, and Two Gray Hills regional styles. The color scheme of Moore's Crystal weavings was usually a combination of hand-spun wool colors—natural white, black, and brown with carded grays and tans, and synthetic dyed red or orange. The weavers at Two Gray Hills used the natural shades of hand-spun wool but rarely used the colors red and orange, and to this day, a Two Gray Hills weaving is characterized by the use of no dyes at all, whereas the

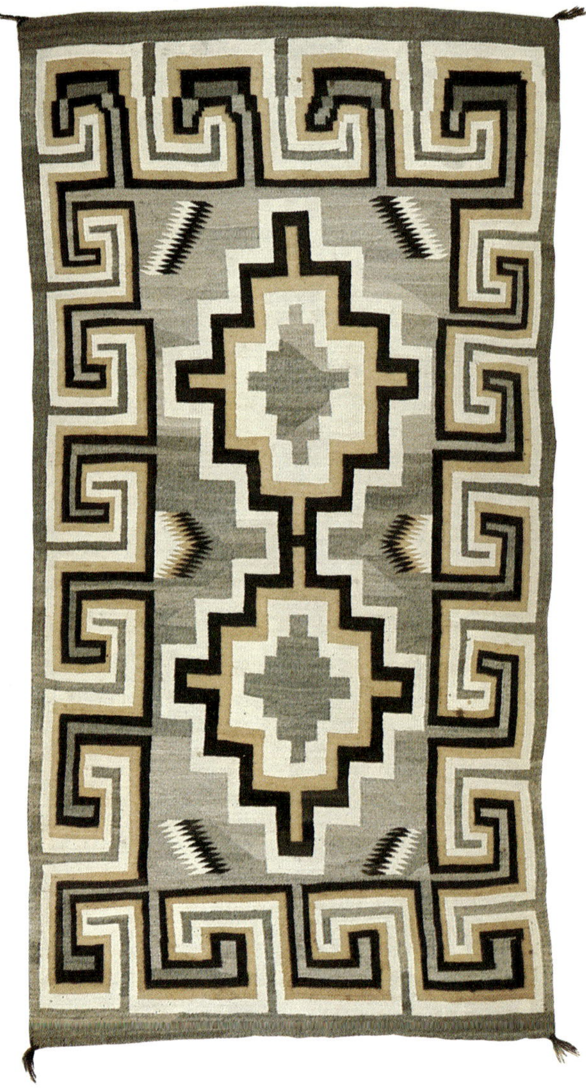

119. Crystal rug, c. 1910. 62″ x 34″. 8 warp/in.; 28 weft/in. The regional style of rug that later became known as Two Gray Hills developed out of rug patterns and coloration like those of this Crystal rug. Woven of natural shades of hand-spun wool yarns. (Collection of Arizona State Museum, University of Arizona)

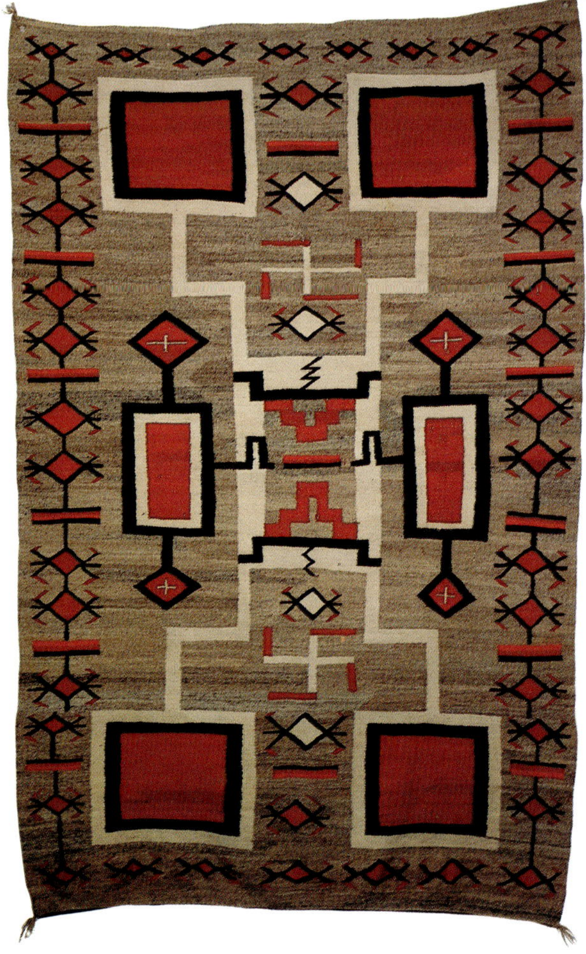

120. Crystal rug, c. 1910. 69″ x 46″. 12 warp/in.; 32 weft/in. Although uncertain, the origin of the "storm pattern" rug design can probably be attributed to J. B. Moore, who published a storm pattern in his 1911 catalogue. Woven of synthetic-dyed red and orange and natural gray, black, and white hand-spun wool yarns. (Private collection)

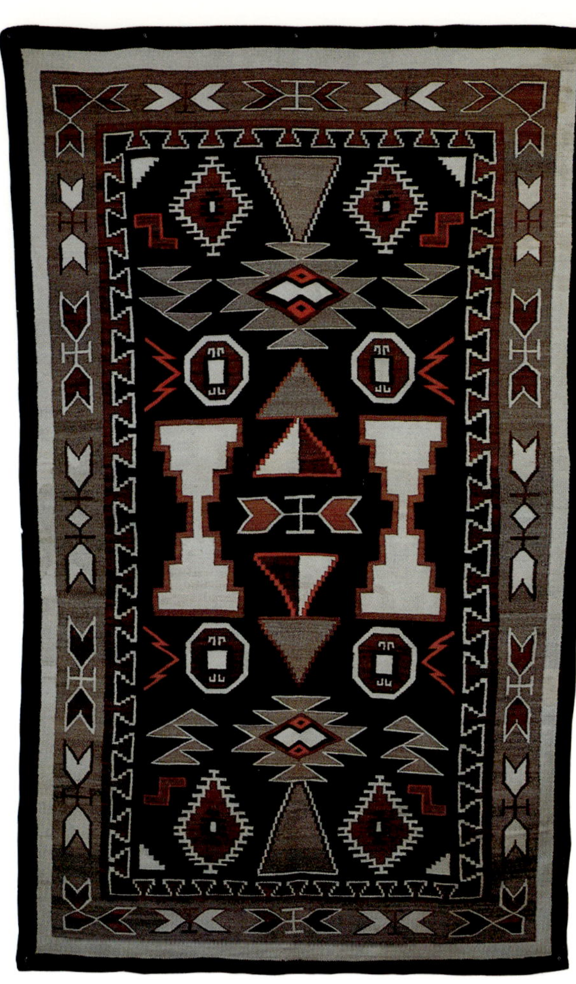

121. Crystal rug, c. 1910. 91″ x 56″. 9 warp/in.; 36 weft/in. One of the unique regional rug styles to develop out of the J. B. Moore Crystal "Oriental" period is the Teec Nos Pos style. Brightly colored complex patterns characterize this style of rug. Woven of synthetic-dyed red, orange with natural brown, black, and natural brown, gray, and white hand-spun wool yarns. (Private collection)

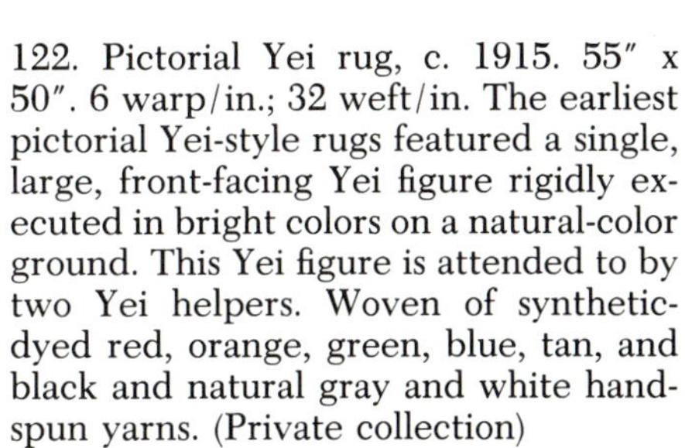

122. Pictorial Yei rug, c. 1915. 55″ x 50″. 6 warp/in.; 32 weft/in. The earliest pictorial Yei-style rugs featured a single, large, front-facing Yei figure rigidly executed in bright colors on a natural-color ground. This Yei figure is attended to by two Yei helpers. Woven of synthetic-dyed red, orange, green, blue, tan, and black and natural gray and white hand-spun yarns. (Private collection)

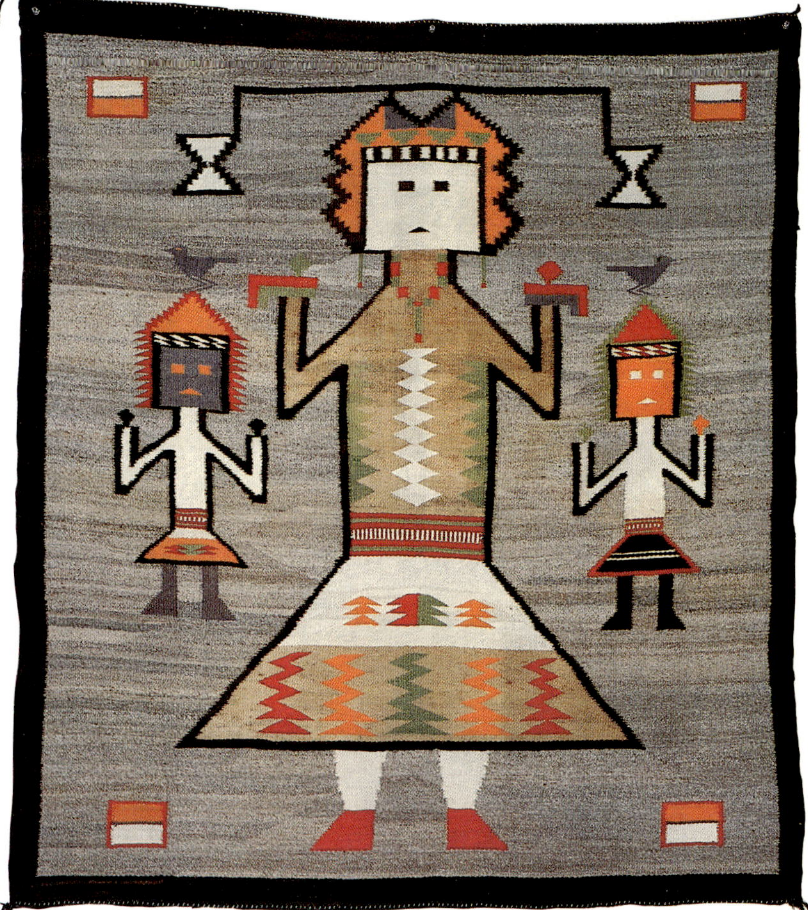

weavers at Teec Nos Pos used bright, synthetic colors on their equally complex-patterned rugs. (As the natural black wool tends to develop a reddish-brown cast, however, many weavers at Two Gray Hills and in other parts of the reservation stabilize the black color with natural or synthetic black dyes.)

Along with Ganado and Crystal, other parts of the Navajo reservation were becoming associated with particular styles. Weavers from the Shiprock and Lukachukai regions both became known for their Yei and Yeibechai pictorial weavings. These quasi-ceremonial weavings have been controversial since they were woven during the early 1900s (figs. 122, 143, and 144).

Yei rugs developed at the same time as and as an offshoot of sandpainting weavings. Yei rugs featured representations of the Yei—the Navajo Holy People—as they are pictured in sandpaintings. Sandpainting textiles were woven versions of some of the dozens of sandpainting designs. Sandpainting is an integral part of a Navajo ceremony performed by medicine men who have memorized the intricate designs that are handed down from generation to generation. Some contemporary art historians claim that Jackson Pollock's painting technique was inspired by the technique of Navajo sandpainters. Navajos believe that the ceremony is only effective if the designs are perfect, yet "earth surface people" are not permitted to create permanent perfection: that is the province of the gods alone. For this reason, sandpaintings must be destroyed after they are created.

It was the permanence of the sacred designs in textile form that made their weaving so controversial among Navajos. Weavers who dared to use these designs were not only flaunting convention, they were defying their holy spirits. No wonder rumors flew among the highly religious/superstitious Navajos about the fate of weavers who took the risk of weaving a sandpainting rug. Arthritis, blindness, paralysis, insanity, and even death were believed to be not only possible but highly probable fates for these weavers.

Although he was not the first to weave either sandpainting tapestries or Yei rugs, Hosteen Klah (literally, Old Left-handed Man) was the first person to become well known for doing so. Klah was a charismatic medicine man. During the 1920s he was the last of his generation to have committed certain of the sacred chants and designs to memory. Male weavers are unusual among Navajos; Klah was even more unusual in that he was reported to be a hermaphrodite. Rather than making him the object of scorn and derision, however, Klah's unusual status made him a very special, even prestigious personage among the tribe.

Klah was first asked to weave a sandpainting textile by the wife of a trader in 1919, after which he was approached by Mary Cabot Wheelwright, a Boston patron of and dealer in Indian art who wanted to establish a "Museum of Navajo Ceremonial Art" in Santa Fe. Not only did Klah survive the weaving of the sandpainting tapestries with all his faculties intact, but so did his two nieces, Mrs. Sam and Mrs. Jim Manuelito, whom he enlisted to help with Mrs. Wheelwright's project. Permanent versions of the sacred sandpaintings were created for her museum, now called The Wheelwright Museum of the American Indian (figs. 145 and 146). The continued good health and prosperity of Hosteen Klah and of the Manuelito sisters opened the floodgates to other weavers, and to the weaving of sandpainting tapestries, Yei rugs, and Yeibechai rugs (in which the figures, usually shown in profile, represent Navajos impersonating the Yei), which are still being woven today.

Mary Cabot Wheelwright also figured in another controversy, another case of tradition versus innovation, as Anglos continued to try to improve the artistic merits of and commercial possibilities for Navajo rugs. In the 1920s Mrs. Wheelwright's and Chinle, Arizona, trader L. C. "Cozy" McSparron's appreciation for Classic Period blankets—and their nostalgia for the past—brought about the development of a new weaving style that helped propel Navajo weaving into the contemporary era.

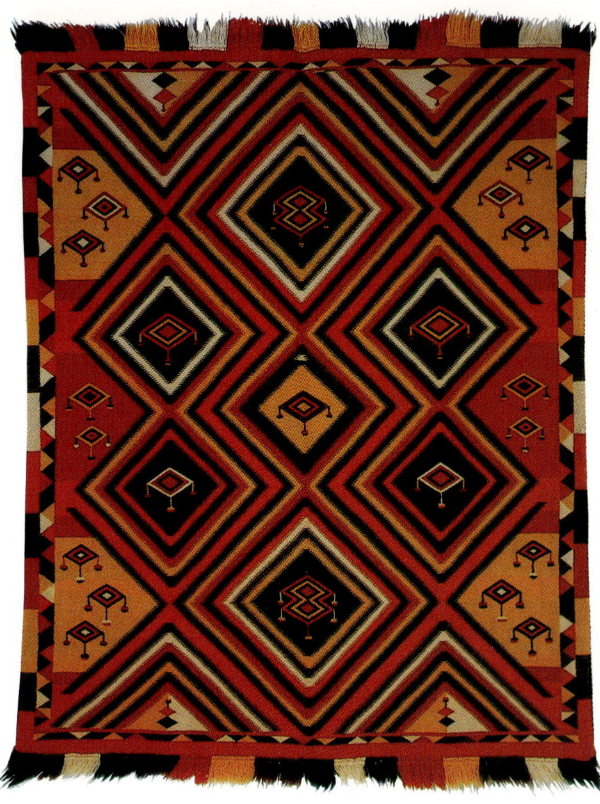

123. Germantown blanket, 1880–1890. 72″ x 55″. 12 warp/in.; 44 weft/in. The combining of Oriental rug and Navajo blanket designs often results in a unique pattern, but not always as successful as in this example, with its optically complex border. Woven of four-ply commercial synthetic-dyed red, purple, yellow, blue, tan, and white wool yarns. (Private collection)

124. Germantown blanket, 1880–1890. 54″ x 39″. 12 warp/in.; 52 weft/in. An example of artistic license carried to the extreme. The weaver of this blanket attempted to fit in as many design elements, including pictorial ones, as possible. Saltillo influence is clearly visible in the border and serrate diamond designs. Woven of four-ply commercial synthetic-dyed red (two shades), purple (two shades), green (two shades), blue, yellow, orange, brown, and white wool yarns. (Private collection)

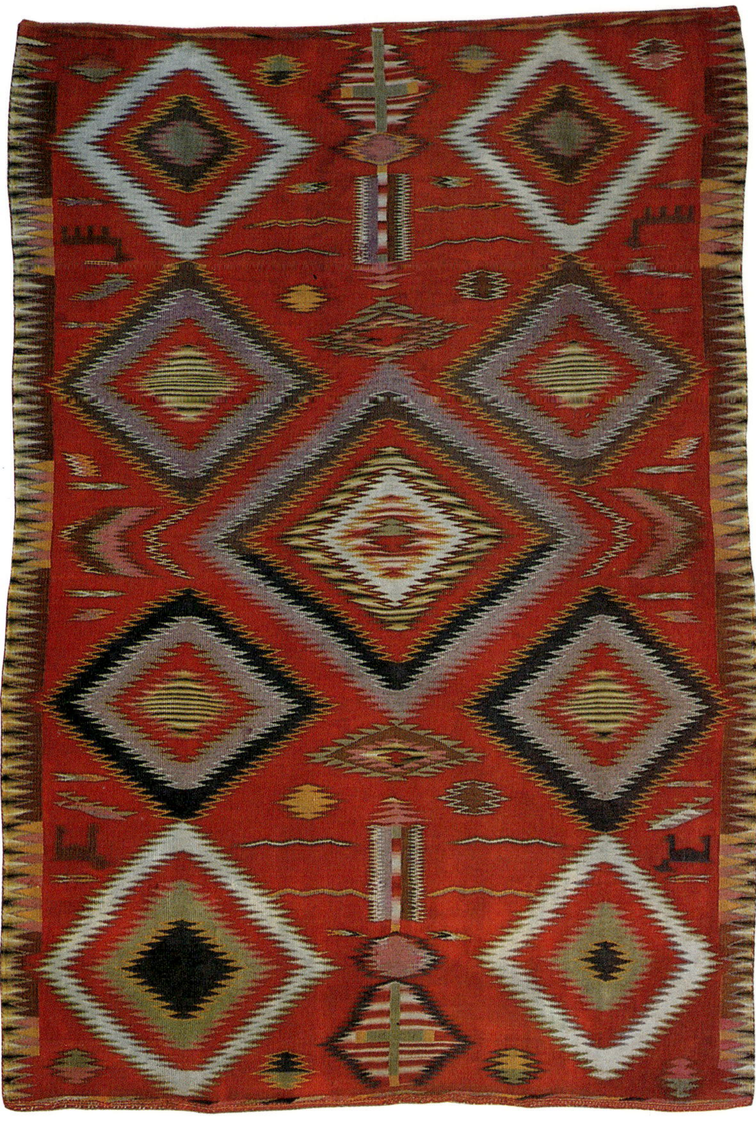

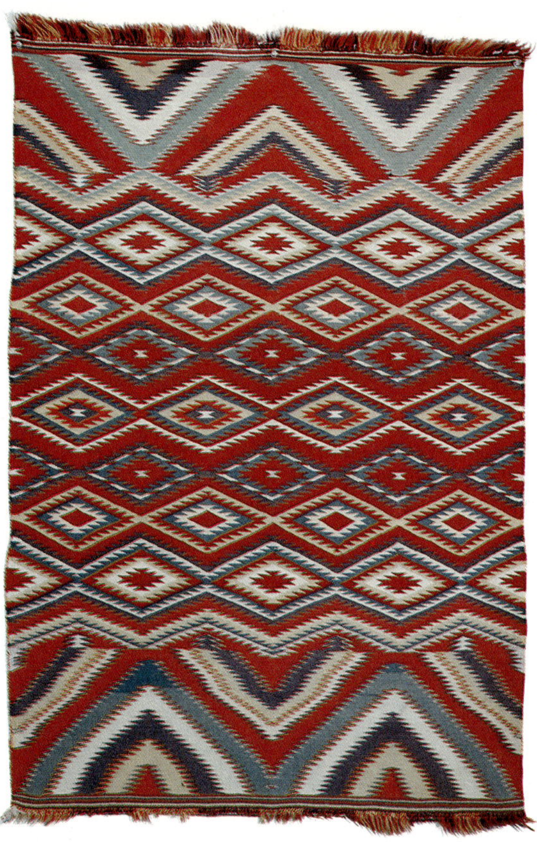

125. Germantown blanket, 1880–1900. 53″ x 36″. 12 warp/in.; 50 weft/in. Many of the smaller fringed Germantown blankets, commonly referred to as saddle blankets, never saw such use, instead ending up on the chairs, tables, and floors of Victorian homes. Woven of four-ply commercial synthetic-dyed red, blue (two shades), purple, yellow, and white wool yarns. (Private collection)

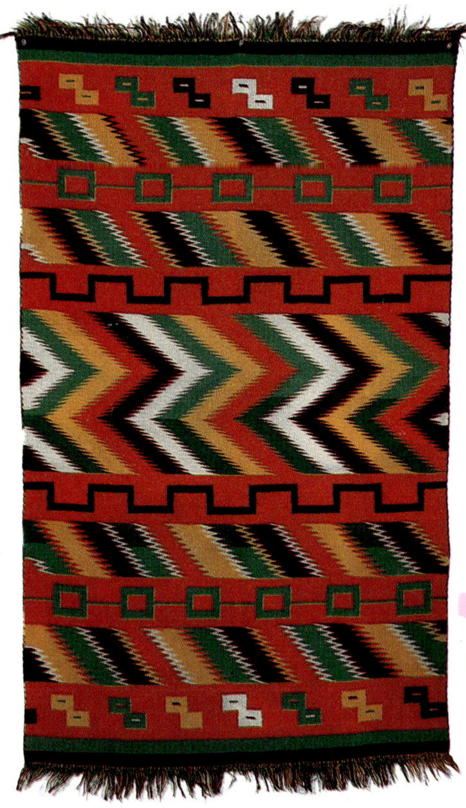

126. Germantown blanket, 1880–1900. 63″ x 36″. 11 warp/in.; 42 weft/in. A forerunner of Op art, the push-pull horizontal movement in this small blanket grabs the eye. In order to save time and expense, many Germantown blankets of this period were woven on a commercial cotton warp, making them more susceptible to eventual deterioration. Woven of four-ply commercial synthetic-dyed red, green, orange, tan, black, and white wool yarns. (Private collection)

127. Germantown blanket, c. 1890. 73″ x 48″. 13 warp/in; 40 weft/in. Large outline, cross-design elements have become a recognized symbol of the trader at the Ganado Trading Post, J. L. Hubbell. The unusual white background was also a trait of the Ganado Germantown. Woven of four-ply commercial synthetic-dyed red, purple, black, and white wool yarns. (Private collection)

128. Germantown Chief blanket, 1890–1900. 58″ x 75″. 11 warp/in.; 44 weft/in. Woven of slightly heavier Germantown yarns, this Late Classic revival-style Chief pattern was intended not to be worn but for floor use. Woven of four-ply commercial synthetic-dyed red, purple, black, and white wool yarns. (Private collection)

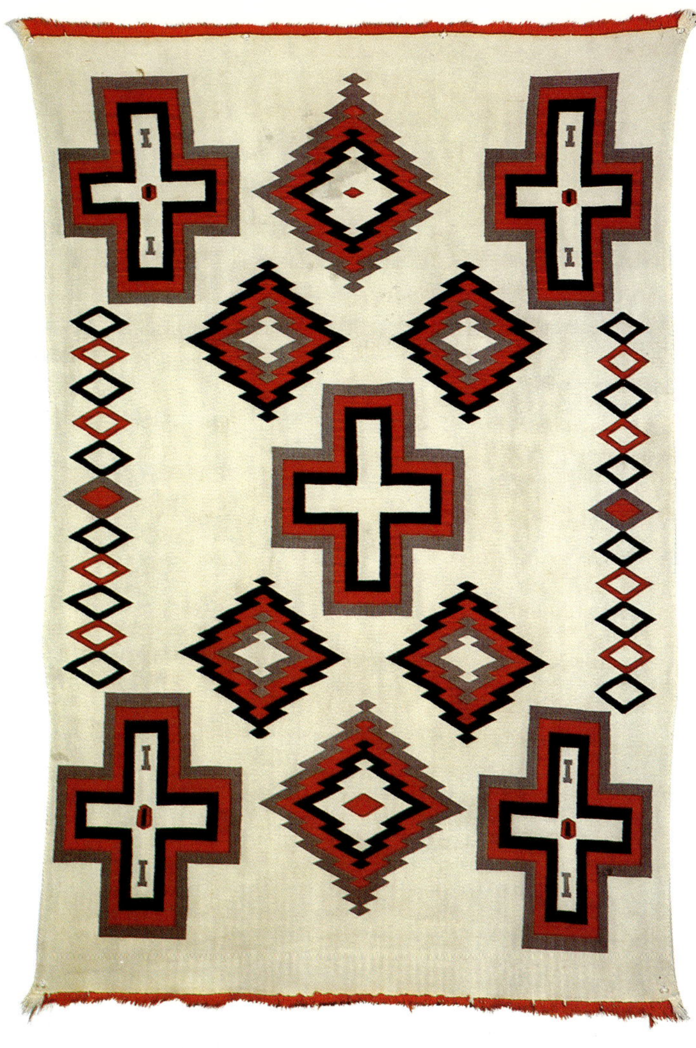

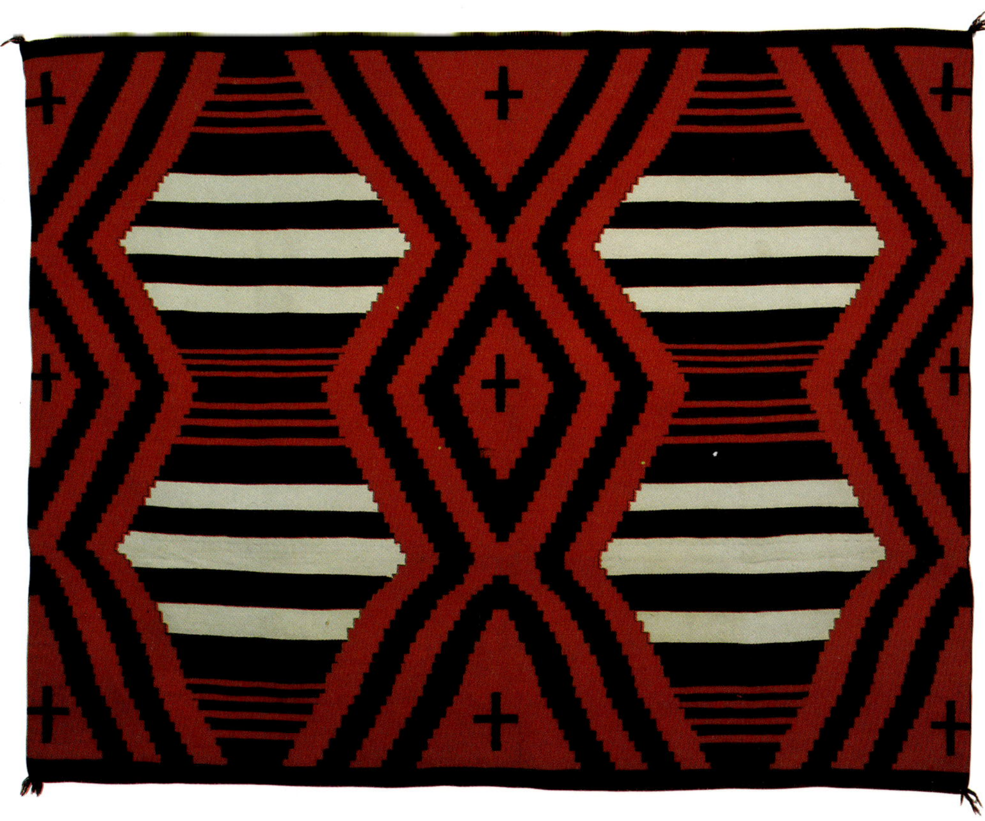

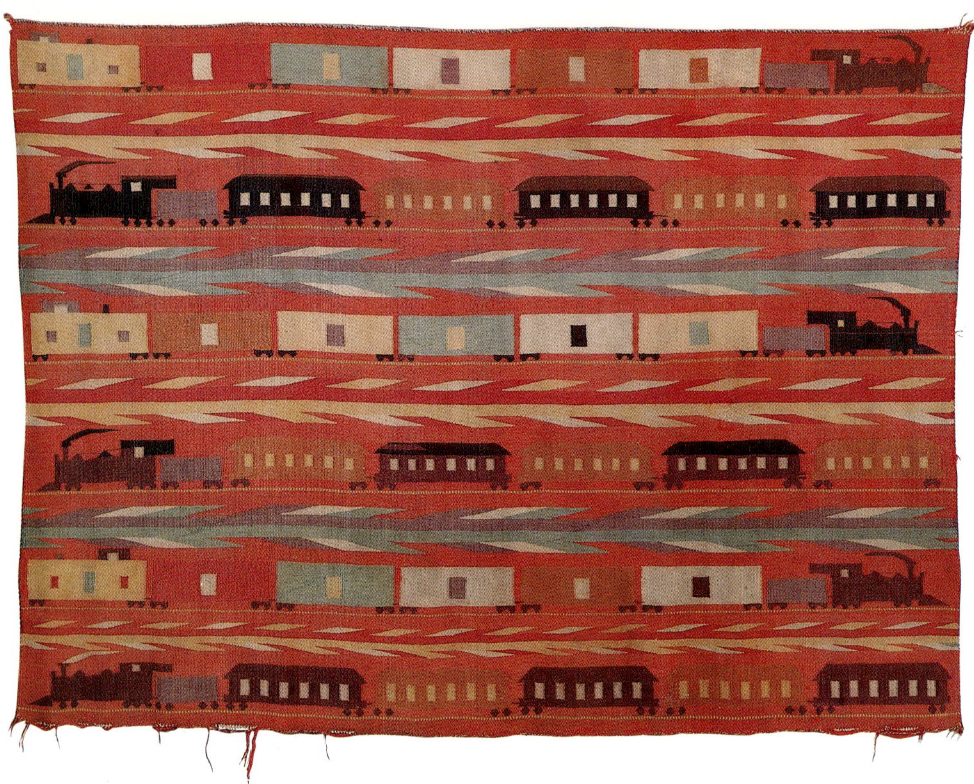

129. Germantown blanket, c. 1890. 45″ x 62″. 11 warp/in.; 52 weft/in. The arrival of the railroad in the Southwest was a major historical event, here documented by a Navajo weaver, that forever changed the lives and life-styles of the Navajos. Woven of four-ply commercial synthetic-dyed red, yellow, green, purple (two shades), pale brown, and white wool yarns. (Private collection)

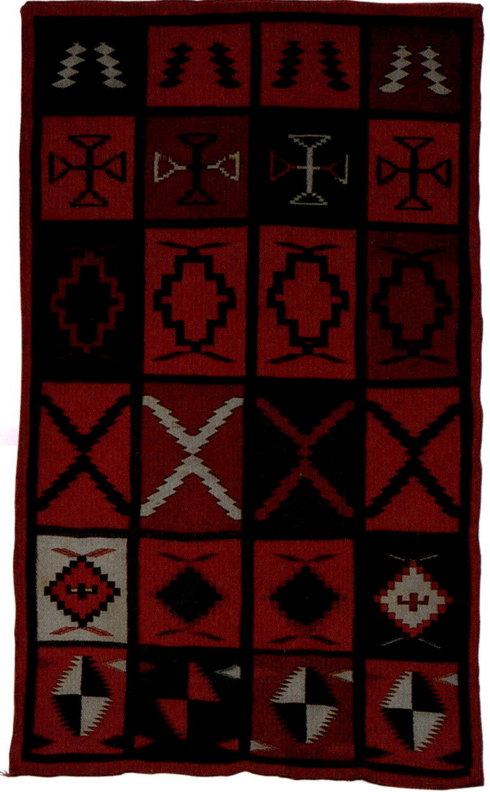

130. Germantown blanket, 1890–1900. 56″ x 45″. 11 warp/in.; 44 weft/in. To promote the sale of Germantown blankets, some traders had Navajo weavers make miniature "samplers" to be shown to prospective clients. This blanket appears to be a collection of sampler patterns woven into one blanket. Woven of four-ply commercial synthetic-dyed red (two shades), green, purple, black, and white wool yarns. (Private collection)

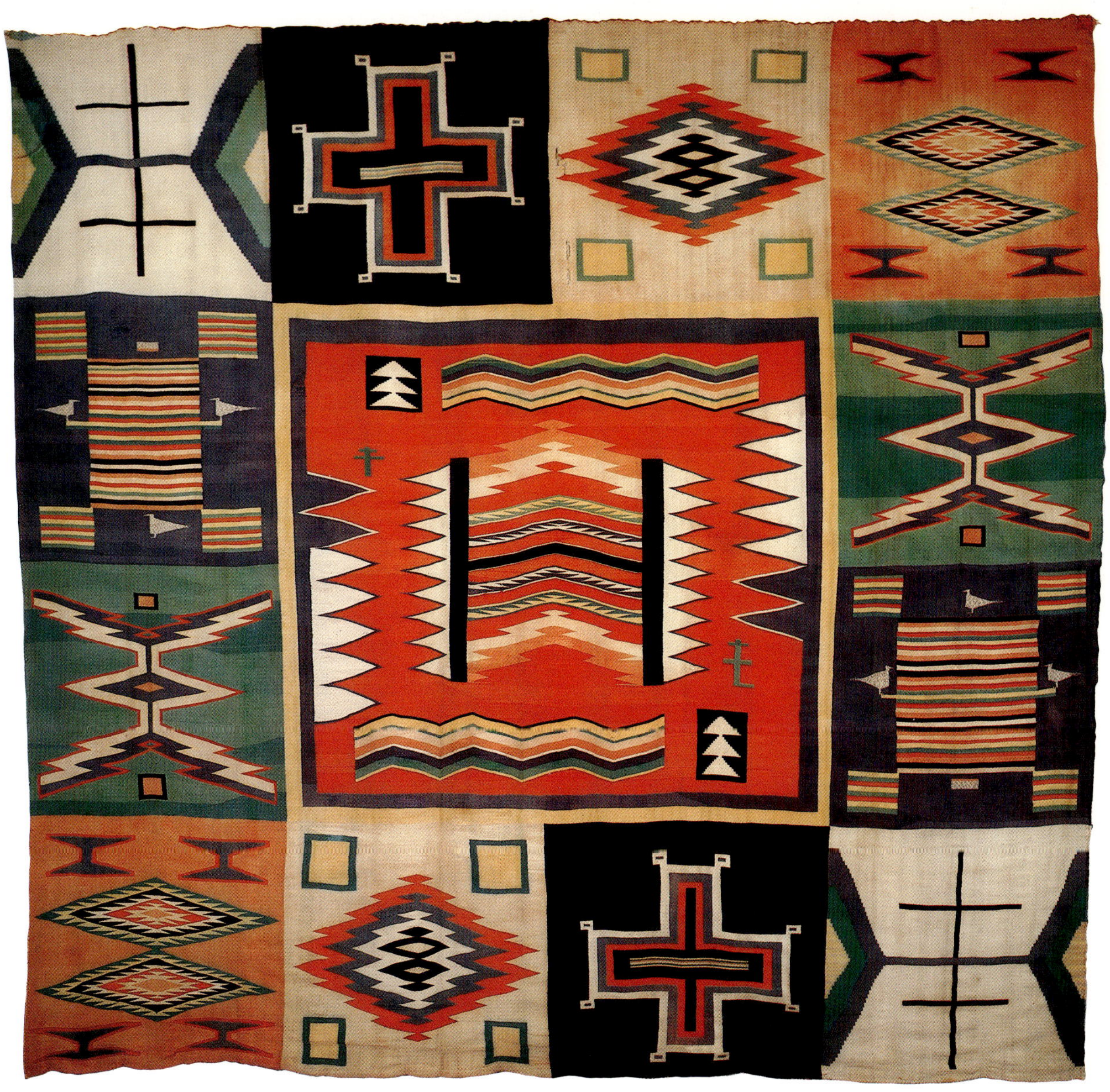

131. Germantown blanket, 1880–1900. 100″ x 135″. 11 warp/in.; 44 weft/in. Extraordinarily large and complex for the period in which it was made, this multipatterned weaving was possibly a special-order item for a particular client. J. L. Hubbell was known to have had large rugs made to order in the late nineteenth century. Woven of four-ply commercial synthetic-dyed red, yellow, purple, green, orange, pink, black, and variegated black-and-white speckled wool yarns. (Private collection)

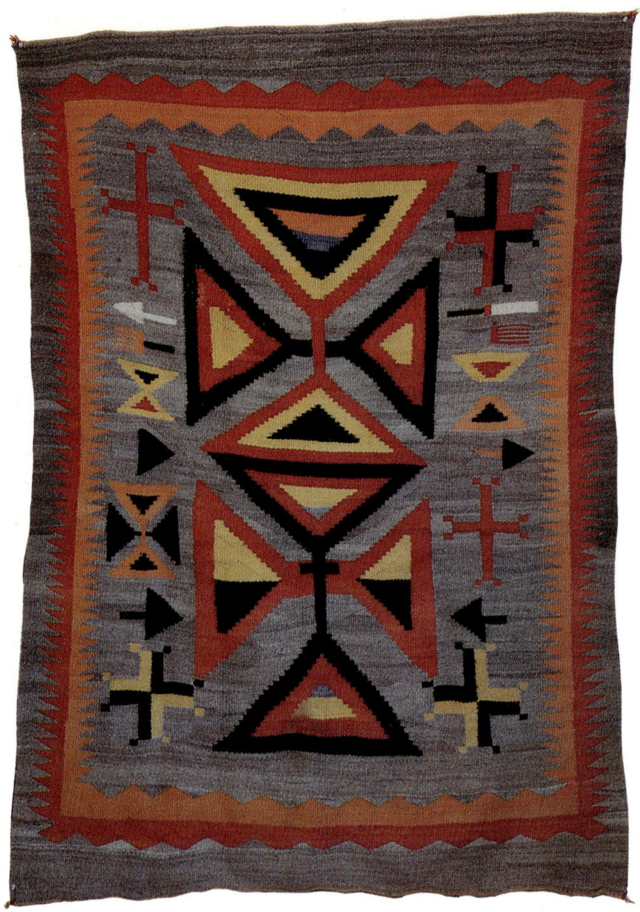

132. Blanket/rug, c. 1900. 77″ x 55″. 6 warp/in.; 16 weft/in. Many of the popular Navajo design elements of the late nineteenth century were referred to as having symbolic meaning. Often it was the traders themselves who suggested that these "symbols" be incorporated into the design repertoire to increase the salability of their rugs to naïve tourists. Woven of synthetic-dyed red, orange, yellow, and blue and natural brown and gray hand-spun wool yarns. (Private collection)

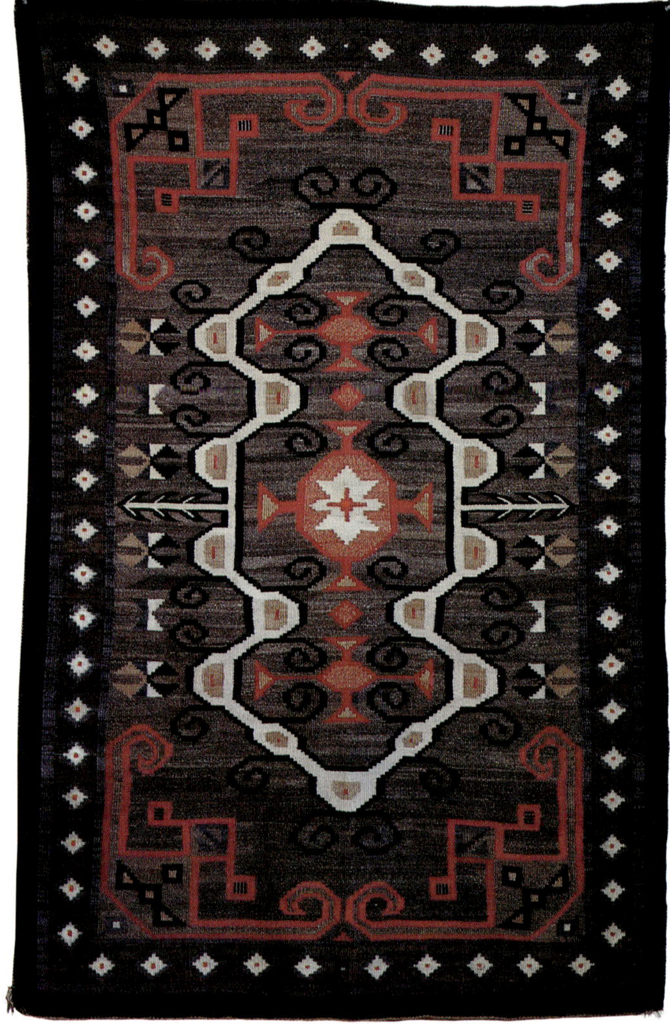

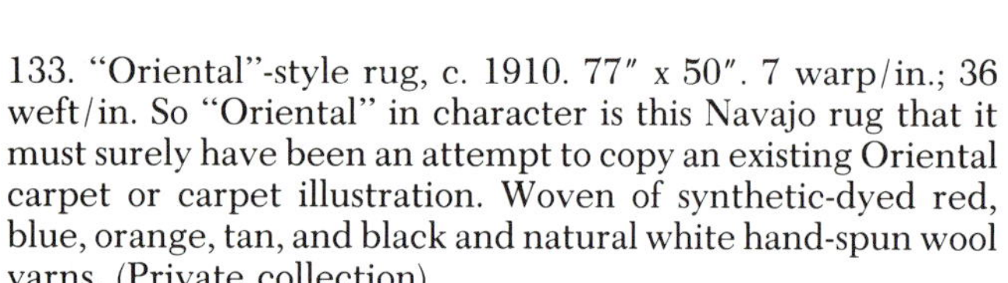

133. "Oriental"-style rug, c. 1910. 77″ x 50″. 7 warp/in.; 36 weft/in. So "Oriental" in character is this Navajo rug that it must surely have been an attempt to copy an existing Oriental carpet or carpet illustration. Woven of synthetic-dyed red, blue, orange, tan, and black and natural white hand-spun wool yarns. (Private collection)

134. Crystal rug, c. 1910. 80″ x 55″. 10 warp/in.; 40 weft/in. The use of only natural colors in this 1911 J. B. Moore catalogue Crystal rug indicates that it was probably woven in the Two Gray Hills region. Woven of natural white, gray, and brown and overdyed black hand-spun wool yarns. (Private collection)

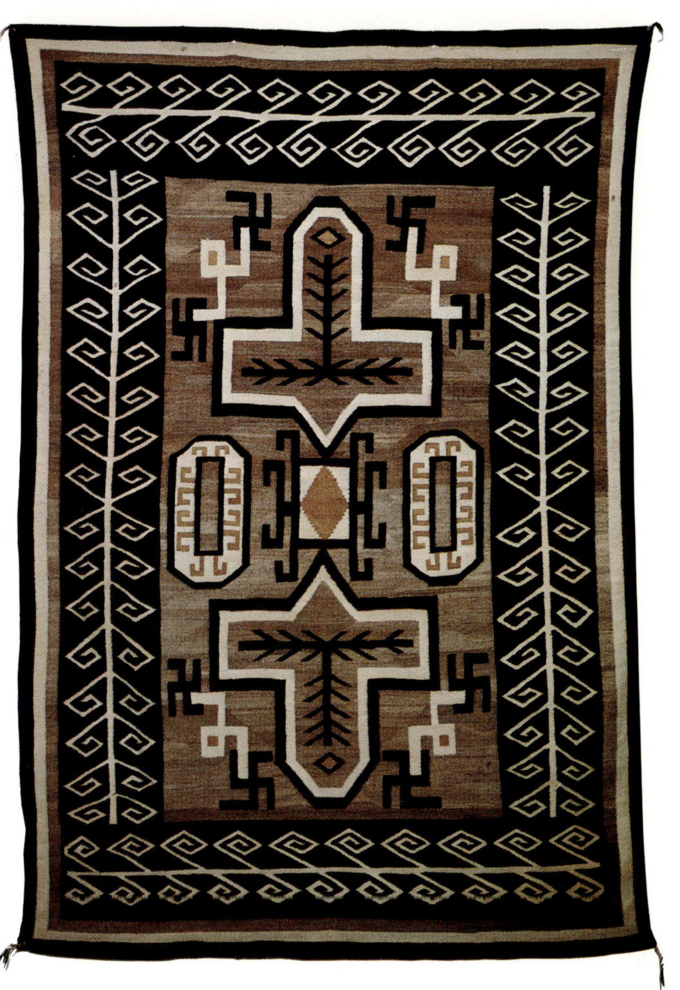

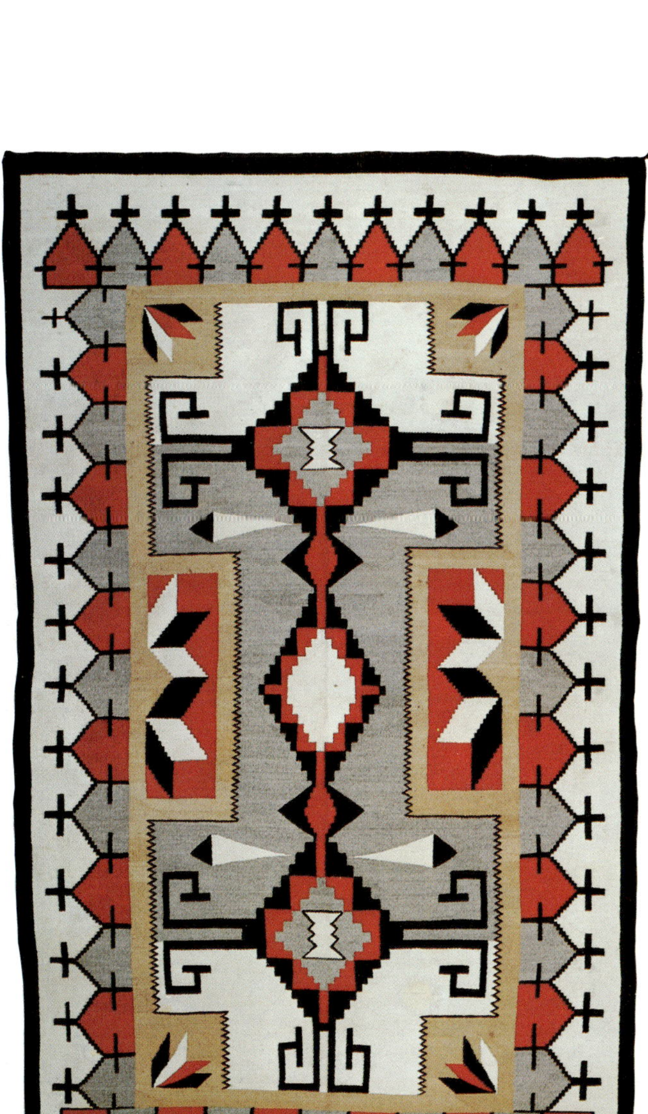

135. Crystal rug, c. 1910. 88″ x 52″. 8 warp/in.; 40 weft/in. This finely woven and executed Crystal rug shares design elements with both the Crystal and Ganado styles. Woven of synthetic-dyed red and black and natural gray, tan, and white hand-spun wool yarns. (Private collection)

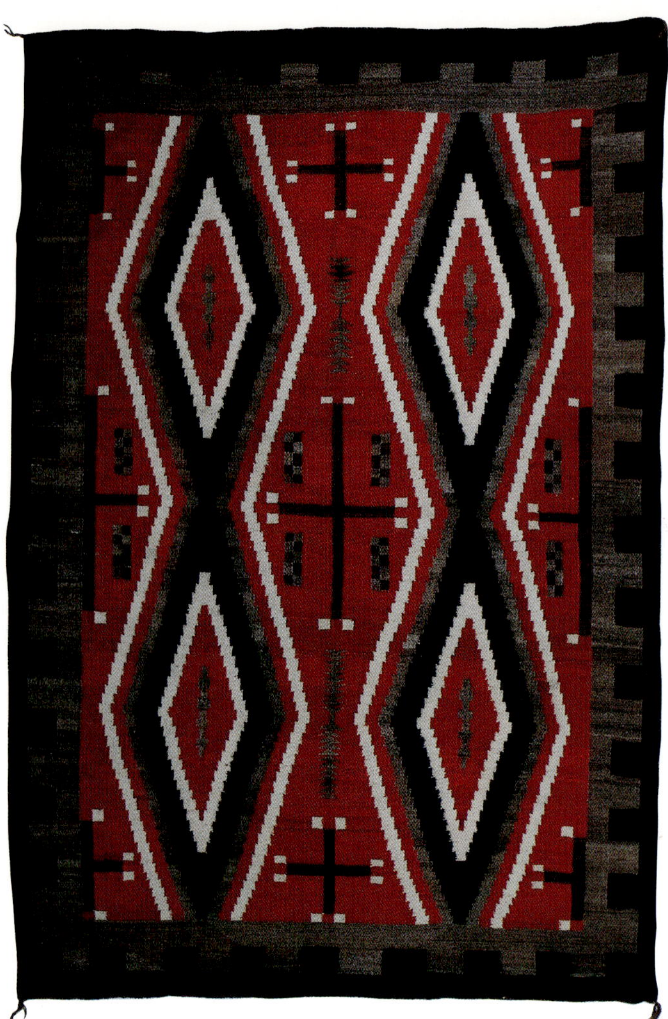

136. Crystal rug, c. 1910. 92″ x 63″. 7 warp/in., 28 weft/in. The Ganado style of rug, having proven its popularity with the Anglo market, was borrowed by and incorporated into the J.B. Moore catalogue inventory of available styles of mail-order rugs. Woven of synthetic-dyed red and black and natural white hand-spun wool yarns. (Private collection)

137. Crystal rug, c. 1910. 72″ x 47″. 8 warp/in.; 32 weft/in. The central medallion or "Vallero star" design in this Crystal rug is of Rio Grande origin. Storm pattern design influence and Two Gray Hills coloration are also evident. Woven of natural gray, brown, and white and overdyed black hand-spun wool yarns. (Private collection)

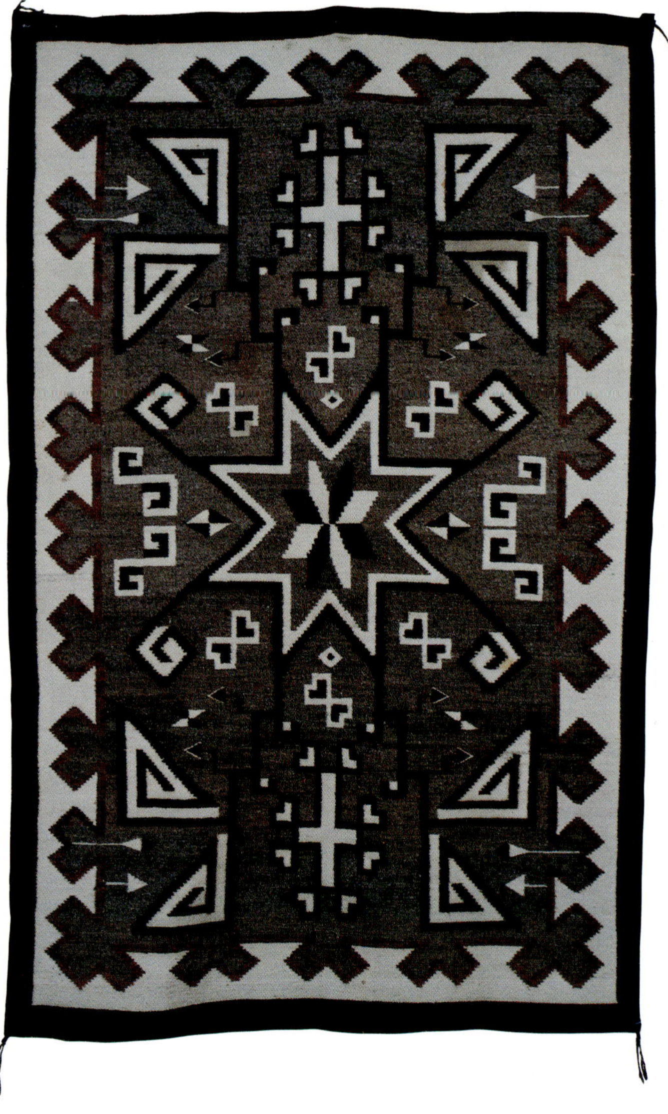

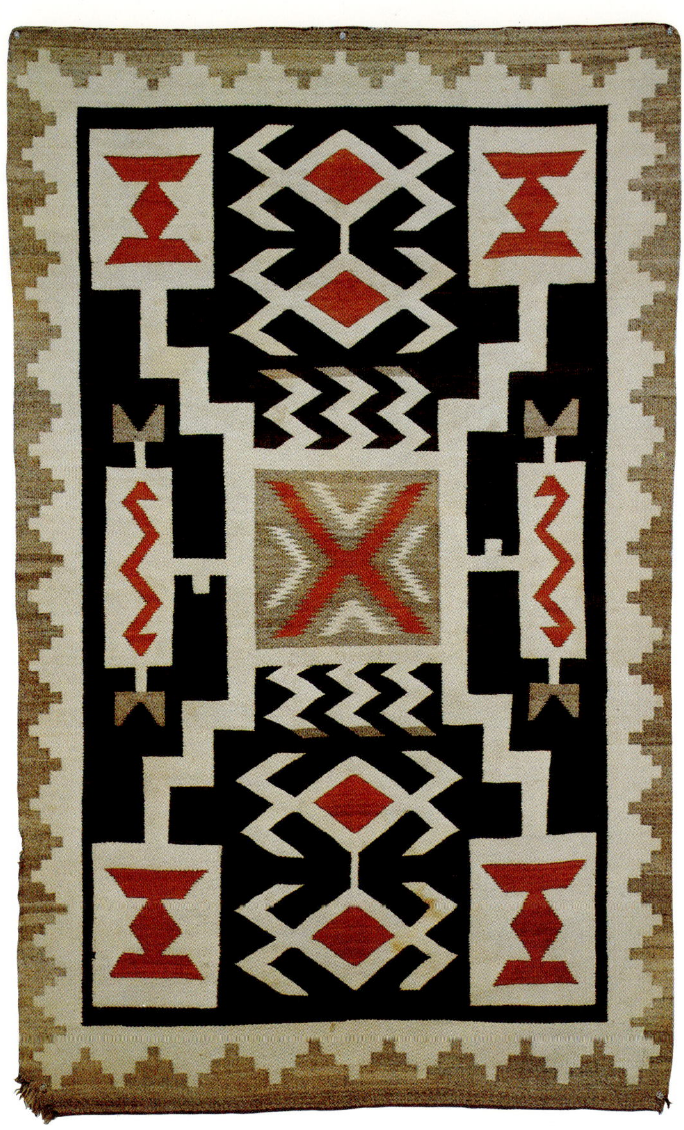

138. Crystal rug, c. 1910. 68″ x 43″. 8 warp/in.; 26 weft/in. This storm pattern Crystal rug, lacking the usual red color, was probably made in the Two Gray Hills region. In later years the storm pattern rug was produced in all parts of the reservation. Woven of natural brown (2 shades), gray, and white hand-spun wool yarns. (Private collection)

139. Red Mesa rug, c. 1910. 98″ x 61″. 6 warp/in.; 32 weft/in. This early Red Mesa "outline" rug is a direct outgrowth of the nineteenth-century "eyedazzler" style of weaving. Woven of synthetic-dyed red (two shades), orange, yellow, green, purple, and gold and natural gray and white hand-spun wool yarns. (Collection of Maxwell Museum of Anthropology, University of New Mexico)

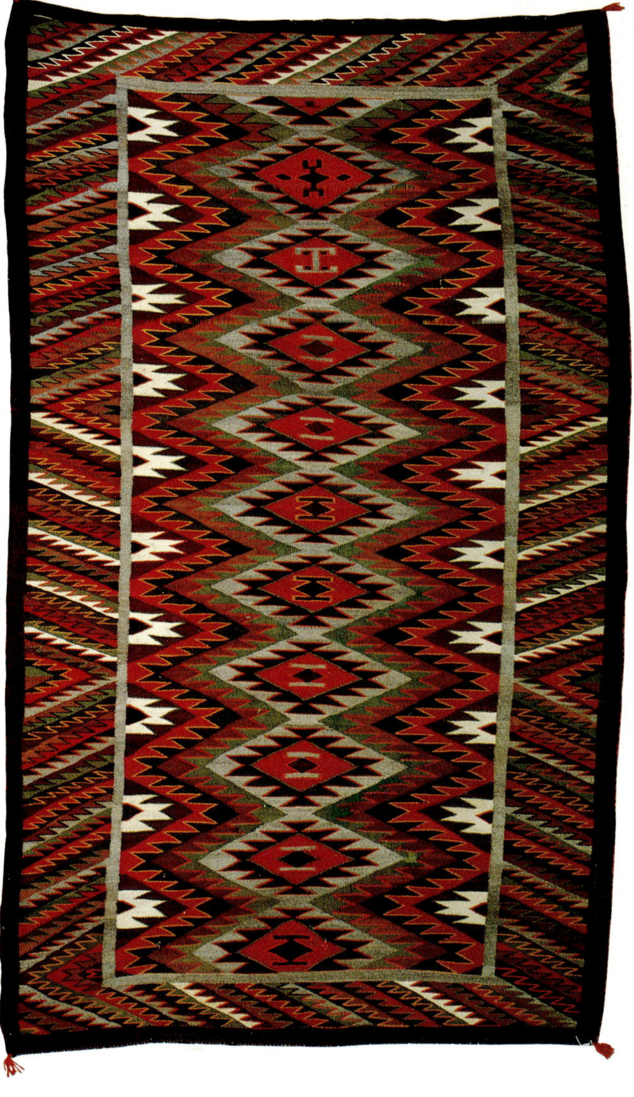

140. Red Mesa rug, c. 1915. 67″ x 46″. 8 warp/in.; 36 weft/in. With little variation, these designs and colors can still be found today on contemporary rugs from this region. Woven of synthetic-dyed black, orange, red, and purple hand-spun and four-ply commercial synthetic-dyed green and yellow wool yarns. (Private collection)

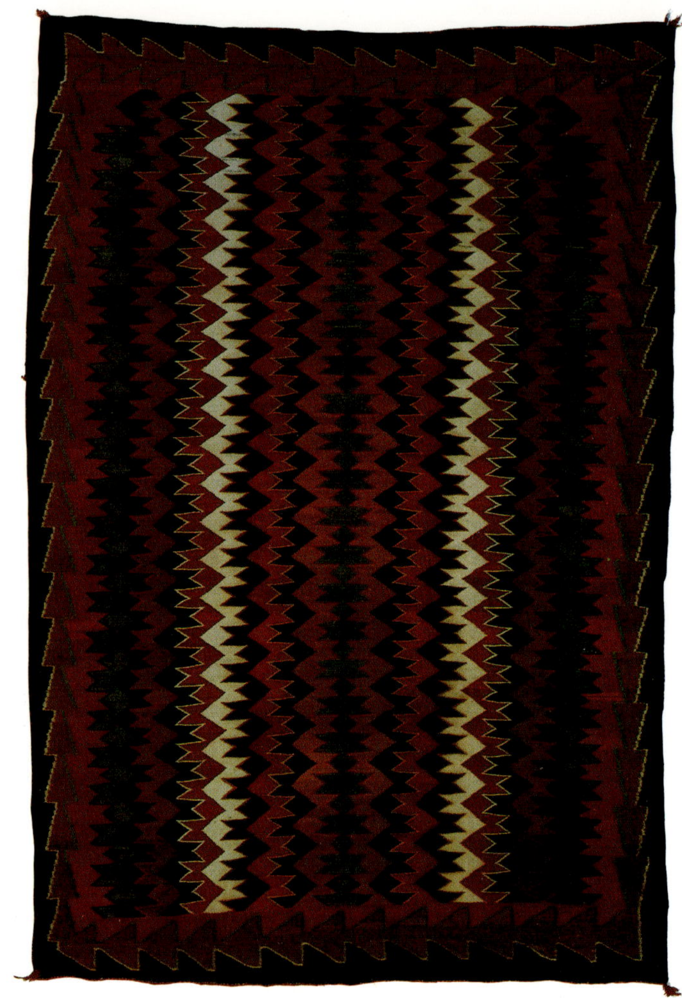

141. Teec Nos Pos rug, c. 1925. 83″ x 53″. 10 warp/in.; 53 weft/in. Like many regional-style rug patterns, the Teec Nos Pos pattern increases in complexity over time. Woven of synthetic-dyed red (two shades), blue (two shades), green, tan (two shades), orange, and yellow hand-spun wool yarns. (Private collection)

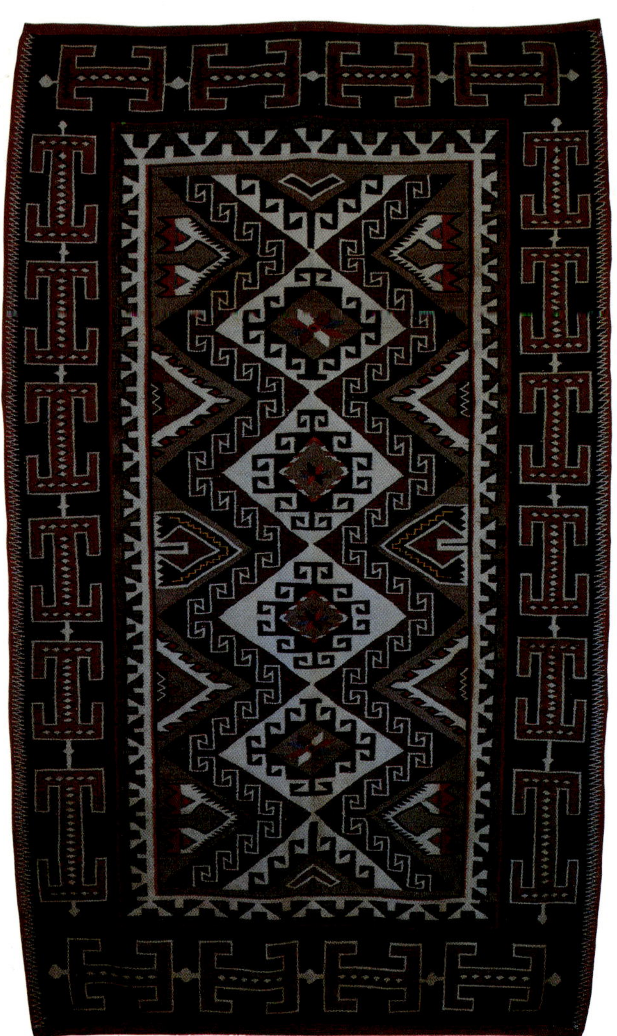

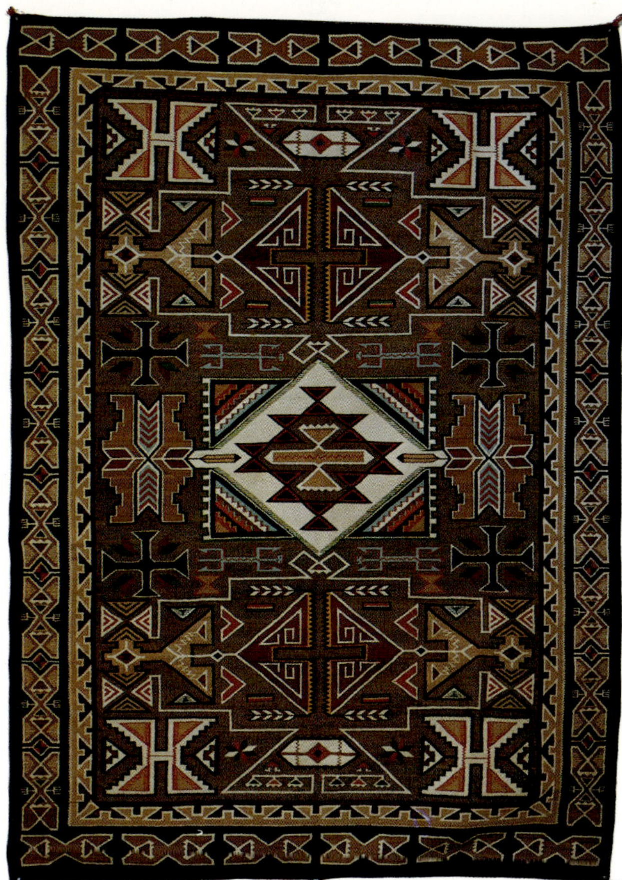

142. Teec Nos Pos rug, c. 1930. 99″ x 72″. 12 warp/in.; 40 weft/in. By 1930 the Teec Nos Pos rug had become the most colorful and complex of all the regional-style rugs. Woven of synthetic-dyed red, green, blue, yellow, orange, and black hand-spun, four-ply commercial synthetic-dyed pale blue, and natural brown, gray, tan, and white hand-spun wool yarns. (Private collection)

143. Pictorial Yei rug, 1915–1920. 55″ x 39″. 12 warp/in.; 52 weft/in. Yeibechai dancers are depicted in full costume in this unusual double-row arrangement of the figures. Woven of four-ply commercial synthetic-dyed red, green, orange, brown, gray, and white wool yarns. (Private collection)

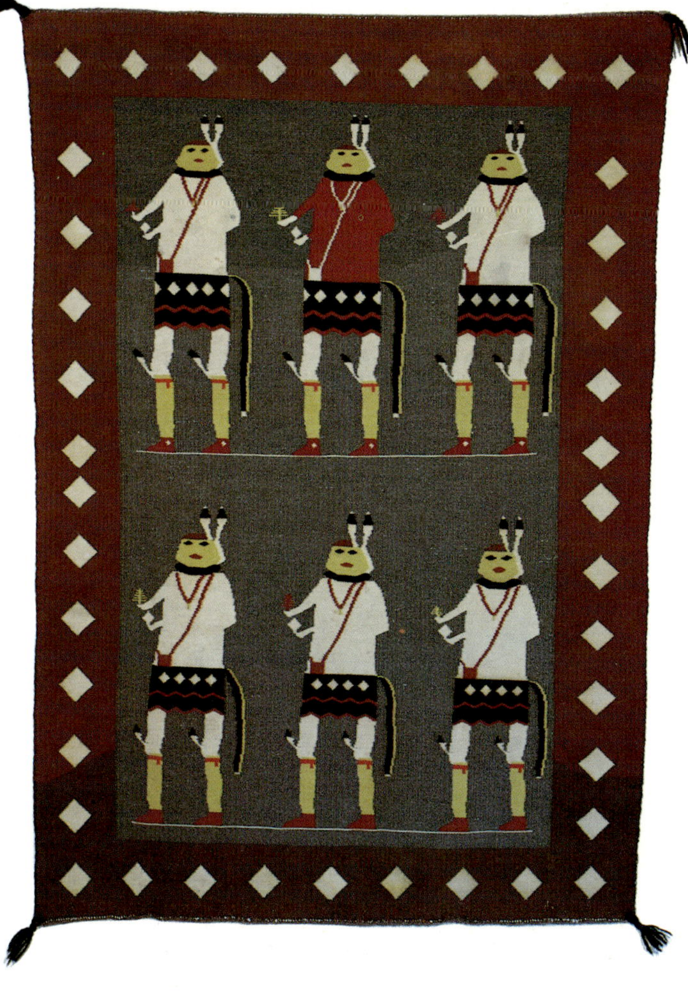

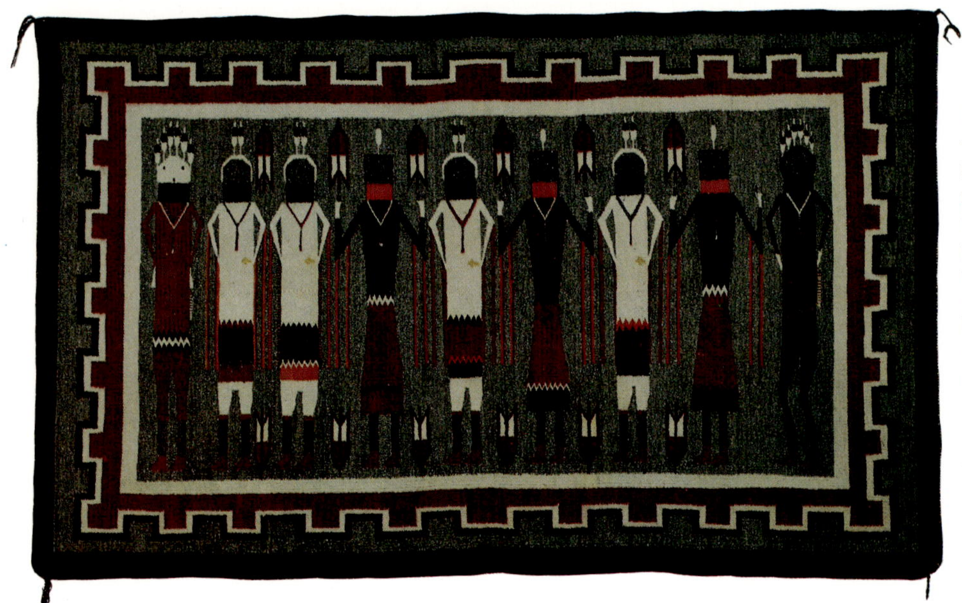

144. Pictorial Yei rug, c. 1920. 46″ x 78″. 8 warp/in.; 36 weft/in. Yeibechai dancers are often more slender and delicately detailed than their Yei counterparts. Woven of synthetic-dyed red, yellow, purple, orange, gold, and black and natural brown, gray, and white handspun wool yarns. (Private collection)

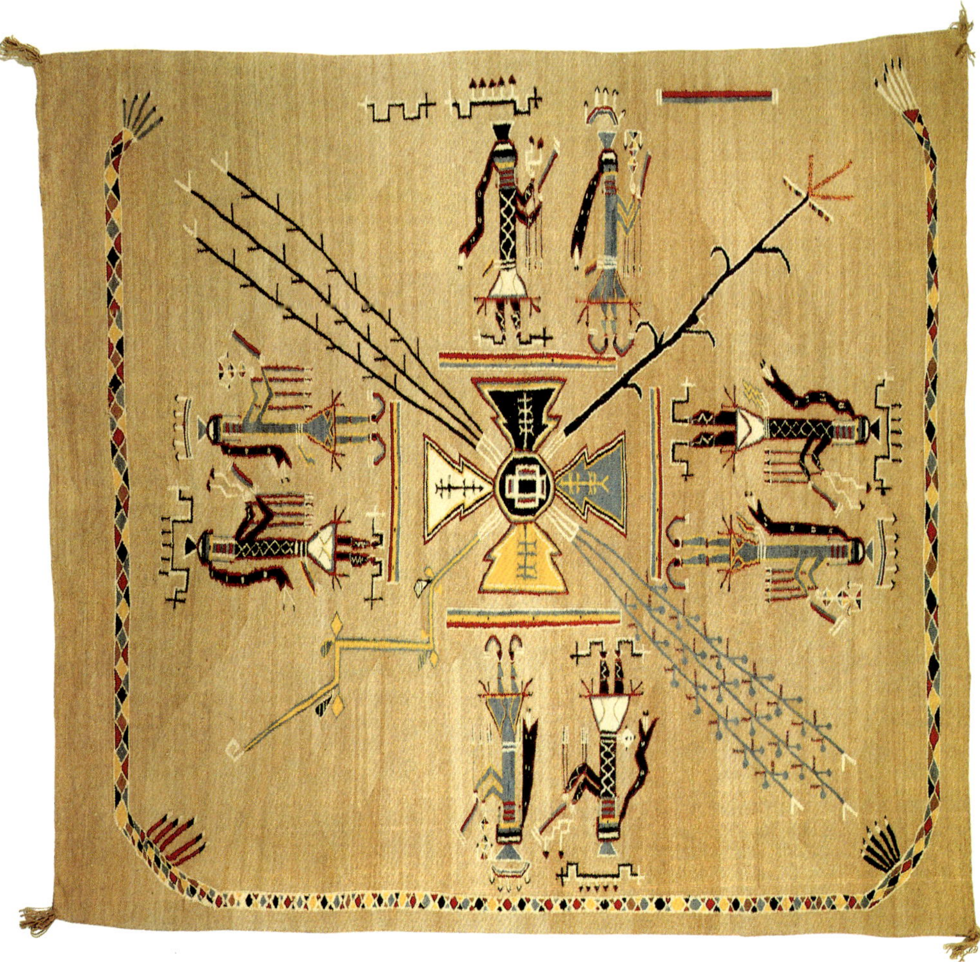

145. Pictorial sand-painting tapestry, by Hosteen Klah, 1925–1930. 88″ x 98″. 8 warp/in.; 36 weft/in. This tapestry, woven to preserve a record of one of the ceremonial sandpaintings, is of the Water Chant. Woven of synthetic-dyed red, yellow, blue, green, and black and natural light brown and white handspun wool yarns. (Collection of Museum of Northern Arizona)

146. Pictorial sandpainting tapestry, by Hosteen Klah, 1925–1930. 83″ x 83″. 8 warp/in.; 36 weft/in. The Nightway, sandpainting of the night sky used in the peacemaking ceremony following the war between the Thunders in Navajo mythology. Woven of synthetic-dyed red, yellow, and purple, overdyed black, and natural light brown and white wool yarns. (Collection of Museum of Northern Arizona)

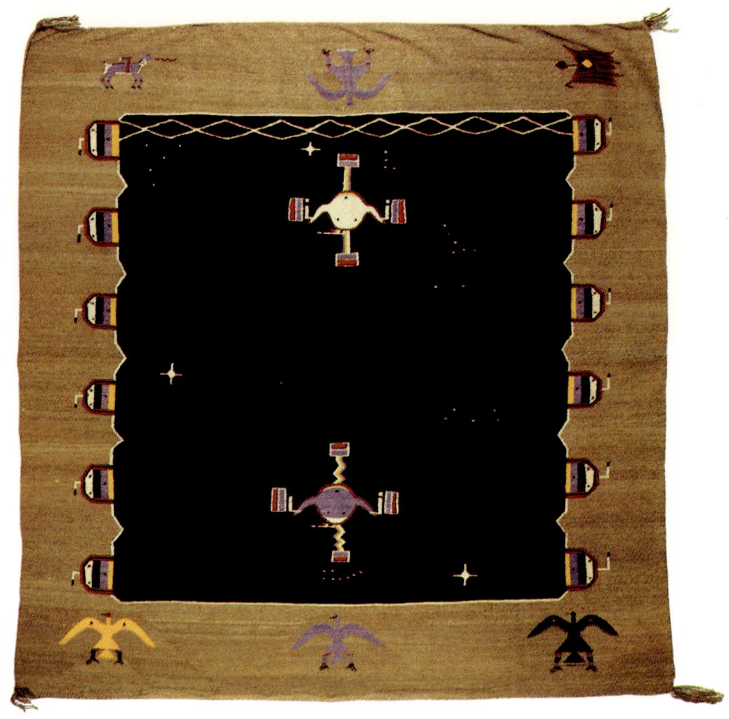

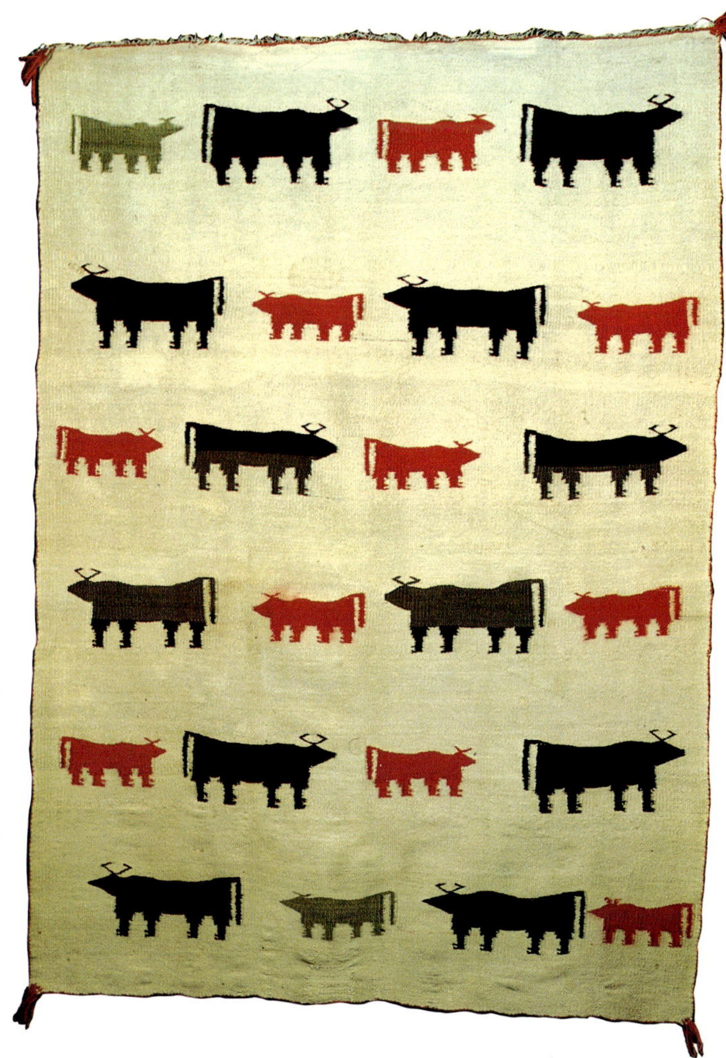

147. Pictorial rug, c. 1915. 74″ x 55″. 7 warp/in.; 28 weft/in. Cattle were a common sight on the Navajo reservation where, like sheep, they represented personal wealth and status. Woven of synthetic-dyed red and green and natural brown and white hand-spun wool yarns. (Collection of Heard Museum)

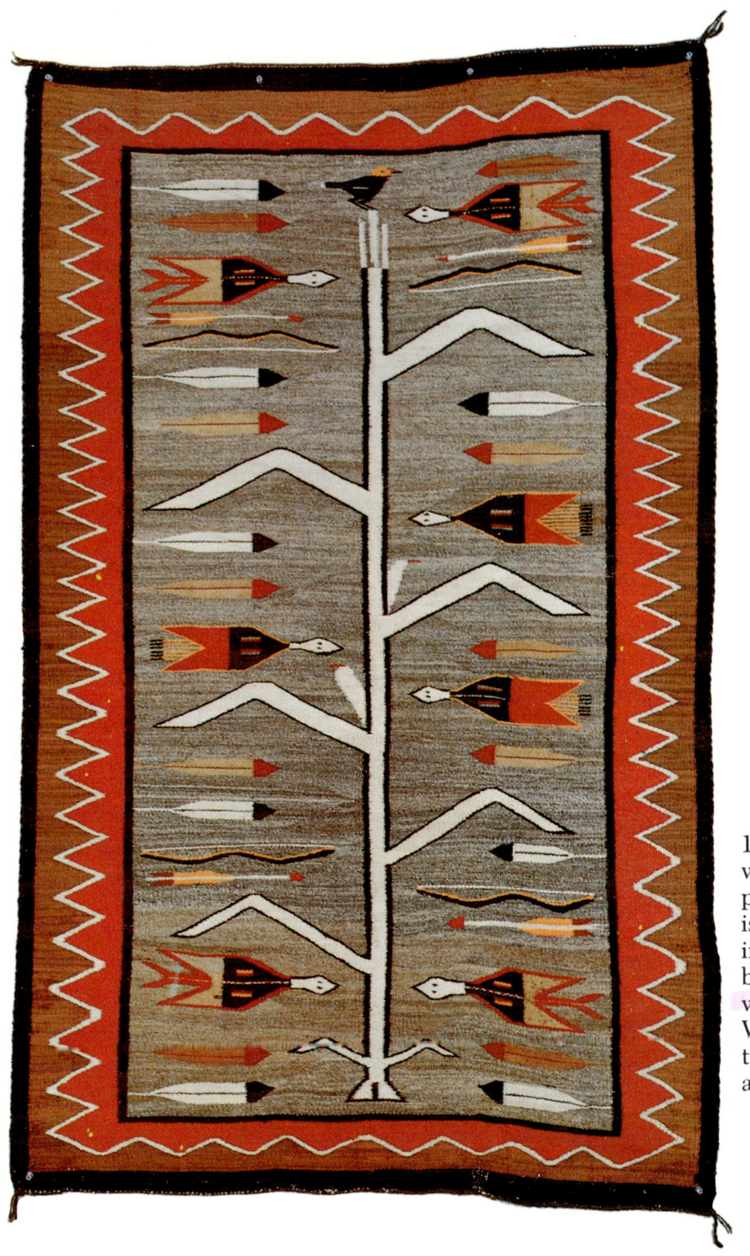

148. Pictorial rug, c. 1920. 70" x 44". 8 warp/in.; 36 weft/in. This pictorial "corn plant" is the roost for stylized birds. Corn is both a staple of the Navajo diet and an important ceremonial substance. The bows and arrows and the feather designs were popular with the Anglo market. Woven of synthetic-dyed red, orange, tan, brown, and black and natural gray and white wool yarns. (Private collection)

149. Pictorial rug, c. 1920. 82″ x 52″. 8 warp/in.; 36 weft/in. The weaver of this rug was most likely influenced by the designs on an Oriental "tree of life" carpet. Woven of synthetic-dyed red and orange and natural gray, brown, and white hand-spun wool yarns. (Private collection)

150. Pictorial rug, c. 1921. 93″ x 64″. 9 warp/in.; 40 weft/in. This rug represents a Navajo weaver's attempt to reproduce an American folk art tapestry illustrated in a 1921 issue of *Delineator Magazine.* No attempt was made to copy the illustration exactly, only to re-create the feeling of the illustrated tapestry. Woven of synthetic-dyed red and blue and natural brown, tan, light brown, and white hand-spun wool yarns. (Private collection)

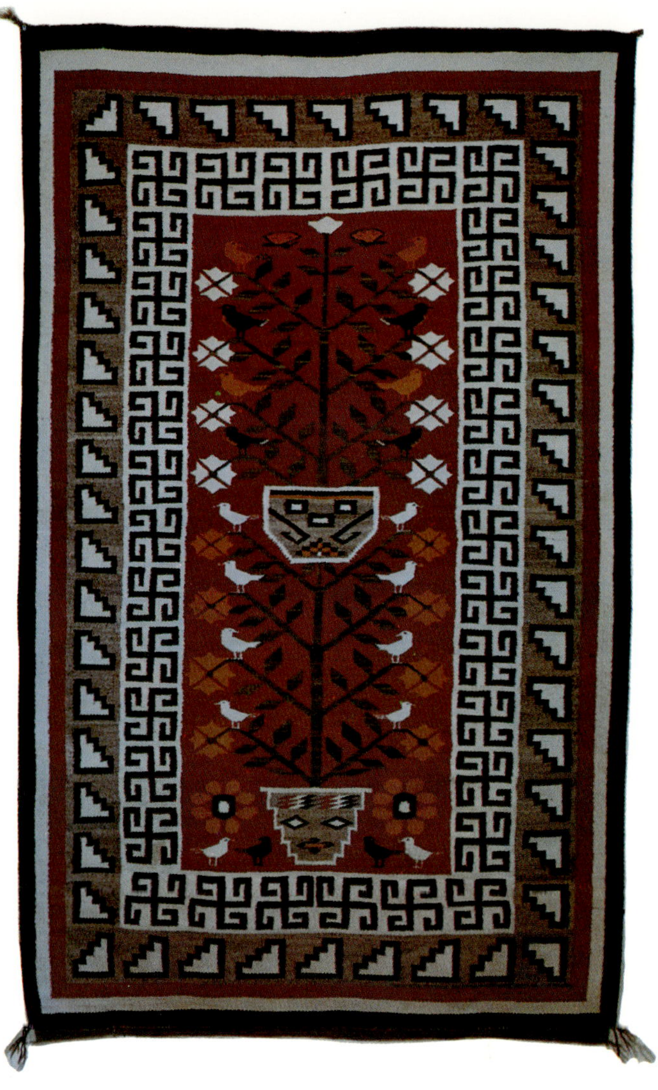

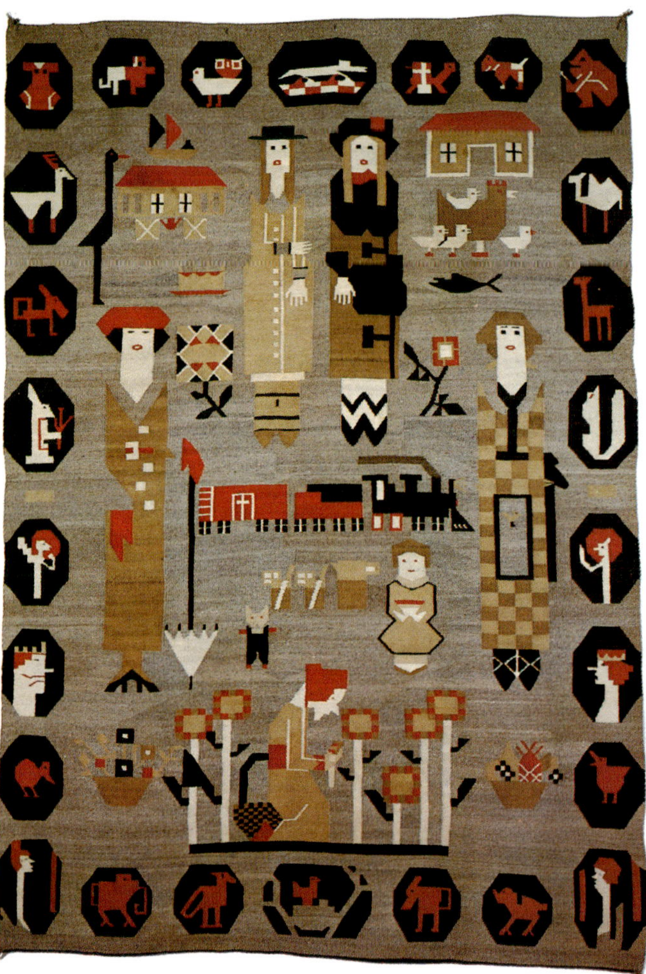

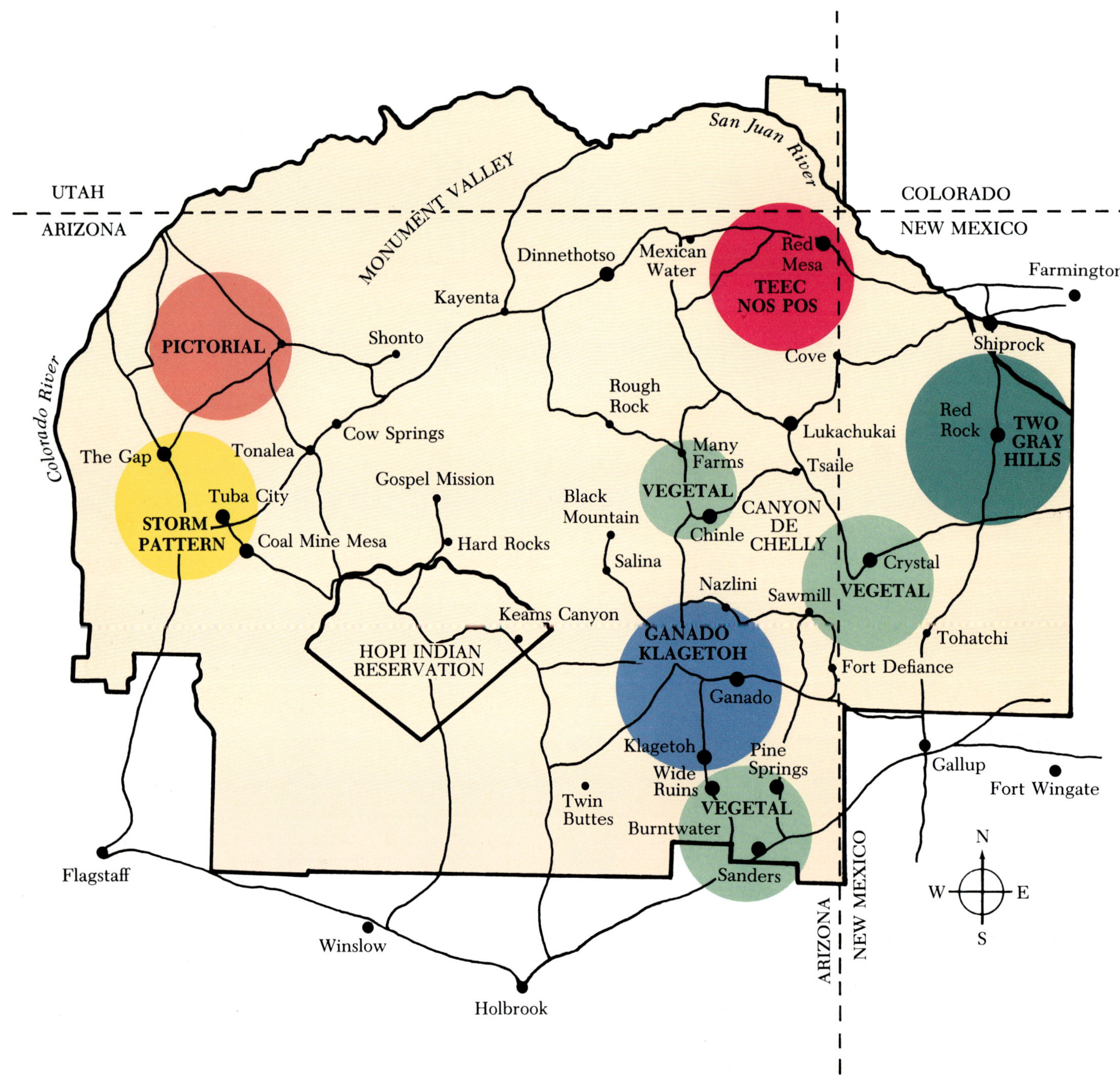

151. Regional rug style weaving areas.

6
CONTEMPORARY NAVAJO WEAVING

> In 1950 I used to visit the trading posts in a panel truck. It was a rare day of buying in which I did not fill that truck to capacity.
>
> Today, I drive a station wagon, and it takes several days of running around the reservation to get a load of rugs.
>
> "The old blankets are passing away," lamented Lorenzo Hubbell in 1902. To which, 60 years later, we can sadly add: "And so is Navajo weaving." May the gods of the Navajo, who walk in beauty, grant us 60 more years!
>
> Gilbert S. Maxwell, 1963[31]

During the 1920s Mary Cabot Wheelwright looked at her collection of Classic Navajo blankets and at the selection of Navajo rugs being sold at trading posts and at Fred Harvey outlets, and found the new rugs lacking. She felt (and other collectors of old Navajo blankets agreed) that contemporary weaving had reached a low point in the history of the art. Many early twentieth-century Navajo rugs were large (six by nine feet was a common size) and coarse: the pound rug had eclipsed the fancy blanket. The colors were harsh. The use of individual synthetic dye packets was almost universal on the reservation (with the exception of the area around Two Gray Hills), and the quality of the dyes and of the dyeing process was often poor. Designs were usually simplistic and lacking in originality and artistic integrity: bordered, endless repetitions of stereotypical geometric elements.

Preferring the old unbordered, banded designs of nineteenth-century weaving, Mrs. Wheelwright proposed to trader "Cozy" McSparron that he persuade the weavers from the Chinle area to return to these old patterns.[32] As models for the weavers, Mrs. Wheelwright copied the patterns of her own Classic weavings onto brown wrapping paper. No actual blankets were given to the weavers because none was available. By the 1920s most of the old blankets were already in the hands of collectors and museums.

In an attempt to reproduce the soft, rich colors characteristic of the Classic Period—the natural dyes used in Saxony yarns, the natural reds raveled from bayeta, the natural blue of indigo—Mrs. Wheelwright also turned to natural sources. Nineteenth-century Navajo weavers traditionally used natural yellow dyes from native plants. Why not expand the palette of natural colors?

With the help and encouragement of Mr. and Mrs. McSparron, Chinle weavers learned to produce soft shades of earth tones ranging from browns to pastels by experimenting with many previously untried native plants as their dye sources (fig. 152).

After a few years the range of colors that could be obtained from plants expanded dramatically. In 1940 a tribal project resulted in the distribution of a booklet listing "recipes" for making vegetal dyes in scores of colors, from light greenish-yellow (that is, "2 pounds actinea leptoclada [blossoms and leaves], ¼ cup raw alum, 1 pound yarn") to soft brown (that is, "2 pounds alder bark, 1 pound yarn").[33] A few years earlier the du Pont Company and the Diamond Dye Company introduced lines of synthetic dyes made to reproduce the

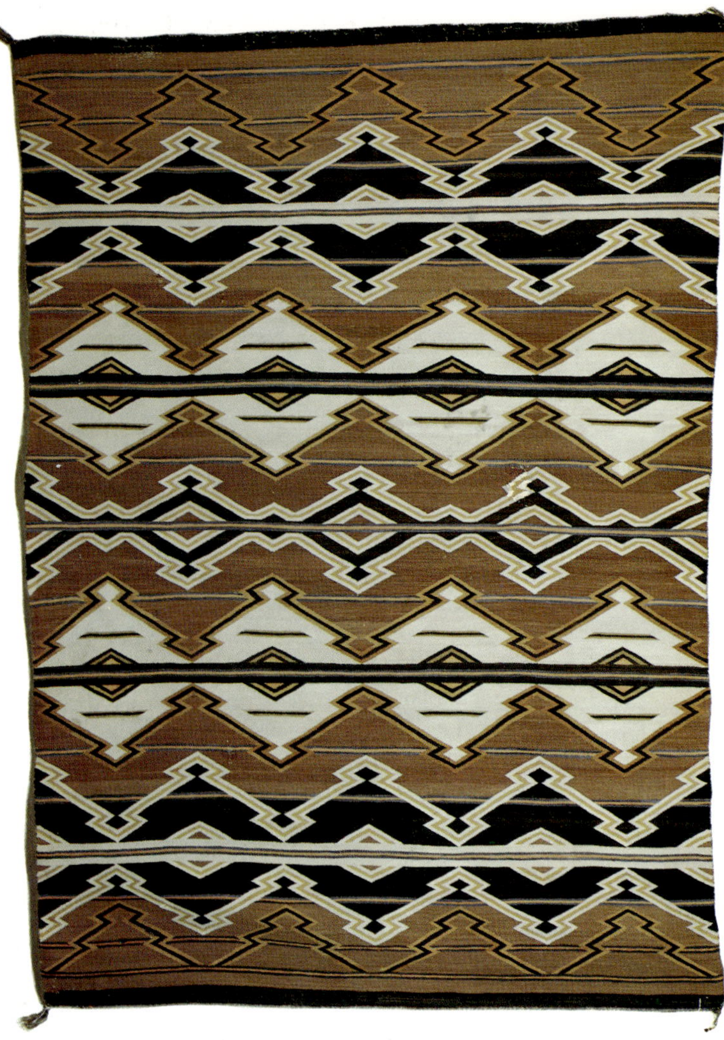

152. Chinle rug, c. 1935. 90″ x 68″. 9 warp/in.; 30 weft/in. Returning to the Late Classic Period style of unbordered banded patterns, the Chinle "revival" rugs ushered in a new era of non-traditional coloration. Woven of synthetic-dyed pale blue and pale orange, vegetal-dyed light brown and beige, and natural brown and white hand-spun wool yarns. (Collection of Maxwell Museum of Anthropology, University of New Mexico)

soft, subtle vegetal colors that had become popular at Chinle (fig. 153). For a brief period in the 1930s vegetal and synthetic dyes were in use together, but soon the use of only vegetal dyes became dominant.

Because the vegetal-dyed "revival" rugs were experimental when they appeared on the market, they were somewhat controversial at first. Some traders were perfectly satisfied with the Navajo rug market as it was. The new Chinle "revival" style did not so much resemble the Classic blanket style as it was a new style of weaving. Perhaps the addition of a new style would confuse the buying public. After all, all Anglos knew that Indian rugs were brightly colored. Would these new earth tones and sophisticated pastels "look Navajo"? Why, they didn't even have borders!

Because of the effort and the risk involved in producing the earliest Chinle "revival" rugs, Mrs. Wheelwright promised McSparron that she would buy the "mistakes" herself. But public acceptance of the rugs was almost immediate, and Mrs. Wheelwright's encouragement resulted in the birth of a new, high-quality regional style that would expand the market for Navajo rugs and would eventually become the dominant style of Navajo weaving. Spreading from Chinle, banded, borderless, vegetal-dyed rugs soon became the specialty of the weavers of the Wide Ruins, Crystal, and Pine Springs areas.

In 1938 the Wide Ruins trading post was purchased by Bill and Sally Lippincott, friends of McSparron who wished to emulate his success selling vegetal-dyed rugs. Using McSparron's methods, the Lippincotts educated the weavers in the Wide Ruins area in making and using vegetal dyes, and worked with the weavers to expand the range of colors available. The Lippincotts insisted on borderless, banded designs; within the design bands, Wide Ruins weavers incorporated chevrons, arrows,

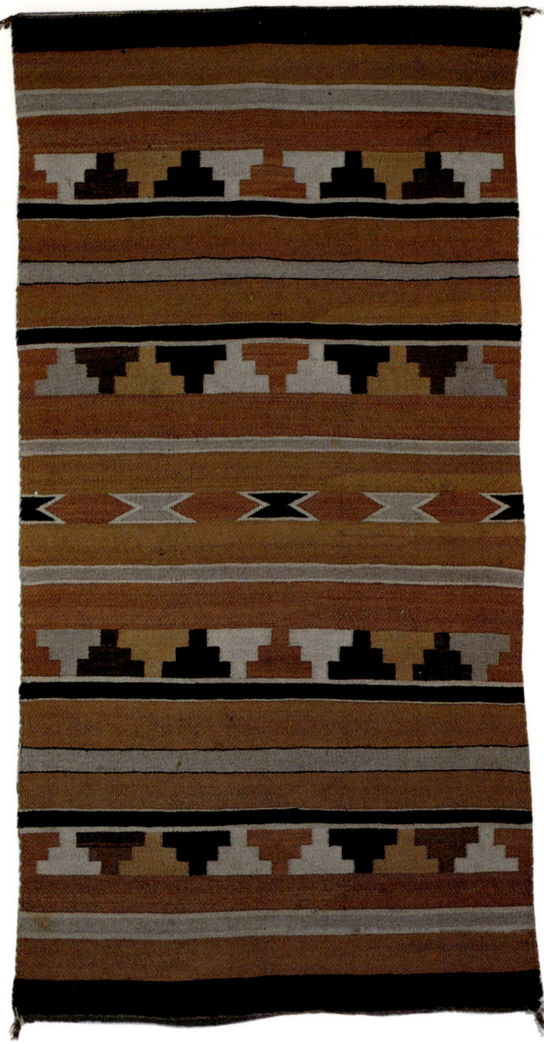

153. Chinle rug, c. 1935. 63″ x 32″. 7 warp/in.; 28 weft/in. Dyed with synthetic Diamond brand dyes or dyes developed by the du Pont Company, the dyes in this rug are the product of an attempt to save time and effort in the production of vegetal-style rugs. Woven of synthetic-dyed yellow, orange, tan, brown, and black and natural white hand-spun wool yarns. (Private collection)

squash blossom figures, and serrate diamonds in soft pastel shades of hand-spun pink, yellow, brown, coral, and green. Tight, even, fine weaving was encouraged, and finely woven vegetal-dyed tapestries became a specialty of the Wide Ruins region (see figs. 163 and 167–170).

The Lippincotts' success at Wide Ruins was not wasted on the trader and the weavers at nearby Pine Springs. A rug style similar to the Wide Ruins style was developed, but because of the differences in local flora, Pine Springs rugs tended to be more green in color than brown and pink.

The J. B. Moore days of glory had been over at Crystal for decades when Don Jensen bought the old post and started developing and promoting a "new" Crystal rug. Borderless, banded, and finely woven from soft, subtle earth and pastel vegetal colors, the Crystal rug is a direct descendant of the Chinle/Wide Ruins rugs. Wavy lines, created by alternating weft colors every few wefts, and the frequent use of a hook design element reminiscent of J. B. Moore's rugs help differentiate Crystals from other vegetal-dyed styles (figs. 155 and 171–174).

The culmination of the vegetal-dye movement was the invention of the Burntwater style, which was developed south of Pine Springs in the 1970s. Combining pastel and earth-tone vegetal dyes for the first time with the ornate bordered designs made popular by weavers and traders from Ganado and Two Gray Hills, the Burntwater rug has become a leading contemporary style of Navajo weaving. Weavers from all parts of the reservation have abandoned other regional styles to begin weaving the quick-selling Burntwaters.

Today, Burntwater weavings are characterized by their high quality. Many are finely woven tapestries displaying complex designs within multiple borders, with some extraordinary examples executed in more than twenty shades of vegetal color (see figs. 156 and 175–181).

Although the vegetal styles would come to predominate, the earlier regional styles still continued to be woven and sold from the 1920s through the 1980s. Over the years, these familiar styles were experimented with and perfected, and the best contemporary regional weavings are the finest, both technically and artistically, to be woven during the rug era.

Ganado rugs and tapestries continue to be very popular with collectors. With minor variations in color and pattern, this style has also become associated with the trading posts at Klagetoh and Piñon. But the style is not limited to these areas. Today, weavers from many parts of the reservation weave in the Ganado style. In fact, geographical diffusion is one of the hallmarks of the contemporary era. Due to increased awareness brought about mainly through increased mobility and improved communications, weavers are very aware of what is being made and sold. A contemporary weaver from any area of the reservation will most likely have at least two or three different regional styles in her repertoire.

Although the contemporary Ganado rug is recognizable as a descendant of the Hubbell original, the newer rugs tend toward more complex patterns, which approach the complexity of weavings from Two Gray Hills and Teec Nos Pos regions. The Hubbell color scheme still survives; like their predecessors, contemporary Ganado rugs come in combinations of deep Ganado red, overdyed black, and natural carded gray, white, and brown (see figs. 157 and 182–185). The trend at

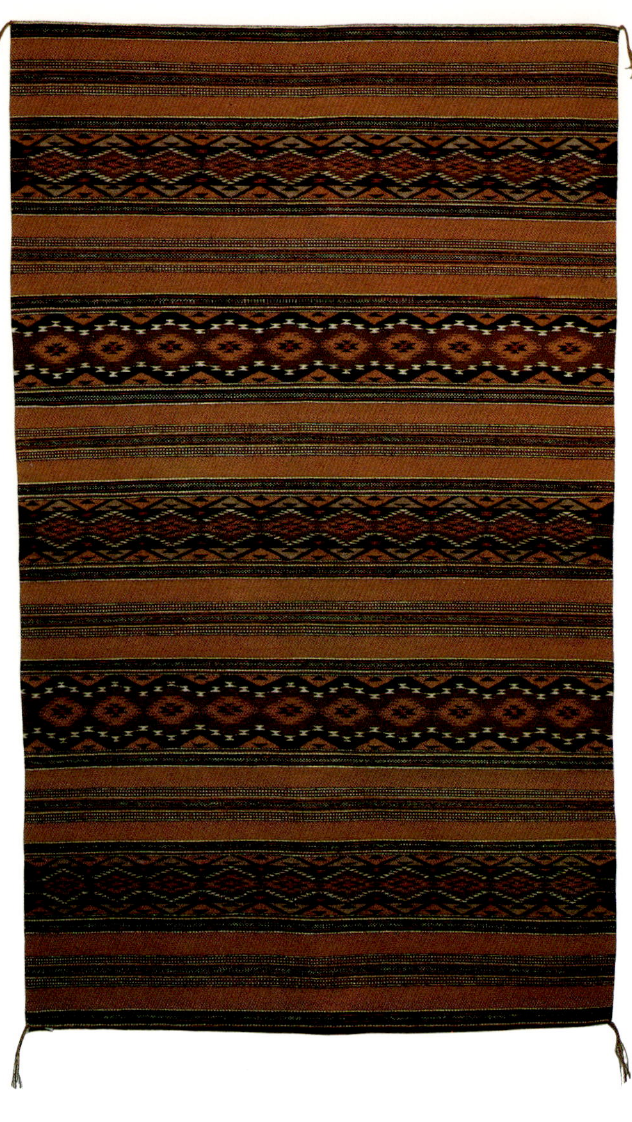

154. Wide Ruins rug, contemporary, by Annie Tsosie. 57″ x 36″. 12 warp/in.; 40 weft/in. The preference for finely detailed designs within narrow bands is characteristic of the Wide Ruins style. Woven of vegetal-dyed shades of yellow and brown and natural white hand-spun wool yarns. (Private collection)

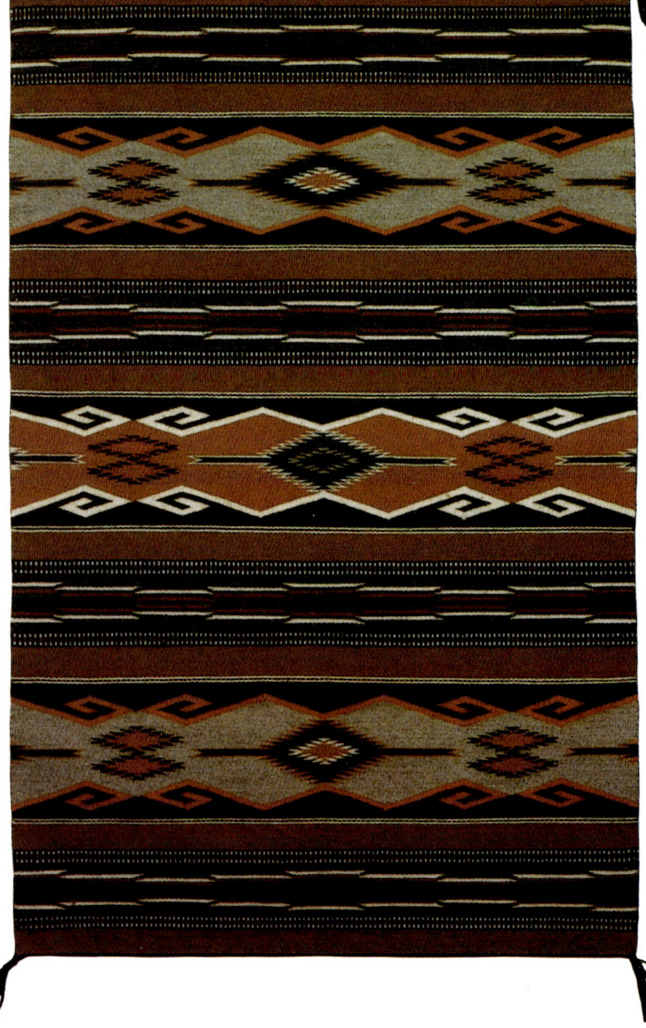

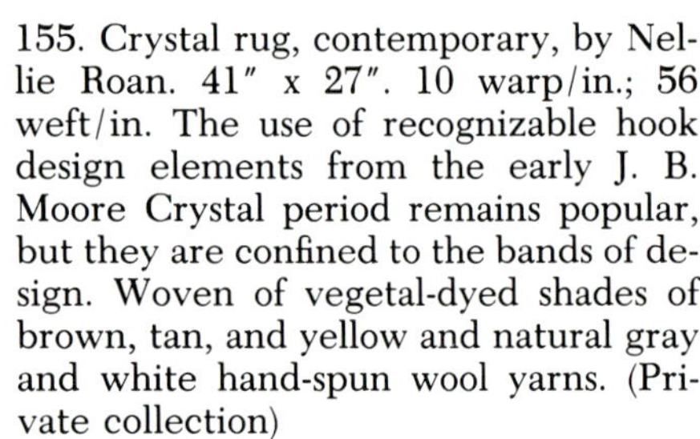

155. Crystal rug, contemporary, by Nellie Roan. 41″ x 27″. 10 warp/in.; 56 weft/in. The use of recognizable hook design elements from the early J. B. Moore Crystal period remains popular, but they are confined to the bands of design. Woven of vegetal-dyed shades of brown, tan, and yellow and natural gray and white hand-spun wool yarns. (Private collection)

156. Burntwater rug, contemporary, by Virginia Yazzie. 59″ x 37″. 10 warp/in.; 56 weft/in. Twelve different vegetal dyes were used to dye the yarn in this typical Burntwater-style rug. Woven of vegetal-dyed shades of beige, yellow, pink, tan, and green, synthetic-dyed blue, and natural white hand-spun wool yarns. (Private collection)

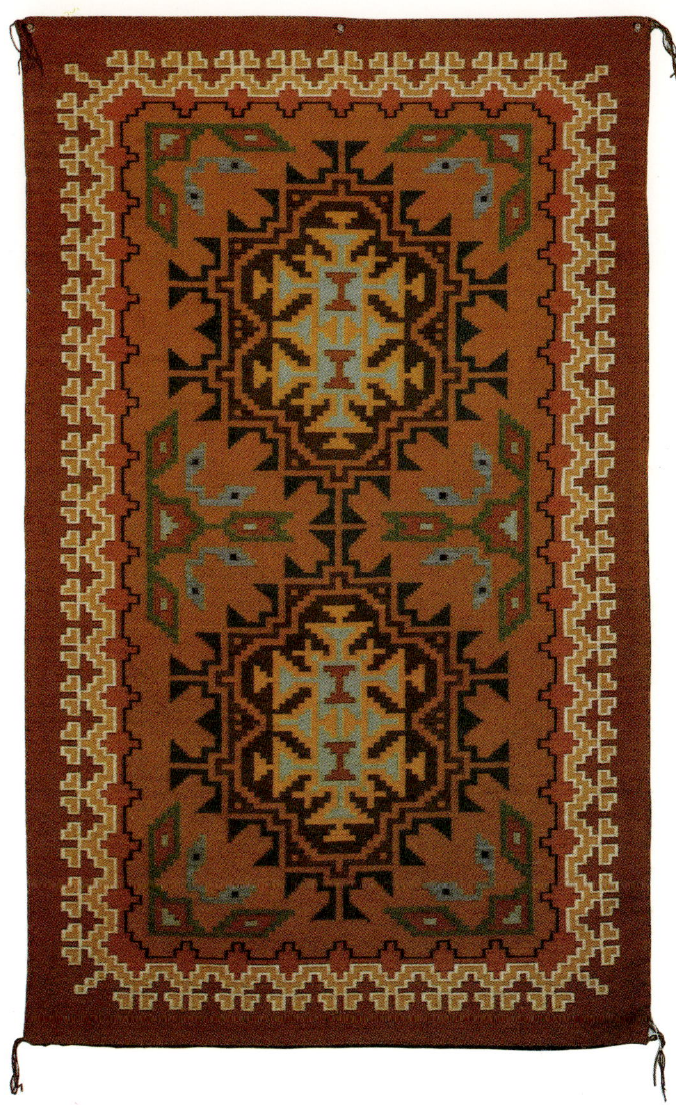

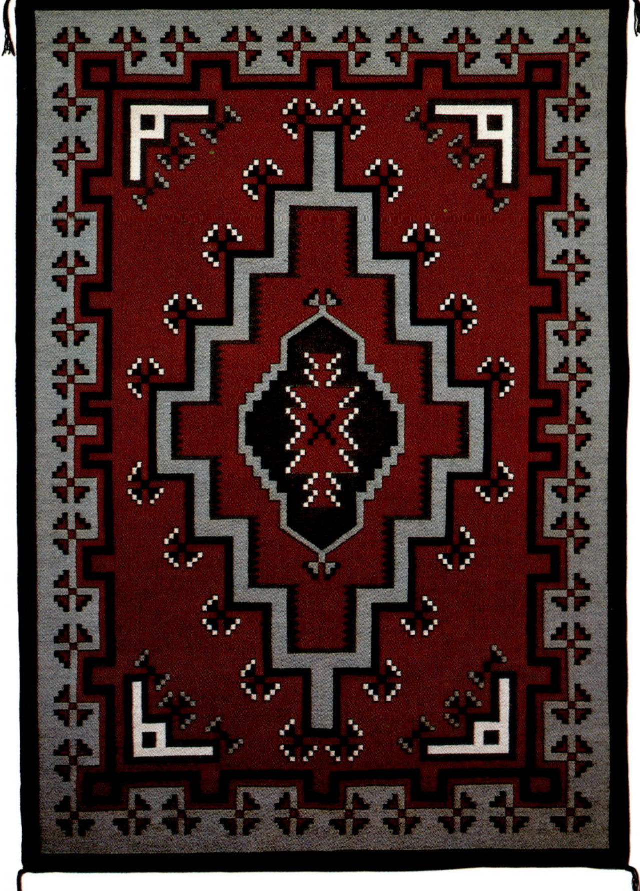

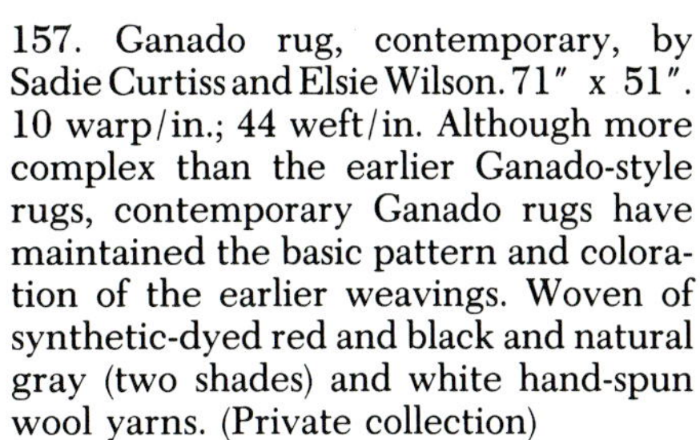

157. Ganado rug, contemporary, by Sadie Curtiss and Elsie Wilson. 71″ x 51″. 10 warp/in.; 44 weft/in. Although more complex than the earlier Ganado-style rugs, contemporary Ganado rugs have maintained the basic pattern and coloration of the earlier weavings. Woven of synthetic-dyed red and black and natural gray (two shades) and white hand-spun wool yarns. (Private collection)

Ganado, as in other parts of the reservation, is toward weaving tapestries rather than rugs. Too fine to be walked on, these tapestries are clearly intended to be hung on a wall (figs. 158, 181, 184, 188, 195, and 197).

By 1925, the distinctive Two Gray Hills style that was born at J. B. Moore's Crystal Trading Post had become indelibly linked with the trading posts at Two Gray Hills and Toadlena, New Mexico. Although Two Gray Hills designs remained fairly constant through the years, no other regional weaving style achieved such an improvement in technical quality. Weavers of this region were encouraged to spin their yarn finer and finer and to make their weaving tighter and tighter. Prize-winning Two Gray Hills weaver Daisy Taugelchee and others have produced tapestry weaves of more than one hundred weft stitches per linear inch. Like the other regional styles, Two Gray Hills–style weavings are now made in all areas of the reservation with many of the best ones still the product of the older more experienced Two Gray Hills weavers (figs. 159 and 186–189).

The origin of the Teec Nos Pos style is mysterious. H. B. Noel, the trader at the Teec Nos Pos trading post, took no credit for the development of the ornate style, insisting that the inspiration came from a missionary. J. B. Moore's ornate Crystal rugs seem to have influenced the development of the Teec Nos Pos designs, and it has been suggested that the local weavers developed the style themselves, using Moore's rugs as models. Similar in appearance to Oriental rugs, these bordered rugs were usually woven in a combination of synthetic- and vegetal-dyed hand-spun yarns, natural hand-spun yarns, and commercial yarn. By 1930 the Teec Nos Pos outline style was well established as a distinct regional style (figs. 160 and 190–192).

Weavers from the area surrounding the Red Mesa trading post, fifteen miles west of Teec Nos Pos, also produced a long-enduring and distinctive style of their own. Red Mesa weavings are characterized by bright synthetic-colored hand-spun or commercial yarns and serrated patterns that resemble nineteenth-century "eyedazzler" weavings (see fig. 190).

158. Three "tapestry"-weave rugs, contemporary, by *(left to right)* Priscilla Taugelchee, Ruby Manuelito, and Priscilla Taugelchee. 29″ x 18″, 21″ x 24″, 29″ x 17″. 16–18 warp/in.; 80–100 weft/in. Today virtually every regional style of weaving is produced in the tapestry weave, with many weavers producing more than one style. (Private collection)

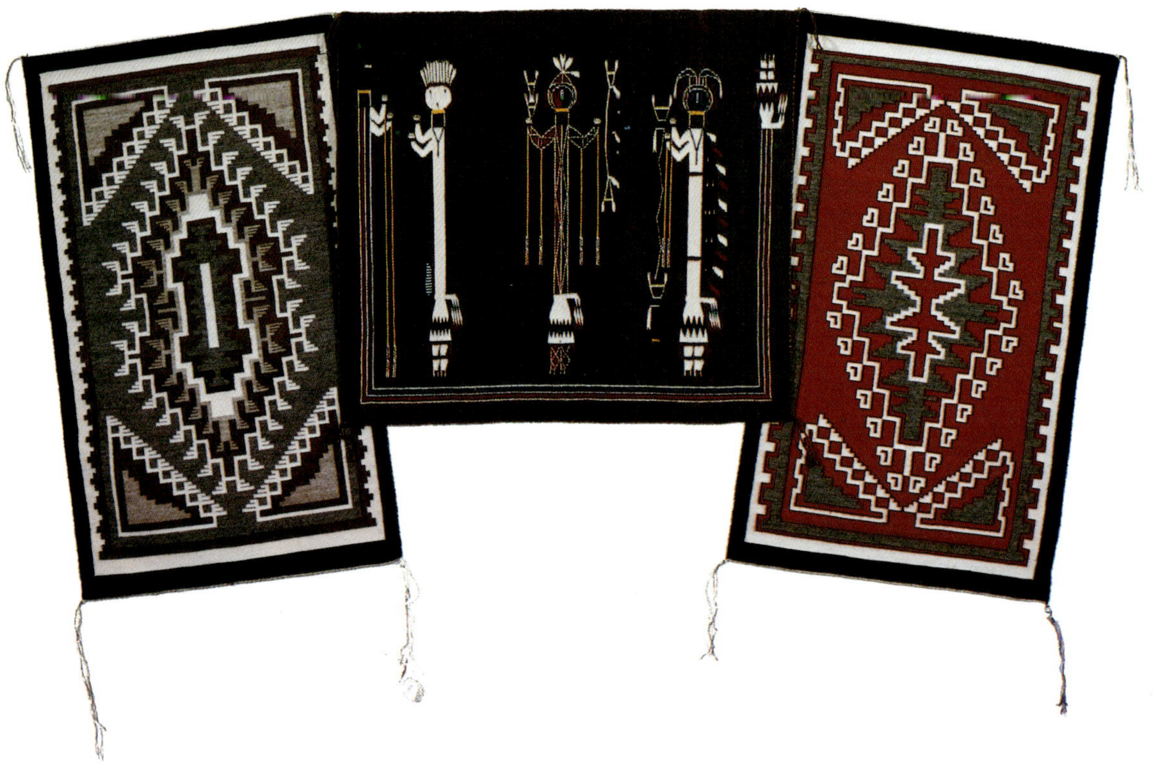

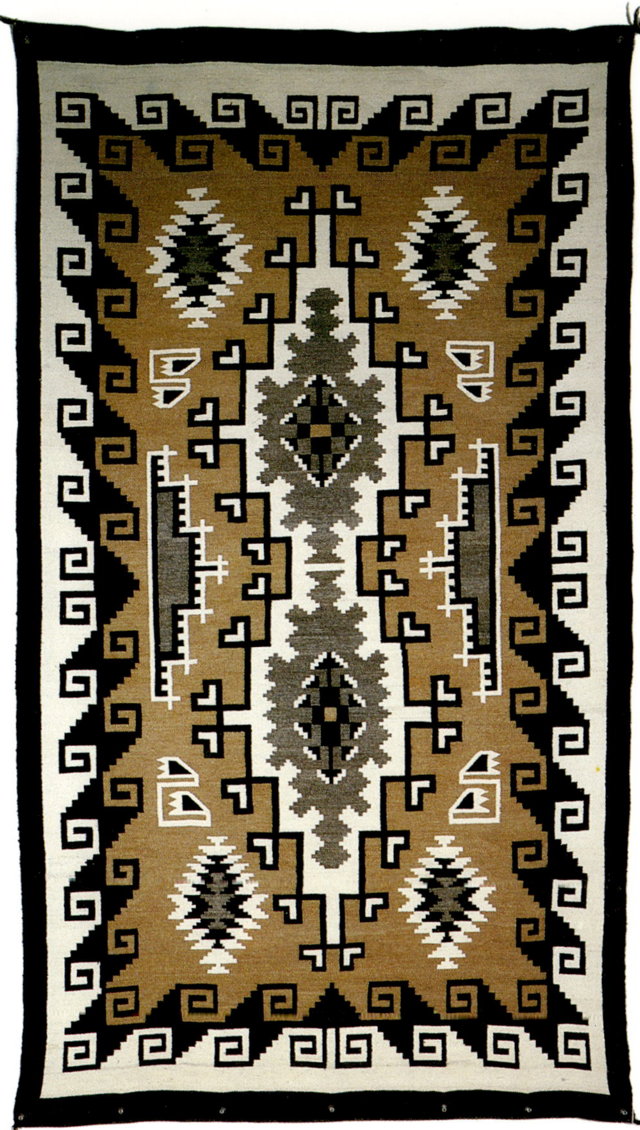

159. Two Gray Hills tapestry, c. 1960. 68″ x 40″. 15 warp/in.; 75 weft/in. One of the earlier Two Gray Hills tapestries produced, this weaving approaches, in fineness of weave, the finest Classic Period blankets. Woven of natural brown and white and overdyed black hand-spun wool yarns. (Private collection)

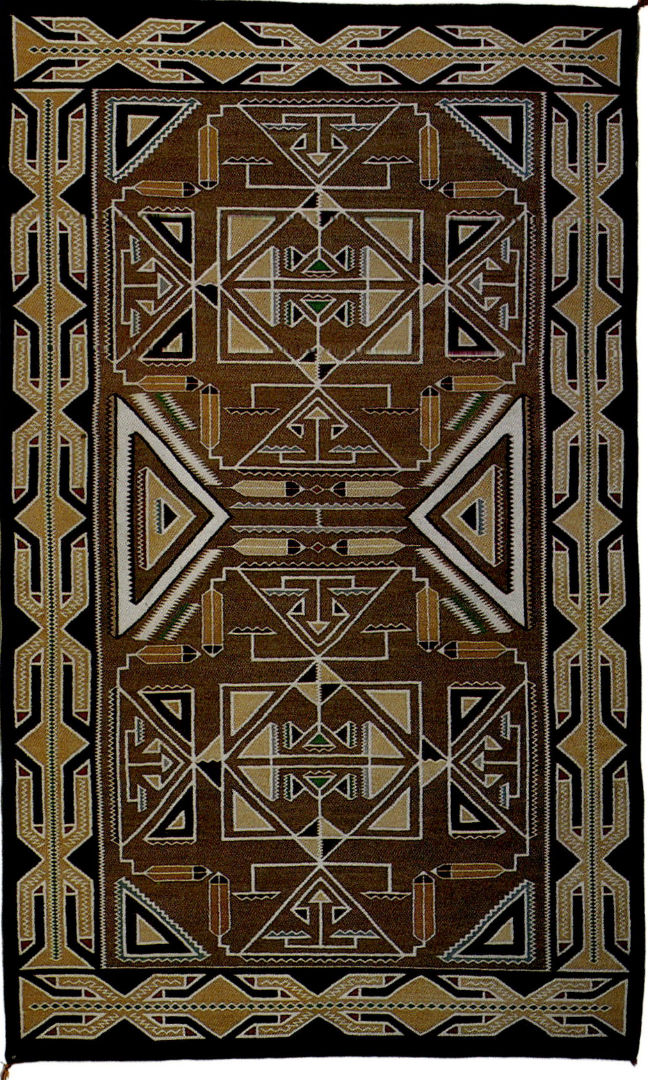

160. Teec Nos Pos rug, c. 1940. 107″ x 66″. 8 warp/in.; 32 weft/in. Almost schematic in appearance, this Teec Nos Pos rug has thin white lines that carve up the background color into a virtually undecipherable pattern. Woven of four-ply commercial synthetic-dyed red, green, pale blue, and black, vegetal-dyed tan, and natural gray and white hand-spun wool yarns. (Private collection)

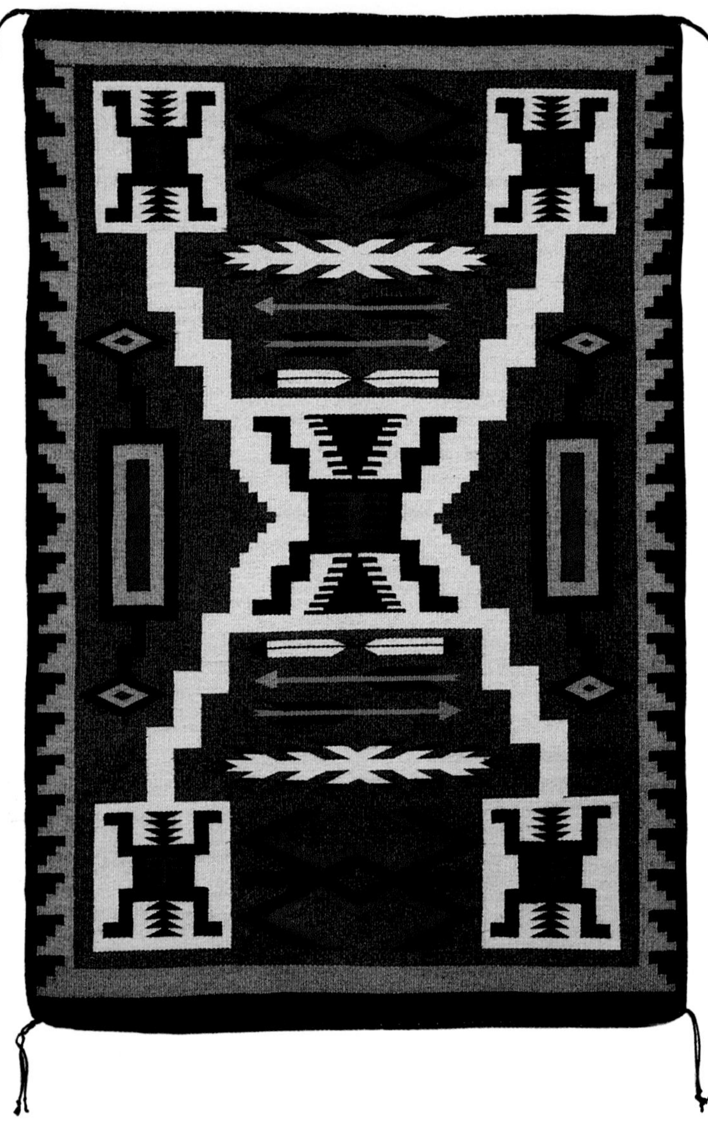

161. Storm pattern rug, contemporary, by Betty Russell. 48" x 33". 9 warp/in.; 32 weft/in. Were it not for the yarns used and the precision of the design execution, this rug could easily be mistaken for a much earlier storm pattern rug. Woven of synthetic-dyed red, tan, and black and natural gray (two shades) and white processed wool yarns. (Private collection)

The storm pattern rug, which would become associated with the western reservation area, is another style whose origins have been the subject of debate for decades. Some say that the style is sacred: that the central rectangle represents the Navajo hogan and the rectangles in each corner represent the four sacred mountains of Navajo legend. The connecting lines between the central rectangle and the corner rectangles are said to be lightning bolts carrying blessings between the mountains and the hogan. Other interpreters of Navajo design find this explanation fanciful; they believe the storm pattern design was influenced by the designs on flour sacks found on the trading post shelves. J. B. Moore featured a storm pattern rug in his 1911 catalogue, and some believe that the design was Moore's own. Almost certainly, the symbolism credited to the storm pattern rug is a product of imaginative Anglo marketing (see figs. 161, 193, 194, and 209). Storm pattern rugs are generally woven from natural wool colors and synthetic-dyed red hand-spun yarns.

Outside of the development of the Burntwater and other vegetal-dyed styles, probably the most interesting developments in Navajo weaving have been in the Yei and pictorial styles. Will Evans, the trader at Shiprock from 1912 to 1948, is believed to have developed the Yei-style rug in the 1920s, once the stigma of this type of weaving had been lifted by the example of Hosteen Klah and his nieces. The first Yei rugs were often almost square in shape, with a single, front-facing Yei (Holy Person) figure woven in bright, synthetic colors on a gray background. Shortly thereafter, weavers from the Shiprock area replaced the single-figure Yei with a line of slender, brightly colored Yei figures on a white or light field. The figures are often depicted wearing feathers and carrying cornstalks. A slender Rainbow Goddess figure partially encloses the line of Yeis (figs. 162 and 196).

Yeibechai rugs, also developed at Shiprock, are similar to Yeis, but the figures depicted are of Navajos impersonating the Yei in the ceremonial dance not of the Yei, or Holy People, themselves. These dancers are usually depicted in profile (figs. 195 and 197). Today, both the Yei and Yeibechai styles are often woven entirely from commercial yarns.

A second style of Yei rugs was developed in the 1930s in the region around the Lukachukai, Upper Greasewood, and Round Rock trading posts. Woven primarily from hand-spun yarns, these generally coarser, larger than Shiprock-style rugs usually have a red, gray/brown, or black field and a simple, banded border. The figures themselves tend to be simpler and less stylized than the figures found on Shiprock Yeis. The Yeibechai style is also produced in this region.

Because of increased communication on the reservation, more contemporary weavers are able to produce more accurate sandpainting textiles than was possible for weavers in the past. The weavers of the 1920s and 1930s who dared to break with the old ways and weave one of the sacred designs had to rely on memory and description. Today, outstanding weavers are exposed to permanent versions of these designs, usually in the form of illustrations from books or from photographs (see figs. 163, 198, and 199).

This increased ability to communicate, and the changes in Navajo reservation life in the last hundred years, also had a significant effect on the weavers of pictorial rugs. The first documented use of pictorial design is found in a sarape collected in 1864 that had belonged to Chief White Antelope, an Indian who died in battle wearing the sarape. Two small, bird designs

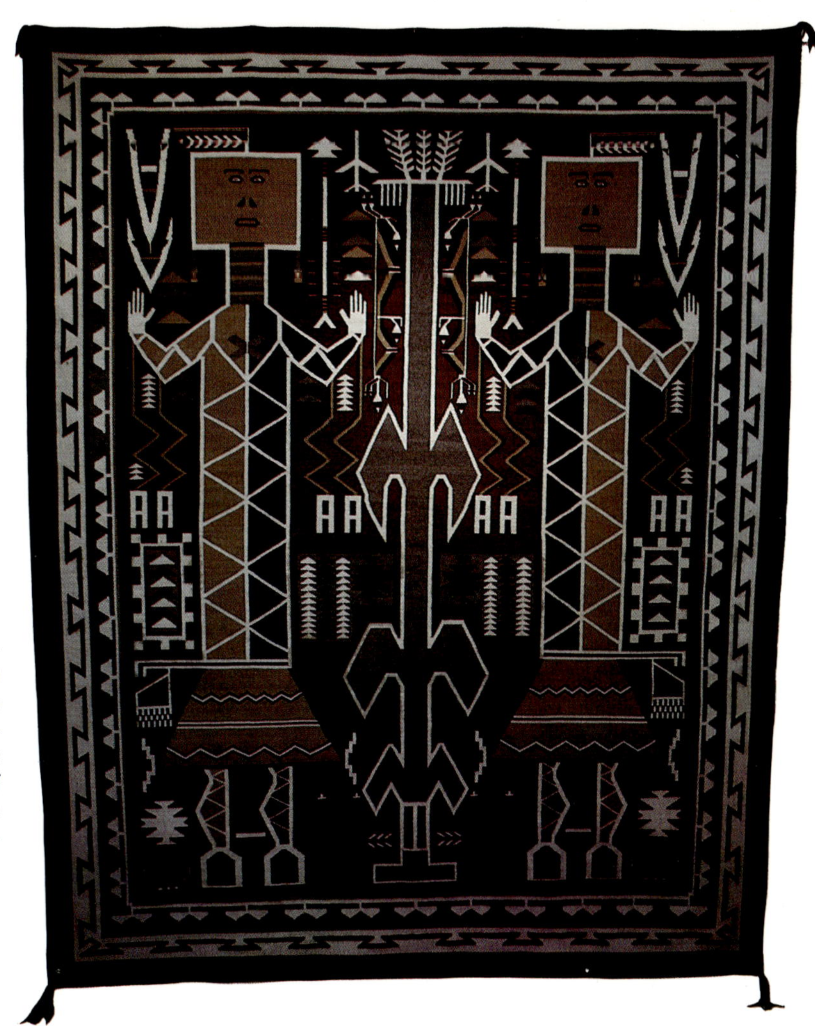

162. Pictorial rug, c. 1950, by Mary Charlie. 98″ x 80″. 12 warp/in.; 50 weft/in. Woven in the Two Gray Hills region, this exceptionally large and well-illustrated Yei-style pictorial rug took more than two years to weave. Woven of natural shades of brown, beige, and white hand-spun wool yarns. (Private collection)

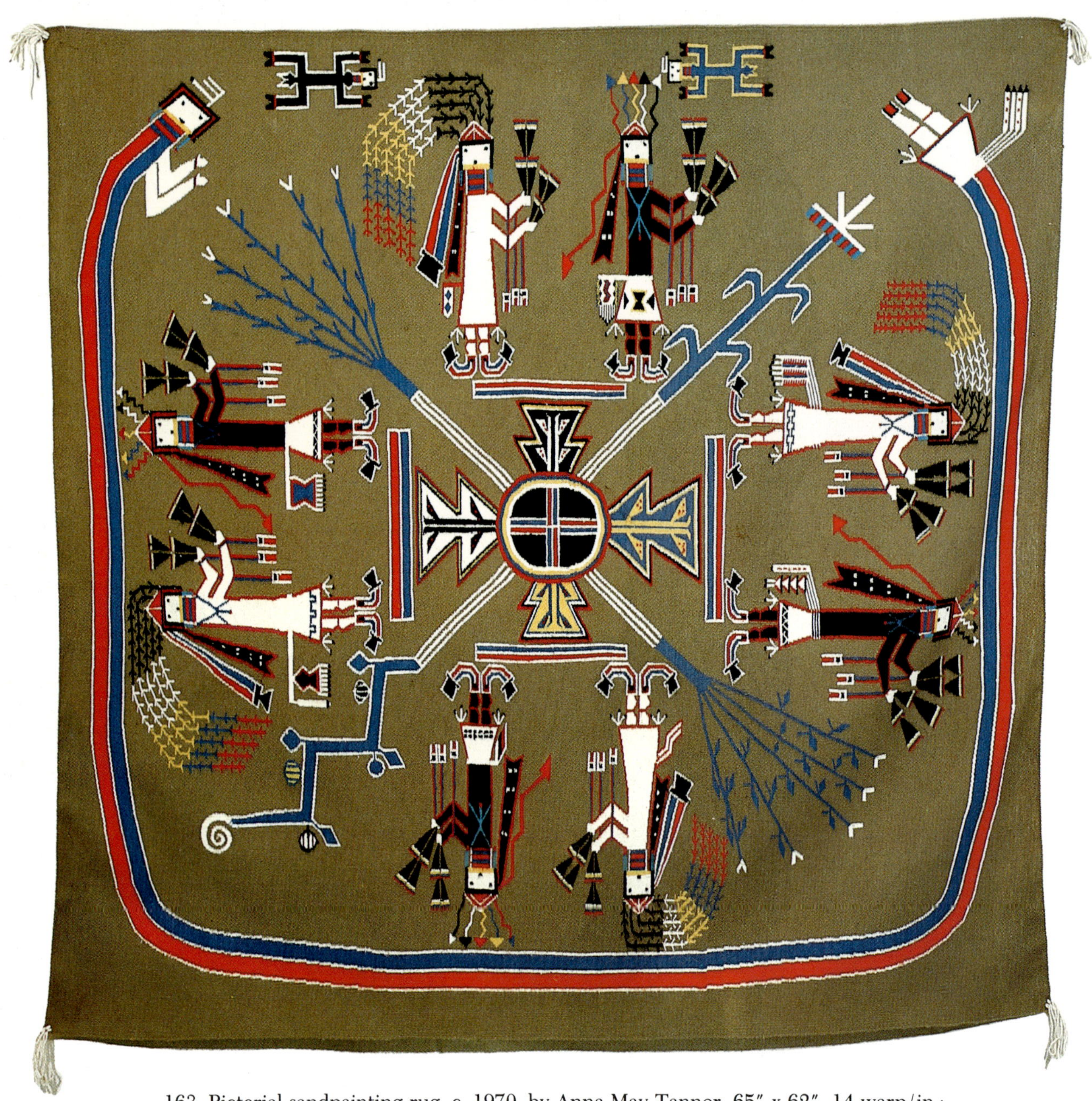

163. Pictorial sandpainting rug, c. 1970, by Anna May Tanner. 65″ x 62″. 14 warp/in.; 56 weft/in. Woven in the Red Rock region, this brightly colored rug is of the Navajo Water Chant. Woven of synthetic-dyed red, yellow, blue (2 shades), and black and natural white hand-spun wool yarns. (Collection of Maxwell Museum of Anthropology, University of New Mexico)

164. Contemporary off-reservation Indian shop/gallery, exterior. A typical off-reservation retail gallery outlet for quality Indian goods. (Photograph courtesy Garland's Navajo Rugs, Sedona, Arizona)

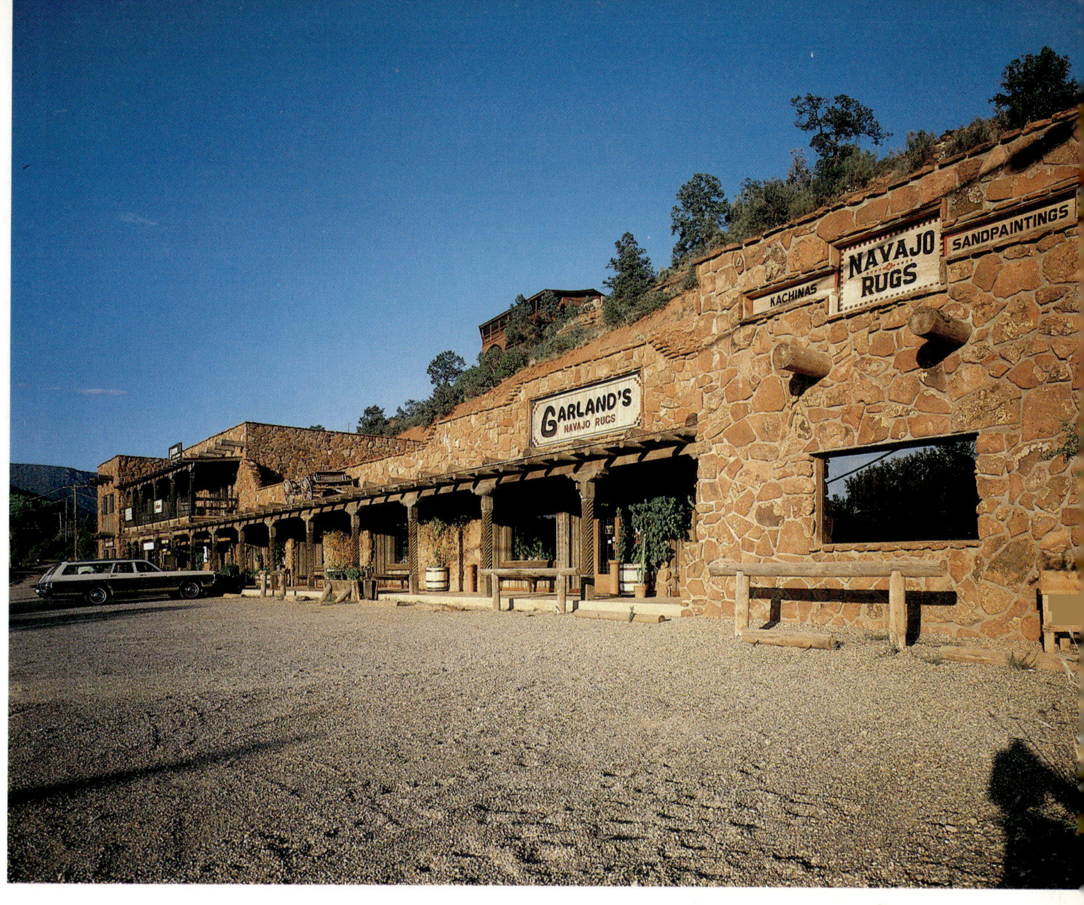

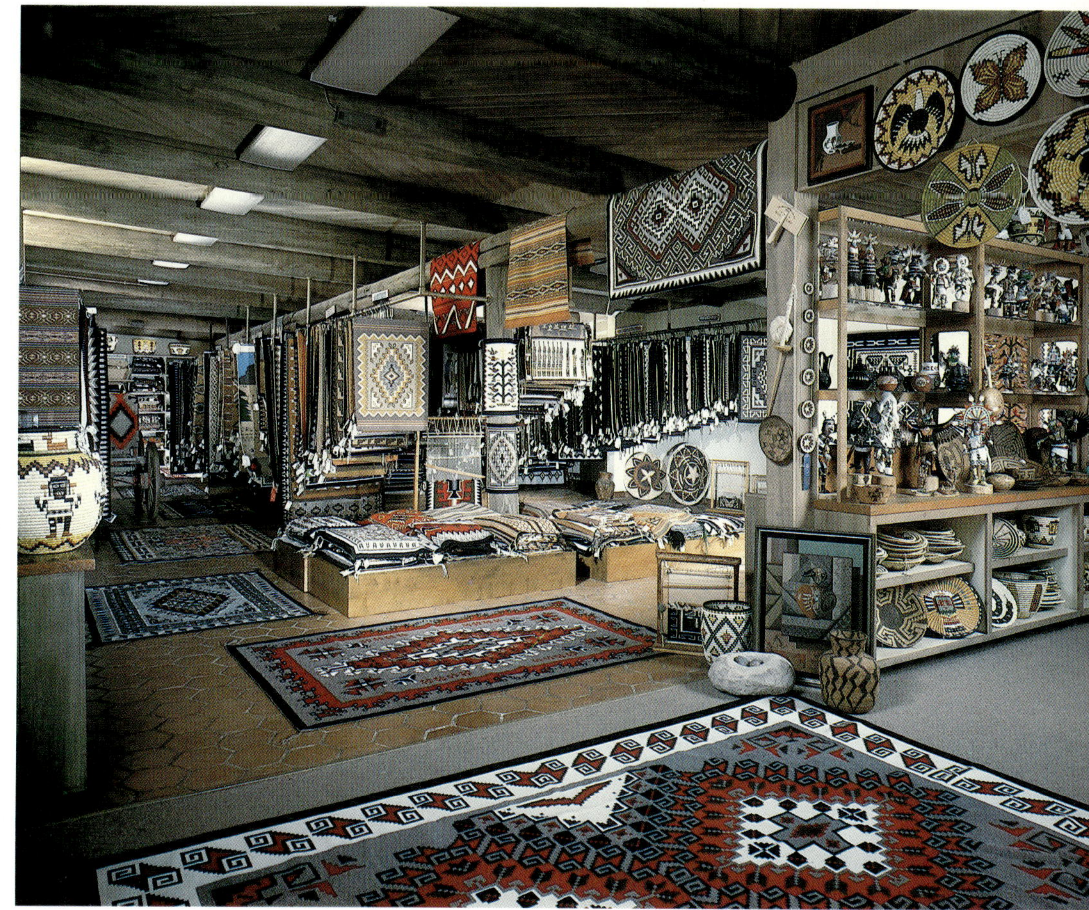

165. Contemporary off-reservation Indian shop/gallery, interior. Amid a profusion of new and old baskets, kachinas, pottery, and rugs Navajo rugs are by far the most popular Indian-made decorative item displayed. (Photograph courtesy Garland's Navajo Rugs, Sedona, Arizona)

are incorporated into what is otherwise a Late Classic sarape pattern. With the arrival of the railroad in the 1880s many weavers began to depict railroad tracks and trains on their textiles, creating a whole new style of representational weaving that was usually executed in synthetic-dyed hand-spun and Germantown yarns (see fig. 129). Pictorials displaying the Navajo life-style with farm animals, landscapes, and depictions of powwows and Squaw Dances have become popular in the last decade (fig. 202). Because of the naïve quality of these images, pictorial weavings are reminiscent of American folk paintings.

The changes in Navajo life are reflected in pictorial weavings. By the 1950s pickup trucks, airplanes, helicopters, and school buses started to appear on pictorial rugs. In the mid-1960s a weaver named Suzy Black made the transition from literal pictorials to pictorials inspired by her own imagination. Instead of using hogans, horses, mesas, and sheep, Black decorated her weavings with butterflies, exotic birds, lions, and tigers. The freedom to explore new motifs is a radical departure for Navajo weavers, and many devoted enthusiasts of contemporary Navajo weaving hope to see this trend developed further (see fig. 201).

For many generations, weaving has been an integral part of the fabric of Navajo life. Monetary rewards are only a small part of the Navajo woman's desire to weave. Weaving is a unifying force, an expression of personal pride and cultural identity, a spiritual experience, a tradition. Because of the increase in education and mobility on the reservation, many alternative sources of income have become available to Navajo women. Although the prices of quality Navajo rugs and tapestries have increased dramatically in the last two decades, it is estimated that Navajo weavers earned only $2 an hour in 1980. Only the very best weavers, whose work has increased in value by as much as 500 percent in the last ten years, earn $30,000 or more a year at the loom. Many of these top weavers are older women, and as they stop weaving, they are not being replaced by younger weavers who are capable of or have the desire to produce textiles of equal quality.

Total weaving production is on the increase, however, because of the introduction of tribally sponsored classroom instruction, tribal help in acquiring weaving materials, and Navajo-run retail outlets and auctions. There are indications that some of the members of the younger generation of weavers will take the time and effort to improve the quality of their weaving in the years ahead in order to carry on the proud Navajo tradition.

During the 1970s and 1980s Navajo weavers have begun to express their individuality as never before. Recognition for individual weavers has become commonplace as these artists travel hundreds of miles to sell their weavings to galleries in Santa Fe, New Mexico, or Scottsdale and Sedona, Arizona, rather than to the nearest trading post. A dealer used to refer to weavings by their regional style. Today dealers and collectors alike refer to an outstanding contemporary weaving as a "Sadie Curtiss," a "Daisy Taugelchee," or an "Agnes Smith." Some weavers have become so outstanding that their work is often sold before it is woven.

Increased mobility, the change from a barter system to a cash economy, and the establishment of tribally operated reservation stores have all led to the decline of the old trading-post system. One third of the trading posts have closed in the last ten years, and the Navajo tribe renegotiated the remaining trading post leases in 1983. Although some of the long-established family-owned trading posts will probably remain open for some time to come, the profitability of such posts appears to be diminishing.

One of the most significant trends in contemporary Navajo weaving is the use of processed yarn. This yarn is made from bulk Navajo wool that is sent to a commercial plant where it is cleaned, spun, and sometimes dyed. Processed wool and commercial yarns have been used by Navajo weavers for more than a century, but in the 1980s they have become the dominant yarns, replacing hand-spun yarns in more than 80 percent of the top-quality weavings submitted for judging in both the 1983 Gallup Intertribal Ceremonial and the 1983 Navajo Craftsman Show sponsored by the Museum of Northern Arizona, in Flagstaff.

Using processed or commercial yarn saves as much as 50 percent of the time required to produce a Navajo weaving from sheep to loom to the finished product. The time saved can be put into actual weaving, thus increasing the number of textiles a weaver can produce and also increasing her income. Many dealers and collectors will not buy weavings made with processed or commercial yarns, and are particularly fussy when it comes to the Burntwater and other vegetal-dyed styles. Weavings made from processed or commercial yarns are valid Navajo weavings, but should be clearly marked as to type of yarns used. Accordingly, the prices of these weavings should reflect the nature of the materials used. Most dealers and collectors believe that the higher prices commanded by weavers who do produce an entirely handmade textile will encourage younger weavers to take their place in the Navajo textile tradition, creating rugs and tapestries with all the beauty, technical quality, and character that make Navajo weaving a great art.

166. Chinle rug, contemporary, by Marie Shirley. 62″ x 44″. 9 warp/in.; 40 weft/in. The placement of two design bands next to each other creates a larger than normal pattern for this style of rug. Woven of vegetal-dyed shades of yellow and brown and natural gray and white hand-spun wool yarns. (Private collection)

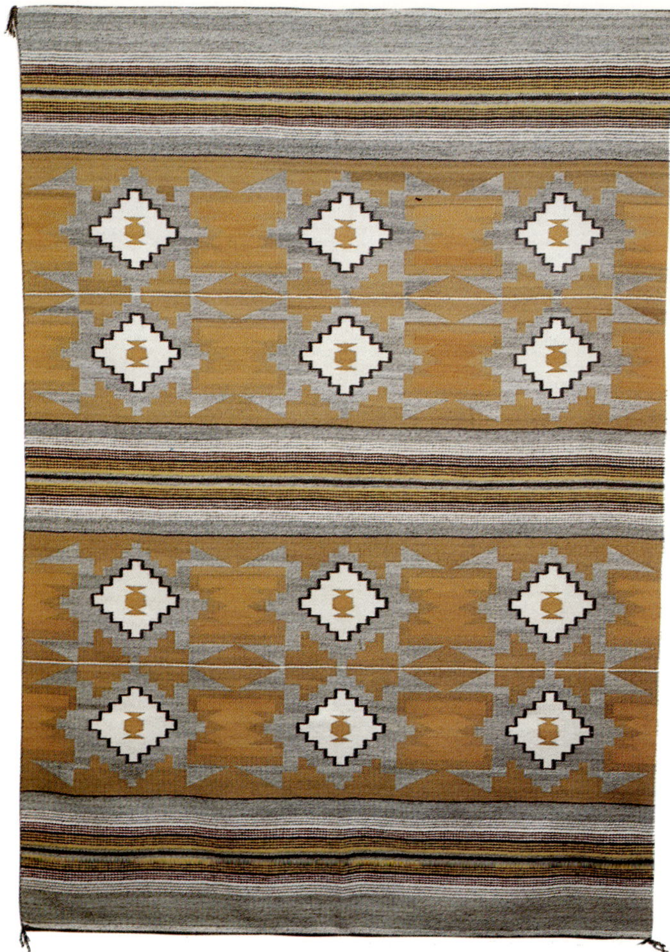

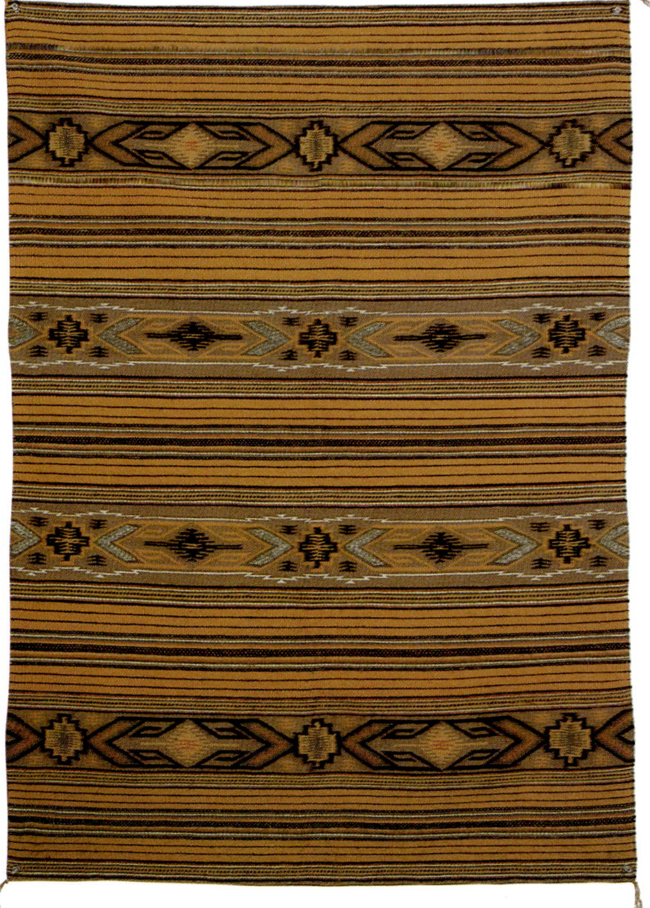

167. Wide Ruins rug, contemporary, by Agnes Smith. 48″ x 35″. 10 warp/in.; 36 weft/in. Vegetal-pattern rugs, like this one, have proven to be extremely popular for use in contemporary interiors. Woven of vegetal-dyed shades of brown, green, yellow, and rose and natural white hand-spun wool yarns. (Private collection)

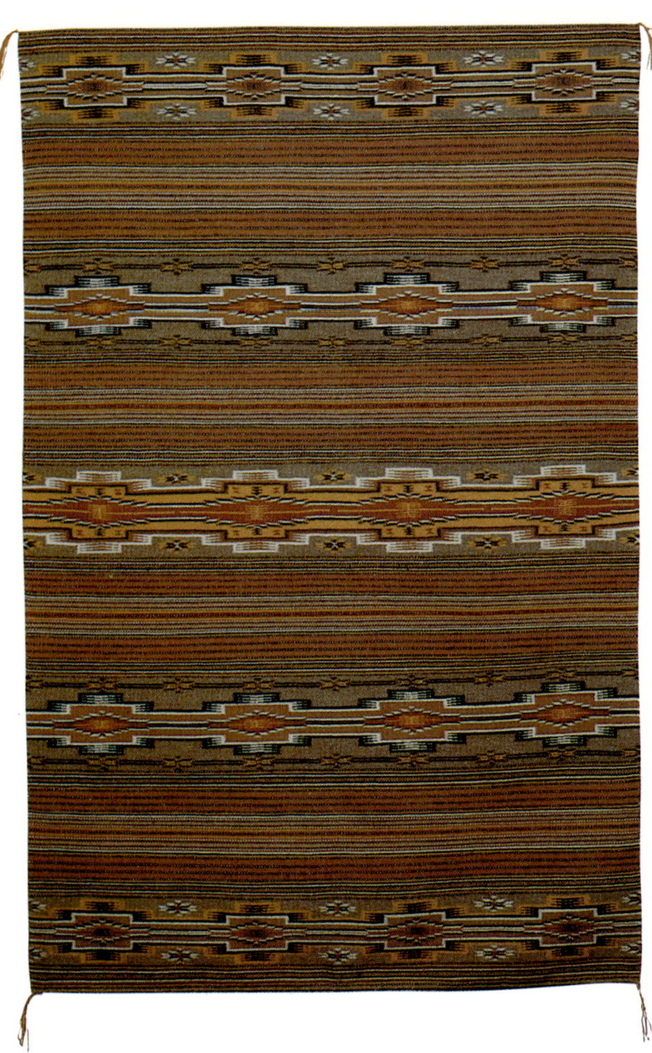

168. Wide Ruins rug, contemporary, by Agnes Smith. 55″ x 36″. 10 warp/in.; 48 weft/in. Each vegetal-style rug weaver possesses a number of dye recipes that she regards as her own and will not readily share with other weavers. Woven of vegetal-dyed shades of brown, tan, yellow, and green and natural white hand-spun wool yarns. (Private collection)

169. Wide Ruins rug, contemporary, by Ellen Smith. 49″ x 35″. 11 warp/in.; 48 weft/in. Wide Ruins rugs are generally considered to be the finest woven of the vegetal-dyed rugs. Today, Ellen Smith and her three sisters are among the top weavers of Wide Ruins rugs. Woven of vegetal-dyed shades of brown and yellow and natural gray and white hand-spun wool yarns. (Private collection)

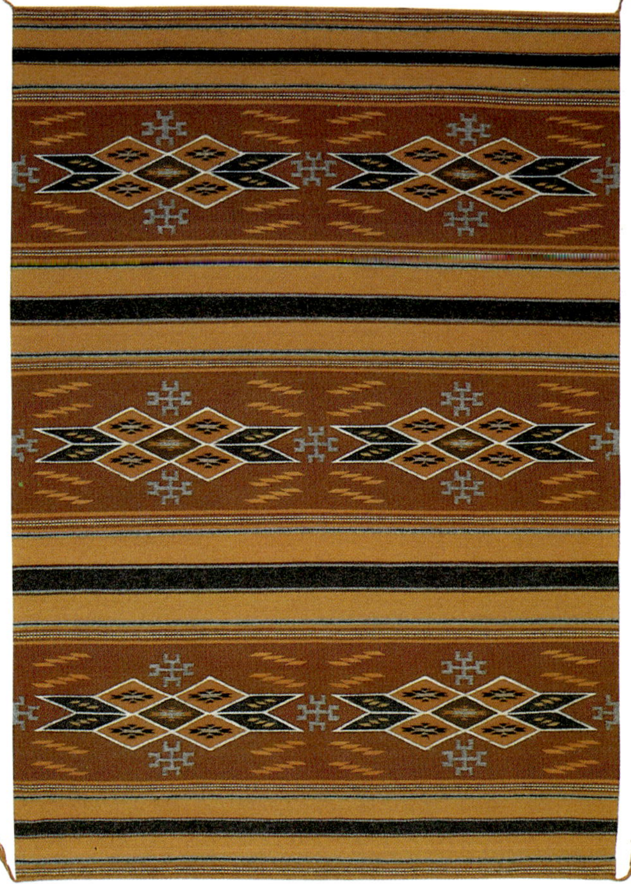

170. Wide Ruins rug, contemporary, by Ellen Smith. 49″ x 39″. 13 warp/in.; 52 weft/in. The best contemporary Navajo weavers are producing rugs that, as personal expressions of the individual weaver's art, transcend the regional styles. Woven of vegetal-dyed shades of orange, brown, and yellow and natural gray and white hand-spun wool yarns. (Private collection)

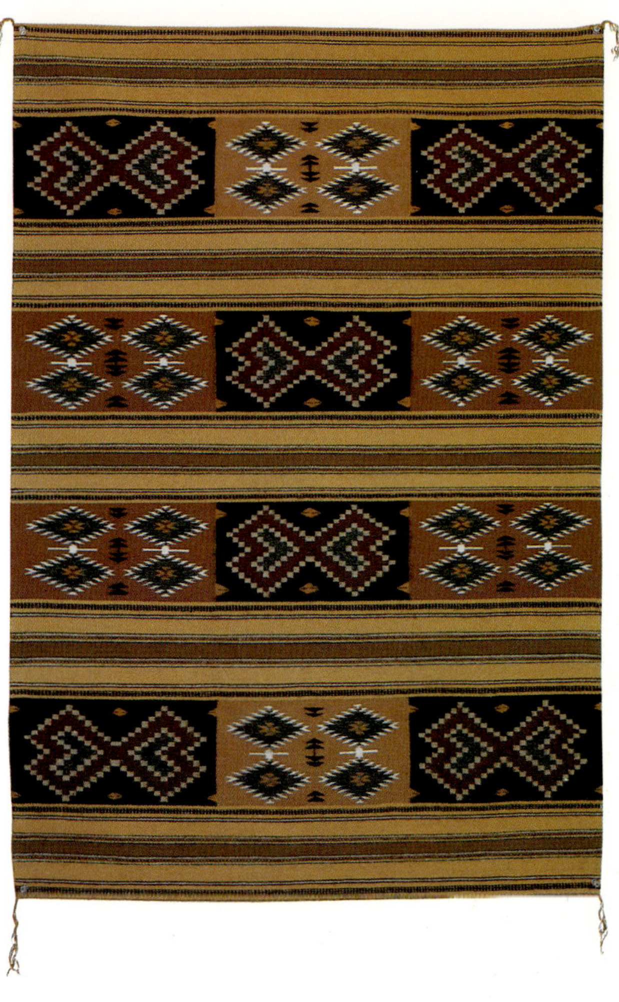

171. Crystal rug, contemporary, by Sarah Begay. 71″ x 49″. 9 warp/in.; 56 weft/in. Having little in common with the J. B. Moore Crystal rugs of the early twentieth century, the new Crystal style was developed in response to the increasing popularity of vegetal-dye rugs. Woven of vegetal-dyed shades of yellow, brown, green, and brown and natural gray and white hand-spun wool yarns. (Private collection)

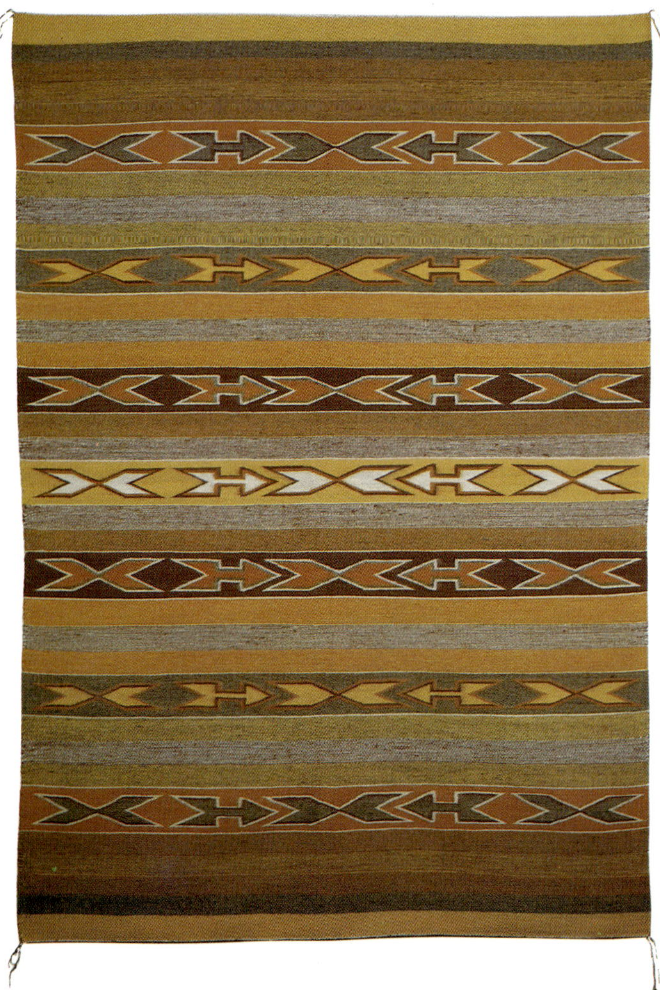

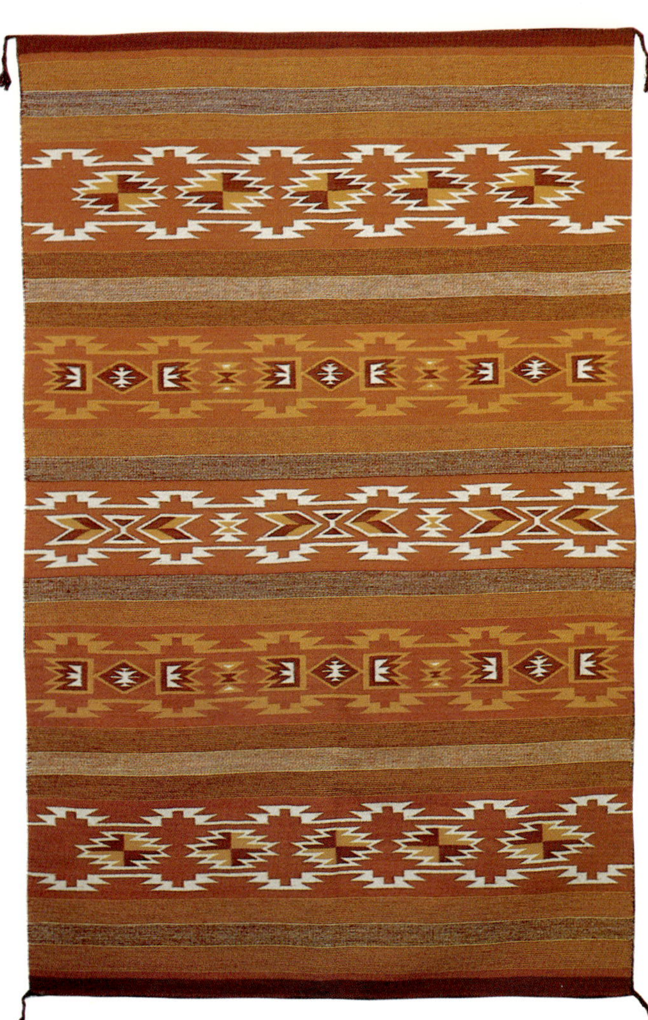

172. Crystal rug, contemporary, by Sarah Begay. 59″ x 38″. 13 warp/in.; 44 weft/in. The design elements in Crystal rugs tend to be larger and less constrained within the bands than those of the neighboring Wide Ruins rugs. Woven of vegetal-dyed shades of yellow and brown and natural gray and white hand-spun wool yarns. (Private collection)

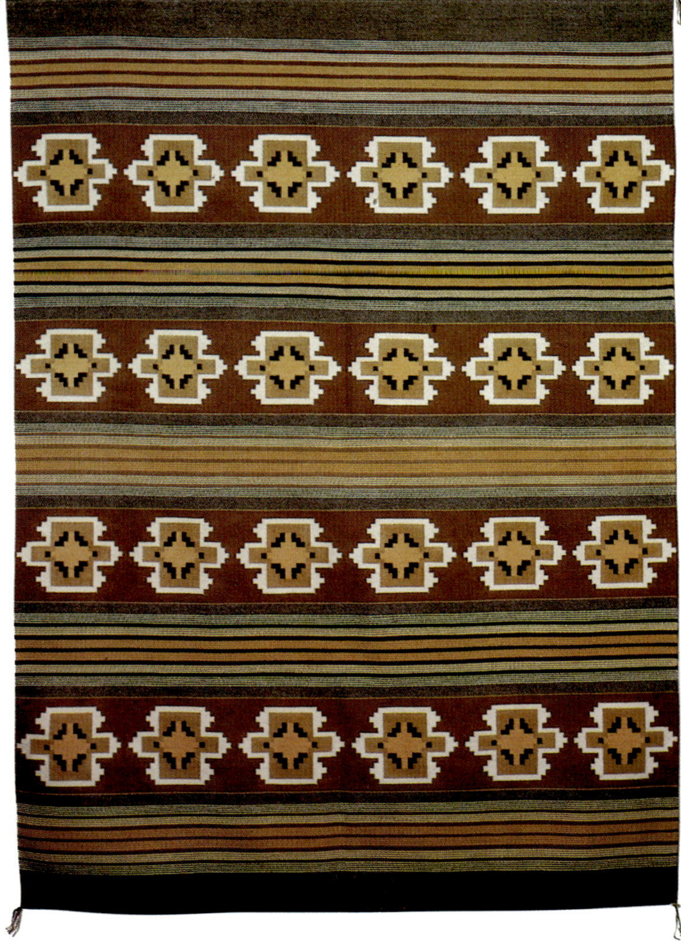

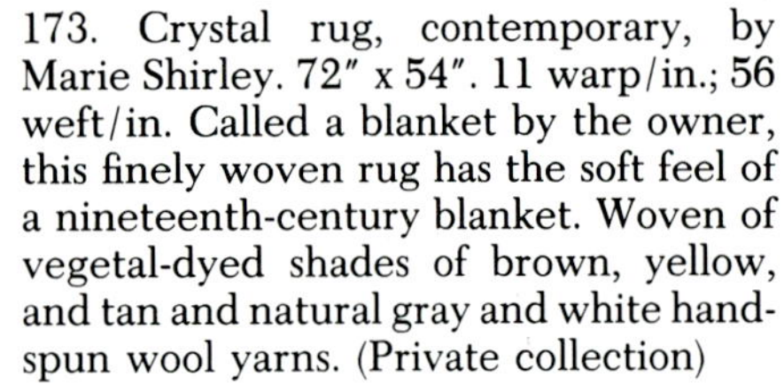

173. Crystal rug, contemporary, by Marie Shirley. 72″ x 54″. 11 warp/in.; 56 weft/in. Called a blanket by the owner, this finely woven rug has the soft feel of a nineteenth-century blanket. Woven of vegetal-dyed shades of brown, yellow, and tan and natural gray and white hand-spun wool yarns. (Private collection)

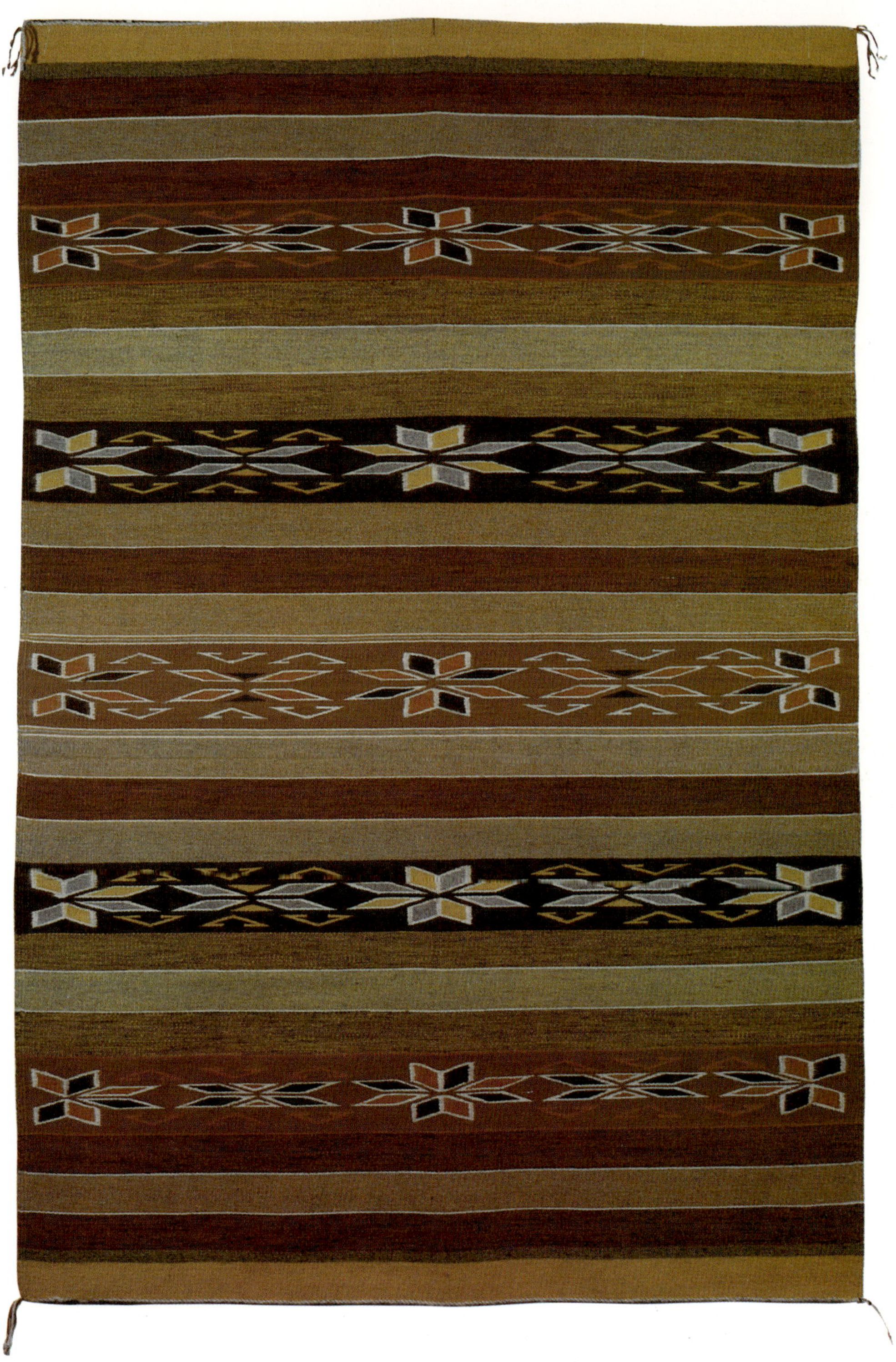

174. Crystal rug, contemporary, by Sarah Begay. 71″ x 49″. 9 warp/in.; 56 weft/in. Squashed Vallero star designs, a carry-over from earlier J. B. Moore Crystal days, are used in the bands of this vegetal rug. Woven of vegetal-dyed shades of brown, tan, yellow, green, and red and natural gray and white hand-spun wool yarns. (Private collection)

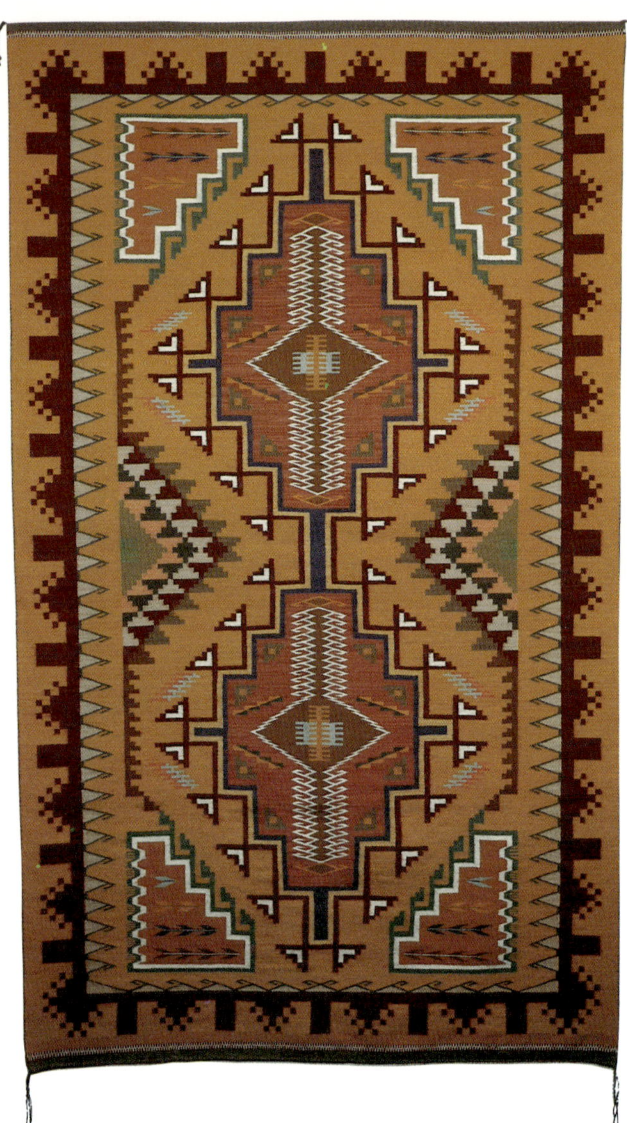

175. Burntwater rug, contemporary, by Sadie Curtiss and Helen Kirk. 83″ x 50″. 9 warp/in.; 56 weft/in. Six different women contributed the many vegetal dyes used in this elaborate Burntwater rug. Woven of vegetal-dyed shades of brown, yellow, pink, orange, green, and blue and natural hand-spun wool yarns. (Private collection)

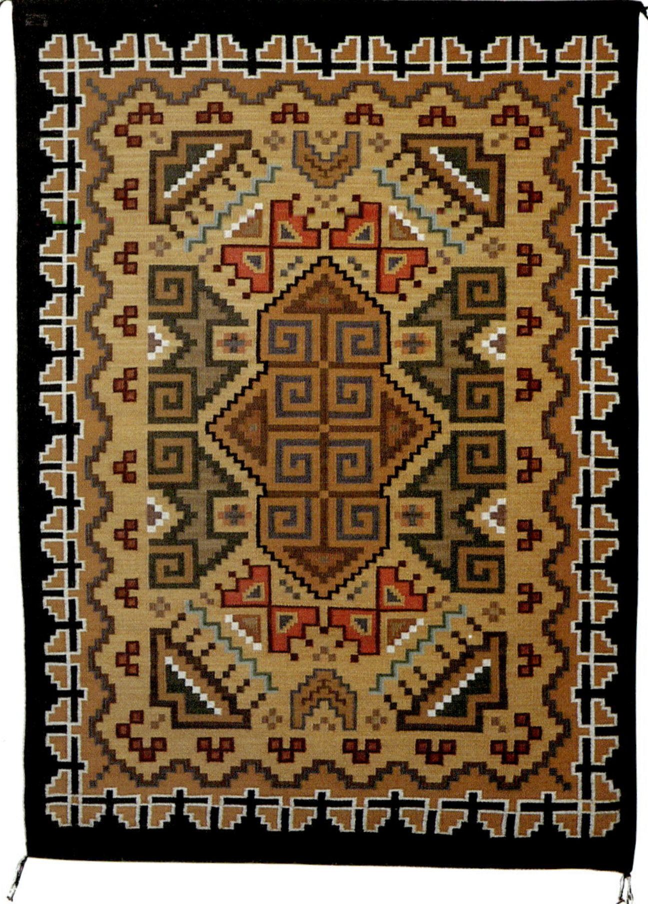

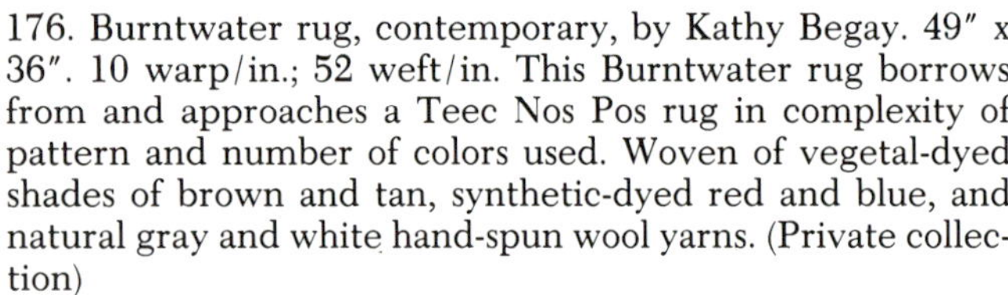

176. Burntwater rug, contemporary, by Kathy Begay. 49″ x 36″. 10 warp/in.; 52 weft/in. This Burntwater rug borrows from and approaches a Teec Nos Pos rug in complexity of pattern and number of colors used. Woven of vegetal-dyed shades of brown and tan, synthetic-dyed red and blue, and natural gray and white hand-spun wool yarns. (Private collection)

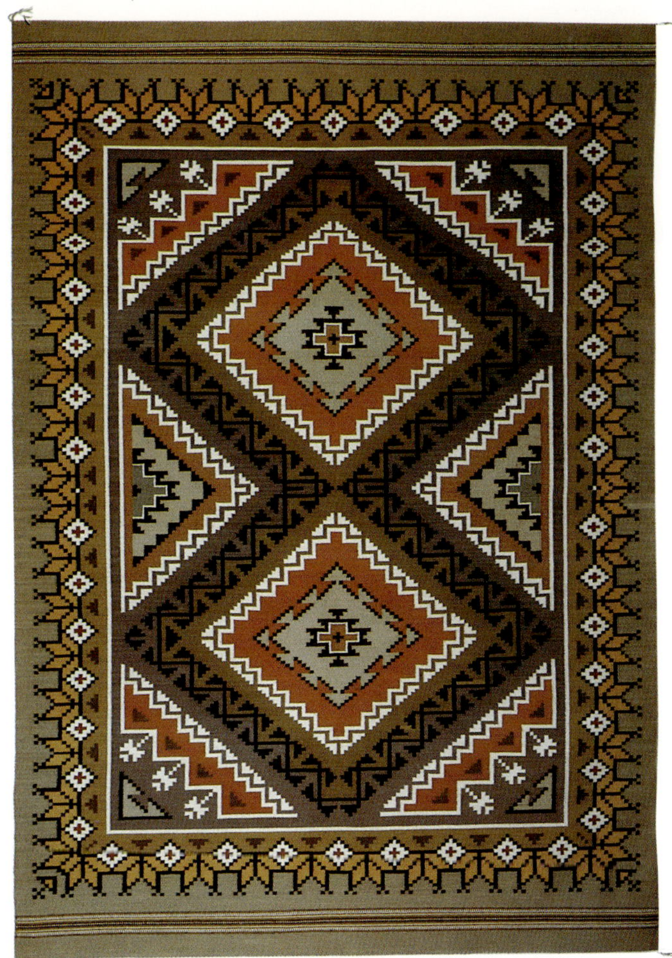

177. Burntwater rug, contemporary, by Winnie James. 84″ x 59″. 12 warp/in.; 36 weft/in. Increased complexity in both color and pattern appears to be the trend in contemporary Burntwater weaving. The predominance of green color indicates that this rug was probably woven in the Pine Springs region. Woven of vegetal-dyed shades of green, yellow, and brown and natural gray and white hand-spun wool yarns. (Private collection)

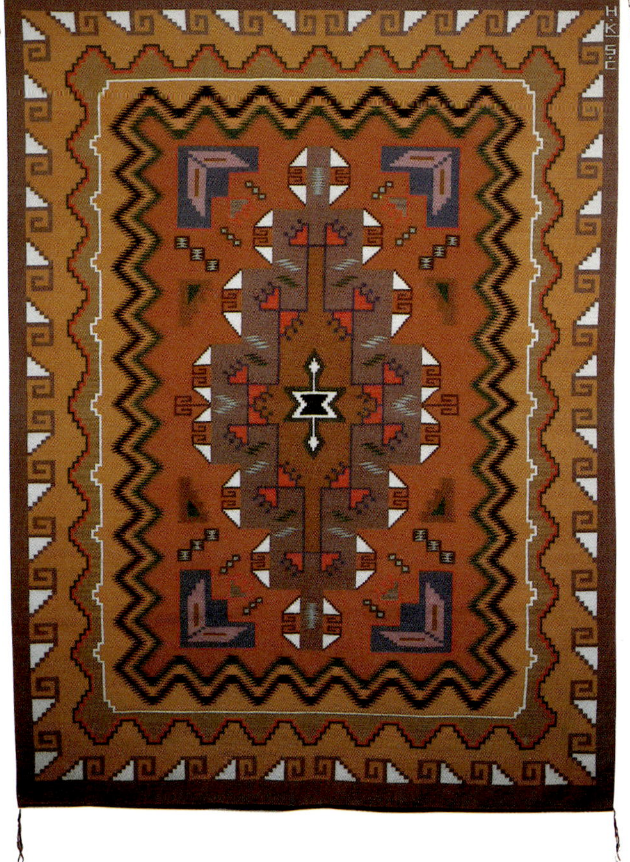

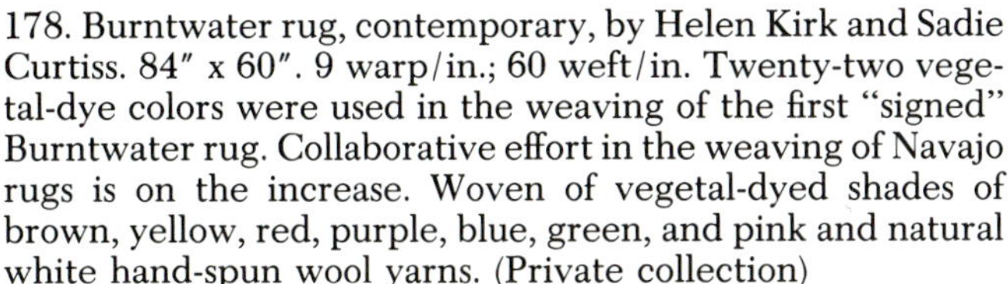

178. Burntwater rug, contemporary, by Helen Kirk and Sadie Curtiss. 84″ x 60″. 9 warp/in.; 60 weft/in. Twenty-two vegetal-dye colors were used in the weaving of the first "signed" Burntwater rug. Collaborative effort in the weaving of Navajo rugs is on the increase. Woven of vegetal-dyed shades of brown, yellow, red, purple, blue, green, and pink and natural white hand-spun wool yarns. (Private collection)

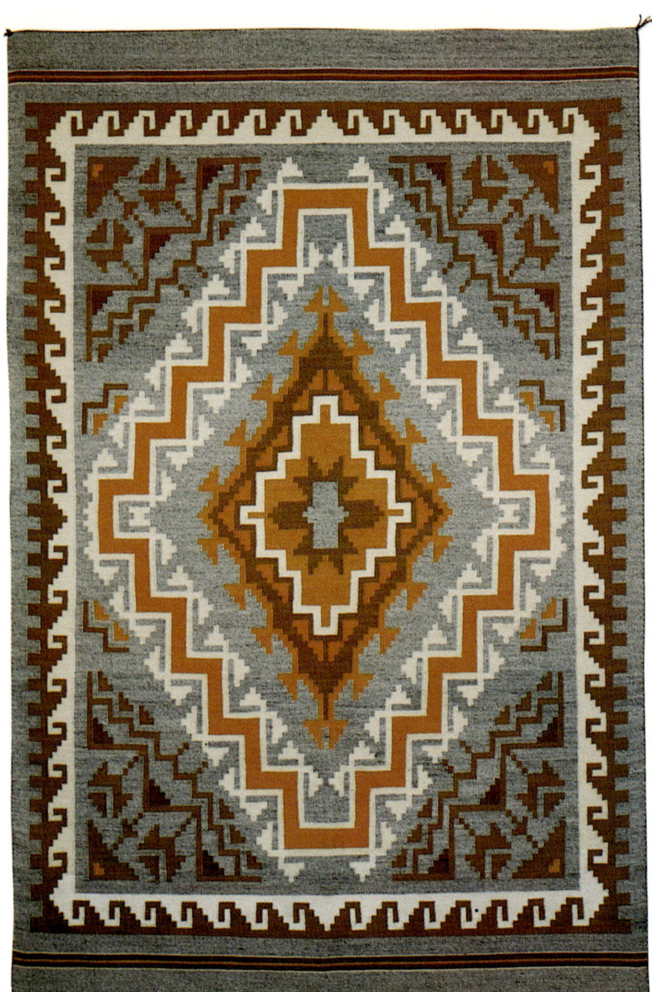

179. Burntwater rug, contemporary, by Marie Shirley. 63″ x 42″. 12 warp/in.; 40 weft/in. Burntwater weavers are unrivaled in their experimentation with color and pattern, as demonstrated in this Two Gray Hills style of Burntwater rug. Woven of vegetal-dyed shades of yellow and brown and natural gray and white hand-spun wool yarns. (Private collection)

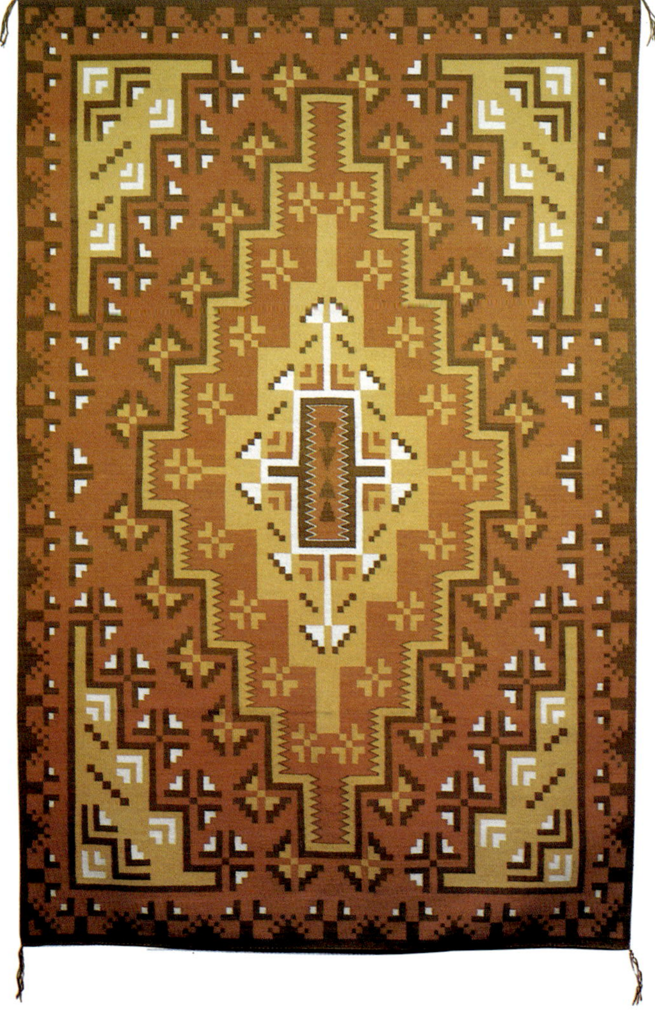

180. Burntwater rug, contemporary, by Stella Bia. 72″ x 48″. 12 warp/in.; 60 weft/in. A recently developed variety of Burntwater rug, the Three Turkey Ruin type, uses typical Wide Ruins coloration. Woven of vegetal-dyed shades of brown, yellow, and red and natural white hand-spun wool yarns. (Private collection)

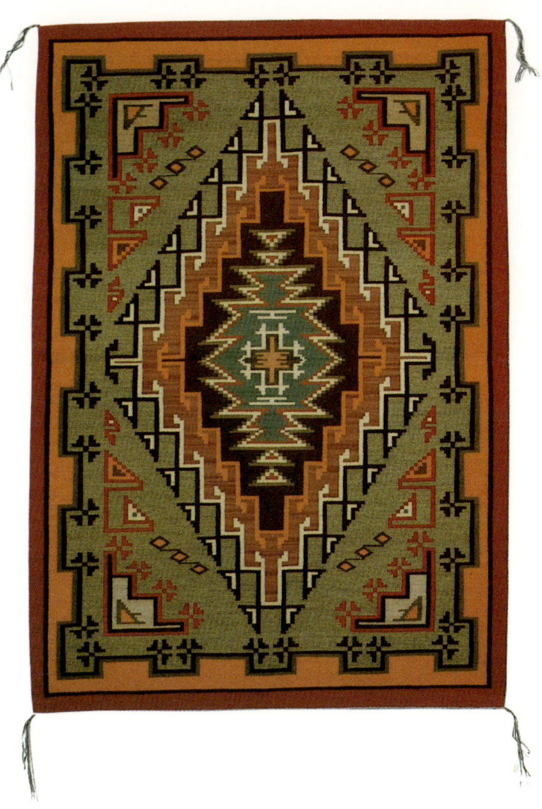

181. Burntwater tapestry, contemporary, by Stella Arizana. 41″ x 30″. 14 warp/in.; 96 weft/in. A rare example of a Burntwater tapestry weave. Tapestry weaves were not, until recently, a part of the Burntwater weaver's traditional repertoire. Woven of vegetal-dyed shades of brown, yellow, green, red, and blue and natural gray and white hand-spun wool yarns. (Private collection)

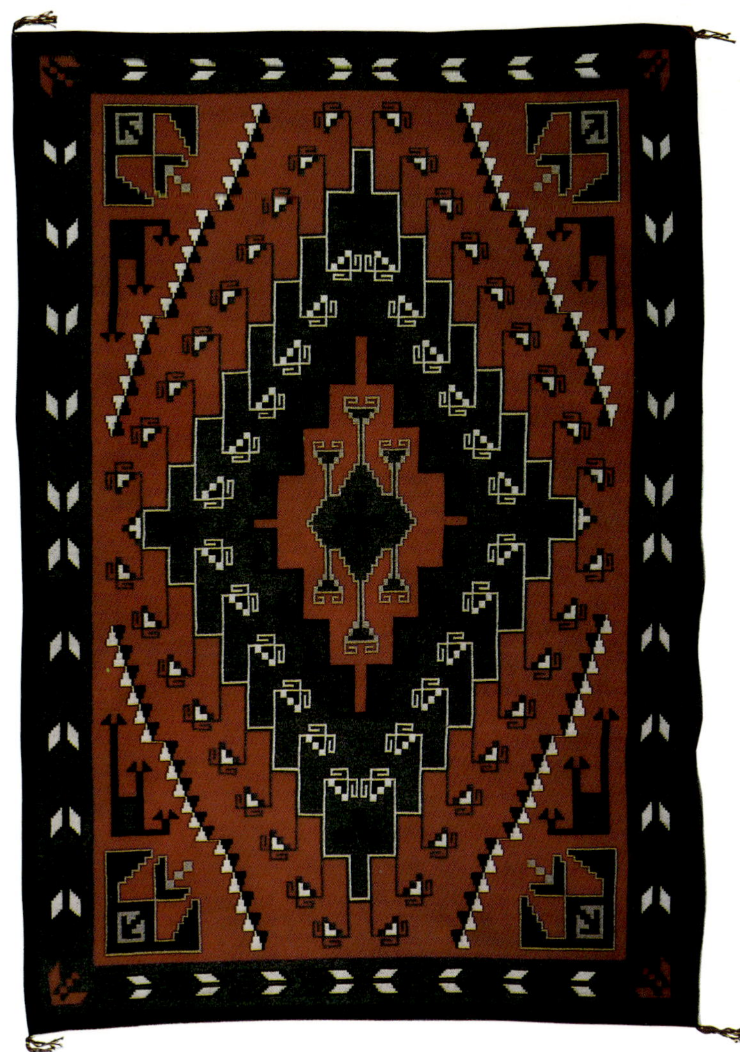

182. Ganado rug, contemporary, by Elsie Wilson. 81″ x 57″. 11 warp/in.; 48 weft/in. A hallmark of the Ganado rug, the dominant rich red color, often referred to as Ganado red, was encouraged by J. L. Hubbell at the turn of the century and is still a recognized criterion today. Woven of synthetic-dyed red and black and natural gray (two shades) and white hand-spun wool yarns. (Private collection)

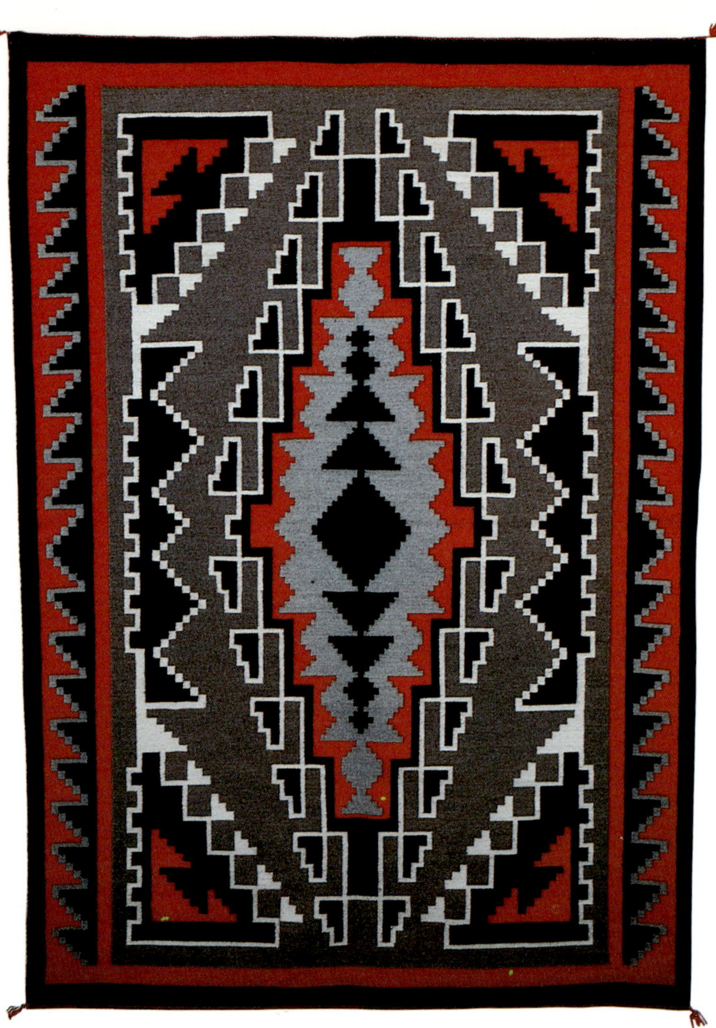

183. Klagetoh rug, contemporary, by Marie Lee. 67″ x 49″. 11 warp/in.; 52 weft/in. Preferring a more somber tone, the weavers at Klagetoh use more gray, particularly as a background color, in their rugs. Woven of synthetic-dyed red and black and natural gray (two shades) and white hand-spun wool yarns. (Private collection)

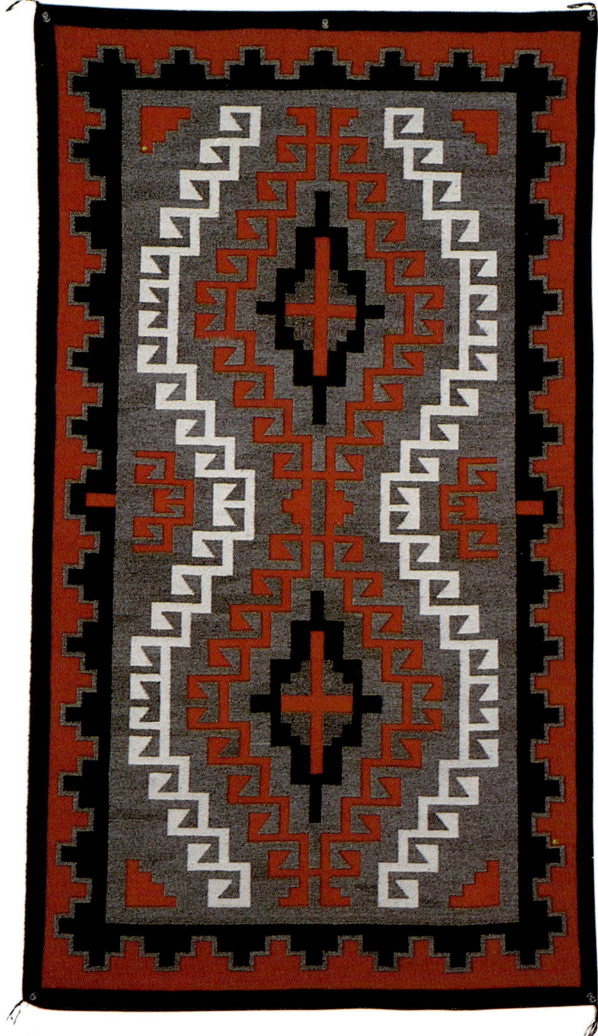

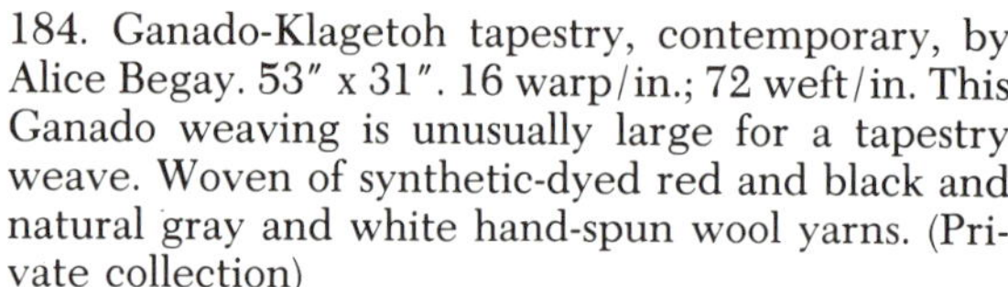

184. Ganado-Klagetoh tapestry, contemporary, by Alice Begay. 53″ x 31″. 16 warp/in.; 72 weft/in. This Ganado weaving is unusually large for a tapestry weave. Woven of synthetic-dyed red and black and natural gray and white hand-spun wool yarns. (Private collection)

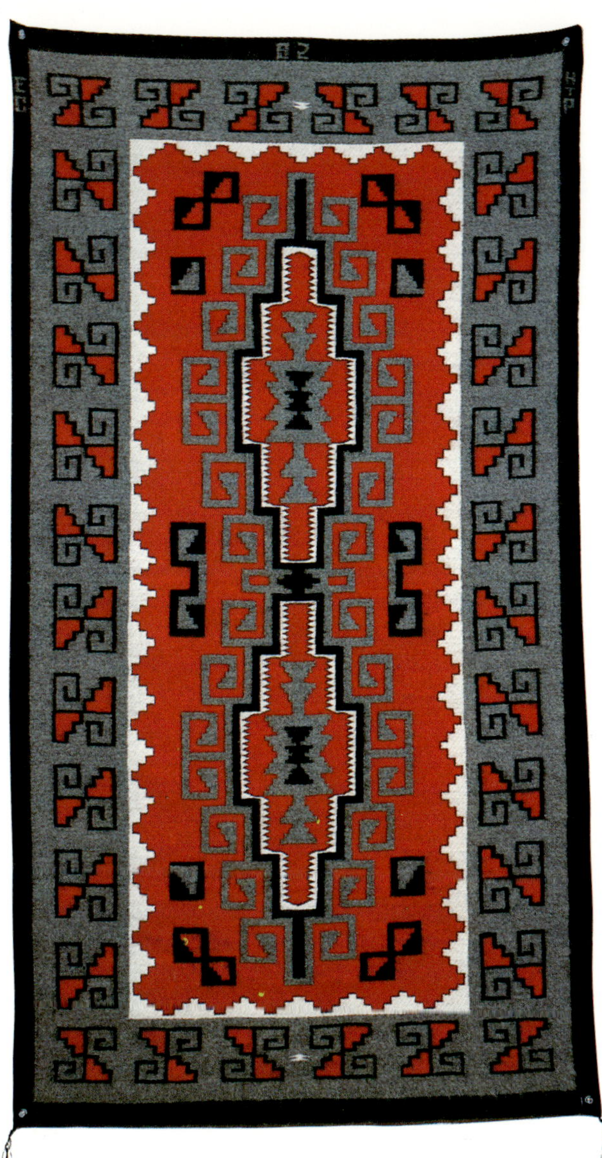

185. Ganado rug, contemporary, by Evelyn Curley. 62″ x 33″. 8 warp/in.; 40 weft/in. A recent development at Ganado is the signing of rugs with initials. This example is signed E.C. (Evelyn Curley) and dated '82. Also noted is the trading post for which it was made: H.T.P. (Hubbell Trading Post). Woven of synthetic-dyed red and black and natural gray and white hand-spun wool yarns. (Private collection)

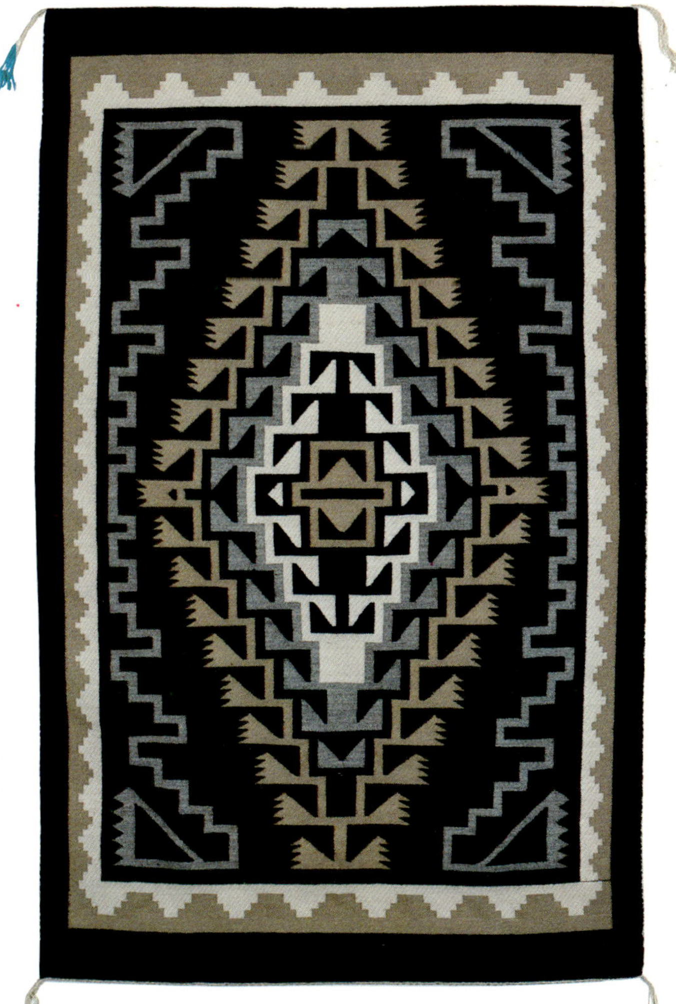

186. Two Gray Hills tapestry, contemporary, by Mildred Natonie. 37″ x 24″. 21 warp/in.; 80 weft/in. Developed in the Two Gray Hills region, superfine tapestry weaves are often framed and mounted behind glass. Woven of natural shades of brown, gray, and white and overdyed black hand-spun wool yarns. (Private collection)

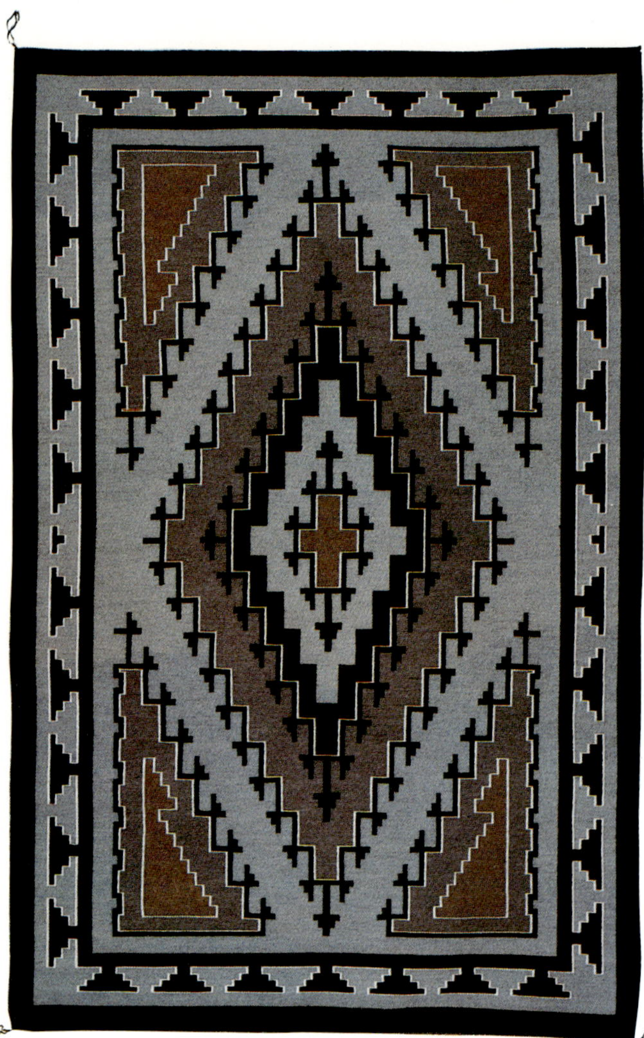

187. Two Gray Hills rug, contemporary, by Helen Allen. 69″ x 46″. 12 warp/in.; 36 weft/in. This relatively uncomplex Two Gray Hills rug is reminiscent of rugs woven in this region prior to 1940. Woven of natural shades of brown, gray (two shades), and white and overdyed black hand-spun wool yarns. (Private collection)

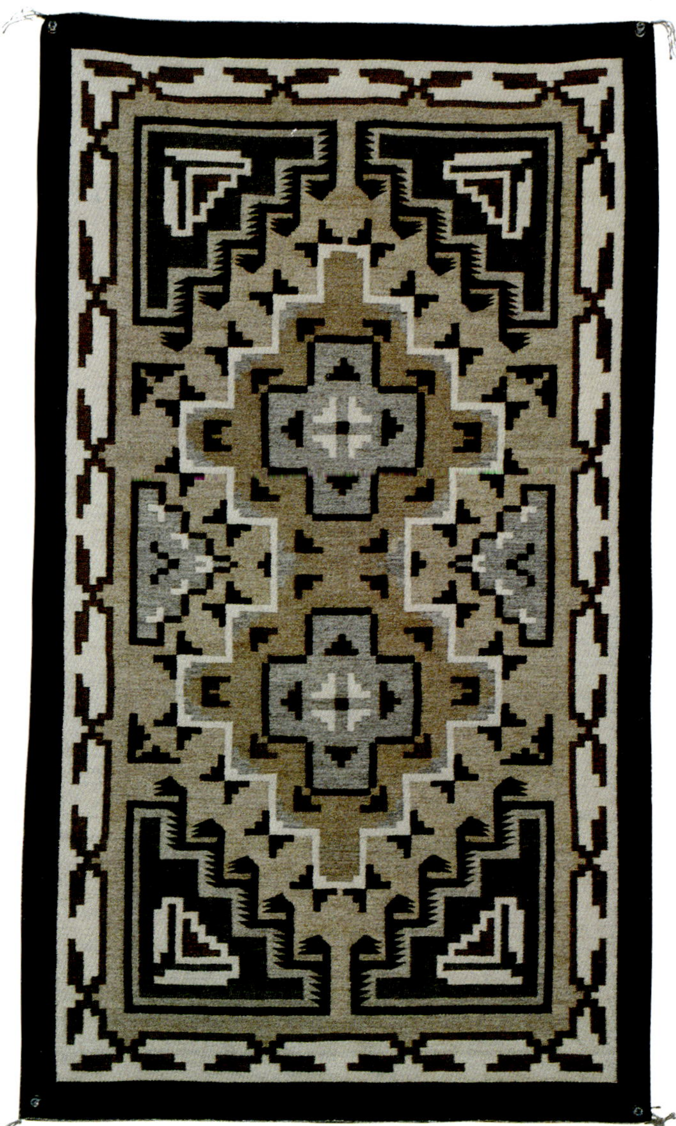

188. Two Gray Hills tapestry, contemporary, by Katherine Nataanie. 40″ x 23″. 16 warp/in.; 60 weft/in. A first prize winner at the 1979 Gallup Intertribal Ceremonial, this tapestry-weave pattern uses the two connected diamonds commonly associated with the Two Gray Hills style. Woven of shades of natural brown, gray, and white and overdyed black hand-spun wool yarns. (Private collection)

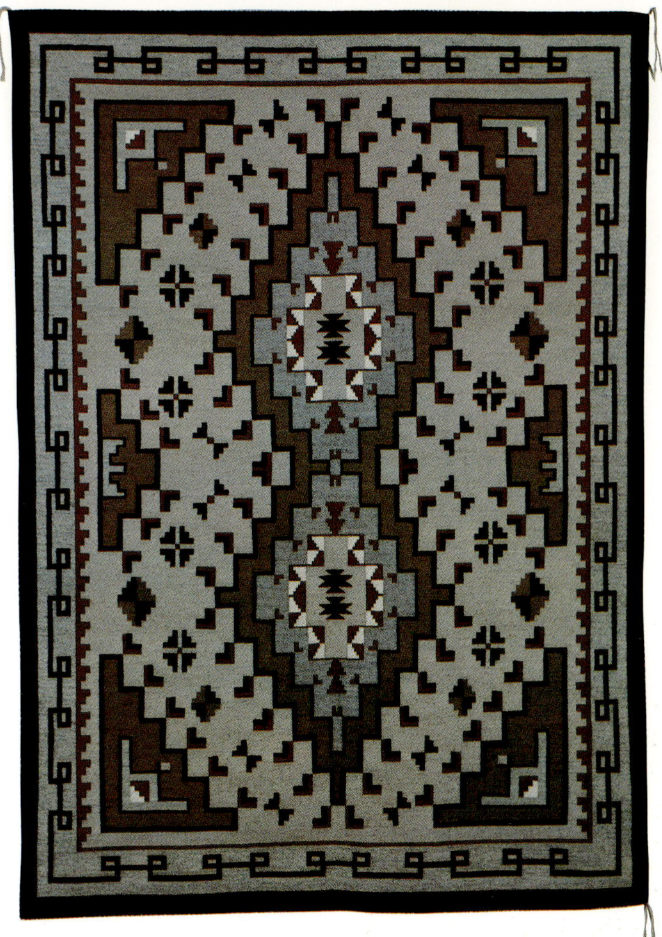

189. Two Gray Hills rug, contemporary, by Lucy Tsosie. 59″ x 43″. 12 warp/in.; 76 weft/in. The finest woven rugs consistently come from the Two Gray Hills region. This full-size rug would almost qualify as a tapestry weave had it been woven in a different part of the reservation. Woven of natural shades of brown and white, vegetal-dyed red, and overdyed black hand-spun wool yarns. (Private collection)

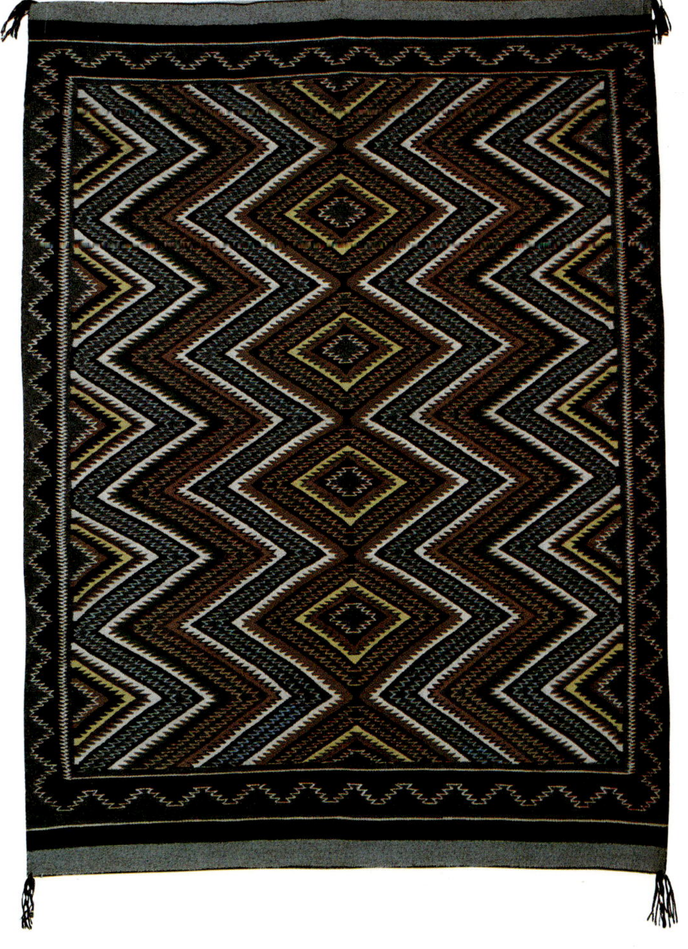

190. Teec Nos Pos rug, contemporary, by Sarah Yazzie. 59″ x 44″. 11 warp/in.; 56 weft/in. Of all the regional styles of weaving, the Red Mesa variety of Teec Nos Pos rug has shown the least amount of pattern change over time. Woven of four-ply commercial synthetic-dyed yellow, green (two shades), brown (two shades), pale blue, and black and natural white and gray hand-spun wool yarns. (Private collection)

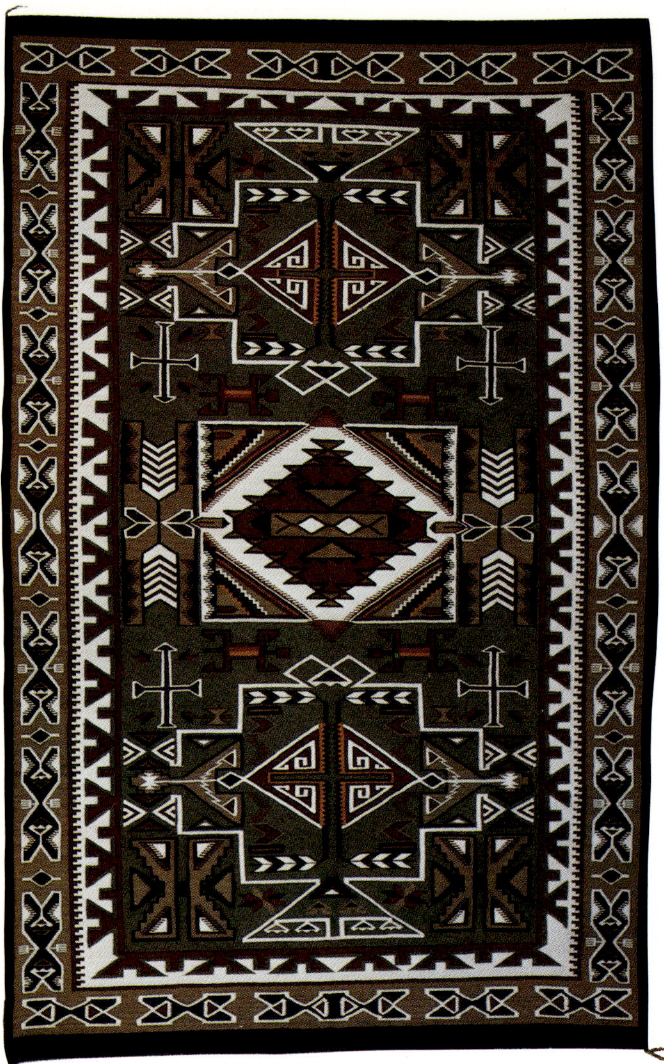

191. Teec Nos Pos rug, contemporary, by Wanda Begody. 110″ x 72″. 9 warp/in.; 28 weft/in. The weaving of large-size rugs has been a trait of the Teec Nos Pos weaver for more than fifty years. The unusual use of predominantly vegetal-dyed hand-spun yarns is in keeping with the current trend in rug coloration. Woven of vegetal-dyed rust, gold, brown, and mauve, synthetic-dyed black, and natural gray and white hand-spun wool yarns. (Private collection)

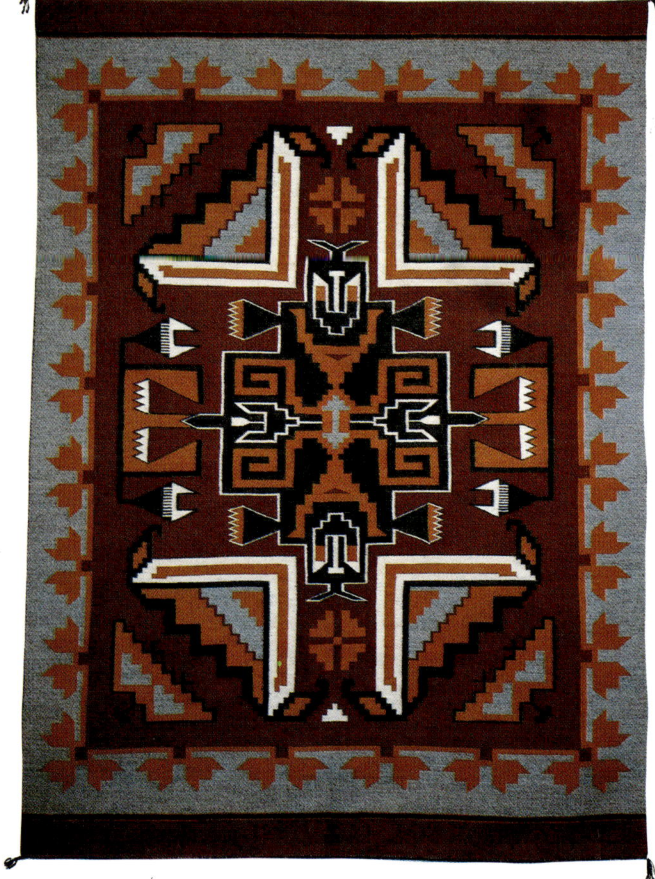

192. Teec Nos Pos rug, contemporary, by Marie Shirley. 60″ x 44″. 11 warp/in.; 52 weft/in. In addition to the increased use of vegetal dyes, Teec Nos Pos weavers are experimenting with new patterns. Woven of vegetal-dyed brown and tan, synthetic-dyed black, and natural gray and white hand-spun wool yarns. (Private collection)

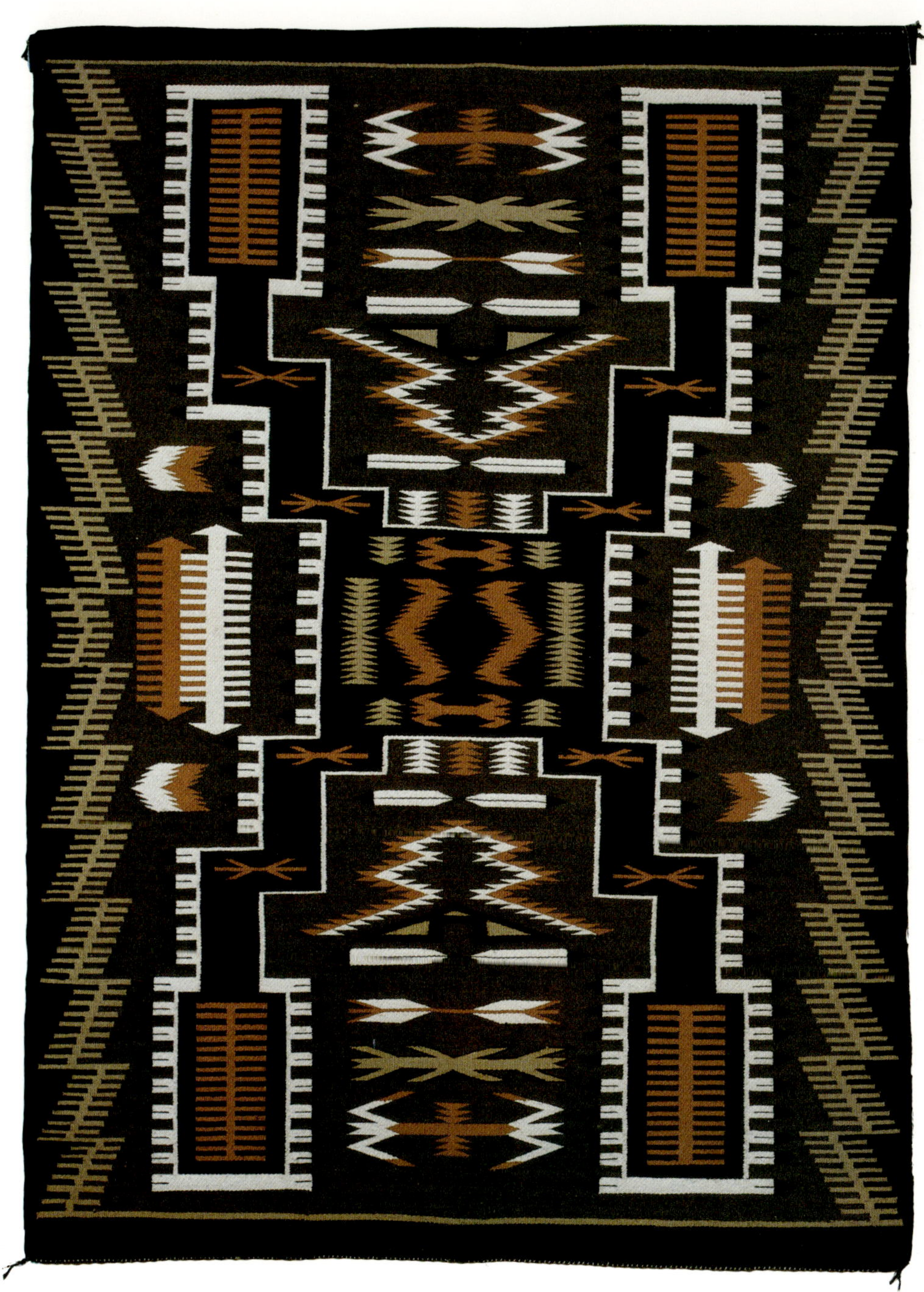

193. Storm pattern rug, contemporary, by Anna Barton. 62″ x 47″. 8 warp/in.; 52 weft/in. This vibrant storm pattern rug still retains many of the symbols originally touted as having ceremonial significance. Woven of vegetal-dyed shades of brown, synthetic-dyed black, and natural gray and white wool yarns. (Private collection)

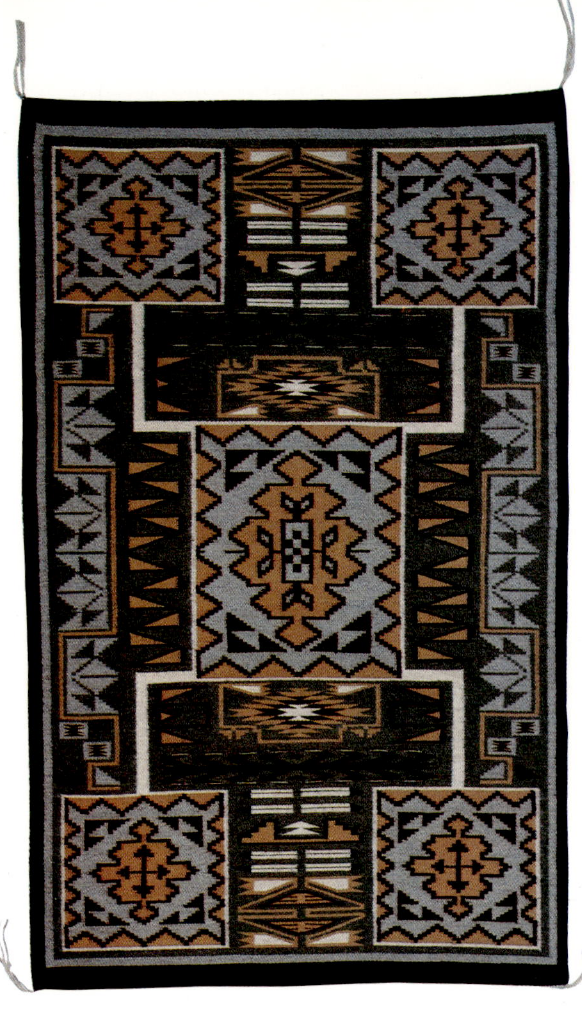

194. Storm pattern rug, contemporary, by Mary Wilson Begay. 46″ x 29″. 9 warp/in.; 54 weft/in. Woven at Dinnebito, this rug shows strong Burntwater influence in both design and color. Woven of synthetic-dyed red, tan, and black and natural gray (two shades) and white hand-spun wool yarns. (Private collection)

195. Pictorial Yeibechai tapestry, contemporary, by Della Woody Begay. 31″ x 38″. 12 warp/in.; 100 weft/in. This Yeibechai tapestry is actually a landscape pictorial of two Navajo women displaying a Yeibechai rug. Woven of synthetic-dyed purple, olive, red, yellow, pink, green, blue, brown, and black and natural white hand-spun wool yarns. (Private collection)

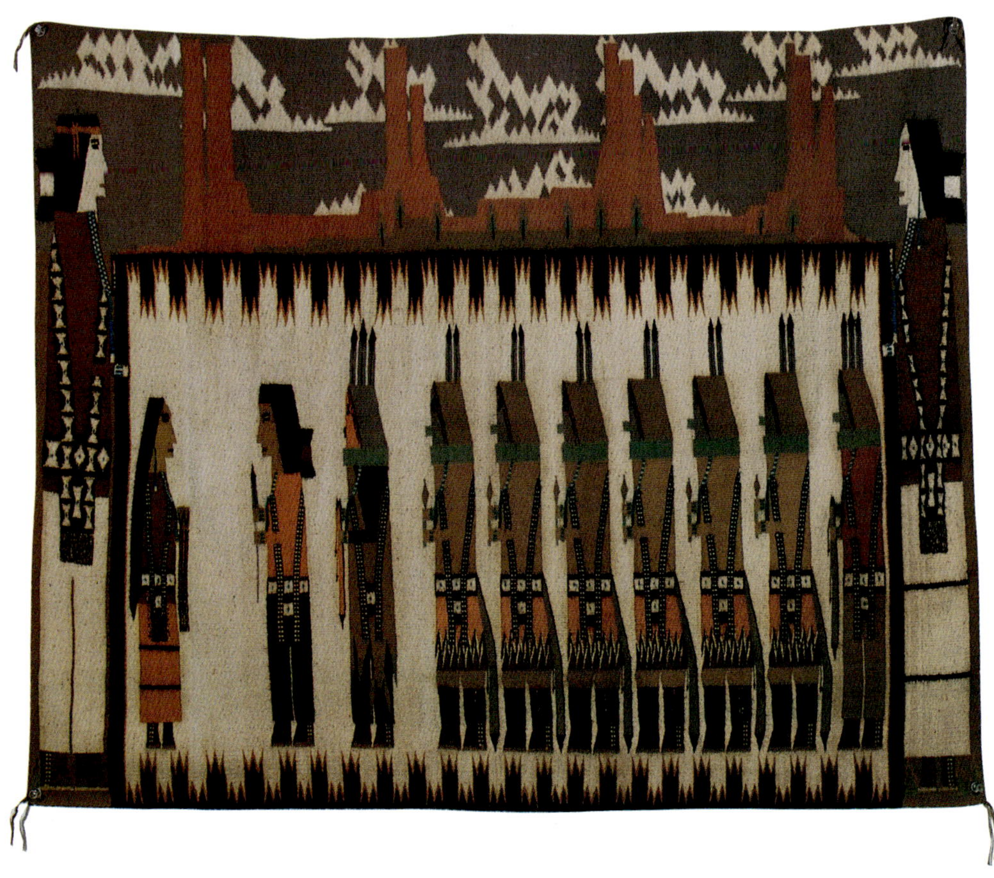

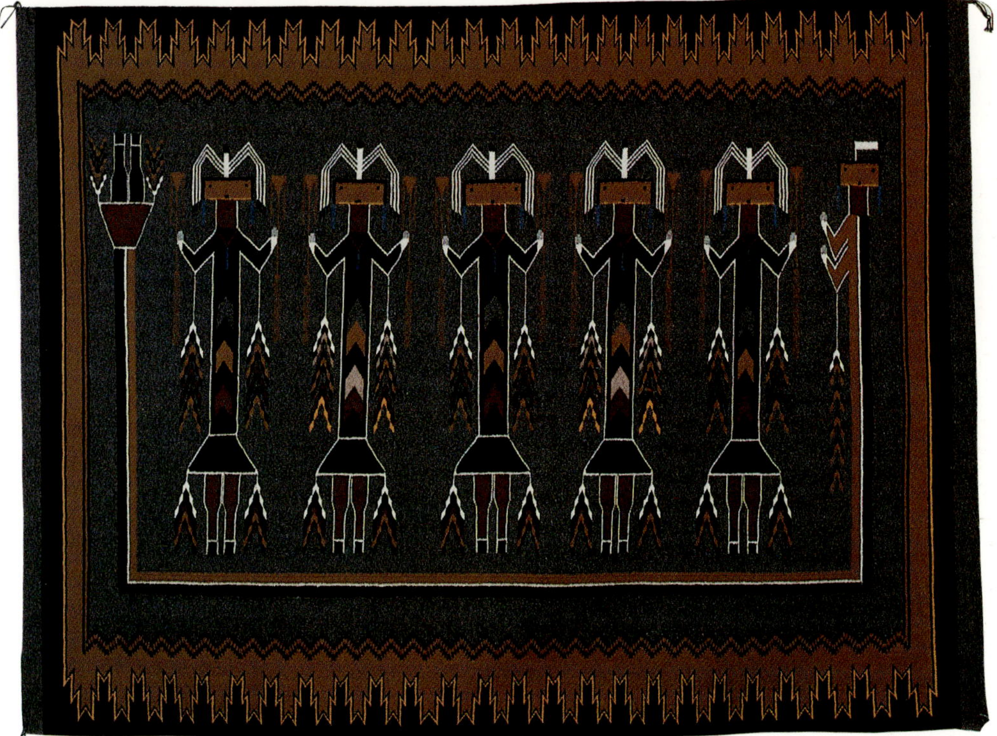

196. Pictorial Yei rug, contemporary, by Mary Long. 46″ x 63″. 16 warp/in.; 40 weft/in. Vegetallike in color, the colored yarns in this rug are actually processed yarns dyed with synthetic dyes. The dark background color indicates that this Yei rug is of the Shiprock variety. Woven of synthetic-dyed green, brown, orange, red, and black and natural gray and white hand-spun wool yarns. (Private collection)

197. Pictorial Yeibechai tapestry, contemporary, by Nellie Yazzie. 32″ x 51″. 10 warp/in.; 66 weft/in. Pictorial Yei and Yeibechai rugs and tapestries are viewed 90 degrees from the way they are woven. The dancers depicted are from the Nightway ceremony. Woven of synthetic-dyed yellow, brown, green (two shades), pink, and blue and natural white hand-spun wool yarns. (Private collection)

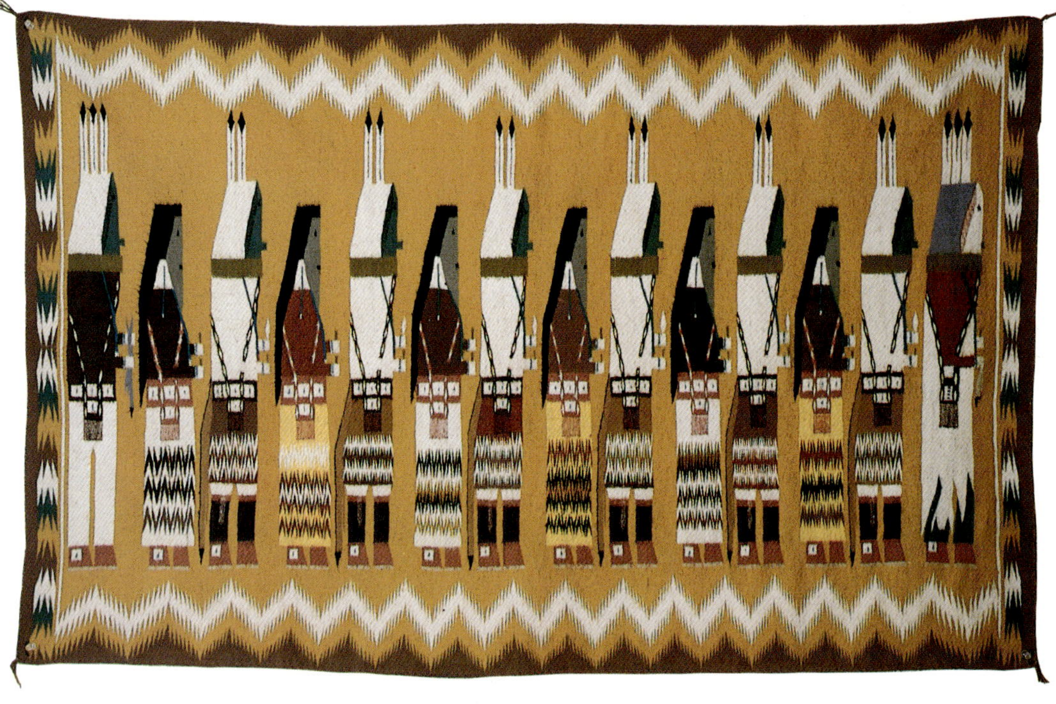

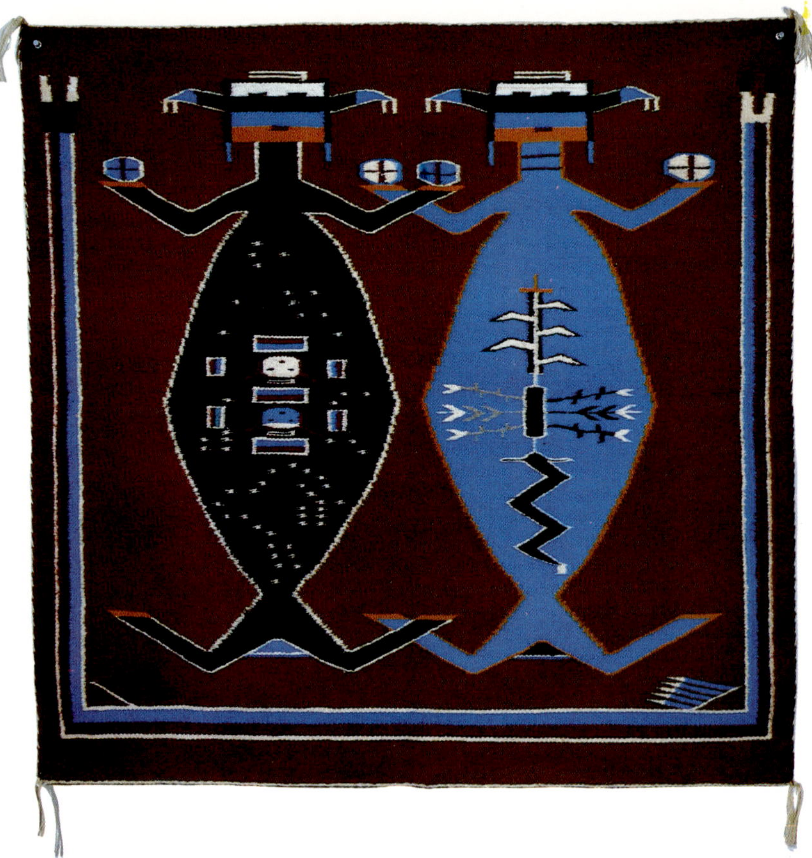

198. Pictorial sandpainting rug, contemporary, by Grace Benally. 36″ x 37″. 11 warp/in.; 32 weft/in. A depiction of the Mother Earth and Father Sky sandpainting. So as not to offend the deities, sandpainting rugs are never totally complete in pattern, as the actual sandpainting would be. Woven of four-ply commercial synthetic-dyed blue, brown, orange, red, and black and white wool yarns. (Private collection)

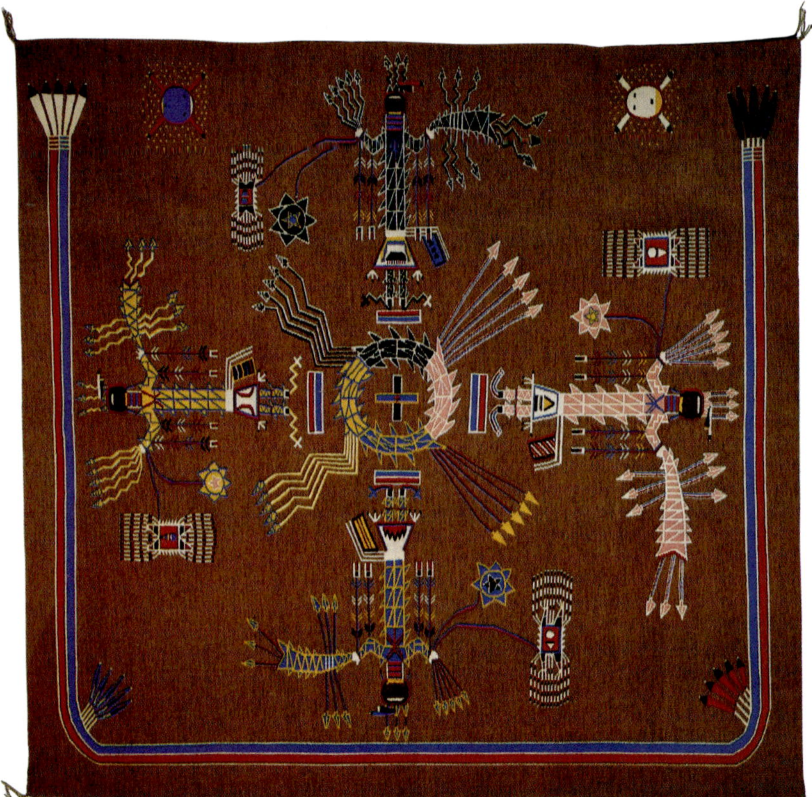

199. Pictorial sandpainting rug, contemporary, by Anna May Tanner. 60″ x 60″. 13 warp/in.; 60 weft/in. Woven in colors Hosteen Klah might have chosen, this sandpainting rug is probably of the Windway ceremony. Woven of four-ply commercial synthetic-dyed brown, red, blue, burgundy, yellow, pink, purple, and white wool yarns. (Private collection)

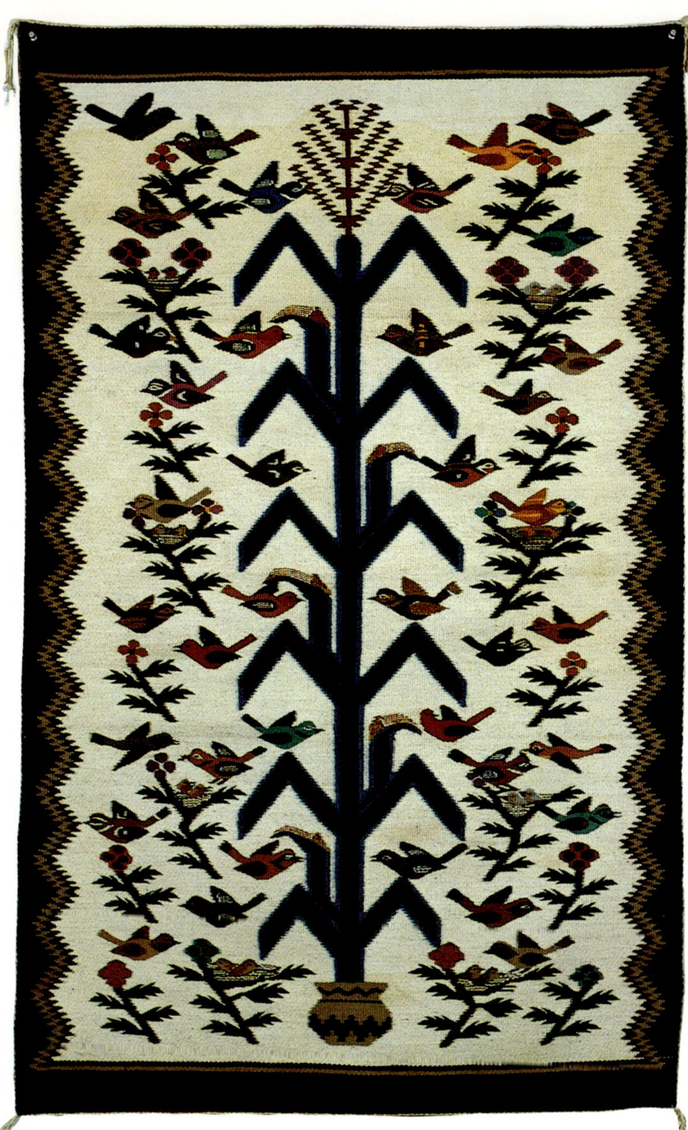

200. Pictorial rug, contemporary, by Bessie Sellers. 50″ x 31″. 10 warp/in.; 32 weft/in. A more naturalistic portrayal of the long-popular "corn plant" pictorial, this rug is easily identifiable as being in the Bessie Sellers style. Woven of four-ply commercial synthetic-dyed red, blue, yellow orange, and pink and natural white and brown hand-spun wool yarns. (Private collection)

201. Pictorial rug, contemporary, by Suzy Black. 85″x 65″. 8 warp/in.; 30 weft/in. Suzy Black is a weaver noted for her original style of pictorial rug. This example reminds one of the famous American folk painting *The Peaceable Kingdom* by Edward Hicks. Woven of synthetic-dyed orange, yellow, blue, tan, gray, brown, and white hand-spun wool yarns. (Private collection)

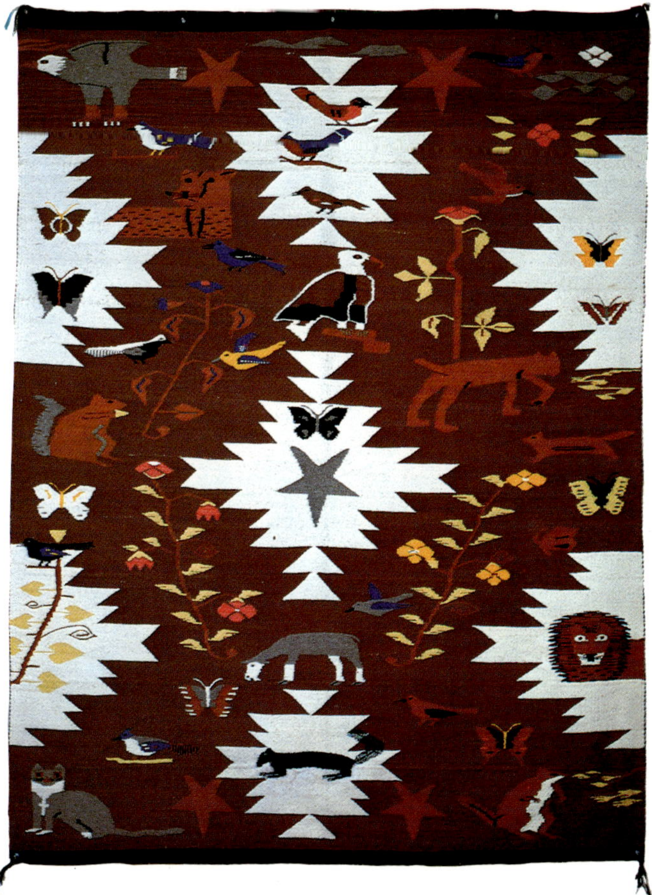

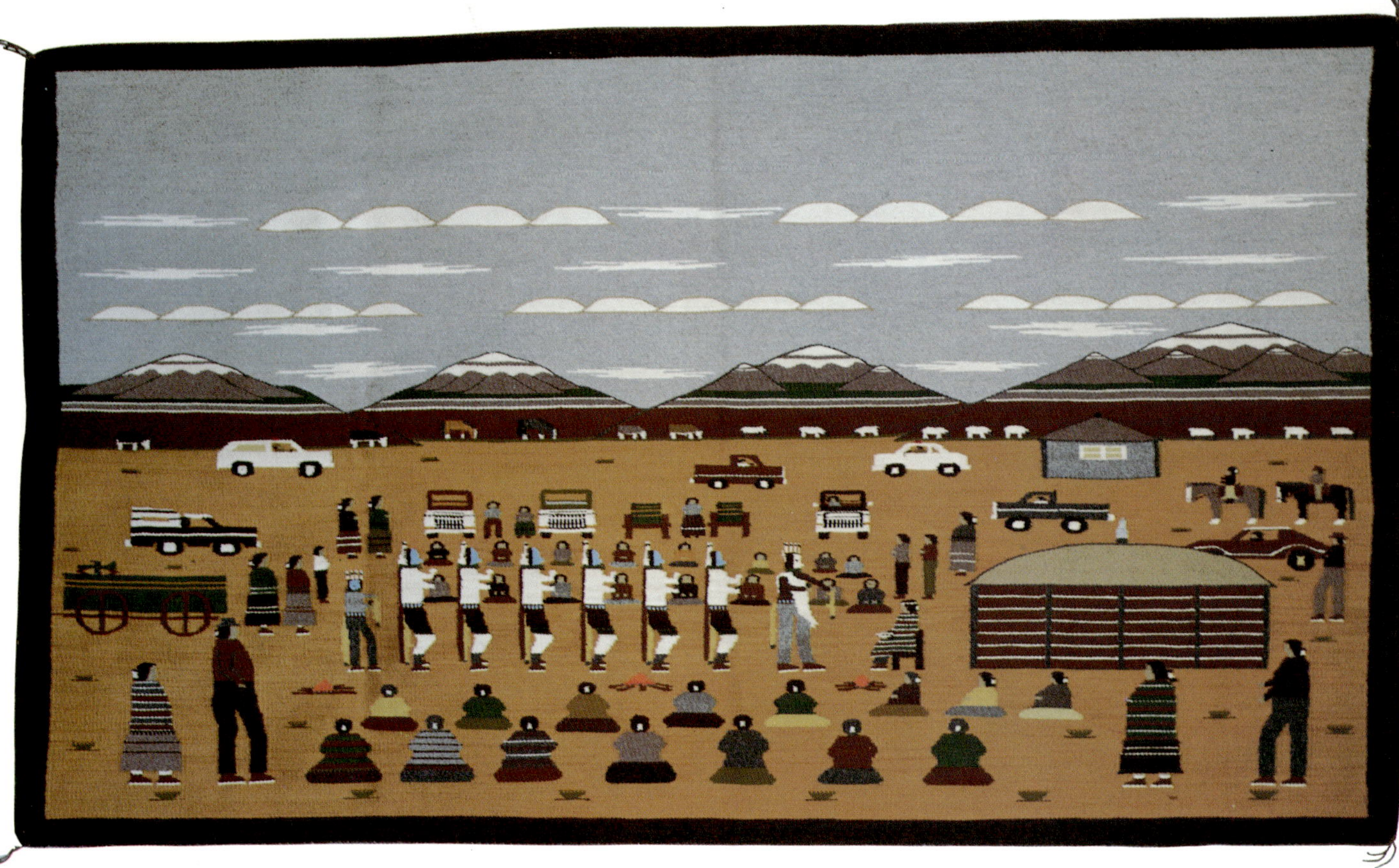

202. Pictorial rug, contemporary, by Isabel John. 46″ x 80″. 9 warp/in.; 52 weft/in. A recent development in Navajo weaving, the landscape pictorial rug usually depicts an important social event in the lives of the Navajo, in this instance a Yeibechai dance. Woven of four-ply commercial synthetic-dyed yellow, green, tan, pale blue, and white, vegetal-dyed gold, mauve, and pale yellow, and natural gray and brown handspun wool yarns. (Private collection)

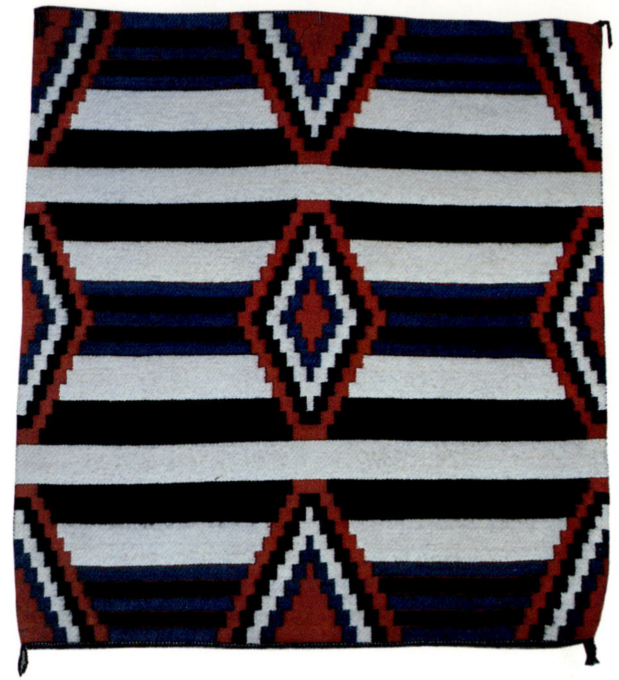

203. Chief pattern rug, contemporary, by Elsie Sherlock. 45″ x 44″. 7 warp/in.; 32 weft/in. Contemporary revivals of Classic Period blanket styles provide a similar look without the great expense. Woven of synthetic-dyed red, blue, and black and natural white hand-spun wool yarns. (Private collection)

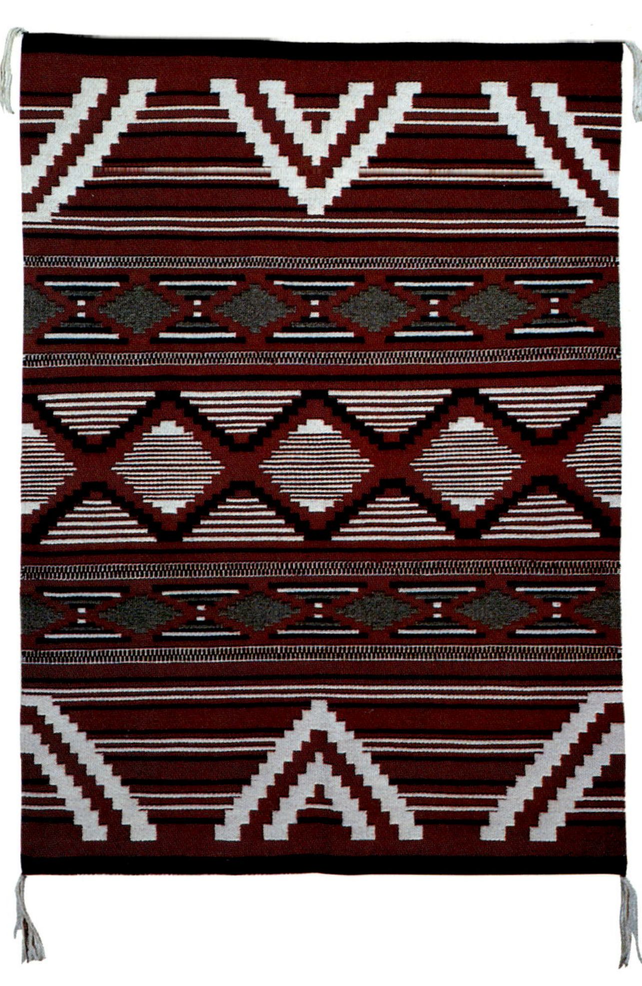

204. Sarape pattern rug, contemporary, by Evelyn Yazzie. 47″ x 34″. 8 warp/in.; 36 weft/in. Few examples of Classic Period blankets exist on the reservation today, so weavers must go to museums or study illustrations in books to familiarize themselves with the Classic Period patterns. Woven of synthetic-dyed red, blue, and black and natural white hand-spun wool yarns. (Private collection)

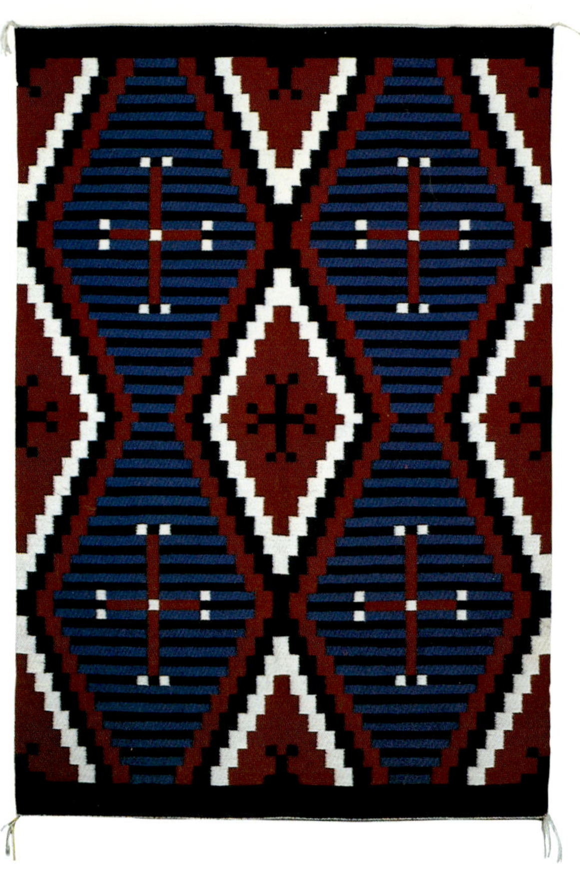

205. Moki sarape pattern rug, contemporary, by Sadie Curtiss. 60″ x 48″. 12 warp/in.; 48 weft/in. A revival of a revival-style Moki rug popularized in the late nineteenth century by the trader J. L. Hubbell. Woven of synthetic-dyed red, blue, and purple and natural white processed wool yarns. (Private collection)

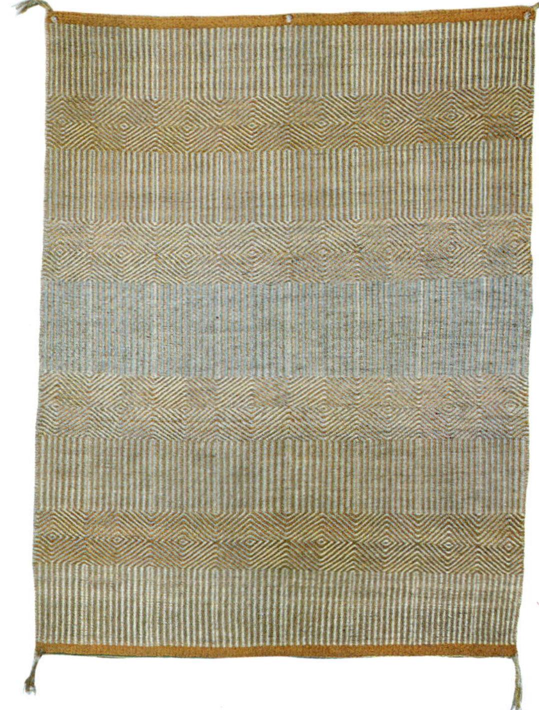

206. Twill rug, contemporary. 47″ x 37″. 8 warp/in.; 20 weft/in. Employed mostly in the production of saddle blankets, diamond-twill and vertical-twill techniques are combined in this vegetal-dyed floor rug. Woven of vegetal-dyed tan and brown and natural gray and white handspun wool yarns. (Private collection)

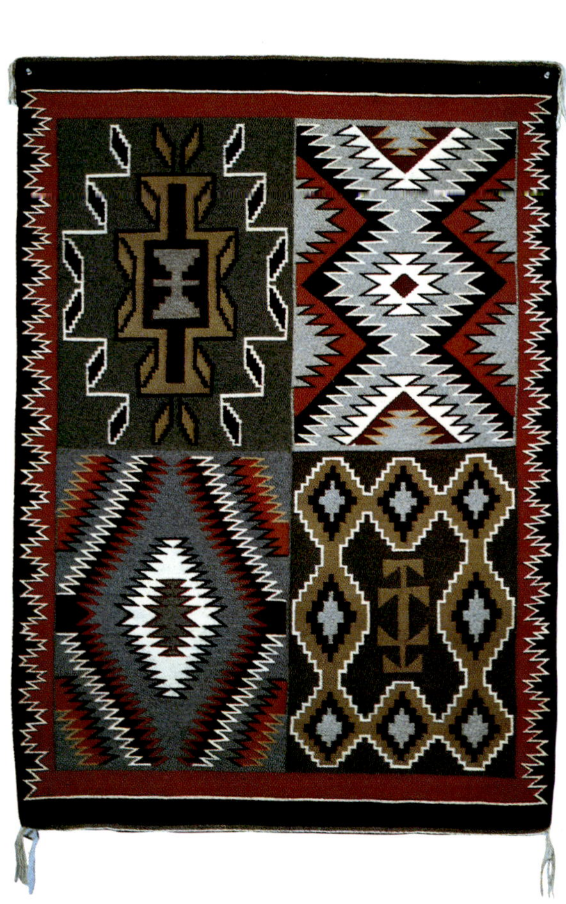

207. Four-in-one rug, contemporary, by Mary Gilmore. 54″ x 39″. 11 warp/in.; 32 weft/in. A carry-over from the late nineteenth-century Germantown multiple-pattern blankets, the rare examples of contemporary multiple-pattern rugs usually consist of only four panels of design. Woven of synthetic-dyed red, tan, gray, and black and natural white processed wool yarns. (Private collection)

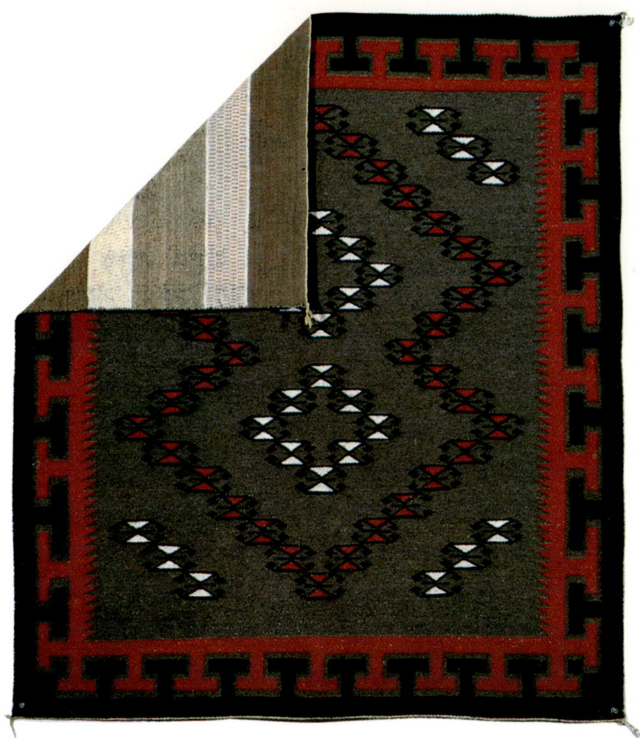

208. Two-faced rug, contemporary, by Audrie Wilson. 52″ x 46″. 8 warp/in.; 20 weft/in. First produced in the late nineteenth century, possibly in response to commercial two-faced Pendleton blankets, two-faced rugs are actually two attached rugs with distinct patterns produced on the same loom at the same time. Difficult to weave and expensive, these rugs are primarily a collector's item. Woven of synthetic-dyed red and black and natural brown, tan, gray, and white hand-spun wool yarns. (Private collection)

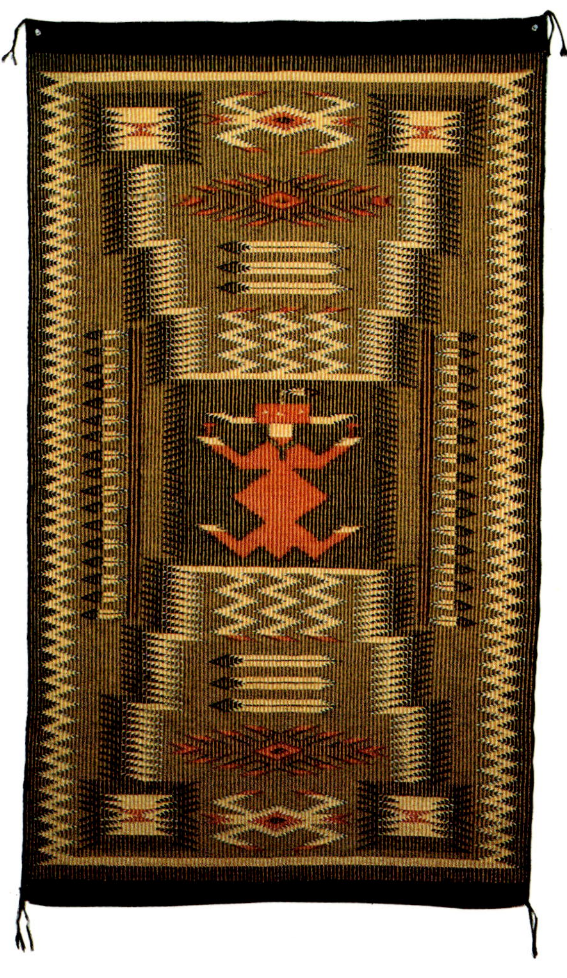

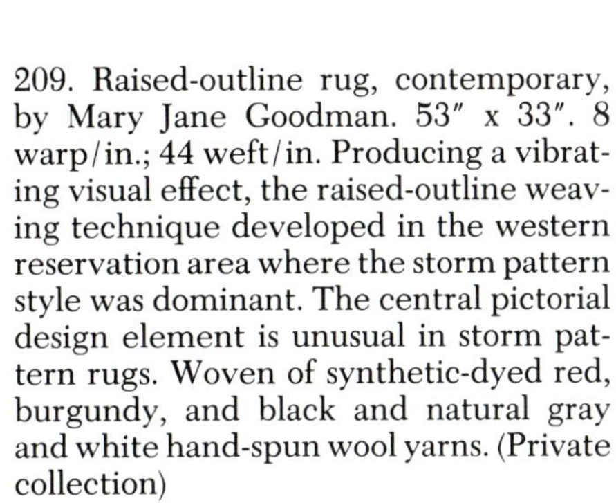

209. Raised-outline rug, contemporary, by Mary Jane Goodman. 53″ x 33″. 8 warp/in.; 44 weft/in. Producing a vibrating visual effect, the raised-outline weaving technique developed in the western reservation area where the storm pattern style was dominant. The central pictorial design element is unusual in storm pattern rugs. Woven of synthetic-dyed red, burgundy, and black and natural gray and white hand-spun wool yarns. (Private collection)

7

THE WEAVING PROCESS—TOOLS, TECHNIQUES, AND MATERIALS

Spider Woman instructed the Navajo women how to weave on a loom which Spider Man told them how to make. The crosspoles were made of sky and earth cords, the warp sticks of sun rays, the heddles of rock crystal and sheet lightning. The batten was a sun halo; white shell made the comb. There were four spindles: one a stick of zigzag lightning with a whorl of cannel coal; one a stick of flash lightning with a whorl of turquoise; a third had a stick of sheet lightning with a whorl of abalone; a rain streamer formed the stick of the fourth, and its whorl was white shell.

Navajo legend[34]

Almost from infancy female Navajos begin to learn the Navajo weaving tradition. Bound in their cradles, the infants rest beside their mothers as they work at the loom. By the time they are young girls they will have assisted their mothers in the preparation of the wool and will have received direct instruction in the weaving process. Many girls of fifteen are able to produce complete blankets and rugs.

The Navajo weaving technique varies little from household to household, and except for periodic changes in materials, tools, and design, the process has remained essentially unchanged for centuries (see fig. 210).

Navajo women traditionally own and care for the sheep, and a family's wealth is measured by the size of the flock. Not all families own sheep and some must purchase wool from a family that does. It is estimated that one adult sheep produces eight to ten pounds of wool, and that it requires the wool from two to three sheep to produce a three-by-five-foot saddle blanket.

WOOL

Introduced into the Southwest by the Spanish, churro sheep provided soft, long, straight, virtually greaseless wool for hand-spinning into natural shades of white, brown, and gray (dark brown and white mixed). Wool from the churro sheep readily accepted hand-dyeing with both natural and synthetic dyes.

In the 1860s, when the Navajos were interned at Bosque Redondo, the U.S. government introduced merino sheep to the Navajos. Interbreeding of churro and merino sheep led to a deterioration in the quality of Navajo wool and a decline in the use handspun yarn.

About 1910 the U.S. government introduced the French rambouillet sheep to the Navajos. Although they proved to be a good source of mutton, the rambouillet sheep possessed a short, oily fleece, difficult to clean and spin and resistant to dyeing. This led to a further decline in the quality of the Navajo hand-spun weavings.

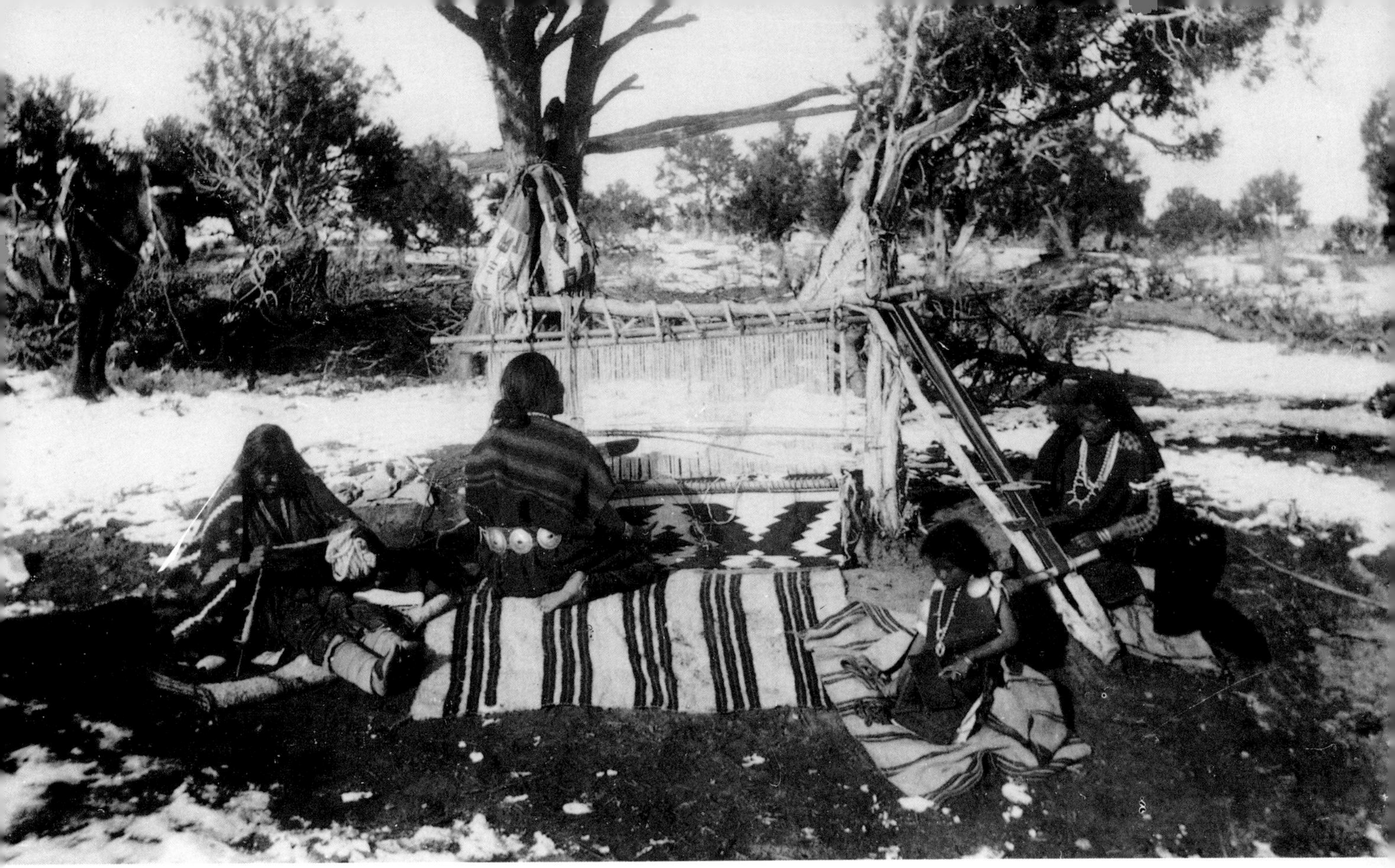

210. Navajo women carding, spinning, and weaving, c. 1893. The Navajo weaving process from sheep to finished product on the loom has remained essentially unchanged since its inception. Note the belt or sash loom set up at the right side of the blanket loom. (Photograph courtesy Smithsonian Institution)

211. Enlarged detail (3" horizontal section from fig. 47) showing fine raveled S-spun bayeta on top, hand-spun wool below. In this instance, several strands of bayeta are grouped together to equal the diameter of the hand-spun yarn. All Navajo hand-spun wool is Z spun, spun from right to left, as is the earliest bayeta of Southwest and Mexican origin. Most bayeta raveled during the Classic Period is S spun, spun from left to right, with later varieties of bayeta being predominantly Z spun. S spun Z spun

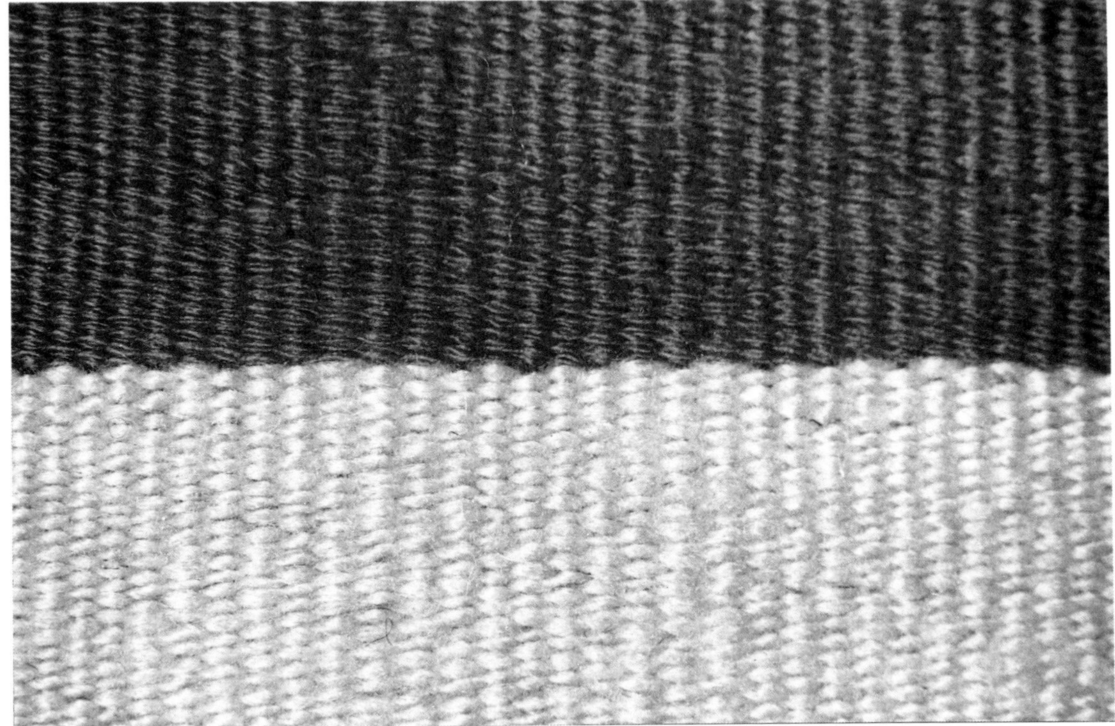

In 1934 the government established a sheep-breeding laboratory on the Navajo reservation to improve the breed, and such experiments continue into the 1980s.

Shearing. The shearing of sheep usually takes place in the late spring or early summer when the wool is thickest. In the early years any sharp-edged instrument was used. By the late nineteenth century metal shears were available through trading posts and the hiring of professional shearers who worked for a percentage of the wool became a common practice.

Cleaning. The initial cleaning process of raw wool was accomplished by shaking out the dirt and picking out by hand any entangled foreign objects such as twigs and burrs. The wool was washed only if it was too dirty to be carded and spun or if the wool was to be dyed. Most of the wool shorn from mixed breeds had to be washed. In the early periods the wool was washed with a native soap solution that was usually made from the dried, powdered root of one of the Spanish amole or yucca plants. In more recent times commercially available detergents have been used. The wool must be thoroughly rinsed before it is dyed.

Carding. Carding, or the straightening, aligning, and further cleaning of wool fibers in preparation for spinning, was accomplished in the early period with brushes made of rows of thistle burrs lashed to a wooden frame modeled after the Spanish/Mexican type of brush. Since the late nineteenth century metal-toothed "tow cards" were available through the traders.

Spinning. Both in tools and techniques, the hand-spinning of yarns is done in the same way as it has been done for centuries. The use of the compact and portable spindle whorl, used natively in North and South America since prehistoric times, offered obvious advantages to the traditionally mobile Navajos over the cumbersome European spinning wheel. The twisting of parallel wool fibers into a suitable yarn fine enough for use as weft material usually requires at least two spinnings, with three spinnings being normal to create yarn fine enough to use as warp. Several thousand yards of yarn are needed to produce a good-quality four-by-six-foot weaving. Only the amount of yarn needed for each weaving is actually spun, and the spinning process often goes on while the weaving is in progress. Spinning is sometimes done by a young girl or by an older woman family member who is no longer capable of weaving herself.

Today, many weavers send out their wool to be processed. This wool is returned to the weaver cleaned, carded, spun, and sometimes dyed.

COMMERCIAL MATERIALS

Bayeta. Any commercially produced wool trade cloth raveled by Southeast weavers, bayeta was first introduced into the Southwest by way of Mexico by the Spanish. The earliest bayeta was probably of European origin. In time, bayeta was produced not only in Europe but also in different parts of the New World, including Mexico and Santa Fe, New Mexico, where by the early nineteenth century cochineal-dyed red woolen bayeta was being produced. The dominant material raveled by Classic Period Navajo weavers, however, was worsted bayeta dyed red with Asian lac dye. Red woolen bayeta dyed with lac/cochineal mixed or pure cochineal dye began to replace lac-dyed worsted bayeta in Navajo weaving by 1860. In the 1860s and 1870s along with raveling bayeta, it was also a common practice to card raveled red bayeta with native white wool to produce a pink yarn. American-made bayeta, much of which is often referred to as American flannel because of its fuzzy texture, was introduced to the Navajo in 1867. Much of the American bayeta was dyed with the newly developed synthetic dyes and was often red-orange in color. Lower grades of bayeta were sometimes raveled, recarded, and respun to make a sturdier and finer yarn, or were cut into strips and woven whole into the coarser utility blankets such as the diyugi.

Saxony. Produced in Europe, Saxony yarns were three-ply commercial yarns spun from merino wool and dyed with presynthetic natural dyes. These yarns are characterized by their fine, silky texture and appearance (see fig. 212). Saxony yarns were shipped to the Southwest, first by way of the Spain–Mexico–New Mexico trade route, and after the Mexican-American war by way of the Eastern United States. Although used by New Mexican weavers as early as the seventeenth century the use of Saxony yarn in Navajo weaving is very rare prior to 1846. Saxony yarns were manufactured in many colors with all colors used occasionally by Navajo weavers, but cochineal-dyed red was the favorite, as it was often used in place of bayeta. The first use of synthetic-dyed yarn in Navajo weaving occurred with the introduction of a synthetic-dyed violet color Saxony-type yarn in the 1860s.

Germantown. Early three-ply Germantown yarns, the products of Eastern U.S. textiles mills, were introduced to Navajo weavers after 1863. Germantown, Pennsylvania, was one of the major American textile-producing centers, and the yarns that were supplied to the Navajos, first by the U.S. government and later by reservation traders, came from many different mills in the Eastern United States. Although Germantown yarn is

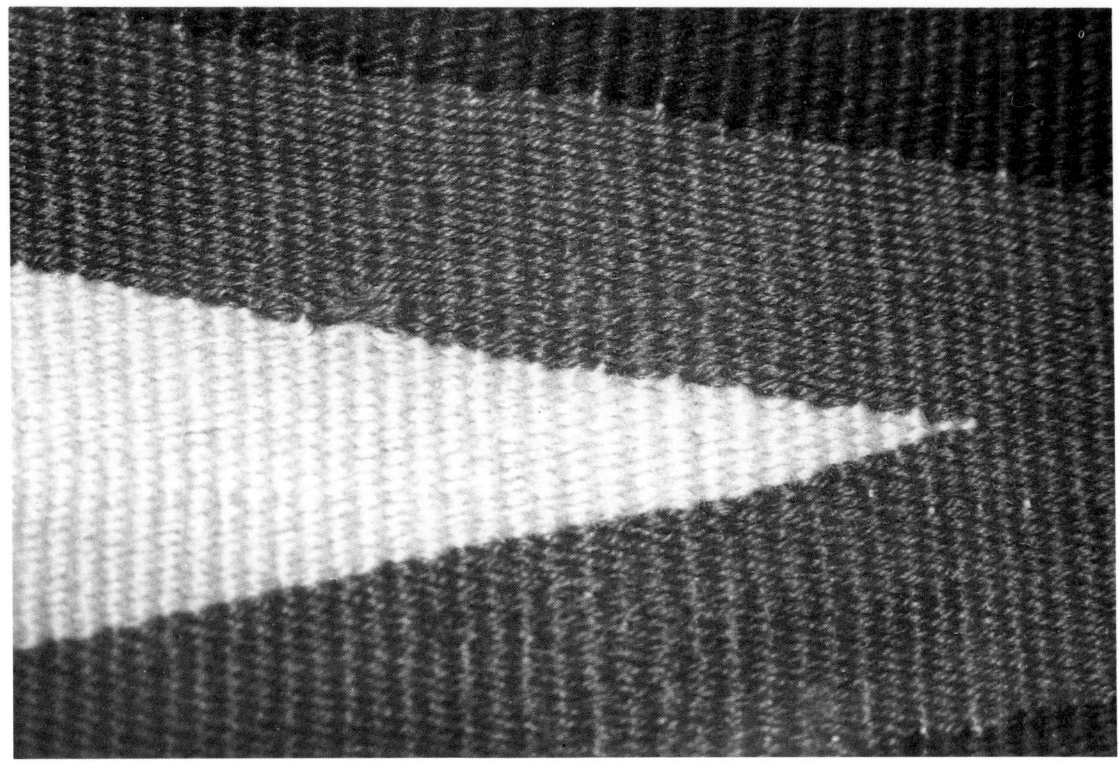

212. Enlarged detail (3″ horizontal section from fig. 66) showing three-ply commercial Saxony yarn sandwiched between two colors of hand-spun yarns.

213. Enlarged detail showing four-ply commercial Germantown yarn at left, coarse raveled American Z-spun bayeta or flannel at right. Note the diagonal or serrate lines separating the two materials, typical in Late Classic/early Transitional Period weaving.

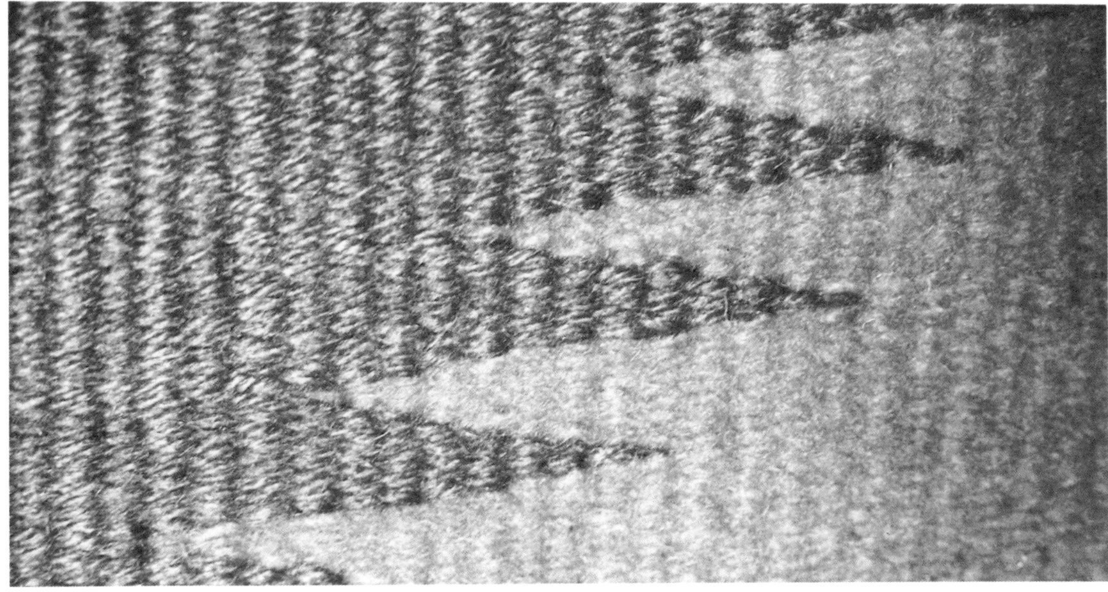

known for its wide range of synthetic-dyed colors, for the first five to ten years of the production of this yarn in the three-ply form, cochineal was often used as the red dye source.

Navajo weavers first used Germantown yarn in combination with hand-spun, Saxony, and raveled bayeta yarn. Three-ply Germantown yarn is larger in diameter and coarser to the touch than three-ply Saxony yarn. By 1875 four-ply Germantown yarn in an even wider range of bright, synthetic, dye colors was available to Navajos (fig. 213). The early synthetic dyes used on Germantown yarn were prone to fading and bleeding.

Processed wool. Wool produced from the various breeds and crossbreeds of Navajo sheep was sometimes commercially cleaned, cleaned and spun, or cleaned, spun, and dyed, and returned to the Navajo weavers for use in their textiles. In the last few years most processed wool has taken the form of cleaned, spun (usually into plies), and dyed yarn, colored with synthetic dyes to resemble soft vegetal-dyed or strong synthetic-dyed hand-spun yarns.

DYES

Presynthetic. *Blue:* The indigo plant, which was cultivated by the Spanish in the Old World, produced a rich blue color. The indigo dyestuff was expensive and complicated to use: the leaves of the indigo plant were first fermented, dried, and cut into cubes before being exported to the New World initially through the Spanish Colonial trade network. Although indigo dye does not require a mordant, or fixative, the dye does require the addition of a strong alkaline solution as a carrier. For this purpose, Navajos would store and ferment urine. In solution with the urine, the dye itself appears green, but once the yarn has soaked for several days and is hung to dry, exposure to the air oxidizes the dye and the colored yarn turns blue. Indigo blue is very stable and rarely fades or bleeds. It was used by Navajo weavers until the late nineteenth century.

Red: Although red is the predominant color associated with nineteenth-century Navajo blankets, before 1863, strong red color was obtained only by raveling predyed bayeta trade cloth or the use of cochineal-dyed three-ply Saxony yarn. The predominant red dye type used to dye the bayeta for Navajo blankets prior to 1860 was an Old World commercial dye made from the powdered, dried carcass of the Near Eastern lac or kermes beetle. About 1860 lac dyes were gradually replaced, first by a lac-cochineal dye mixture, and then about 1865 by pure cochineal dye as the red dye type used to dye the bayeta in Navajo blankets. Cochineal dye was a product of an insect similar to the lac beetle but native to the New World. Both cochineal and lac dyes produced a range of color shades from pale pink to orange to dark maroon, depending on the fixative, or mordant, used in the dyeing process. Although cochineal dyes were stronger than lac dyes in color, unlike lac dyes they were subject to fading. The mixing of the two dye types produced a color that was both rich and resistant to fading. Synthetic dyes all but replaced lac and cochineal dyes by 1880.

Recent chemical dye analysis of red yarns used in early Navajo blankets, documented as to date of collection, has made it possible not only to determine dye type (that is, lac, cochineal, lac/cochineal mixed, or synthetic) but also to generalize more accurately about when the various dye types were in popular use. Comparative studies of design elements and patterns, materials, and dye types have made it possible to date more accurately most early Navajo blankets.

Yellow: Shades of pale yellow obtained from a variety of wild plants, primarily rabbit brush, were the only native vegetal colors known to have been used by Navajo weavers in the nineteenth century. The flowers of the rabbit brush were boiled down to a strong color, a fixative such as native alum was added, and natural white hand-spun yarn was hot-dyed for several hours before being hung to dry. The shade and intensity of the yellow obtained depended on the dye strength, the amount and type of fixative used, and the duration of immersion time. If properly produced, native yellow was resistant to fading and bleeding. Most examples of existing Classic Period Navajo textiles employing yellow date after 1850. The use of vegetal yellow diminished at the end of the nineteenth century only to be revived during the period of vegetal-dye experimentation in the 1920s.

Green: Shades of green color were produced by mixing vegetal yellow dye with indigo blue dye. The ratio of dyes mixed, the strength of the dyes, and the duration of yarn immersion determined the shade of green. Overdyeing of vegetal yellow yarn with indigo blue dye would also produce shades of green. Few existing Classic Period textiles made before 1850 contain any green-dyed hand-spun yarn. Like vegetal yellow, presynthetic green was resistant to fading and bleeding. Raveled vegetal-dyed green bayeta occurs usually in small quantities in some Classic blankets, mostly those woven after 1850. The use of vegetal/indigo green diminished in the late nineteenth century.

Black: A very dark brown, almost black color could be obtained by dyeing natural hand-spun brown wool with a mixture of boiled-down native sumac or piñon

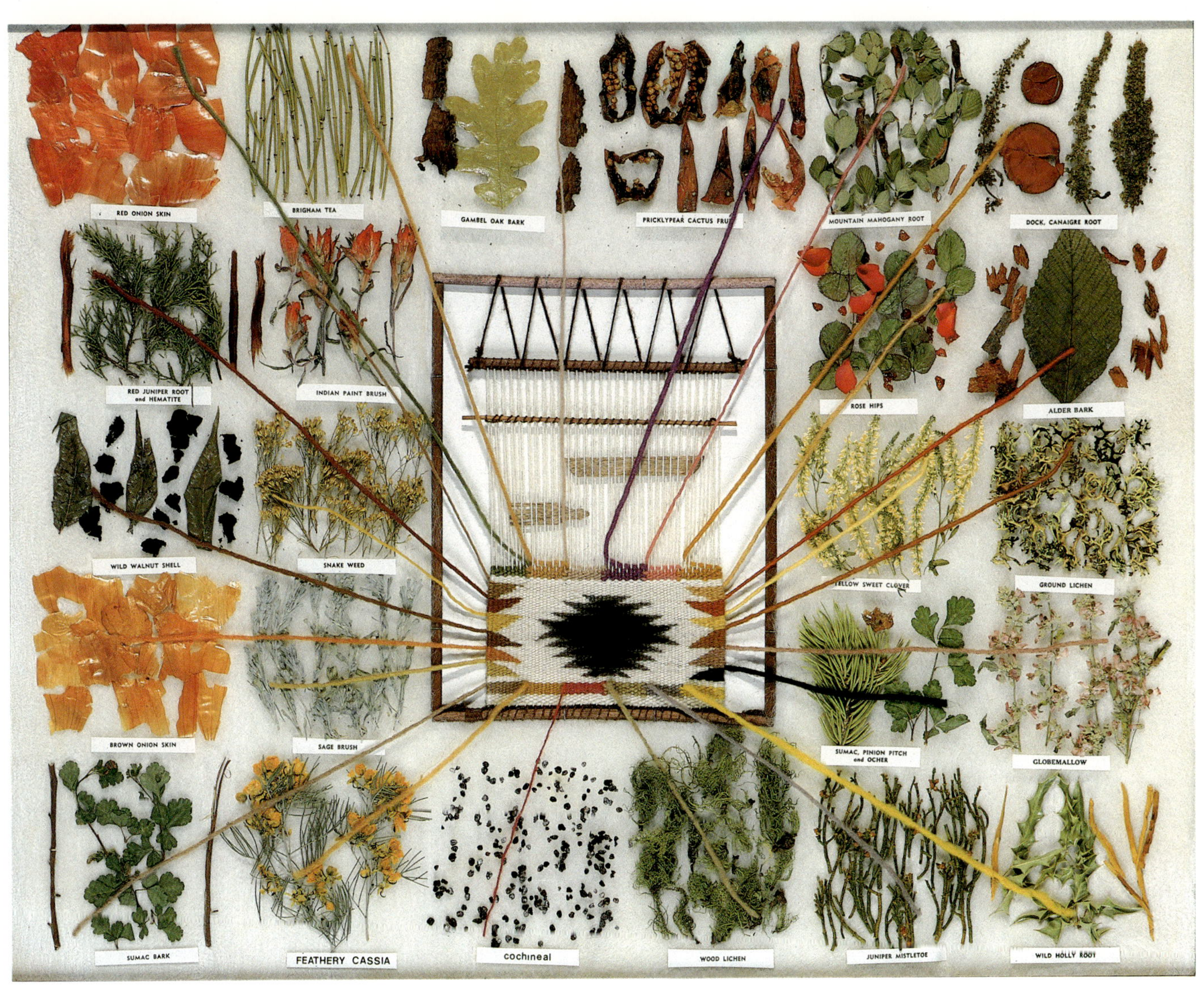

214. Vegetal dye samples. Twenty-four samples of plants and vegetal colorations commonly used by weavers of contemporary vegetal-dye rugs. (Photograph courtesy Garland's Navajo Rugs)

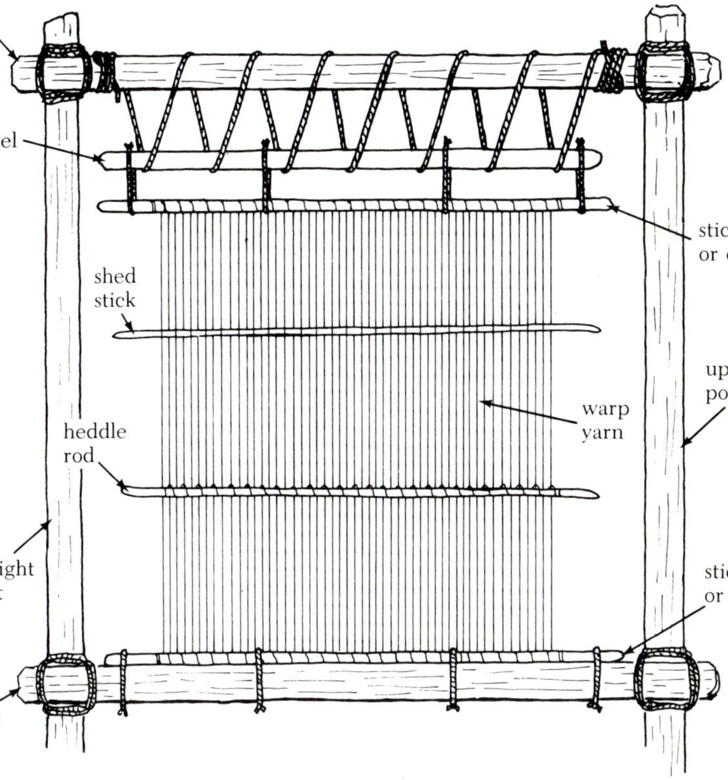

215. The Navajo loom.

pitch and native yellow ochre mineral. The overdyeing of natural brown hand-spun wool to darken it to black increased in popularity after 1865, but decreased in the late nineteenth century when the overdyeing was more easily accomplished with synthetic black dyes.

Synthetic dyes. The first synthetic dye was a violet color dye that was accidentally discovered in 1856 by William Henry Perkin in England as a by-product of the distillation of coal. The range of colors that could be synthesized rapidly expanded, and by the time synthetic dyes reached the Navajos a whole new spectrum of color was available. Although the early synthetic dyes were inexpensive to produce, they were not easy to use, as is indicated by their general absence from Navajo hand-spun yarns until the late 1870s when packets of dyes were supplied to the Navajo by the traders for dyeing white hand-spun yarn. All that was needed to produce a strong color was hot water and a brief immersion time. Unfortunately, early synthetic dyes tended to fade badly and to bleed when exposed to moisture. After a period of experimentation with bright color (1875–1890), most Navajo weavers settled on a smaller number of their traditional favorite colors. Red and red/orange were the dominant synthetic colors of the late nineteenth and early twentieth centuries. The 1930s saw the development of new commercial synthetic dyes with subtler color tones that resembled native vegetal dyes. Synthetic dyes of both the strong and subtle types continue to be used in contemporary weaving. Most of the new synthetic dyes are resistant to both fading and bleeding.

Vegetal dyes. Although Navajo weavers flirted with native yellows during the Classic Period, widespread use of vegetal dyes did not occur until the 1920s, and the use of these colors was a result of Anglo taste and encouragement. Virtually any part of the native plants—leaves, stems, roots, nuts, berries, or flowers—could be used to produce a potential dye source. More than 250 native vegetal-dye colors have been discovered to date. The predominant colors being produced today are soft shades of yellow, beige, brown, tan, rose/red, green, and orange.

Among the factors that determine which color will be produced are: (1) plant type or species; (2) season harvested as well as region harvested from; (3) dye strength (the amount of plant material used and which parts of the plant used); (4) mordant type (alum, baking soda, juniper ash) and quantity; (5) length of time of immersion in dye bath; (6) mixture of dye types; and use of fresh versus dried plant material.

Most dye baths are prepared hot. After the yarn has soaked for several days, it is hung to dry. Some early vegetal dyes were known to fade, but most contemporary vegetal dyes are resistant to both fading and bleeding.

THE LOOM

By the tenth century the Pueblo Indians of the Southwest were producing cotton textiles on the upright loom, which, with little modification, was adopted by Navajo weavers and is still used by them today. Portable and easy to assemble, the Navajo loom consists of a rectangular outer and inner frame. The outer frame is constructed from two sturdy vertical supports, traditionally made from piñon logs. Occasionally two young living trees that grew conveniently near each other were used, but usually two logs were embedded in the earth or supported with boulders. Lashed to the vertical supports are two horizontal crossbeams, the bottom one usually larger in diameter than the top beam, to aid in the anchoring of the loom. The inner frame, upon which the warp is strung, consists of two smaller (approximately one inch), smooth, straight sticks. The width and length of the weaving is determined by the length of these sticks and their distance from each other (see fig. 215).

To facilitate the warping process, the inner frame is laid out parallel to the ground. The warp yarn is strung in a continuous figure-8 manner between the two beams. Five to twenty warps per inch is standard. Once the warping of the inner frame is completed, two thin, round sticks (or shed rods) are inserted into the upper and lower cavities between the front and back sets of warps created by the warp beams to preserve the two distinct sets of warps once the warp beams are removed.

The four edges of a Navajo weaving are reinforced with the application of a doubled selvage cord that is applied in an intertwining manner with the top and bottom selvage cords catching each warp to maintain proper warp spacing prior to the removal of the top and bottom warp beams (fig. 216). Reattachment to the inner frame is made by lashing a new set of warp beams to the top and bottom selvage cords, thus allowing the entire length of warp to be used in the weaving process.

The inner frame is now ready for incorporation into the larger outer frame. The top warp beam is lashed to an intermediary tension beam that hangs loosely from the top outer frame cross member and allows the weaver continuously to adjust the tension of her warps and to lower the weaving to within reach as the work progresses. The bottom warp beam is lashed directly to

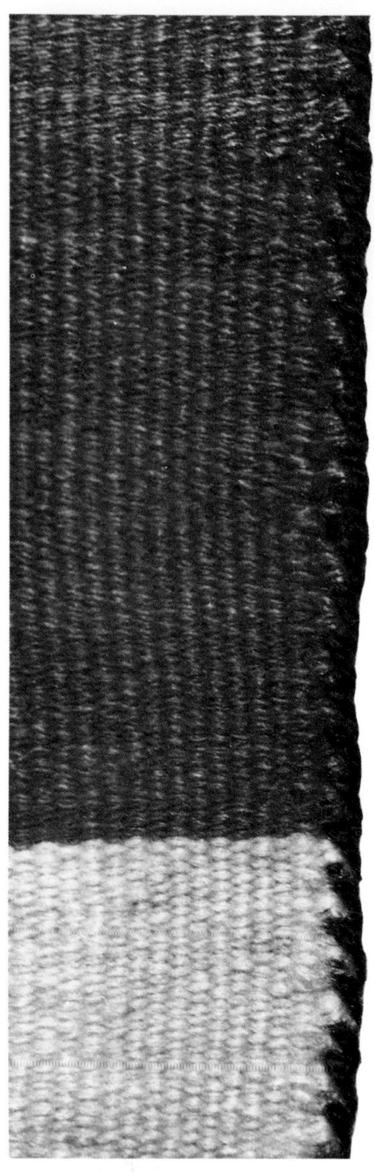

216. Enlarged detail (3″ vertical section from fig. 47) showing Navajo side selvage binding (two cords of three plies each).

217. Enlarged detail (3″ horizontal section from fig. 47) showing "lazy" line created by weaving on the diagonal within the same color—a common characteristic of Navajo weaving.

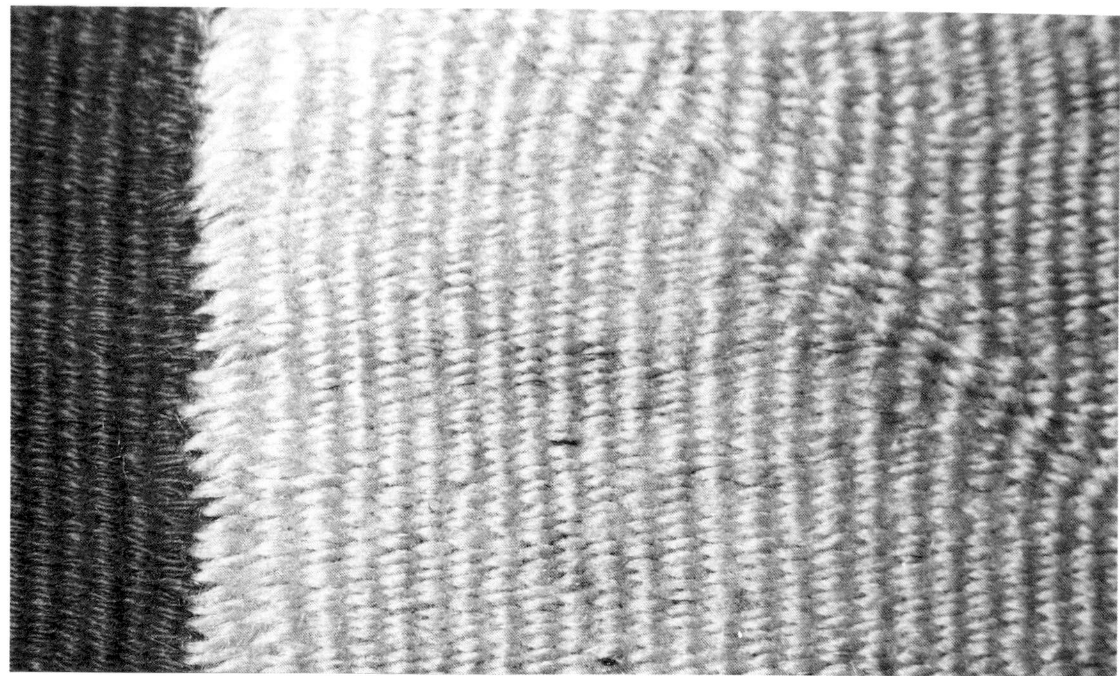

the bottom outer frame cross member. A long, doubled selvage cord, which hangs next to each side warp and is intertwined with each weft element, is attached to the top warp beam at both the left and right corners.

Once the inner frame is mounted in the outer frame the upper shed rod is often replaced by a flatter, wider shed rod. A heddle rod is attached to the rear set of warps with continuous loops of fine warp yarn, allowing the weaver to create a second shed by pulling forward the back set of warps, thus creating an additional space through which to pass her weft yarn. The heddle rod must be moved occasionally as the weaving progresses so that the weaver can maintain a large enough shed space through which to pass her weft. As a result, a lasting physical impression of the previous heddle positions may remain visible in the finished textile. This loom trait is especially noticeable in finely woven nineteenth-century blankets, but is usually less noticeable and better concealed in contemporary weaving.

WEAVING TECHNIQUES

Plain Weave. The most basic and earliest of all weaving techniques, plain weave grew out of the simple over-and-under plaited basketry-weave technique, which leaves both the warps and wefts clearly visible. Navajo weavers abandoned the plain-weave technique early on, but Pueblo weavers continue to use it, especially in the production of cotton ceremonial garments.

Tapestry weave. The tapestry-weave technique has been the dominant Navajo weaving technique for the last two hundred years. In tapestry weave the weft elements are packed down so tightly that the warp is not visible. The Navajo weaver executes the tapestry technique by inserting her batten between the front and back warp sets to create a shed. She then loosely lays in her weft and packs it down with the fork. The weaver then repeats the process in the opposite direction through the second shed created by pulling the rear set of warps forward, which she maintains with the batten. Patterns are created by changing the color of the weft yarns. An experienced weaver can expect to complete up to one square foot of woven area per day, depending, of course, on the complexity of the pattern and the fineness of the weave. This fineness can vary from six to more than one hundred weft elements per linear inch. Unlike her Pueblo teachers, the Navajo weaves a small area at a time (how small is determined by her reach), often changing from one color to another, before physically moving to weave in the next area of the textile. This technique leaves visible lines in the weaving, which are called lazy lines and are unrelated to the pattern itself (fig. 217).

Twill weave. Predominant in Pueblo textiles from the days of the Anasazi through recent times, the various twill-weave techniques were rarely used by Navajo weavers after 1800 but made a brief resurgence in popularity in the 1870s, particularly in the weaving of saddle throws and women's mantas. Twill weaves are considered to be sturdier than tapestry weaves, making this technique particularly appropriate in the making of saddle throws. The twill-weave mantas of the 1870s appear to be a revival of the earlier Pueblo style. Occasionally a finely woven wearing blanket will display one of the twill techniques either overall or in small banded areas.

All twill weaves are produced by floating the weft elements over more than one warp at a time to create a raised pattern of color and texture. Three twill-weave techniques were used by both Navajo and Pueblo weavers: plain twill forming diagonal floats; herringbone twill, in which the diagonal floats alternate direction to form a vertical zigzag or chevron pattern; and diamond twill, in which the herringbone patterns are woven in such a manner as to create concentric diamond patterns (fig. 218).

A new style of rug weaving that developed out of combining twill techniques is the double-weave rug, named for its color reversal from one side of the textile to the other. The pattern remains the same on both sides, but by alternating the color of the weft throughout the width of the sheds, two distinct sides are obtained. Many of the weavings done in this style bear an uncanny resemblance to early American coverlets.

A recent development in the use of a floating weft to create a three-dimensional impression is the raised-outline technique, developed in the vicinity of the Coal Mine Mesa area of the Navajo reservation in the 1950s. Wefts of two different colors, one from each shed, are floated over two warps of each design edge to further emphasize the outline of the design in this otherwise normal tapestry-weave technique. The raised outline occurs only on the front (or weaver's) side of the textile (see fig. 209).

Pulled-warp or wedge-weave technique. This innovative but short-lived variation on the tapestry-weave technique came into limited popularity in the 1870s. Pulled-warp weaving required the weaver to force the normally vertical warps into a diagonal position. Packing the weft in place while the warps were on a diagonal kept the warp cords from returning to the vertical posi-

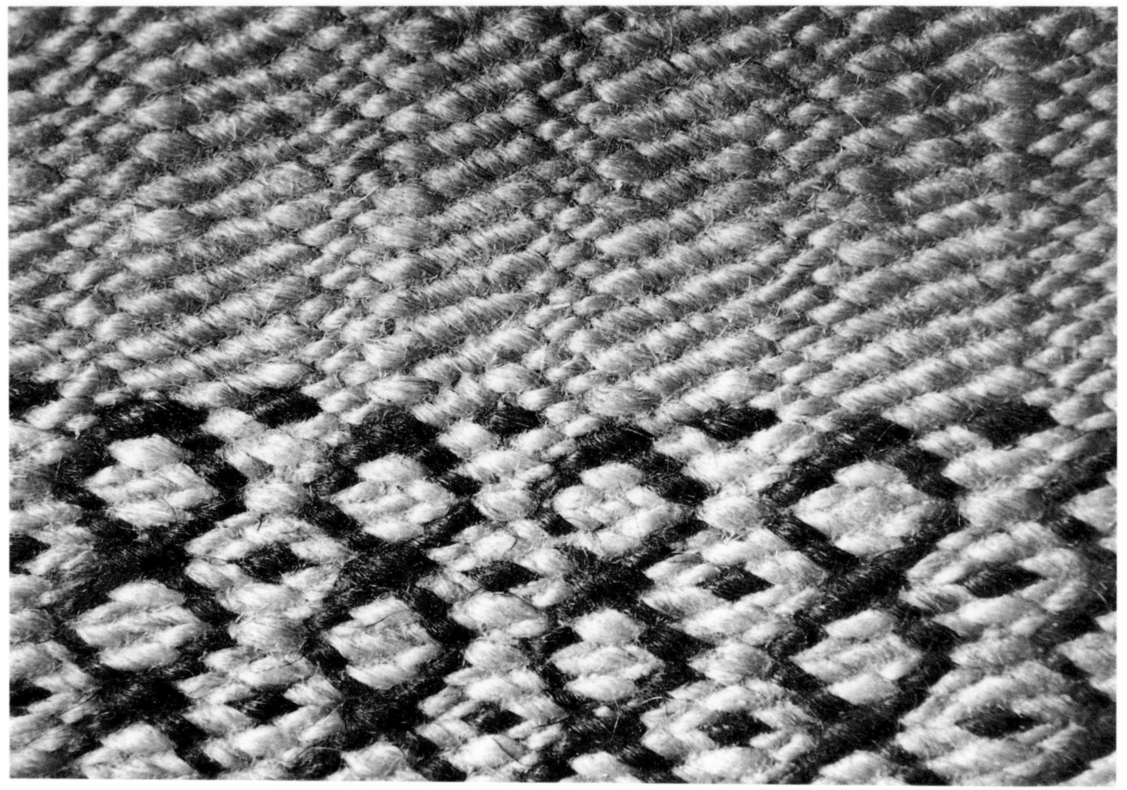

218. Enlarged detail (3″ horizontal section from fig. 100) showing diamond and herringbone twill techniques.

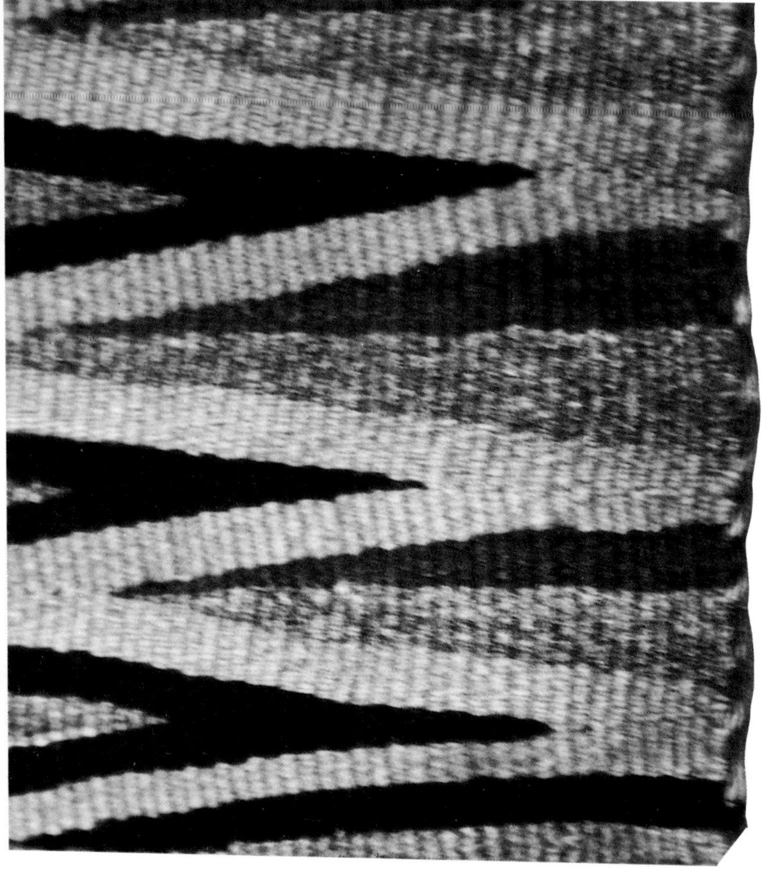

219. Enlarged detail (approximately 6″ vertical section from fig. 96) showing pulled-warp technique. Note the wavy nonlinear arrangement of the unexposed vertical warps.

tion. The end product was a series of diagonal or zigzag stripes running vertically either overall or restricted to bands, the bands usually alternated with bands of natural white or gray. These visually dynamic weavings were often executed in all hand-spun yarns, usually in combinations of bright aniline colors and natural wool colors. By 1900 the pulled-warp technique had been abandoned (see figs. 95 and 96).

Another technical innovation of the late nineteenth century was the two-face weave, which was the weaving of two separate textiles with entirely different patterns on the same loom. This was achieved by using four separate sets of warps with two sets of wefts, one placed behind the other. Two-face rugs are still being made today (see fig. 208).

In concluding this chapter it would be remiss not to at least mention two final and highly unusual weaving techniques, the Tufted rug and the Circular rug. The Tufted rug resembles a shag carpet with long strands of angora goat hair woven into the weft during the weaving process to produce a thick stringy surface. The Circular rug is the unique creation of a handful of weavers who secretly guard their technique. Circular rugs are usually woven with a Ganado-like pattern in a regular tapestry weave and rarely exceed three feet in diameter.

220. The Vanishing Race, by Edward S. Curtiss. c. 1909. (Photograph courtesy University Museum, University of Pennsylvania)

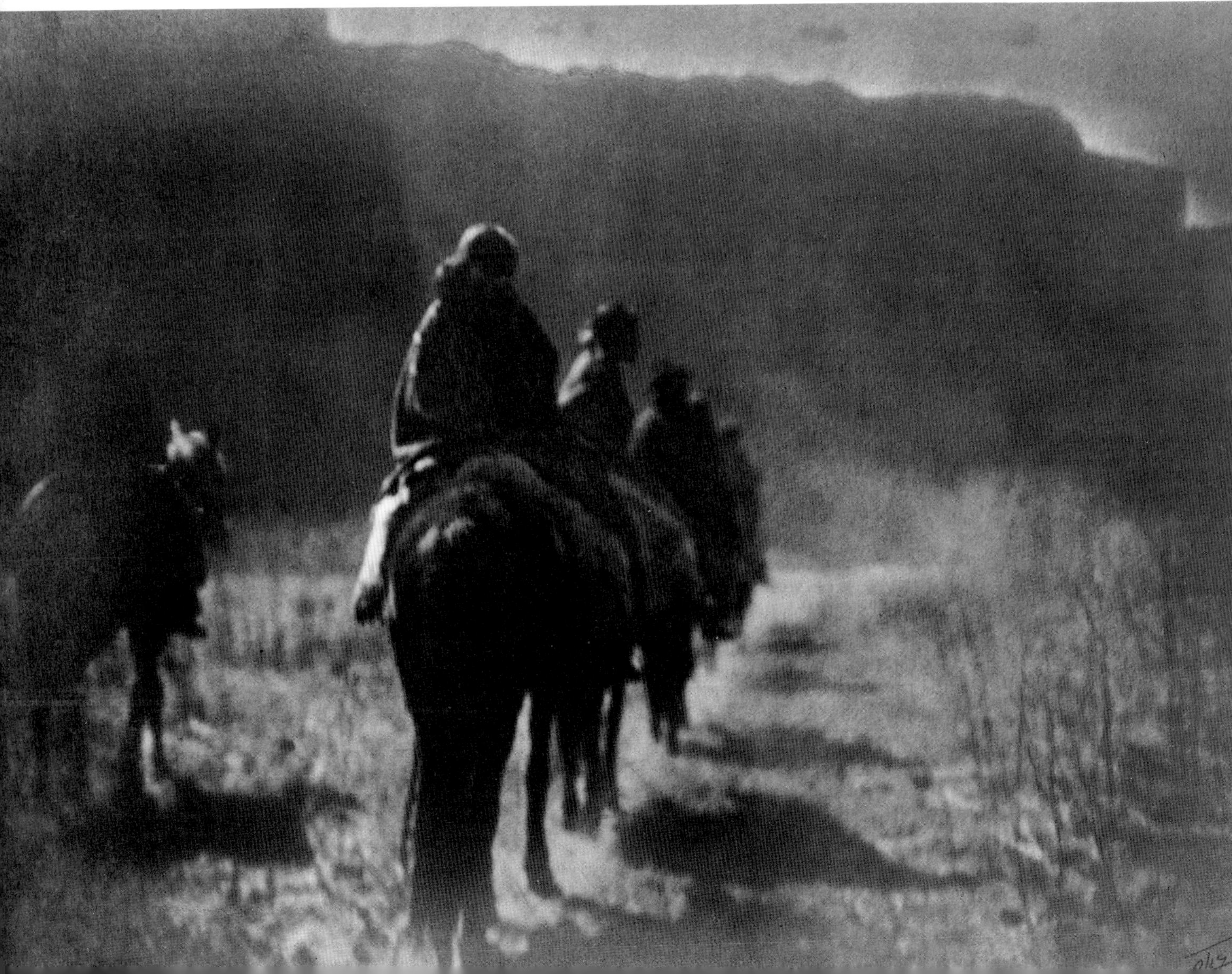

NOTES

1. Dr. Washington Matthews, *Third Annual Report of the Bureau of Ethnology 1881–1882* (Washington, D.C.: Government Printing Office, 1884), p. 375.
2. John Adair, *The Navajo and Pueblo Silversmiths* (Norman: University of Oklahoma Press, 1944), p. 135.
3. This and the other Navajo chants in this chapter are quoted from Marcia Keegan, *Mother Earth, Father Sky* (New York: Grossman Publishers, 1974).
4. John Upton Terrell, *The Navajos* (New York: Weybright & Talley, 1970), p. 20.
5. Joe Ben Wheat, "Rio Grande, Pueblo and Navajo Weavers: Cross Cultural Influences," in *Spanish Textile Tradition of New Mexico and Colorado* (Santa Fe: Museum of New Mexico Press, 1979), p. 30.
6. Kate Peck Kent, "From Blanket to Rug: The Evolution of Navajo Weaving After 1880," in *Tension and Harmony: The Navajo Rug, Plateau* 52, no. 4 (Flagstaff: Museum of Northern Arizona Press, 1981), p. 18.
7. Quoted in Charles Avery Amsden, *Navaho Weaving: Its Technic, and Its History* (Glorietta, N.M.: The Rio Grande Press, 1974), p. 132.
8. *Ibid.*, p. 133.
9. Terrell, *The Navajos,* p. 56.
10. Amsden, *Navaho Weaving,* p. 153.
11. Terrell, *The Navajos,* p. 50.
12. Joe Ben Wheat, *Navajo Blankets from the Collection of Anthony Berlant* (Tucson: University of Arizona Museum of Art, 1974), Introduction.
13. *Ibid.*
14. Nora Fisher and Joe Ben Wheat, *The Materials of Southwestern Weaving: Spanish Textile Traditions of New Mexico and Colorado* (Santa Fe: University of New Mexico Press, 1979), p. 199.
15. Wheat, *Navajo Blankets,* Introduction.
16. Amsden, *Navaho Weaving,* pp. 97–98.
17. Quoted in Amsden, *Navaho Weaving,* p. 159.
18. Quoted in *ibid.,* p. 164.
19. Quoted in Terrell, *The Navajos,* p. 196.
20. Wheat, "Rio Grande, Pueblo and Navajo Weavers," p. 33.
21. Terrell, *The Navajos,* p. 159.
22. Gerald Thompson, *The Army and the Navajo* (Tucson: University of Arizona Press, 1976), p. 14.
23. Quoted in Amsden, *Navaho Weaving,* p. 160.
24. Thompson, *The Army and the Navajo,* p. 102.
25. *Ibid.,* p. 122.
26. Robert M. Utley and Wilcomb E. Washburn, *The American Heritage History of the Indian Wars* (New York: American Heritage, 1977), p. 230.
27. Jules Loh, *Lords of the Earth* (New York: The Macmillan Company, 1971), p. 129.
28. "New Tribe Leader Picked by Navajos," *The New York Times,* November 4, 1982, p. A16.
29. Amsden, *Navaho Weaving,* p. 179.
30. *The Romantic Story of Pendleton Blankets* (Pendleton Woolen Mills, Pendleton, Ore.).
31. Gilbert S. Maxwell, *Navajo Rugs, Past, Present, and Future* (Palm Desert, Calif.: Best West Publications, 1963), pp. 61, 63.
32. Amsden, *Navaho Weaving,* pp. 227, 225.
33. Nonabah G. Bryan, *Navajo Native Dyes, Their Preparation and Use* (Palmer Lake, Colo.: Filter Press, 1940), pp. 19, 21.
34. Washington Mathews, *Navajo Legends* (Boston: American Folklore Society, 1897).

GLOSSARY

Anasazi Navajo term for "the ancient ones," the prehistoric Pueblo Indians who built and lived in the great masonry towns of the American Southwest.

aniline dye A type of early synthetic dye commonly used in the last quarter of the nineteenth century to dye both commercial and hand-spun wool yarns.

bayeta Spanish term for English baize; in fact, any commercially produced wool cloth, raveled by Southwest weavers and incorporated into their own textiles.

Bazan brothers Spanish Colonial master weavers sent from Mexico to Santa Fe in the early nineteenth century to revive the declining Colonial weaving industry.

blanket dress The traditional Navajo woman's dress form by 1800, made from two identical rectangular front and back blankets, joined at the shoulder and sides.

Bosque Redondo Spanish for circle of trees. A place in eastern New Mexico near Fort Sumner where the Navajos were interned from 1863 to 1868.

Chief blanket A striped wearing blanket descended from the Pueblo manta, woven wider than long and worn horizontally. The Chief blanket underwent three distinct design phases as well as many innovative variations during the second half of the nineteenth century.

child's sarape A small, finely woven wearing blanket approximately two and a half by four feet, patterned after larger sarapes and woven to the proportions of a child.

"Chinle revival" Beginning in the late 1920s, a movement to return to the unbordered, banded patterns reminiscent of Classic and Late Classic blanket patterns began in the Chinle region of the Navajo Reservation and subsequently expanded to surrounding areas. The yarns used in these rugs were largely colored with native vegetal dyes.

churro sheep The small, strong breed of sheep introduced into the Southwest by the Spanish in the 1500s, whose long, straight, greaseless wool was ideal for weaving.

Classic Period The period from 1800 to 1865 in Navajo weaving, characterized by the development of the Chief blanket and sarape patterns and the use of bayeta, Saxony yarns, and indigo dye.

"Classic revival" weavings Late nineteenth- and early twentieth-century copies of Classic or Late Classic Period blankets, usually woven with Germantown synthetic-dyed and natural hand-spun yarns.

cochineal dye A natural (presynthetic) source for the color red produced from powdered carcass of the New World cochineal insect.

commercial yarn Any machine-spun and plied wool yarn.

Dine, Dinetah *Dine* is the Navajo word for the People, meaning the Navajos; *Dinetah* is the land of the Navajos.

diyugi Coarsely woven, everyday, all-purpose, utility blankets.

"eyedazzler" A Navajo weaving style begun in the last quarter of the nineteenth century, largely as a result of the influence of the serrated-diamond style of Rio Grande/Saltillo weaving and the introduction of multiple colors of bright synthetic dyes.

Germantown The generic term for commercial three- and four-ply, synthetic-dyed wool yarns, manufactured in the Eastern United States after 1863.

hand-spun yarn Yarn produced by hand from raw wool, usually in the form of a single ply.

indigo A plant dye source for the color blue, introduced to the Southwest by the Spanish and widely used in Navajo weaving until the end of the nineteenth century.

lac dye A natural (presynthetic) source for the color red produced from the powdered extracts of the Asian lac insect.

Late Classic Period The period 1865 to 1875 in Navajo weaving characterized by dramatic cultural change and the introduction of new design elements (crosses, meanders, interrupted diagonal stripes, vertical zigzags) and new weaving materials into the earlier Classic Period style.

manta A woman's shawl or cape, woven wider than long, produced by both Navajo and Pueblo weavers.

meander A repetitive up, across, down, across, angular (always at right angles) horizontal wavy stripe design element commonly found in Late Classic blankets.

"Moki" sarape A blue, brown, and sometimes with white banded background blanket style, influenced by striped Rio Grande blankets, and often elaborated on by the Navajos with the introduction of terraced or serrate design in red.

mordant A substance, usually added to a dye bath, which helps the dye adhere to the yarn.

overdyeing The dyeing of natural brown hand-spun wool yarn with either natural or synthetic black dyes to intensify the color. Also refers to the application of a second dye color on top of a previous dye color to effect a color change.

Pendleton blanket A colorful, commercially manufactured wool trade blanket produced by the Pendleton Woolen Mills, Oregon, popular with American Indians in the late nineteenth and twentieth centuries.

pound rug Coarsely woven and often simply patterned rugs made between 1890 and 1920 and sold to reservation traders by the pound.

presynthetic dyes Dyes produced from organic, naturally occurring substances.

processed wool Commercially cleaned, and sometimes spun and dyed Navajo wool.

rabbit brush A yellow flowering plant native to the Southwest, which produces a yellow dye used by Classic Period Navajo weavers in the nineteenth century and revived by vegetal-dye weavers in the 1920s.

Rio Grande weavings Blankets woven by Spanish Colonial weavers on the European horizontal loom in settlements along the Rio Grande in New Mexico.

saddle blanket The most commonly produced type of Navajo weaving, often woven in a thick, sturdy hand-spun twill weave for use under the saddle.

Saltillo sarape Finely woven, complex-patterned, colorful sarapes produced in weaving centers throughout Mexico that directly influenced Rio Grande weaving and indirectly the style of Navajo weaving in the second half of the nineteenth century.

sandpainting weaving A woven approximation of one of the many Navajo ceremonial sandpaintings.

sarape A finely woven, often complexly patterned wearing blanket, woven longer than wide and worn horizontally, wrapped about the shoulders. Poncho sarapes, woven with a central slit opening for the head, were worn draped front and back.

Saxony A fine silky, European commercial three-ply yarn spun from merino wool usually dyed with presynthetic natural dyes.

slave blanket Blanket woven by Navajo women servants in Spanish households. Woven on the Navajo upright loom, these blankets display both Navajo and Spanish design characteristics.

synthetic dyes Dyes produced synthetically from inorganic substances.

trade cloth Any machine-spun and -woven cloth, usually available in bolt form, traded to the various groups of American Indians. Bayeta is a generalized type of trade cloth.

Transitional Period The period from 1875 to 1890 in Navajo weaving, characterized by the transition from the production of blankets to that of rugs, the establishment of the Navajo Reservation and reservation traders, and the development of the Anglo rug market for Navajo rugs.

vegetal dye Any dye made from a plant source. In Navajo weaving, vegetal dye usually refers to dyes made from plants native to the Southwest.

Yei The Navajo Holy People, often depicted in twentieth-century Navajo pictorial Yei, Yeibechai, and sandpainting weavings.

zone An area of a Navajo blanket or rug defined by larger or more complex design elements or grouping of elements, often confined within bands or isolated by simple stripes or areas of solid color.

SELECTED BIBLIOGRAPHY

Adair, John. *The Navajo and Pueblo Silversmiths.* Norman: University of Oklahoma Press, 1944.

Amsden, Charles Avery. *Navajo Weaving: Its Technic, and Its History.* 1934. Reprint. Glorietta, N.M.: The Rio Grande Press, 1974.

Bennett, Kathy. "Navajo Chief Blanket: A Trade Item Among Non-Navajo Groups." *American Indian Art Magazine* 7, no. 1 (1981), 62–70.

Berlant, Anthony, and Kahlenberg, Mary Hunt. *The Navajo Blanket.* New York: Praeger Publishers in association with the Los Angeles County Museum of Art, 1972.

———. *Walk in Beauty: The Navajo and Their Blankets.* Boston: New York Graphic Society, 1977.

Brody, J. J. *Between Traditions: Navajo Weaving Toward the End of the Nineteenth Century.* Iowa City: Stamats Publishing Co. for the University of Iowa Museum of Art, 1976.

Bryan, Nonabah G., and Young, Stella. *Navajo Native Dyes: Their Preparation and Use.* 1940. Reprint. Palmer Lake, Colo.: The Filter Press, 1978.

Cerny, Charlene. *Navajo Pictorial Weaving.* Santa Fe: Museum of New Mexico, 1975.

Gilmour, Frances, and Wetherill, Louisa Wade. *Traders to the Navajo.* Albuquerque: University of New Mexico Press, 1953.

Halpern, Katherine Spencer, McGreevy, Susan, Parezo, Nancy, and Parrish, Rain. *Woven Holy People: Navajo Sandpainting Textiles.* Santa Fe: Wheelwright Museum of the American Indian, 1982.

James, George Wharton. *Indian Blankets and Their Makers.* 1914. Reprint. Glorietta, N.M.: The Rio Grande Press, 1974.

James, H. L. *Posts and Rugs: The Story of Navajo Rugs and Their Homes.* Globe, Ariz.: Southwest Parks and Monuments Association, 1976.

Jeter, James, and Juelke, Paula Marie. *The Saltillo Serape.* Santa Barbara, Calif.: New World Arts, 1978.

Keegan, Marcia. *Mother Earth, Father Sky.* New York: Grossman Publishers, 1974.

Kent, Kate Peck. *Prehistoric Textiles of the Southwest.* Santa Fe: School of American Research, 1983.

———. *Pueblo Indian Textiles: A Living Tradition.* Santa Fe: School of American Research, 1983.

———. *The Story of Navajo Weaving.* Phoenix: Heard Museum of Anthropology and Primitive Art, 1961.

Loh, Jules. *Lords of the Earth.* New York: The Macmillan Company, 1971.

Matthews, Washington. *Navajo Legends.* Boston: American Folklore Society, 1897.

———. *Third Annual Report of the Bureau of Ethnology 1881–1882.* Washington, D.C.: Government Printing Office, 1884.

Maxwell, Gilbert S. *Navajo Rugs, Past, Present, and Future.* Palm Desert, Calif.: Best West Publications, 1963.

McNitt, Frank. *The Indian Traders.* Norman: University of Oklahoma Press, 1962.

———. *Richard Wetherill: Anasazi.* Albuquerque: University of New Mexico Press, 1957.

Mera, H. P. *Navajo Textile Arts.* Santa Fe: School of American Research, 1948.

———. "Pueblo Indian Embroidery." *Memoirs of the Laboratory of Anthropology* 4 (1943).

———, and Wheat, Joe Ben. *The Alfred I. Barton Collection of Southwestern Textiles.* Coral Gables, Fla.: Lowe Art Museum, 1978.

Museum of International Folk Art. *Spanish Textile Traditions of New Mexico and Colorado.* Santa Fe: University of New Mexico Press, 1979.

Museum of Northern Arizona. "Tension and Harmony: The Navajo Rug." *Plateau Magazine* 52, no. 4 (1981).

Parezo, Nancy J. *Navajo Sandpaintings: From Religious Art to Commercial Art.* Tucson: University of Arizona Press, 1983.

Reichard, Gladys A. *Navajo Shepherd and Weaver.* New York: J.J. Augustin, 1963.

Rodee, Marian. *Southwestern Weaving.* Albuquerque: University of New Mexico Press, 1977.

"Southwest Indian Weaving." *Arizona Highways* 50, no. 7 (1974).

Terrell, John Upton. *The Navajos.* New York: Weybright & Talley, 1970.

Thompson, Gerald. *The Army and The Navajo.* Tucson: University of Arizona Press, 1976.

Tyrone D. Campbell Newsletter 1, nos. 1–5 (1981); 2, nos. 1–6 (1982).

Utley, Robert M., and Washburn, Wilcomb E. *The American Heritage History of the Indian Wars.* New York: American Heritage, 1971.

Wheat, Joe Ben. *Navajo Blankets from the Collection of Anthony Berlant.* Tucson: University of Arizona Press, 1974.

———. "The Navajo Chief Blanket." *American Indian Art Magazine* 1, no. 3 (1976), 44–55.

Wyman, Leland C. *Southwest Indian Drypainting.* Santa Fe: School of American Research, 1983.

INDEX

Page numbers in **boldface** refer to illustrations.